Telephone: MOUntview 3343.

HIGHGATE LITERARY & SCIENTIFIC INSTITUTION

11, SOUTH GROVE, N.6.   4484

Time allowed FOURTEEN Days

Date Issued	Date Issued	Date Issued
29 OCT 1949	9 APR 1958	
15 NOV 1949	4 AUG 1961	
26 NOV 1949	17 AUG 1961	
20 DEC 1949	8/24	
3 JAN 1950		
14 JAN 1950		
21 JAN 1950		
21 FEB 1950		
31 MAR 1950		
20 DEC 1951		
29 DEC 1951		
5 JAN 1952		
11 JAN 1952		
29 JAN 1952		
18 APR 1952		
10 MAY 1952		

Alexander ꝑꝑa. VI

THE BORGIA POPE

ALEXANDER THE SIXTH

By
ORESTES FERRARA

Translated by
F. J. SHEED

LONDON
SHEED & WARD
1942

FIRST PUBLISHED JANUARY 1942
BY SHEED & WARD LTD.,
110/111 FLEET STREET
LONDON, E.C.4

PRINTED IN GREAT BRITAIN
BY LOWE AND BRYDONE PRINTERS LTD.
LONDON, N.W.10

CONTENTS

Contents

CHAPTER I

Reputation

THE Borgias are among history's favorites. The story
in which they are the principal characters is so out-
standingly criminal that they interest the public in much
the same way as that public is interested by the outstand-
ing sanctity of St. Francis of Assisi. Alexander VI and his
children (if they were his children) Cesar and Lucretia
especially, have captivated many minds at least to the
point of putting them to endless trouble in the study of
their actions, the search for their motives, the examination
and judgement of their lives. That these same minds have
fallen into a mass of errors, exaggerations, and distortion
of facts does not alter the magnitude of their labors. Few
characters of history have been the object of so much
study.

The Borgias indeed have become the types of an age.
When we speak of "the time of the Borgias" or "the
Borgia age," we do not use these phrases simply to indicate the space that lies between two dates in the past; we
are defining the methods of government and the social
conditions by which in our minds that particular space of
time was marked. For public life, the word Borgia calls up
a vision of poison and dagger, of malevolent cunning, incest, fratricide, perfidy unlimited; and for the Church,
simony, nepotism, utter want of belief, something very

1

close to atheism. In common opinion, the comparatively short period in which Pope Alexander occupied the throne of Peter was a time of abomination so immeasurable that other ages, no matter how notorious their infamy, can only approach and never equal it. The example he set incited the basest men of the lowest passions to employ the worst means to attain their perverted ends. If Machiavelli is the theorist of methods repudiated by the human conscience, the Borgias represent the full practice of precisely those methods.

According to the legend one Rodrigo Llansol, a kind of soldier, a cross between a bandit and a gentleman, vicious and violent, one day changed his second name to Borgia and entered the Church at the instance of his uncle, Pope Calixtus III, who proceeded to confer the purple upon him against the will of the Sacred College.

The new Cardinal led a debauched life, in which lust and greed for money strove for first place. Emboldened by continuing success, he bought the Conclave on the death of Innocent VIII and made himself Pope. Under the name of Alexander VI he murdered many of his former colleagues in the Consistory and others besides, using a poison called *cantarella*; he involved his son Cesar in the most sordid adventures; and like Cesar committed incest—and with the same woman, his daughter, the unspeakable Lucretia. He seized the money of all his victims. He never kept his word. A great hypocrite, he was a secret accessory in the murders attributed to his son, whom he continued to love and to raise to the highest honors, though he knew perfectly well that that base man had had another of his children, the Duke of Gandia, murdered. He destroyed the peace of Europe, invited the barbarians to the conquest of Italy, stole the Church's temporal goods for the enrichment of Cesar, and robbed many princes of their towns, their castles, and their houses. In the end he died, a victim of his own poison, just when under the thrust of his cupidity he was preparing the destruction by this same poison of a Cardinal and other dignitaries of the Church. As everybody was in terror of him and no one could be sure of seeing the next day dawn as long as he lived, his death was a glorious relief for Rome and all Europe.

There you have in its main lines, the story of the Borgias, as it has come down to us. You will find it in history books, in popular tradition, in melodrama, in fiction.

To attempt a revision of traditional ideas is not easy. History is at once an art and a science; and when these two mental disciplines are bent upon the same study, the former, representing the slow adaptation of our collective tastes to the external world, is nearly always too strong for history as a science, constituted by individual investigations having a purely objective end. My desire is to take up the study of Alexander VI from original documents, discover how the legend has been formed upon each event, and by an impartial criticism get at the real proportions of acts long regarded as monstrous. And all this means in some sense the dissipation of an illusion, the dislocation of an artistic whole which has for long thrilled authors and readers, playwrights and spectators, and in our own day the not very mature public of the cinema.

Yet it is quite certain that the palpitating story that now occupies the general mind is a sheer invention. What passes for the history of the Borgias is a legend, in part invented by contemporaries and added to by later authors; a legend which, like all legends, has taken shape gradually. To make it plausible it has been necessary little by

3

little to add imaginary acts to real acts, then to alter proportions, turn guesses into realities, and finally, with the aid of distance, transform the whole thing into a piece of drama. The history of Alexander VI as it has reached us is a tissue of inaccuracies, extraordinarily easy to disprove the moment recourse is had to contemporary documents in a spirit of sane criticism.

Accusation after accusation collapses, not only for want of proof, but still more because it was evidently impossible for him to have committed the crime in question. In fact as we come to see the truth, we begin to realize that in the whole Renaissance period there was no man who had a loftier idea of the liberty of the Church, of States and of individuals; no man who had a truer appreciation of the evil to be feared from the powers of the period which aimed at hegemony; no man who used more strength and skill than he in the effort to preserve Italy from the disaster of foreign domination.

Alexander was a jovial, far-sighted, moderate man, well-balanced in mind and body. Having lived nearly half a century in Rome, and having been for almost the whole of his life part of the ecclesiastical organization, he had come to a profound respect for all the interests of the Catholic Church, a respect greater than for his own life. He was prepared to compromise upon all purely human questions, but inflexible upon whatever concerned the rights of religion. He was the type of "political priest," cautious and slow to act in face of the unforeseen, but brave to the point of heroism in defense of the great Institution whose direction had been entrusted to him.

Thoroughly versed in the politics of his day and the needs of the Church, he tried to prevent evils which were to afflict Italy for four centuries after. If his policy

4

of international balance had remained that of the Vatican, if Julius II had not destroyed it by his temper and his utterly chaotic mind, the Church and Italy would have been spared much suffering.

He succeeded in doing more for other countries indeed than for Italy. In Spain he helped most effectively towards national unity; and in the Americas he fixed the line of demarcation for the possession of newly discovered lands. In the purely ecclesiastical domain, he drew up a program of religious reform not vastly improved upon either by the Reformation or the Counter-Reformation. He was the great precursor of the Council of Trent. With paternal indulgence, he pardoned the two-fold treason of certain cardinals, towards the States of the Church and towards himself. He never showed the harshness and cruelty normal at the time, save when it was a question of delivering Rome from the factious tyranny of the great nobles, a truly sordid crew. He was no mystic and no saint. He had the merits and the faults of a man of action aiming at success. He was a Pope, and a great Pope, of the Renaissance. He was a nepotist and a temporal prince, a lover of work, a lover of pleasure, inflexible upon the interests of religion, a legalist in public affairs.

Thus there is a huge contrast between the reality and the legend. And the contrast cannot fail to trouble the mind of every reader and every writer. It troubled my own mind. It is to this that we owe the kind of uncertainty to be found in many modern historians, who when they come to speak of the Borgias deny and affirm the same facts, and are guilty of incredibly contradictory judgements.

As the legend of Alexander VI has become by force of repetition a fact of common opinion, his true history gives an effect of novelty; it has been necessary to construct it

5

in complete freedom of mind, and after that kind of patient analysis of ancient documents which the modern reader finds least to his taste. I have had to be constantly on guard against myself, lest in the heat of controversy I should be drawn into the opposite error.

But if in the order of facts, I have felt justified in setting down definitive conclusions, the question of how a general opinion has managed to arise so utterly opposed to the truth also has to be treated. Even if an explanation can be found of the erroneous judgement on each incident, yet all these explanations together do not seem sufficient to reveal the underlying cause of the general and continuing hostility towards the Borgia Pope and his family. For unanimity of opinion is also a fact of history, and has to be accounted for. An examination of this problem before we come to the actual narrative will help to an understanding of the historical fantasy with which posterity has been duped.

The Borgias were Spaniards. Two of them were Popes, at an interval of thirty or forty years. To be Pope at that period meant the possession of temporal power. The Pope was a prince exercising authority over a rich territory. He received tribute from the farthest corners of the Christian world. According to the doctrine of the Roman Church, he was "the Supreme Government of the world, the Father of Princes and Kings, and the Vicar upon earth of Jesus Christ, our Saviour." Like all princes the Popes were nepotists, they favored their families and their fellow countrymen, their friends and former dependents. Nor have popular governments acted otherwise; for with the coming of democracy the power has passed from one set of politicians to another who all alike have used and abused the power which the ballot boxes have temporarily given them for their own profit and the profit of their friends and relations.

The choice of the Conclave gave the elected man the power to distribute benefices, prebends and such like favors entirely at his own will or whim. The result was that every new Pope brought within the orbit of power a group of his own relations and friends and partisans. Everyone at the time found all this perfectly normal and natural. The refined and artistic Lorenzo the Magnificent considered that the Pope had not only a right but actually a duty to grant honors and profits to his family: to do otherwise would have been no virtue, but a want of heart and humanity.[1]

Thus with the second Borgia as with the first, Spain penetrated into the Vatican. In fact the Borgias entered Rome with cohorts of Catalans, as the Spaniards in Italy were then called. It is to be noted that if no foreigner was esteemed by the Romans, the Catalans were literally hated. In a general way, the Italians feared the French and barely tolerated the Germans, but they abhorred the Spaniards. The Italian peninsula was not a political unity, but it regarded itself as the expression of a civilization superior to that of the States beyond the Alps and beyond the sea. The Renaissance of classicism had strengthened this feeling of superiority. As in antiquity, the name of barbarians was given to all who were not the direct descendants of Rome.

Spain was regarded as an inferior nation even by comparison with the rest of the barbarians, because it was the latest in date in the totality of countries of high civilization.

7

The opinion, clearly a false opinion, held of the Spaniards by the Italians of that day finds expression in a book by Antonio de Ferrariis, bearing the title of *Galatea*. There were some Italians, either better instructed in the reality of things, or financially bound to the Spanish cause in Italy, who did not share the view of Ferrariis; but it is clear from what is said by many writers and from what we can learn from popular feeling as shown by the behaviour of the mass, that he expressed the feeling of the great majority of his countrymen. Philology even bears testimony to this contempt, since the Spanish words which have made their way into the Italian vocabulary are not words which stand for honorable actions or good habits.

Ferrariis gives us a veritable philippic, all the more serious since it does represent general opinion. I quote it because it defines the spirit then reigning:

> The Spaniards claim to be Goths and so they are, apart from a very small number of cultivated and moral people. The greater part are certainly uncultivated and desire to remain so; they have no aspiration for learning; they feel no need either of refinement of manners or improvement of life. The young people are not educated to this end but on the contrary are degraded; for instead of sending them, as is done in the rest of Europe, to be prepared for life by people of nobler condition, they are kept with their own inferiors, who teach them all the ways of evil. Among them it is a virtue to know how to deceive and to rob one's neighbor with skill and cunning. Their highest level of sociability consists in telling amusing stories. Gaming is their habitual distraction, and the best way of being able to go on gambling for

8

long hours by day and night is to get money by borrowing and not pay it back.

They are pompous and sensitive to affront; barbarians, and like all barbarians lustful; old and young sing beneath their mistresses' windows. Their poetry is worthless, for the Spanish poet is no more than a maker of songs. Their music is languorous, effeminate and melancholy. Their idea of a tourney comes to this: "You advance, I withdraw; you withdraw, I advance!"—all this with turbans on their heads and the utterance of frightful Arab cries.[2]

It could not have been easy for a Spaniard to rule a country where such opinions were held, particularly when he had to rule not by material arms or right of conquest, but by moral authority alone.

Calixtus III was the first to make his way in a Rome where that was the atmosphere. A man of rare ability and great legal learning, he was elected Pope in April, 1455. His election was a surprise, of the sort that often happened in Conclaves. The conflict between two candidates of equal strength issued in the election of an old man in broken health. The populace received the news with the liveliest displeasure, and one of the Orsini showed the most startling disrespect towards the new Pope's authority, by presenting himself during the ceremony of enthronement fully armed and in a threatening attitude.

Many personages of the period loved him and admired him, remembering that he had been professor at the University of Lerida and president of the Sacred College of Naples, an institution for higher legal studies. But the great public could find for this professor of canon law, this counselor of kings, this distinguished diplomat, no better title

9

than "the Barbarian Pope." And the nickname stuck to him for long.

He aggravated his offense of intruding upon the Throne of Peter by maintaining abuses already existent, justified by Italian Popes. He immediately showered ecclesiastical benefices upon his two nephews, Rodrigo Borgia, the future Alexander VI, and Luis Del Mila. Shortly after he made them Cardinals. He named another of his nephews, Pedro Luis, Captain General of the Church and Prefect of Rome. For the three years that Calixtus was Pope Rome was governed by Spaniards. Carlo de Ponte tells indignantly that in this sinister hour for Italians, only Catalans were to be seen in Rome. In spite of the fact that his short Pontificate was devoted principally to the preparation of a Crusade against the Turks, a fact which in itself would have made him popular, Calixtus III was even more detested at his death than at his election. The moment he was dead, the Romans set up a cruel and persistent persecution of his fellow-countrymen. The houses of Spaniards were pillaged, the greater part were dispossessed of their goods and a certain number murdered. All this took place some thirty-five years before the triple crown was placed upon the head of Rodrigo Borgia.

During the long years he was in Italy, Alexander VI had assimilated all the psychology of the Roman curia, which is essentially Italian. There remained in him nothing Spanish save his affection for Spain. But for popular opinion he was a Spaniard. And popular opinion was in the outcome not entirely wrong.

During his Pontificate he elevated nineteen Spaniards to the cardinalate. His advisors were for the most part Spaniards; so were the best soldiers of Cesar, Gonfalonier of the Church, and the men who had been his instructors,

10

and the maids of honor of Lucretia. With his intimates, Alexander spoke Spanish or Valencian. I repeat, all the external part, all the sentimental part of his life was Spanish and thus a great irritation to the nobility and people of Rome. It meant little to them that his policy was entirely Italian, as well as his culture and mental habits.

In public life, which is a mixture of sentiment and self-interest, nothing is more irritating than an intruder, real or supposed. Eneas Silvius, who became Pius II, has written that the Italians willingly obey their fellow-countrymen but not foreigners. A foreigner Alexander VI was, though he had lived in Spain only up to his seventeenth year and had spent the rest of his life in Italy. In spite of his personal qualities, he could neither be esteemed nor loved; for he was not only a foreigner, but the worst kind of foreigner, a Spaniard. Just as his uncle in spite of his learning was nicknamed "the Barbarian Pope," so Rodrigo in spite of his noble birth was nicknamed "the Marrano Pope."

It is true that at the moment of his election he was loudly acclaimed, for he had a sound reputation as a man of learning and a man of action, and his elevation to the Pontificate was looked upon as the end of government by irresponsible coteries. But excessive applause is a bad beginning for a statesman. Once the great wave of enthusiasm had flowed by, the new Pope was once more the Catalan intruder who was usurping the wealth of Italy for himself and his friends.

But whereas Calixtus III had got himself to some extent tolerated and consequently forgotten—partly because of the shortness of his reign, partly because of his preparation for the Crusade—Alexander VI whipped hatreds to fury by the terrible audacity with which he set about transforming the political system of a country not his own,

B

in the light of his own conception of the Church's universality and permanent needs.

This attitude was at the origin of the evil renown which weighs upon his memory and was most certainly its determining cause.

The political program of the new Pope was clearly shown from the very beginning. At Rome, the Pope must govern. Factions must disappear. The Pope does not need the help of powerful families, these families must not be powerful. It matters nothing that Lorenzo Valle discovered that the famous Donation of Constantine was false so that Rome did not belong juridically to the successor of Peter. In hard fact, Rome was abandoned by the civil authority during the later Empire and remained under the jurisdiction of its Bishop, as happened with so many other European cities in the early Middle Ages.

Outside Rome, Alexander's view equally was that the Pope must govern the traditional possessions of the Church, even if he must use Vicars as intermediaries. The territories of Ravenna and the Pentapolis had been granted to the Sovereign Pontiff by Pepin the Short, after he had driven out the Lombards who had previously usurped them from the Roman Emperor in the East. It is true that Pepin had no prior legal right to his conquest. But this was as unimportant as the discovery that the Donation of Constantine was false. In the religious domain the Church insists upon the immanence of moral principles. But in the matter of property rights, she admits that force can create such rights and time can legalize them. If the Pope possessed of right these temporalities in the Romagna and elsewhere in central Italy, he must possess them in fact. If he did not effectively claim them, not only would he cease to fulfill his primary obligation to defend the Church, but he would abandon whole populations who trusted him to the ferocity and rapine of such classical tyrants as the Baglione, the Bentivoglios, the Malatestas, the Varanos, and the rest. This idea was not new in Alexander VI. Certain previous Popes had thought likewise. They had even tried to put the thought into effect, but their strength was less than the strength of the usurpers.

The so-called Vicars had occupied cities, territories and strongholds by violence, assassination, treachery—and also through papal nepotism. Little by little, they had become independent of Rome. Bent only upon a life of luxury, they tyrannized over their peoples and bled them white. They were feudal lords, but by now they were a class of usurpers. They had once been necessary for war, but from that point of view they were now merely survivals of no practical value. They were organs which had ceased to be useful and hence had degenerated; and they continued to exercise their art, which was war, by selling their swords to the highest bidder, and making treason their principal source of income. Alexander decided from the beginning to destroy them the moment he had the strength for it.

So much for Rome. So much for the Papal States. For the rest of the world, Alexander wanted no invasions; he defended the status quo and aimed at such a balance of material power, that the moral power of the papacy (though weakened by the new form of the national state and by the lessening of religious faith) might be decisive at least in the hour of great decisions if it could not be so continuously.

A program of this sort maddened everybody. It ran counter to the designs of the kings of Europe, especially those of France and Spain who were in process of founding a new all-conquering imperialism upon the ruins of the Holy Roman Empire. It collided with the designs of Venice, which was at that very moment ambitious of becoming a great power on the mainland since the Turk was driving it out of its maritime possessions. It collided with the designs of Naples, then under the rule of the insatiable King Ferrante, who meant to take Benevento and thus establish easy contact with the territory of Florence and be in a position to exercise an influence upon the north of Italy. But above all, Alexander's program threatened at the very foundation of their existence the great princely houses of Rome, and the still more numerous great houses of central Italy. For these families were the richest and most aggressive and had in their pay the best troops, the best poets and the best pamphleteers of the peninsula.

And he actually fought on two fronts, since he not only assailed the nobility but was determined to repress the excesses of the populace. He strictly maintained the law's authority over the lower classes. Though these lower classes were the objects of continual vexations, yet they had been allowed an evil latitude in the matter of obedience to the law, provided their breaking of the law did not damage the interest or caprice of the lord upon whom they depended. Alexander organized the administration of the city, expelled the men-at-arms who had come to sell themselves in this market of revolts, and vigorously prosecuted malefactors—who in all this moral confusion and absence of authority were protected by the victims themselves.

His offensive, rapidly put into action, was aimed principally at Italian elements. The author of the offensive was a foreigner, of a race held as inferior. Furthermore, order destroys usages and harms interests just as disorder does; imposed rapidly and over a whole field, it always causes

14

unpopularity. The reaction was bound to be as vigorous as the offensive.

The Roman families fought against Alexander VI sword in hand with more or less success; but the combat they waged against him by false and dishonoring rumors was totally successful. To overcome him, they had to destroy his prestige, since his power lay principally in the prestige arising from his high office. The ancients crowned their victims with flowers before leading them to execution; but in an age when principles are abandoned, men cover their victims with mud.

Rome was in a ferment. Discontent against a government which insisted upon being a strong government gradually spread outwards from Rome to the rest of Italy and then over the Alps. The Pope's nepotism exposed an obvious flank for attack. And then began the great flood of: "it is said," "we hear," "everybody thinks." Diplomats, to satisfy the avidity of their governments for intrigue and their political interests, gathered up such rumors, even the feeblest, with all the more satisfaction because the Pope was haughty in manner and bore himself as a supreme Lord who admits no equals.

The world reacted swiftly against Alexander's policy. The Orsini, the Colonna and other families now had a common enemy, so that we find them fighting on the same side, a thing unknown for centuries. King Ferrante of Naples, the incarnation of all abuses, a tyrant utterly vile and corrupt, turned into a moralist when the Pope checked his advance against the Papal States; and he wrote a letter for the Spanish sovereigns, which was the first calumnious document, denouncing the Pope's private life. To discredit the Pope, the Venetians united with the Lords of the Romagna who were tyrannizing over their country,

15

and against all decent usage informed the King of France of the secret discussions they had with the court of Rome. The Florentines, peaceful merchants, looked with an unquiet eye upon a Pope who wished Rome strong in the temporal order and ruled a vast region by which their own State was completely surrounded; they made use of Savonarola to combat him. The Kings of France designed to invade Italy and occupy the Kingdom of Naples and the Duchy of Milan, and only the Pope was in their way. The King of Spain wanted to have a subordinate in Rome in the person of this Spaniard, while in Rome the Spaniard in question had precisely the opposite view.

In the sphere of action, Alexander VI strove with consummate skill against all these difficulties; but in the sphere of opinion, against whispered slander and the calumny of anonymous pamphlets, he did not bother to make any reply at all. It is a weakness that sometimes goes with greatness to believe that a cause can defend itself by its own justice. Thus it was that there began that process of accusation in which only evidence adverse to him was held valid.

Yet it is certain that the false rumors, the epigrams, the clandestine publications, even the interested calumnies of diplomats and chroniclers would have been rectified by the calm judgment and good sense of the majority if the age had not been exceptional, essentially revolutionary. At a normal time, the public rumors of one period are not regarded as unquestionable facts in the next, any more than the fact of being born in another country transforms a decent man into a criminal once time has weakened the passion of the moment. But the Renaissance was not a normal period. It was an explosion of the whole content, good and bad, of the human soul, a period in which nothing that happened is to be measured by ordinary standards of honor and obligation.

In the long passage of history, there are hours when all the dykes of intellectual and moral principle, built with such patience and great toil by preceding ages, are utterly broken. New needs and new aspirations come into collision with principles built up in the past and these yield little by little. The first thing to crumble in a revolution is the code of rules of living which custom, even it may be ill-custom, maintains; these rules, by the very fact of their fixity, are always superior to those substituted for them in periods of transition. From this state of moral license completely unchained, there arise all the impetuosities and audacities, which, the one canalized and the other brought within some sort of uniformity, ultimately produce a forward movement of human society. This forward movement, once it is consolidated, creates a new harmony with other principles and other rules of life, in a word, another order. But in the interval? Until the confused initiatives of so many unbridled minds are disciplined for the creation of a new moral and juridical climate, there is a chaos of mean passions, wild ideas, criminalities, lying, poverty of ideas, human beings sacrificed, passionate hatred for whoever stands in one's way, private interests sordid and triumphant.

To explain the repulsive crimes of the Malatestas, Bentivoglios, Oliverotto, and so many others—or rather all others—we are driven to imagine some kind of universal hysteria. Their cruelty was the expression of a spirit for which no satisfaction was possible; for every barrier having broken, desire, even the most perverse and diabolical desire, was not limited by this or that definite end to be achieved, but spilled over into madness.

17

Under the influence of this collective psychology, truth and lying were now merely intellectual variants; reality and theory only degrees of knowledge whose difference did not signify. And that is why the great men of the period were men of fluid convictions. The greatest, Erasmus, did not know whether to remain with Rome or to oppose; and the most dynamic, Luther, long hesitated between total rebellion and merely partial apostasy. Where there are no stable principles, no uniform rules of life, there will be no interest for truth, which means that there will be no fact universally held as certain. At such a moment truth is nothing more than the opinion of the men who write, the men who have the public ear—that is to say ultimately the men who rule.

Alexander's pontificate coincided with the period of greatest fermentation of the whole Renaissance. And the Renaissance continued after his death, and his enemies were the greatest rulers of the day, their court poets and chroniclers, and the salaried historians who wrote of the past and used it as a peg upon which to hang their commentaries on present affairs.

The acts and events of his life, already falsified in their own time, made an excellent basis for the wildest accusations in the time that followed. Provided it was about him, any hypothesis might pass for certain fact, nothing was too incredible to be accepted and spread abroad. Rumors, invented by the vilest self-interest or the most fantastic folly, were solemnly written down as indisputable truths. In 755 Pope Stephen II had written to King Pepin the Short: "In this age, honest men themselves believe in fiction when they judge it useful to their own interests."[3] The same was true of the whole of the sixteenth century.

It cannot be said too often that if part of the legend took

shape during the lifetime of Alexander VI, the other part was invented later. New calumnies began under the pontificate of Julius II, that is to say during the government of his bitterest enemy. We may compare it with the history of Robespierre, composed under the influence of the reaction which followed upon his death. It is as if we were to write the history of Napoleon according to English newspapers of the period, or the biography of Catiline according to Cicero's speeches. And to obviate any misunderstanding as to the real date of the accusing documents it must be noted that many of them, which appear to be of Alexander's period, were actually written later. For the journals and collections of letters of that time were subjected to later revision and alteration. And many of these journals and letters have reached us not in their original form but in the form of summaries made by others than their writers, or copies made by unscrupulous scribes whose habit it was to introduce their own ideas into the manuscripts they were copying. This literature has had a considerable influence upon the reputation of the Borgia Pope and his relations, because it appears as the direct statement of men in a position to know. They are credited with that spontaneity which comes from facts immediately experienced.

Among all the documents thus altered and added to, there is one of especial importance. It is one of those historical papers to which fortune has been kind—though its fortune must be attributed to the fact that it is the first attempt at a biography of Alexander VI. It is anonymous, and copies are found in different libraries with texts which do not agree. The copyists have done their usual job of interpolation and alteration. Serious authors are generally ashamed to quote it; but they are clearly inspired by it.

19

Its title is: "Life of don Rodrigo Borgia, later Pope Alexander VI, and of Cesar Borgia and his brothers, sons of the said Pontiff, with Memoirs of the most secret events that took place during this pontificate, the whole drawn from manuscripts in the Vatican Library."

The work is short and contains summaries of all the supposed crimes of the Pope and his family. The writing is lively, and the book admirably suited to the historian who wishes to present, in good literary prose, facts not verified by himself but strongly to the taste of his readers. It is impossible to imagine a document more crammed with errors, put together with less care, more contradictory of all that is known with certainty about the Borgia family. Everything in it is anti-historic. The author brings the Pope's father on to the stage several years after his death, presents young Rodrigo as a bandit in the Spanish countryside at a time when he was receiving ecclesiastical dignities; puts him, at eighteen, at the head of certain affairs although he was at the time only a student at Rome or Bologna; has him a lawyer in Spain and later a soldier. As if all this were not sufficient activity for a young man, he makes him page to King Alfonso V. He makes him live twenty-eight years in Spain, although unquestionable documents establish that by that age he was already a cardinal living in Rome. He also places in Spain his relations with Vannozza, a piece of gallantry in which Rodrigo appears as lover of the mother and her two daughters at the same time. Calixtus III, ignorant of what was happening—says our anonymous author—died while Rodrigo was still in Spain, and the Conclave elected Innocent VIII. Thus the pamphleteer suppresses three Popes, Pius II, Paul II and Sixtus IV. Over and above these historical errors, we have the string of assassinations, poisonings, incests, so piously

20

repeated by the historians of that day and handed on as a priceless legacy to their successors.

These absurdities could not have appeared save at a moment when any slander against Borgia was sure to be well rewarded. The author, whoever he was, had doubtless taken up his pen with no higher ambition than to amuse some Lord who kept or protected him, and with no vision of the success his work was to have throughout the centuries. The pamphlet had no historical pretensions; it was simply a writing job, bought and paid for.·

Other documents have had more or less influence upon the fame of the Borgias and especially of Alexander VI. Setting aside Pontano and Sanazzaro, who instead of relating facts merely hurl insults, it seems to me that three sources of information have been particularly effective in this sinister work of moral demolition.

Infessura treats in his *Journal* of the first years of the Pope's reign. Upon the value of his work, it may be enough to say that Muratori would not include it in the collection of "Rerum Italicorum Scriptores," because of its lack of respect for truth.

The *Letter to Silvio Savelli*, also anonymous, pretends to be addressed to the said Savelli, at that time a refugee in Germany, the Pope having confiscated his goods and sent him into exile. When Alexander VI read the document, he laughed heartily because the whole thing seemed to him absurd. Later he received Savelli back in Rome and it is even probable that he protected him.

Finally, there is the diplomatic correspondence of Giustiniani, which simply attests the blind hatred of this representative of Venice towards the Pope and his relations.

But these three writers, like the later Giovio, Guicciardini, Bembo and others are men of their time. They

21

had no notion of rational criticism. Their object was polemic.

The death of Julius II and the disasters suffered by the Church under later Popes did not have the effect one might have expected. It did not bring about the more calm and balanced judgement of a posterity not worked upon by the passions of their predecessors. On the contrary it provoked a fresh stream of calumnies, fantasy no longer being checked by the sense of shame which must always tend to cramp the style of a man, however irresponsible, who really knows what happened. The mystical reaction through which men passed at the time of the Reformation and the Counter-Reformation had to find one man whom it could regard as the incarnation of the Renaissance wickedness which was now in such ill-odor.[4] Thus that happened to Borgia which had happened to Machiavelli. The two names were indissolubly linked. Machiavelli was seen as the theorist of an age that denied God and all human morality, and the Borgias as the principal actors in the age's drama.

It is not surprising that the effect of all this lasted into the nineteenth century. Historical criticism should then have set about the huge task of rectification, for the facts were beginning to emerge from archives in the form of authentic documents. But it must be remembered that in its first phase, modern historiography had to accept the documentations of the past, more by reason of its quantity than its quality. A document that one had discovered, from the very fact that it was *a document*, seemed to constitute absolute truth. Thus for example, when Ranke read in the dusty archives of Venice the story the Venetian Capello gives of his embassy in Rome, he regarded it as absolutely probative. The great historian did not realize, could not realize, that in passing through the brain and pen of Sanudo, the story had probably lost its original form, since Sanudo is not always exact when he is by way of reproducing a document; nor did it enter his head that Capello and Sanudo were both Venetians, at a period when the Borgias were resisting the imperialist spirit of the Most Serene Republic; and that furthermore Capello speaks of many things he did not know at first hand, since he was not at Rome at the time when they happened, either as orator or ambassador or in any other capacity. Ranke felt the same enthusiasm—remote from any critical sense—that a man would feel today who discovered a document written by Pilate and treating of Christ.

It is only when documentation becomes abundant that one document can be confronted with another, and it is only then that critical history can come into action.

If today men wish to know the things of the past as they really happened, there is only one possible method. They must rid themselves of prejudices no matter how deep-rooted in time, examine the facts at their source, and group them according to the principles of sound criticism. The method of course is well known, but it is not easy to apply. General opinion still hostile to the Borgia, the falsifications that have been made, the destructive work of time upon valuable documents, all hinder our reconstruction of the past. Yet we can by patient analysis discover Alexander VI as he was.

In noting that his Spanish birth was against him as Pope, and that the Renaissance was not a period from which his reputation was likely to emerge scatheless, I do not claim that these facts prove him innocent. Nor does the further fact that his policy set everybody against him with the

23

weapons of calumny then customary, as Savanarola himself admits.[5] The hostility of his successor Julius II and of all the princes at home and abroad who dominated the mind of the age, is not a conclusive proof that he did not commit this or that great crime. Nor is he proved innocent by the extraordinary fact that writers of the highest intellectual quality have agreed in accepting the accuracy of anonymous narratives in which the hand of the paid pamphleteer is only too apparent. All this helps to explain the reputation of the Borgias, though it does not clear them of that reputation. But it should serve to preserve in us a mind free from prejudice in the examination of the successive phases of Borgia's life, to make us realize that his reputation was not necessarily due to any crime he actually committed, finally to bring us by a study of all the documents to the certainty that men and ages have conspired to conceal the truth, and that this truth can now in large part be seen.

CHAPTER II

Youth

THE courier bearing the news of the election of Pope
Alexander VI reached Valencia on August 20, 1492, at
nine in the morning and there was a great celebration
in the cathedral; there was a procession, and the Te Deum
was sung; and the whole town went to greet Dona Beatriz
de Borgia, sister of the pope-elect and wife of Don Ximeno
Perez de Areños, kissing her hands.[1] The news went swiftly
from Valencia to Xativa, the next town, where the people
gathered with great rejoicings, because it was the pontiff's
birthplace. The bells clanged, and processions thronged
the streets singing the Te Deum to give thanks to God
for the happy event.

In these two towns Pope Alexander VI, the one-time
Rodrigo Borgia, had spent his childhood and his early
youth, up to the age of seventeen or eighteen. It was natural that their enthusiasm should at that moment be of a
different quality from that of the cities of Italy, for the
people saw an honor to themselves in the honor accorded
to their fellow-citizen by his elevation to the throne of
St. Peter.

The town of Xativa realized that Rodrigo Borgia was
entering history under a new name, the name of Alexander VI. And it realized another thing: for ordinary mortals
—who arrive at the tomb with nothing but their naked

25

bodies and whatever may happen to be on their conscience at the time—it is not necessary to fix with any great precision either their origin or the various stages of their life; but for men who play a great part in the drama of their age there is no fact however secondary or apparently unimportant that posterity may not need to know. That is why the town had thirteen witnesses affirm under oath that Rodrigo was "son of the noble Jofre and Isabel de Borgia, that he was born in the month of July at midnight" in the house on the square that bears his family name. These witnesses said further, to indicate Jofre de Borgia's degree of nobility, that he had four horses and that his son Rodrigo at the age of eight used to ride through the streets of the town "mounted on a pony"; finally, they mentioned that at the death of Jofre, when Rodrigo was only ten, the whole family moved to Valencia.[2]

Neither the supreme dignity of Alexander VI nor the precision of this and later information have prevented many errors about his birth and his early years. It is interesting to note that writers who have accused the Pope of so many crimes by intention—which after all is a difficult thing to investigate—do not so much as know his proper name, his exact age, his unduly early entry into ecclesiastical orders, the different places where he lived— all of them external facts much easier of investigation than the deep places of a man's soul.

The true name of Alexander VI was Rodrigo de Borja, Italianized as Borgia; but from the Continuator of Platina down to Baron Frederick Corvo, including on the way writers of the importance of Reumond and Von Pastor, the great majority have affirmed that Rodrigo had only adopted the name of Borja in order to obtain greater favors from his maternal uncle of that name, who had become Pope under the title of Calixtus III. The Continuator of Platina was the first to deny to Rodrigo the name of Borgia, calling him instead Rodrigo Lanzol.[3] This error arises from a confusion because Pope Calixtus III did have another nephew, equally favored by him, called Lanzol.[4] With rare exceptions the historians have only too willingly reproduced this error in order to deny Alexander VI noble ancestors.

Yet in all the documents of the time, as in the discourses pronounced in his honor after his election, and in the bulls of his predecessors conferring ecclesiastical benefices upon him, the name used is that of Borgia.[5] The best proof is a document discovered in 1924 in the archives of Valencia concerning a grant made by Cardinal Alfonso de Borgia, later Calixtus III, to his sister Isabel, which confirms his paternal descent. This document proves that Rodrigo's father, well before the birth of his son, bore the name of Borja and not that of Lanzol.[6]

Alexander VI's mother was named Isabella and also belonged to the Borgia family as we have said, there being no possibility of doubt about her name—both because of the document in which the future Pope Calixtus III grants her a dowry at the time of her marriage with Jofre de Borja, and because of the declaration of the witnesses already quoted, made at the time of Alexander's election.

But, as if alteration of facts were de rigueur in writing the history of the Borgias, contemporary writers who, as we have seen, can read the deepest secrets of his heart with ease, call her Juana, confusing her with another sister of Pope Calixtus, while handsomely conceding that "certain other historians gave her name as Isabella."[7]

The ancestral nobility of the Borgia family was, as I think, exaggerated by Pope Calixtus because he intended

c

27

to give one of his nephews, Pedro Luis, either the Kingdom of Naples or some important Duchy like that of Benevento, which indeed he conferred upon him a short time before his death. The historical fact is that the name of Borja arrived at Valencia and Xativa with the numerous members of the family who accompanied King James I of Aragon when he won the whole of Murcia from the Moors and entered Valencia in 1238. From undoubtedly genuine documents we learn that these Borjas held honorable posts and a certain wealth, things which went together when noble families were in question. The Borjas, from whom Alexander VI came, represented the king and the people in the town of Xativa and dwelt in a considerable house in the center of the square which bore their name.[8]

But it is mere guesswork to affirm that these Borjas descended from Ramiro, King of Aragon, and more immediately from Don Pedro de Athares who in 1134 was elected King, was then forced to abdicate, and after his abdication took the title of Seigneur de Borja. All we can say is that there is an identity of name and that there may have been a connection.

It may be that these Borjas of Pope Alexander were citizens of the town of that name, and consequently vassals of the Lord of Borja, who later made the town's name their own; or they may have been of the family of the ex-King Don Pedro. It has been affirmed, though no sources are given, that Don Pedro left no male children and if this were certain it would settle part of the question. But the many grants of land that the Pope's ancestors received at Valencia render it improbable that they were merely vassals serving in the army of King James I. Perhaps they were a bastard branch. With the information we have, the

28

question of royal origin seems insoluble. What we know
for certain is that Calixtus III and Alexander VI believed
in it, and that the Spanish sovereigns, after the death of
Calixtus and before the election of Alexander—that is to
say at a time when there was no Borgia pope—agreed to
the marriage of a member of their own family with a
Borja; and that the arms of the luckless King Don Pedro,
himself descended from King Ramiro, are the same as
those of the Borjas.

Whatever may be the truth, all dimmed as it is by time,
the young Rodrigo was born noble and rich; and his father,
as was normal in families of that sort, had destined him
for the ecclesiastical life, since he was not the eldest son.

We cannot describe Rodrigo as an infant prodigy, for
his fellow citizens, even at the hour of his glory, could
find no exceptional qualities to commemorate.

Rodrigo Borgia was born in 1432.[9] When he was ten,
he left Xativa for Valencia; and at fifteen we find him receiving by a Papal Bull the authorization to accept high
administrative charges and ecclesiastical dignities.[10] Later,
we find benefices conferred upon him by Pope Nicholas V
and, according to a bull of the same Pope confirming an
earlier bull, we are given to understand that even before
his fifteenth year he had received other favors from Pope
Eugenius IV.[11] Thus we must place his entry into the
Church at some date earlier than his fifteenth year, probably at six, the minimum age demanded by the Canons.

Under the protection of Cardinal Alfonso de Borgia,
who was to become Calixtus III, Rodrigo's rise was swift
and brilliant; and in 1449, by a bull of February 17, Pope
Nicholas V authorized Rodrigo Borgia, Canon of Valencia,
to reside outside the places from which his benefices

came.[12] This year, 1449, is the last year of his residence in Spain, apart from the period from 1472 to 1473 when he visited the country as Legate of Pope Sixtus IV.

It may be that young Rodrigo spent some time in Rome immediately following the year 1449 with his uncle, the Cardinal; but not much later we find him studying law at the University of Bologna. To lend point to their accusations of ignorance and to exaggerate the nepotism which so aided his ecclesiastical career, almost all the biographers have him come from Spain to Italy and go to Bologna only after the coronation of Calixtus III, which was in 1456[12a]; but it is quite certain that he came to Italy in 1449, as is shown by the bull already mentioned of Nicholas V, and from a discourse of Jason del Maino;[13] and there is no doubt that he was at Bologna at least as early as 1453.[14] A document in which Calixtus III recommends, as in a kind of diplomatic passport, that every sort of consideration and assistance be given to Rodrigo and his other nephew Del Mila by the officials of the territories through which they must pass on their way from Rome to Bologna in 1455, does not as von Pastor believes apply to his first journey but to a later one. Alexander VI certainly made really considerable studies at Bologna over a space of seven years.

There is to be found at the University of Bologna a document upon which is signified approval of his law studies, together with certain marginal notes indicating the dates on which he was made Cardinal and Pope and the date of his death. These marginal notes belonged to a later period, when the Borgias had already acquired their grim reputation. The last reads like this: "He died in August, 1503, and was buried in Hell." Contemporary writers bear witness that the future Pope passed his various grades with

30

all honors,[15] and we know that Alexander VI was deeply versed in canonical questions and that at an early age he wrote by no means ill upon these subjects.

We have his correspondence with Savonarola, his numerous and voluminous letters to the Franciscan friars, and his letters to the Ruthenians to lead them to abandon the Orthodox rite. All these are documents of considerable value canonically. In addition he has left us two works in defense of the Faith entitled *Clipeus defensionis fidei Sanctae Romanae Ecclesiae* and *Constitutiones Ecclesiasticae*. Further he wrote two books, the first longer than the second, upon ecclesiastical organization together with other less important works.[15a]

Thus all that is historically known of this period proves that Rodrigo de Borgia entered at a very tender age upon the ecclesiastical career. Thanks to his uncle the Cardinal, he received an endless flow of benefices and offices, with the corresponding remuneration.

We know further that at seventeen he received papal authorization to continue drawing the income of his benefices although he was no longer in the appropriate residence and to stay either in Rome with Cardinal de Borgia or in a University.

In fact we find him later at the University of Bologna.

All this, to put it in legal language, is proved by documents irrefutable and not to be questioned; but the legend was inevitable. The lucky document which has served as a foundation for the majority of writers to create that fabulous criminal family, and which deals with this first period of the life of Alexander VI, proves at once the unreliability of its author and his calumnious purpose. It is in reliance upon this document that so many modern writers, from the eighteenth century onwards *but not before*, have held it as certain that young Rodrigo Borgia, either before becoming an ecclesiastic or as an interlude in his ecclesiastical career, had been a soldier and had traveled widely. To which they have added that, giving up the sword for the gown, he turned lawyer in order to defend difficult cases with the subtle skill that was his.[16]

But since tragedy must not be lacking even to his infancy the document just mentioned says that Rodrigo, at the age of twelve, killed another boy of the same age but of a lower social condition. The attack was ferocious and leaves no doubt of the viciousness of his instincts, for he stabbed his victim again and again in the pit of the stomach, trying to find the place where it would hurt most! Nor need we say that the cause of the attack was of the slightest since we are discussing the greatest of history's criminals; it was due merely to disrespectful words. Rodrigo's father inflicted no punishment upon him, nor did the law. The father's failure to punish the twelve year old Rodrigo was perhaps less surprising than the law's, since he died when his son was ten.

The writer of the manuscript prefaces the tragic story with "It is said." The moderns who have copied him at second or third hand suppress this indication of doubt.

As to when and how he could have been a *condottiere* of the Spanish sort in the Iberian peninsula, and an illustrious lawyer in the court of Valencia, we are not told and it is difficult to imagine. He was an ecclesiastic from early childhood; he went to Italy at just over seventeen; he was at Bologna at eighteen—certainly not later than twenty-one; he was a Cardinal at twenty-four. And by a strange chance Alexander VI, differing in this from that curious person Julius II, has put it on record that he had no knowledge of military affairs. In his letters to princes as in his conversations, he affirmed at different periods that having belonged to the Church from childhood and throughout his life, he had no understanding of such questions.

The election of Pope Calixtus III was decisive for the future of his nephew Rodrigo, then at the University of Bologna. The College of Cardinals, after a close struggle between two opposing groups had chosen the aged Cardinal Alfonso de Borgia, precisely because he was aged. He was seventy-six. Aspirants to the Papacy sometimes adjourned the combat in this way, in the hope that the interval would be brief as the advanced age of the new Pope promised. This time the interval lasted only three years. But Rodrigo Borgia passed from being a young ecclesiastic with powerful connections to the rank of a relation of the Pope, who, let us remember, was a temporal prince uniting the highest spiritual authority in the world with an effective territorial rulership. Alexander made haste to leave Bologna and come to Rome. But the Pope sent him back to his studies with the promise that he would certainly not neglect his future. And in fact rich benefices began to fall upon his head in extraordinary abundance.

Calixtus III was elected on April 8, 1455, and crowned on April 20. As early as the tenth of May he had nominated his nephew protonotary apostolic, a very high dignity directly depending upon the Vatican. A little later—in January of the following year—he made him priest and canon of the cathedral of the united dioceses of Segovia and Albarazin. Later he gave him the parish of Quart in the Diocese of Valencia. All this, you understand, in consideration of his virtues and for the services he had rendered to the Church and to the Pope. In plain fact, Rodrigo was at that time nothing but a serious studious young man, preparing for his doctorate; but nepotism always found fine words to justify itself.[17]

Excessive as all these favors were, they by no means exhausted the desires of Calixtus' family, nor indeed did they completely satisfy the affection the pontiff had for his nephew. He was old and ill; and he knew, as Lorenzo the Magnificent had reminded Innocent VIII, "that he was not immortal and that while a Pope possesses all the power he likes, yet he cannot render his office hereditary nor turn into personal property anything but the honors and riches he gives his family while he is alive."[18] From the first hour of his pontificate Calixtus III had decided to make Cardinals of his two nephews, Rodrigo and Luis Juan del Mila. That is to say, he meant to confer upon them the highest dignity in his power; but at the same time he wanted to see them finish their studies. A man of high culture and a jurist habituated to the observance of forms, he did not want them to cut short their time at Bologna; and it was only later and with a certain hesitancy that he decided to place the red hat upon these youthful heads still bending over their books. In a consistory held February 20, 1456, the Pope named three cardinals—Luis Juan del Mila, Rodrigo Borgia, and don Jaime of Portugal, son of the Infanta don Pedro. They were all young men—Mila twenty-five, Rodrigo twenty-four, and don Jaime twenty-three. Later other cardinals were named even younger, for at that time the cardinalate was not the supreme reward for a life devoted to faith and worship; it was something much more complex. A cardinal often had the function of a prince or territorial ruler and in some instances he acted as papal commissary with the armies.

These three new cardinals were named *in petto,* an

uncommon form, but used to indicate that for the moment
the appointments were not to be made public.

The secret consistory and the nomination *in petto* have
led the biographers to some highly dramatic interpreta-
tions. Even some of the moderns say that there was a
strong opposition to these nominations and that finally,
since the will of the Pope was not to be resisted in such
a matter, the cardinals gave way in the hope that, as the
nominations had been made *in petto*, so ill a man as the
Pope might die before publication; in support of this, it
is pointed out that the Pope actually announced the nominations publicly in the month of September, a time when
the hygienic conditions of the Rome of that day kept the
cardinals of the opposition out of the city. All this is sheer
invention. In the bull creating Rodrigo Borgia a cardinal,
the Pope affirms the unanimity not only of the other cardinals present but even of the single absentee, the Cardinal of Ostia; and their signatures are at the end of the
document.[19] It is possible that there may have been a
strong preliminary opposition to this act of obvious family
favoritism; but all that we actually know is that the nomination was made in a form which may have been unusual
but had been used in a good many other cases, and with
every safeguard for the cardinal-elect in the event of the
Pope's death. Anyhow Calixtus III could die happy. Not
having the right to choose, like a good worldly prince, a
direct and immediate successor from among his own family, he at least created potential inheritors. Time and the
tenacious will of one of them did ultimately bring a second Borgia to the Papal throne.

At this moment of his nomination as cardinal, no one
could have judged the future Alexander VI with severity.
Only writers of later ages, in their condemnation of real

or supposed actions of his maturity, have chosen to slander his early youth. In this year 1456 there was no pretext for an accusation against the young man preparing to take his doctorate at the University of Bologna, who was being elevated to so lofty a charge by the Pope and King his uncle.

Obviously, the nomination of a boy of twenty-four to such a dignity was an act of sheer favoritism, but no pope of the period was free from that fault. And it is strange but true that the most important popes of the Renaissance came precisely from among the young men whom nepotism had raised to the purple.

CHAPTER III

The Cardinal

Rodrigo was too young for the burden laid upon his shoulders. But under the direction of his uncle, the Pope, and with his own highly cultivated intelligence and above all with his imposing appearance, not less imposing for the cardinal's scarlet, his novitiate was easy. He did not need long training for a career of command. Besides, in the exercise of government success is not difficult for a man well tutored if his will is strong. Rodrigo had the character needed for any high enterprise.

Some months after having published the new cardinal's nomination, Calixtus III appointed him as Papal Vicar in the March of Ancona, with full temporal and spiritual powers; and under this pretext he fairly loaded him with benefices, some of them for a fixed period in order to cover the expenses of that particular mission, some of them permanent. The March of Ancona was at that time in need at once of a strong hand and of good administration, scrupulous and strict. Cardinal Borgia showed himself fully at the level of his task. In one of those conspiracies with which the period swarms, a nobleman of Ascoli had assassinated one Giovanni Sforza, tyrant of the town; he followed up this crime, which he described as a victory for the people, by taking his victim's place and exercising the same tyranny. Another conspiracy threw *him* out, and

37

he barely escaped with his life. But knowing how easily collective passions can change direction, the noble lord attacked and seized hold of the papal fortress which guarded that domain, hoping to return to power and animated by the murderous spirit of revenge normal in such circumstances. Cardinal Borgia passed through Ascoli at the very beginning of his mission and realized that there were two victims in this tragedy, one, *de jure,* the Papacy which was no longer obeyed though it was the rightful sovereign; the other, *de facto,* the people which paid for its master's rivalries with its blood. Undeterred by the difficulties, he ordered the Papal forces to attack the castle. Fortune was with him. The struggle was short, the fortress was captured and the rebel with it. He was not, as usual in those cases, executed but sent to Rome.

If it were my purpose to write novelised history, I should make this incident the key to the whole policy that Alexander VI was later to pursue. It was the first time that Borgia found himself face to face with the sort of tyrant who at that time strove for the possessions of papal Rome by means of assassination, treason and plot. It was the first time he realized that the Church's weakness in the temporal order allowed these abuses, which caused so much misery to cities and so much shame to the Church herself. But, drama apart, it must be granted that in this special case the incident helped toward the formation in him of that psychology which later, nearly forty years later, led him to reverse the temporizing policy of the Popes who preceded him. For it had been their policy to rely upon one tyrant to fight another. He fought them all. Even so early he must have learned that under the name of Vicars were hidden usurpers who dominated the Church in the guise of its defenders.

38

In this first mission the new cardinal gave equal proof of the financial and administrative abilities for which he was later to be so highly appreciated, even by his enemies. He settled the question of the tax on salt and increased its yield. He took up necessary matters of justice; he punished other rebellious nobles and confiscated their goods in favor of Rome. There could not have been a more splendid beginning for his new career.

The old Pope spoke in the consistory of his nephew's success with much pleasure. All the family affection of the Borgia clan, so numerous and so united a clan as it was, poured out in his words.[1] And he rewarded his nephew's success by other well-remunerated offices. Since he could not yet name him bishop, he made him administrator of the diocese of Gerona, in order that he might give him the bishopric when he should have arrived at the canonical age of twenty-seven. But even so many benefices, granted at such a rate, were not enough for the heart of the Pope, who felt certain that he had found the glorious continuator of the illustrious name of Borgia. He did not of course forget his other nephews nor indeed any of his relations. He was mindful in particular of Pedro Luis, for whom as we have seen he even dreamed of the throne of Naples. But Rodrigo stood first. The old Pope knew that in that age there were no honors and successes without peril save in the hierarchy of the Church; and choosing a moment when he thought he could carry the thing through without great opposition, he named him, in 1457, Vice-Chancellor of the Church—the second place in that universal organization.

God's Chancellor upon earth is the Pope. If the Vice-Chancellor was not a vice-pope, he was at least head of the internal organization and his dignity was second only to that of the Sovereign Pontiff. Besides, the office was extremely well paid. Jacapo de Volterra suggests that the income attached to it may have been as high as eight thousand florins a year, a considerable sum for that time.[2]

It must be noted, for the honor of Calixtus III, that his spirit of nepotism did not, in this nomination, involve any sacrifice of the interests of the Church. Whatever opinion may be held of Borgia as Pope, there can be no question that in his present office as in all his functions, ecclesiastical and temporal, his success was complete. In fact he remained Vice-Chancellor all the time that he was a cardinal, that is from 1457 to 1492. In succession Popes Pius II, Paul II, Sixtus IV and Innocent VIII maintained him in the office with the most profuse expressions of approbation and approved the reforms introduced by him into the Chancellery. Pius II had already expressed appreciation of the young Cardinal's work before he became Pope: "Rodrigo Borgia is now in charge of the Chancellery; he is young in age assuredly, but he is old in judgment."[3] Sixtus IV declared that Rodrigo had been Chancellor for many years with the most eminent qualities and the most exact diligence.[4] Pope Innocent VIII believed that Borgia's period of office was the one which had given the Holy See the best information upon affairs.

If the remuneration increased, so also did the expenses —especially at the beginning, when Cardinal Borgia had to build a great edifice which was to remain for long the Vatican Chancellery.

When Borgia was himself elected Pope, he gave this building to Cardinal Ascanio Sforza, who had succeeded him as Vice-Chancellor. This gift is the principal foundation of the accusation that his election to the Papacy was simoniacal. But that was all in the future. For the moment Cardinal Borgia, for all that he was laden with benefices

40

and remunerated on the grand scale as Vice-Chancellor, did not always have enough money for his commitments; he often had to borrow and even at times pawn the future revenues of his many benefices for long periods.

When Calixtus III died he had emptied the vessel of fortune over his nephew's head. He gave him every honor that it was in his power to give, everything needed to make him, in spite of the recency of his nomination, one of the most powerful of the cardinals. And that material force might be added to spiritual and financial, he put him at the head of the whole military organization, while keeping Rodrigo's own brother, Pedro Luis, as the actual chief of the army.

Given the shortness of his pontificate, Calixtus III's nepotism surpassed anything that ever had been seen, or indeed ever was to be seen. Probably the family pressure was more effective upon this pope than upon others because of his advanced age and the infirmities which kept him always in a kind of seclusion. This meant that he never heard those murmurs of envious or dissatisfied courtiers which take the place of public opinion when the free air of the street cannot penetrate the chamber of the great. Calixtus could die happy. The three years of his pontificate had been worth an ordinary quarter century to Rodrigo's career.

Left to stand on his own feet, the young Cardinal proved that he no longer needed either the advice or the powerful protection of the dead pope. After having fulfilled the duties imposed upon him by the triple bond which united him to Calixtus III, who was his pope, his uncle and his protector, he defied the populace when they wished to prevent the obsequies having that degree of pious solemnity which the death of a pope demands. He saved the life of his brother Pedro Luis and managed to secure him a satisfactory financial arrangement with the Holy See. Then he occupied himself energetically with the functions of his office as Vice-Chancellor, maintaining and increasing by his intelligence and ability the position that had come to him so easily.

Our principal knowledge of his work as cardinal concerns the successive conclaves in which he took part. There were four of them, and in all it was he who virtually decided the election. In three of them, he did so at the last moment: in the early ballots he voted against the cardinal who had the greatest number of votes; then, moving neatly and surely he gave him the necessary majority, so that he seemed to settle the matter as an arbiter rather than as a voter. It was in these electoral assemblies that every cardinal in large measure determined his future career. For it was only at the time of election of a new pope that the cardinals were sovereign, as the people are sovereign in our own day only at the ballot box. It was for each cardinal so to act in the conclave as to impose upon the newly elected pope such a moral obligation that though he was an absolute monarch—with no juridical chains to curb him and no moral obligations save such as he recognized himself—he would spontaneously remember the cardinal's good offices.

In the first of these conclaves, Rodrigo, still very young, offered his vote to the Cardinal d'Estouteville. The Cardinals believed that the necessary two-thirds of the votes would almost certainly go to him on the first ballot. Estouteville had, as the phrase then ran, entered the conclave as pope. But as no one wanted too easy an election, they all voted in the secret of the urn against their given word. They even voted for cardinals who had not offered themselves as candidates, and this scattered the votes. Estouteville, who had regarded himself as pope already, was utterly stunned at such perfidy. On the second ballot Cardinal Borgia kept his promise and voted for him. But once more the proverb was confirmed—he who goes into a conclave as pope, comes out as cardinal. Estouteville was not chosen. Instead they chose Eneas Silvius Piccolomini, the Cardinal of Siena, an elegant and learned writer, a highly intelligent diplomat and man of affairs, and in mental quality close to genius.

It is necessary to explain the procedure followed in conclaves if we are to grasp the important role played by young Rodrigo Borgia in this first testing, and see how, although he was opposed to Piccolomini, he was the principal factor in his election.

The pope may be elected in different ways. The first is what in modern terminology is called "election by acclamation." The Church ennobles this with the name "election by inspiration." A great number of cardinals begin to call out the name of one of their members. If these cries issue from the breasts of two-thirds plus one, the necessary number is thus obtained and the bearer of the name is acclaimed as elected. This method is rarely employed in practice and in theory it is useful only when there is a practical unanimity of opinion. In any case it is a dangerous method and the cardinals have often agreed among themselves to exclude it, for it influences the weaker spirits and those who are in terror of not being with the majority.

The second form is styled "by adoration." When the candidate is a deeply respected cardinal, mature in years and venerable and of strong character—the kind of man needed in a crisis—the requisite majority of two-thirds plus

D

43

one rise from their seats and go to kneel at the feet of their chosen colleague.

The third way is by secret ballot. This is the commonest way, especially in the early stages of an election. But there are still two others which may be regarded as supplementary: the one by "accession," the other "by compromise."

Accession is useful when, after many ballots, the necessary majority has not been obtained and the conclave is being unduly prolonged; it is then permissible for a cardinal to announce that he has changed his vote and given it to the one of those who has a majority though not the requisite majority. If one of the cardinals thereby attains the requisite number of votes, the balloting immediately ceases and we have a pope.

The final method is used when it is realized that none of the preceding methods will secure the necessary majority and that the conclave is being prolonged beyond the limits of prudence, with the consequence that there is less food for the cardinals and tumult in the streets. In such an event they name a committee with full power to choose the new pope.

In the contest between Estouteville and Eneas Silvius Piccolomini, the conclave decided after a ballot which gave six votes to one candidate and nine to the other that the election should be completed by accession. In the silence that always falls in that solemn moment, he who takes the initiative of interrupting the reticent waiting in which the great majority have taken refuge commits either an imprudence or an act of decision. While the cardinals were eyeing one another anxiously, as if to read what the intentions of others might be, hesitant yet anxious to be

44

on the victor's side, Rodrigo Borgia rose gravely from his velvet seat and said with all solemnity: "I accede to the Cardinal of Siena." Thus Eneas Silvius came closer to the necessary majority and Estouteville lost a vote, falling back from six to five. That settled it. Immediately Cardinal Tebaldo also acceded to the Cardinal of Siena, and when the majority was virtually certain, Cardinal Colonna likewise went over to the winner.

The legend of course naturally has it that Borgia betrayed Estouteville. But if acts of this sort are regarded as betrayals there would never be an electoral majority. Borgia's action is easy to understand. After a ballot which had given a large majority, he followed that majority. It has been said that both competitors had offered Rodrigo Borgia to maintain him in his office of Vice-Chancellor, but that Eneas Silvius had let him know that Estouteville had given the same promise to another cardinal: this, runs the story, was the cause of Rodrigo's last minute decision. While we are in the realm of guesswork, it is surely more plausible to believe that if Eneas Silvius had known of his opponent's double promise, he would have told Borgia about it earlier; and if Borgia had believed that Estouteville was tricking him, he would have voted against him rather than for him in the earlier balloting.

It has also been said that he was forced to vote for Piccolomini under the pressure of an Italian state, Milan. But again the problem is to know why he waited until the last moment to vote for him, since the conclave was rigorously guarded, completely closed to the outside world, and it was not possible for any influence from the outside to make itself felt once the doors were closed. Eneas Silvius had in fact wished to gain Rodrigo's vote at the start, but he had presented the young Spaniard with an argument

45

which, in view of his own aspirations for the future, was not likely to be convincing: he told him that another foreign pope would be a cause of difficulties for the Church and he asked him at least to give his vote to an Italian. The subtle scholar knew that none of the other Italians was a dangerous candidate and simply wished to weaken Estouteville; but Borgia could not accept the theory that a non-Italian might be a danger to the Roman Curia. It may be that this was the reason why he had voted for Estouteville in the ballots.

Rodrigo took the same position in the election of Cardinal Francesco della Rovere, the next pope but one, who took the name of Sixtus IV. It had seemed that Francesco della Rovere had no chance of success. In the early stages of the conclave other names were discussed. Borgia voted for the Cardinal of Ravenna, but the real contest, which lasted two days, was between the Cardinals Gonzaga and Estouteville. At the end of these two days, Gonzaga put forward as candidate Francesco della Rovere, a Franciscan, an eloquent preacher, of poor family, utterly unversed in politics. Since he saw that he could not himself be pope, Cardinal Gonzaga wished that one should be elected who would be likely to follow his counsels. Rodrigo voted against Francesco but seeing that he had a solid majority, he proposed that recourse should be had to accession to bring the conclave to a conclusion. This having been agreed, he rose and gave his adhesion to the majority; he was followed by Estouteville and by Barbo, nephew of Paul II. So it was that Francesco della Rovere became pope.

In 1484, upon the death of Sixtus IV the conclave was

opened on August 26. Cardinal Borgia was now one of the most powerful elements in it. He was the doyen of the Sacred College and was himself a candidate. Of those who were cardinals at the time of his promotion there remained only himself and his cousin Del Mila who had some time before retired to Spain and took no more interest in Rome and its Court.

Rodrigo pronounced the opening discourse, exhorting all to vote for the man most likely to serve the Church well. The balloting began, and in order to avoid surprises, there was a preliminary agreement that on the first day there should be no recourse to the system of accession. The idea was to give the conclave the necessary time to form a spontaneous majority, so that nobody should be obliged to make his decision under the watchful critical eyes of the rest.

In the early ballots a number of cardinals voted for Marco Barbo, Cardinal of San Marco; some voted for Borgia and some for Giuliano della Rovere, the future Pope Julius II. A few votes were sprinkled round among other cardinals. Night came and the necessary majority had not yet been attained. Then, in private conversations, the two future adversaries, Rodrigo Borgia and Giuliano della Rovere agreed to abandon their personal aspirations— probably because they were pretty sure that they would not be elected anyhow—and decided that the Church would be very well defended by the Cardinal of Santa Cecilia, Giovanni Baptista Cibo.[5] He was descended from a noble family, differing in this from his predecessor; but like him he came from Liguria. Sixtus IV was born at Savona and Cibo at Genoa. Cibo was elected and took the name of Innocent VIII.

The help that Cardinal Borgia gave to Cibo was due not

47

only to the view he had of him as a man of calm and con-
ciliatory disposition (which everybody wanted after the
tempestuous Sixtus IV), but also because he was the man
most likely to defeat Marco Barbo whom he did not want
to see elected. Yet Barbo would have triumphed if he had
not been a Venetian. Sixtus IV had launched an interdict
against Venice only the year before, and this had caused
considerable animosity between the Holy See and the Most
Serene City. The whole policy of Venice ran, at that time
as at many other times, contrary to the policy of the Vatican and the interests of the rest of Italy. In fact in the very
year of this conclave Venice suggested to the French King
Charles VIII to set about the conquest of Naples; and it
signed the Peace of Bagnola against the Italian League in
order to expand its hold upon the mainland by the annexation of Polessini and Rovigo.[6]

A Venetian on the throne of Saint Peter could not at
such a moment be pleasing to the great body of cardinals,
and this factor was the more acute in that the nationalist
spirit—if the word may be used in speaking of a city—
was known to be excessive in the Venetians. The virtues
of Cardinal Barbo himself were overshadowed by these
political considerations. The enemies that Borgia had gathered about him in the centuries since his death had been
quick to see why he opposed Barbo; he was afraid of so
virtuous a man! All the same it was political and not personal considerations which influenced his decision.

Twenty years earlier, in the election of 1464, Borgia had
from the first supported Cardinal Pietro Barbo, another
Venetian and uncle of Marco. He was elected and took the
name of Paul II. Indeed it seems that Borgia was considered the principal factor in his election although a recent
illness, contracted when he was with Pope Pius II in An-

48

cona, meant that he came to the conclave still only convalescent. The envoy of Mantua wrote to his Prince on this
occasion: "The Vice-Chancellor (Borgia) will have a great
influence with this pope, and he has certainly earned it."[7]

The kind of skill we have seen Rodrigo show in these
various elections is a quality of passionless calculating
minds. Such a mind Rodrigo had; and he gathered the
fruit of so many successive victories.

The authority of the cardinals had greatly increased since
the time of the Schisms. They had acquired new prerogatives. The popes, before their election, were obliged to
make many concessions in their favor. They had to fix a
sum to be taken from the papal treasury for those whose
benefices did not suffice for the princely life held proper
to them. In the conclaves, before proceeding to an election,
each cardinal candidate signed a list of obligations. It was
a kind of papal program setting out all that the cardinal
undertook to do for his former colleagues if he became
pope.

In these circumstances it is not surprising that the candidate, either before or during the conclave, should make
known, in that superb indirect style which the Church had
either borrowed from the classics or arrived at as suited to
her own psychology, what he meant to do with such benefices as happened not to be allotted at the time of his election. Further every pope, on ceasing to be a cardinal, had
to give up the benefices he had held; and naturally every
cardinal who was *papabile* generally had a fair number of
benefices, precisely because only an important cardinal was
likely to be *papabile*. Naturally, such offers would be made
indirectly. When one speaks of simony in the conclaves,
we must not understand the putting up of votes for sale.

Obviously the losers and their supporters, disappointed in their hopes, would accuse the winner of corruption and venality. But if corruption it was, then the loser had used it exactly as the winner had: although neither of them really violated, at any rate in form, the law bearing upon the matter.

We find Cardinal Rodrigo Borgia being loaded with favors immediately after each conclave, and indeed throughout the various pontificates. But this was true of the other cardinals in active service who resided permanently at the Roman Court. And it seems that they gave him the most difficult and expensive offices and were invariably satisfied with the zeal, diligence and sound good sense he invariably showed. The bulls in which the missions and benefices are given to him are exactly the same in tone as those signed by the Pope who was his uncle; and they follow one another at intervals of a few months. The praises they lavish upon him might be used for the composition of a historical defense of his character; only that all this was official prose, using stock formulas.

But we have more to rely on than these official texts to show the esteem in which he was held. The popes desired his company, accepted his counsels, charged him with missions of great importance, used him constantly. When they left Rome to visit other parts of the Church's territory, he was practically always with them, whereas the rest of the papal suite was formed of a small number of cardinals who took turns.

He was in relation with the great of this world. He received them when they visited Rome, flinging wide the doors of his magnificent house. In the official programs of such state visits, there was always something on the grand scale at the Borgia house. Ascanio Sforza, of the powerful ducal house of Milan, a man of elegance and refinement, could not refrain from describing to his brother, Ludovico Moro, the beauty of one of these banquets at which he had just been on the occasion of the arrival from Naples of a prince of the house of Aragon.

In religious ceremonies also Cardinal Borgia was pre-eminent. He rolled out his tapestries, filled the streets with flowers, marvelously illuminated the front of his house. His lavishness was hard to distinguish from extravagance.

His private life, on the other hand, was simple to the point of parsimony. Bruchard, Maffei[8] and others tell us that at his own table only one dish was served, and that Cesar Borgia and other cardinals avoided dining with him. Unlike Julius II, whom everybody took care not to meet after meals, Rodrigo drank lightly. In his private life he spent as little as possible; and those around him murmured the word avarice.

His income was enormous but so were his public expenses. He built the episcopal palace at Piensa to please Pius II who wanted for sentimental reasons to "make" that town. He rebuilt the fortresses at Subiaco and the castle of Civitta Castellana. In 1461 he paid for thirty men-at-arms for the war against Sigismond Malatesta, which was more than any other cardinal did. Pius II had made ready a crusade against the Turks, a luckless enterprise which was ended by the plague at Ancona and the Pope's death: Rodrigo provided a galley, which cost him several thousand ducats. He repaired all the churches in his diocese at heavy expense.

Jacopo Gherardi de Volterra has left us a vivid description of Borgia at the time he was a cardinal: "A man of versatile intelligence and greatness of soul, a fluent speaker though his speeches lack true literary value. An ardent

51

temperament but given to careful consideration of matters he is dealing with from the angle of self-interest; clever at finding the best mode of action. Many kings and princes are bound to him in friendship . . . he possesses, especially in Spain and Italy, rich sacerdotal incomes, and he is in charge of three episcopal sees—Valencia, Porto, and Cartagena; further, he receives from the Chancellery a sum which amounts, it seems, to eight thousand ducats. He has vessels of silver, precious stones, vestments of gold and silk, and books of doctrine. So that he is considered as the richest of the cardinals except Estouteville."[9]

CHAPTER IV

Accusations of Immorality

A DAY by day account of Borgia's life would lack historical basis. We simply have not any exact knowledge. And it would be monotonous to describe the routine events of his ecclesiastical life, the religious ceremonies in which he took part, the prebends and benefices he received or resigned. The fact is that the life of a cardinal at that day was lived entirely in the shadow of the Pope, who represented the Church in its totality. In any case the main historic interest of a Borgia lies in the role assigned to him by later writers, and primarily in his private life and the immorality with which he has been so liberally credited. There is no point in talking of this or that journey, or banquet or hunting party. What is interesting at this time is to estimate what truth there is in all that has been written and rewritten about the evidences of debauchery and treachery shown by him before his arrival at the papcy.

But it must be made clear that in all the fantastic pile of accusations, not much was said of these things before Rodrigo had reached the age of sixty; for before the conclave of 1492, at which he attained the tiara, there is not the faintest shadow of a mention of his relations with either Vannozza or Giulia la Bella, who was Giulia Farnese.

I have already shown the absurdity of the accusations concerning his early youth, and these are in fact rejected or at any rate treated as doubtful by the majority of modern writers. We must now examine the very few details, actually given us by history during his life as cardinal, bearing upon the sex attraction ascribed to him—an attraction described by a contemporary author in a phrase that was meant for eulogy but has been used by posterity for slander.

Apart from two episodes more or less reprehensible, we have no trace whatever either of the obscene banquets and festivals beloved of his biographers, or of the quietly respectable "married life" he is supposed by some to have led.

Eneas Silvius, who succeeded Calixtus III under the name of Pius II, had a special regard for Borgia. In his *History of Europe,* he writes of Borgia's nomination as cardinal that though he was very young for such a dignity, there was no injustice in it, given his knowledge, his prudence, and the excellence of his life. He expresses his pleasure at Borgia's appointment as Vice-Chancellor, with the remark that the cardinal is young in age but old in his ways and in his judgement. When he became pope, Eneas Silvius gave Rodrigo clear proofs of affection, continuing the shower of benefices which had begun to fall upon his fortunate head in his uncle's days. He retained him as Vice-Chancellor. At the beginning of his pontificate he had to go to the Congress of Mantua, in order to continue the work of his predecessor and obtain the union of Christian princes in a league against the Mussulman. He asked Cardinal Borgia to accompany him along with other colleagues. Returning from Mantua where he had small success, he went to Siena, still followed by the cardinal. He always liked revisiting his native city but on this occasion he was constrained to it by gout. He wished to take the waters at Petriolo and remain out of Rome to avoid the extreme heat. Borgia stayed with him the whole time.

And now we have for the first time a precise accusation against Rodrigo Borgia.

The Pope was at Petriolo in the month of June, 1460, and Cardinal Borgia was close by at Siena. The incident now to be mentioned is not related by any chronicler of the period and seems to have been unknown to historians practically contemporary with Alexander VI.

But we have the details directly from Pius II himself, who made a collection of facts and documents concerning his person and his time, and they are to be found in a severe letter written directly by the Pope to the cardinal. The latter is regarded as apocryphal by certain Catholic authors, on the ground that the style has not the elegance of this most excellent Latinist. But I am inclined, with von Pastor and L'Espinois, to consider it authentic not only because of the deep feeling it expresses but also because we have not to deal merely with one isolated document. In any event the incident, when we see it in its totality, has not quite the blackness which recent biographers have found in it.

Forgers are in the habit of fabricating isolated documents, but not without a very definite purpose. It may be that this letter has been altered in part, but in the main it is as Pius wrote it. That the style is not worthy of so famous a Latinist is not a strong enough argument. The pope, writing at speed, may very well have lacked the usual elegance of his literary style; or even he may have ordered a secretary to write the letter, since it was a matter of urgency and he was suffering from gout.

This letter contains an account of the incident, and it

seems worth while to reproduce it in its entirety, but translated from the Latin. It shows the severe language used by a pope who loved his Church and was determined to defend its morals against any personal affection of his own. It is not to the point that Eneas Silvius had made ill use of his own youth. In this hour he was Pope; and upon the moral law popes do not compromise.

"We have learned that three days ago a large number of women of Siena, adorned with all worldly vanity, gathered in the gardens of our well-beloved son Giovanni de Bichis, and that your Eminence, in contempt of the dignity of your position, remained with them from one o'clock until six o'clock in the afternoon; and that you had in your company another Cardinal to whom at least his age, if not the honor of the Holy See, should have recalled his duty. We are told that the dances were immodest and the seductions of love beyond bounds and that you yourself behaved as if you were one of the most vulgar young men of the age. In truth I should blush to set down in detail all I have been told of what happened. Not only these things themselves, but the mere mention of them, are a dishonor to the office you hold. In order to have more freedom for your amusements you forbade entry to the husbands, fathers, brothers and relations who came with these young women. You two, with a handful of attendants, were the sole organizers and instigators. It seems that at this moment no other thing is spoken of in the town of Siena and that you are the laughing stock of everybody. Assuredly here, in the baths, where there is a great crowd of ecclesiastics and laymen, you are on everybody's tongue. If I said I was not angry at these matters, I should commit a grave error. We are more angry than we can say, for it is a cause of dishonor to the ecclesiastical state and contempt for our ministry; it gives a pretext to those who accuse us of using our wealth and our high office for orgies, it is such things as these that cause the small esteem in which we are held by princes and powers, the daily mockery of the laity, and the reprobation hurled at our own conduct when we undertake to reprove others. The Vicar of Christ himself is an object of scorn because it is believed that he closes his eyes to these excesses.

"You preside, my dear son, over the Church of Valencia, one of the most important in Spain; likewise you rule the pontifical Chancellery; and what renders your act more reprehensible is that you are stationed close to the Sovereign Pontiff as Counsellor of the Holy See. We leave it to your own judgment to say if it befits your high degree to pay compliments to women, to be sending them fruit, to drink a mouthful of wine and then have the glass carried to the woman who pleases you most, to spend a whole day as a delighted spectator of all kinds of games; and finally, for the sake of more liberty, to exclude from the gathering the husbands and relations of the women who are invited.

"Your faults reflect upon us, and upon Calixtus, your uncle of happy memory, who is accused of a great fault of judgment for having laden you with undeserved honors. Your youth is not to be alleged in your defense, for it is not so tender and you are capable of realizing the responsibilities that your dignity places upon your shoulders. It behoves a cardinal to be irreproachable, to be a salutary example to all in the morality of his life, and the model of an existence which not only is edifying and profitable to the soul but is so exteriorly as well. We are indignant when secular princes approach us for dishonorable reasons, when they do us wrong by coveting our properties and our benefices, and when we must bend to their demands. It is ourselves who inflict upon us the wounds from which we suffer when we so act that the authority of the Church is less respected from day to day. We bear the shame of our conduct in this world, and we shall suffer the punishment we have deserved in the world to come.

"Let your Eminence then decide to put an end to these frivolities; you must remember your dignity and cease to appear among your youthful contemporaries in the likeness of a man of pleasure. If such acts were repeated we should be obliged to show that they happen totally in spite of us and against our will; and our reproaches would be cast in such terms as would put you to the blush. We have always loved you and regarded you as worthy of our protection, because we have taken you for a model of gravity and modesty. Let us long keep this opinion and this conviction, and to this end you must without delay enter upon a much more serious way of life. Your youth, the pledge of amendment, causes us to warn you paternally. If you had allowed yourself such things at the age of your companion, we should no longer be able to do you this charitable service."

Clearly the accusation is harsh and the letter is written in pretty vigorous terms. But upon the gravest point, the

Pope is very careful to say "We have been told," and this is very important, as we shall see. It must be considered too that the letter contains both statements of fact and comments. In letting himself go at length in these latter, the Pontiff, using the always slightly apocalyptic language of the Roman Church, says that a cardinal must not provoke a scandal—and that scandal is even worse in a bishop, who has the charge of souls.

But on the other hand, on the question of fact, he limits himself to saying that Rodrigo and another cardinal advanced in years, took part in a festival in the gardens of a person of distinction loved by the Pope; and here, after having forbidden entry to the fathers, husbands, and such like of the ladies of the party, they were present at improper dances in which were incitements to love—by which he means certain lascivious movements of the figures of the dance. Further, he says, Rodrigo congratulated the girls upon their dance, sending them fruit and having the glass from which he had drunk taken to the young woman of his preference that she might drink from it.

Reading what the pope thinks of all this, one thing is clear—such severity is only shown to persons whose moral reputation is high. It is unthinkable that the Borgia of legend should have received such a letter. Pius II seems surprised at this ill-behaviour of Cardinal Borgia and, having criticized it, tells him with paternal affection that he has always loved him and regarded him as worthy of his protection because he held him for a model of gravity and modesty. Further, he held that the other cardinal present had sinned more gravely, and he indicates that in the matter of Rodrigo he has great hopes for the future. The other cardinal and his morals seem not to interest the Pope—as

E

though he thought him entirely beyond redemption. At this distance of time, it is difficult to imagine the cause of the difference in the Pope's attitude toward the two cardinals, for the reasons he alleges—that one of them is much older than the other—does not seem like very sound logic; but whatever the reason may be, we cannot doubt his esteem for the one and his contempt for the other. In any case, I am inclined to believe that the papal language is largely making use of the apostolic technique of reprimand. In the Church's view, a sin once committed must always be presented in the darkest colors. Read any encyclical or any sermon written or spoken in countries of robust Catholicism and you will begin to wonder about the virtue of even the holiest man. Religious language, and especially Catholic language, is always colorful when it comes to sin. Hence the philippics of Savonarola against a whole society, and even the aggressive sermons of Luther —who, in spite of his rebellion, had not managed to rid himself of old habits.

As to the facts treated, as set out in the letter, it must be realized that what had happened was simply a typical festival of the day. The two cardinals stood apart and admired a spectacle; women danced or executed intricate figures—for such were the dances of the time: their movements were lascivious, with much casting of veiled voluptuous glances; and a sipped wine cup was sent to the one who danced best or took the eye most effectively. Festivals of the same sort took place later even in the Vatican, and under more than one pope.

Rodrigo Borgia wasted no time. He replied to the Pope without delay. His answer has not come down to us. It was certainly preserved by the Pope, but destroyed in the period of hostility to the Borgias in order to damage their defense. Anyhow the Pope's answer to the answer does remain. And obviously he wasted just as little time, since the second letter is dated only three days after the first.[1] The Pope does not withdraw completely from his first position—a pope may well feel like a father, jealous of his authority, who never admits to his son that he has made a mistake. But he admits that Rodrigo's actions may well have been less culpable than he had been told (*licet minus fortasse sit quam fuerit nobis relatum*).

This second letter must also be reproduced, because, read with the first, it proves that if the future Alexander VI had been guilty of frivolousness or even of something more serious, it shows us also that at twenty-eight his moral outlook was very different from what common opinion supposes.

"My dear son. . . . We have received your Eminence's letter and taken note of the explanation you give. Your action, my dear child, cannot be free from fault, though it may perhaps be less grave than I was at first told. We exhort you to refrain henceforth from such indiscretions and to take the greatest care of your reputation. We grant you the pardon you ask; if we did not love you as a son of predilection we should not have uttered our affectionate reproaches for it is written: 'Whom I love, him I rebuke and punish.' So long as you do good and live in modesty, you will have in me a father and a protector whose blessing will be showered likewise upon those who are dear to you. So long as Pius lives, you will not have to regret the loss of your uncle, our predecessor. Given . . . June 14."

61

The difference in tone between the first and second letter is notable. It may be that the Pope had had time to check his information; in any case in the first letter he was judging without having heard the accused, in the second he took account of his explanations. Anyhow this second document allows only one of two deductions: either Pius II was convinced that Rodrigo was guilty only of a slight fault in having been present at a festival gay but not immoral; or else, as some biographers have considered, he chose in a spirit of conciliation to treat the incident as closed. The Pope's true mind is shown in his actions, then and later.

In plain history we find that, as distinct from some others of his colleagues, Cardinal Borgia remained with the Pope until he had finished his tour, and returned with him to Rome by way of Viterbo where both men were on September 30 of that same year 1460. Further while the ink on the harsh letter of June 11 was scarcely dry, the Pope showed Rodrigo new favor: on the road to Rome he signed a bull granting him the administration of the Cistercian Monastery at Tarragona. It is notable that most of the benefices that Cardinal Borgia received from Pius II were given to him after the incident of which we have just spoken.

In a second visit to the town of Siena a short time before his death, the Pope took with him Cardinal Borgia and only four other cardinals. Borgia went with him also to Ancona where the Pontiff, in spite of illness, thought of taking ship to go personally to fight against the Turks. But at Ancona he died, surrounded by the cardinals of his train, themselves ill with the epidemic, probably the plague, which decimated the soldiers and churchmen gathered there. Indeed the plague buried in one tomb the worn-out body of Pius II and his ideal of delivering Christians from the unceasing violence of the Turks.

This journey to Ancona nearly cost Rodrigo Borgia his life. He was so seriously ill that his doctor thought him in danger of death. Given his importance as Vice-Chancellor and the close friendship which bound him to Luigi Gonzaga, Jacopo de Arezzo made haste to inform his prince of the state in which the cardinal was. His letter has been the object of much satire and grave insinuations. Here it is:

> "I also inform Your Illustrious Lordship that the Vice-Chancellor is stricken with the illness, and this is certain: he has a pain in the ear and under the left arm. The doctor who has just seen him says that he has small hope of curing him, especially considering that a little while ago he did not sleep alone in his bed (*non solus in lecto dormiverat*)."[2]

A facile criticism has made the all-too-easy deduction that the illness in question was that which was known as *le mal français*—in plain words venereal. But from 1494 when this disease was first certainly diagnosed—thirty years after the Ancona plague—up to the present time, no one has ever taken as symptoms those which Rodrigo Borgia's doctor indicated as mentioned by Jacopo in his despatch.

On the other hand, the bubonic plague—brought from the East some forty years earlier—did show itself in certain cases, according to popular opinion, by such symptoms as an outbreak under the arm or pains in the ear.

But what are we to make of the observation about the bed which Rodrigo was said to have shared with someone else? The doctor's opinion must not be taken either as a reflection upon his patient's character or as a desire to give away his patient's secrets, but simply as a piece of technical information. Here we must note two things: first it was supposed that the plague came from human contact; and second that at that time it was customary for many people to sleep in one huge bed—and it may well have happened that even cardinals were obliged to sleep in that fashion at Ancona.

Ancona was a small town and Crusaders had gathered there from all sides in great numbers in the hope of drawing pay from the Pontiff. Besides, a vast number of ecclesiastics filled the houses. The Pope himself was obliged to put up with a meagre lodging and the cardinals with their numerous retinues lived in groups in quite small houses. Each cardinal had an escort: at Rome it was enormous, superior in number and quality to that of many princes; and although outside Rome their retinue was less, it was still great enough to strain the accommodation of Ancona beyond all bounds. At that time houses were not large. The Renaissance house did not possess the conveniences that wealth was later to bring. On the other hand, official trains were normally very numerous and we know that often kings and emperors were not able to come together for conference on questions of high importance, because the towns chosen for their meeting were not large enough to contain the number of courtiers indispensable to each monarch.

In short, there was nothing abnormal—given the enormous beds of that period in which, modesty or no modesty, whole families habitually slept—in the Cardinal sharing a bed with other ecclesiastics of his Court. Rather, we should consider it totally abnormal if, while the Pope was dying, in the course of a raging epidemic, in a town which had more than twenty times its usual population, the cardinal had been able to find a room sufficiently secluded and there given himself over to the diversions his slanderers suggest.

Whatever interpretation one chooses to give to the doctor's words, whatever Jacopo actually meant in writing to his Lord who was the Cardinal's intimate friend, it remains that at no time in the history of medicine have the symptoms quoted served to diagnose venereal disease; and it remains, likewise, that amorous pleasure neither causes nor aggravates the plague. And it is worth remembering that Cardinal Scarampo, Cardinal Barbo and others also caught the disease at Ancona, and that later it was recalled that Rodrigo Borgia had had the plague as a young man.

As a proof of Borgia's immorality use is made of another document almost as important as the letter of Pius II. It is a letter of Cardinal Ammanati Piccolomini. In it Borgia is accused of having brought about the election of Sixtus IV[3] by intrigue, cf being vain, malignant, and of having spent the Church's money in his mission to Spain, which his letter describes as futile. Certain authors have taken some words of the cardinal about his and Borgia's changed way of life as evidence that they had both been deeply dissipated. But from the letters I have before me as I write—extracts from the *Cardinalis Papiensis Epistolae et Commentarii* published first at Milan, then at Frankfort—it is clear that the expression "changed way of life" had reference to a change of relations between the two men. The whole letter tends towards this meaning and no other.

But as von Pastor truly says, Cardinal Ammanati is not to be taken very seriously because of the volatility of his ideas, which led him to write in the most opposite senses and to relate the most contradictory happenings. He was in fact an embittered man. He was literary, not practical, not adaptable, especially not likeable, so that he was not built for success at the Roman Court. Extremely sensitive, he made himself enemies over trifles. Thus he accused Rodrigo Borgia of refusing to have anything to do with him because he wanted to cultivate the friendship only of the great, and because he preferred the conversation of another cardinal, more important than himself. He poured ridicule and insult upon Cardinal Bessarion, who was regarded then and later as a saint. But Ammanati Piccolomini did not always have this opinion of Borgia. At another time he wrote to him in Spain during his mission in that country, calling upon him to return because his presence was indispensable in Rome. He told Rodrigo that he had now accomplished his task in Spain and that he must return because "everybody wants to see you here and considers your presence necessary that you may exercise your predominating influence, to prevent the achievement of imprudent designs and in particular to prevent the entry of a natural son into the sacred college." Another time, alluding to quarrels they had had, he asked Rodrigo to forget the past and to take up again their former friendship.[4]

It is a wearisome business in this story of Rodrigo Borgia to expose all these fantastic charges: one has to be constantly denying instead of affirming, scattering smoke clouds. At any rate upon the question of his morals there is nothing alleged against him up to the time of his entering the conclave from which he emerged as Pope, beyond what I have related. I do not say that he may not have been guilty of other matters: but there is not the faintest mention of them prior to his election as Pope.

There are scores of bulls granting him benefices, in which he is spoken of in terms of high eulogy. Five Popes, differing in virtue, intelligence, birth, learning, all treat Cardinal Borgia with the same esteem, admire his work, entrust him with the most difficult missions, shower benefices upon him. Here is a bull of Innocent VIII which is an eloquent summary of his relations with the Popes who over a space of forty years before governed the Roman Church:

"Innocent, Bishop, servant of the servants of God, to his venerable brother Rodrigo, Bishop of Porto and Vice-Chancellor of the Holy Roman Church, health and apostolic benediction. Sometimes we send our thought to you, who are distinguished by noble gifts, abounding in merit and remarkable by your virtues, and it comes to our mind that while you have been clad in the splendor of cardinalitial dignity, you have served the Church of Rome under the Pontiffs of happy memory Calixtus III, Pius II, Paul II, Sixtus IV our predecessor, and also ourself, for almost thirty years. During this time you have aided us to bear the responsibilities of the Church, bending your shoulders in constant labor with unvarying diligence, assisting the Church with your exceptional prudence, your subtle intellect, your prompt judgement, your faithfulness to your sworn word, your long experience, and all the other virtues to be seen in you. Not once have you ceased to be useful to us."[5]

This bull is dated April, 1486. Rodrigo Borgia was then fifty-four years old by my reckoning, fifty-five according to most previous authors. The bull is not written in official formulas. It is a living witness which would honor any man, even if he who uttered it had not the authority of a Pope. Such documents are rare in history, to be found only in exceptional cases where great virtues call for recompense.

CHAPTER V

Two Great Missions

THE period during which Rodrigo Borgia was cardinal is what may be called the period of preparation for the new Crusade. But this Crusade required other motives than the earlier ones, motives outside the religious order. Hence, a great mass of difficulties in the way of its success. There was endless talk, issuing in nothing.

By that day war against the Turk represented a political interest, the greatest of political interests, the defence of Italian territory and the territory round about. The Pope saw a threat to his own throne, for this new power which had in 1453 established itself in the empire of the East was now marching upon the West with steady step. The domains of the sovereign Pontiff and Rome itself might very well find themselves one day within the grasp of the invader; as to the Pope's spiritual dominion, the religious spirit of the masses had diminished so that it was at a considerably lower ebb than in the past. It was all very well for the Pope to invite, as the Popes always had invited, Christian princes and peoples to fight in the name of the Faith; but the princes were occupied in establishing their states under a new juridical form which should assure them absolute and uncontested power; and the people, by the mere fact of the development of learning and the increase of wealth had lost both religious fervor and the powerful cupidity which great poverty inspires—the two forces which had sent them off on earlier crusades.[1]

The Venetians alone strove with energy in the defence of their Mediterranean possessions, resisting with all courage the advance of the Turks. But their city had no hinterland—like Carthage of old which had had to yield the empire of the seas to Rome—and was obliged to withdraw in face of the enormous Mussulman empire, which could continually renew its fleets and never treated any defeat as final. Hungary, likewise defending its own existence, resisted upon land. But apart from those two, the great powers of the period either made a show of obeying the Pope, or else sought pretexts for remaining out of a war which suited them all the less since it was in the back of their minds that they might later enter into arrangements of their own with the Infidel. But the Popes refused to accept the new conditions in which they found themselves.

Calixtus III devoted three years of his pontificate to the work of organizing a crusade with no practical results. Eneas Silvius died on the shores of the Adriatic, abandoned, impotent, at the moment of taking ship himself for the Holy War. Paul II, who was a Venetian, clung to the same hope, with the same success! Sixtus IV, a strong and vigorous man, went further, thinking to bring off a maneuver in the grand style and destroy the enemy with one blow. With the full support of the consistory, he decided as a preliminary step to send five Cardinals to the princes of Italy and all Europe to persuade them of the necessity of the Crusade and to collect the necessary funds. Later— after the reign of Innocent VIII—the Popes came to realize that the times were changed; and, obliged to defend themselves on their own territory against the aggression not of Turks but of Christian princes closer at hand than the In-

fidel, they tended to suggest a Crusade as one more
weapon against their ordinary temporal enemies. So it was
that Alexander VI used it. Or else they used their material
or spiritual arms against their Christian enemies, ignoring
the Turk who was at the time fighting in Asia: so it happened with Julius II. Or finally, when they lacked capacity
for high politics and had abandoned all hope of defending
themselves whether against Turks or Christians, they simply bowed to necessity like Leo X and Clement VII.

The five Cardinals sent by Sixtus IV as legates into the
provinces of his spiritual empire represented the very best
that could be found in the sacred college. One of them was
Rodrigo Borgia. Another was Cardinal Bessarion, who had
been regarded as *papabile*. He was born in the Mediterranean east, and was a respectable and respected man. He
was sent as envoy to the King of France, the King of England and the Duke of Burgundy. Cardinal Barbo, nephew
of the previous Pope, Paul II, was sent to the Emperor,
the King of Hungary and other less important monarchs.
The highly esteemed Cardinal Caraffa was delegated to
the sovereign of his native place, King Ferrante, while
Cardinal Capranica was entrusted with the Italian princes.
Borgia was sent to the Courts of Spain and Portugal. These
choices were received with great satisfaction. There was
only one discordant voice, that of Cardinal Ammanati
Piccolomini, probably because he had wanted to be sent
himself.

Before starting for Spain, Rodrigo Borgia set about obtaining all the powers that a pope can grant to a legate.
In fact he was given all possible powers in the political
sphere and a great number in the spiritual. I think it is
impossible to find in the history of the Church a legate
a latere with more authority. A writer of the period says

that with regard to Spain he might consider himself as actually the Pope.[2] In addition to his task concerning the Crusade, Sixtus IV laid upon him another concerning the political situation in Spain.

At this period the Iberian peninsula was in continual disorder. While King John of Aragon, with the help of his son Ferdinand, was establishing himself strongly in the North and fighting energetically against the rebellious Catalans, the prodigal and effeminate Henry IV occupied the throne of Castile and of Leon, passing from one favorite to the next, keeping his vassals in utter moral and material confusion. The court of Portugal had its eye on Castile in spite of the mutual hatred of the two peoples, a hatred which is none the less real for being not entirely explicable. To the south, in the kingdom of Granada, the Moors defended their pleasant but already precarious civilization; while in the extreme north was the weak kingdom of Navarre and in the border provinces the ever-present threat of war with France.

There were other difficulties still, dynastic difficulties. The King of Castile had an only daughter, whom his people did not regard as his, and the nobles were divided upon the matter of the succession. The higher clergy were as divided as the nobles. Thus while the Archbishop of Toledo was opposed to the King's "daughter," another great prelate, later Cardinal, Pedro Gonzalez de Mendoza, preferred to accept the fiction, maintained by the King himself, that she was his. Public opinion, with or without reason, had given her the name of "La Beltraneja" from the name of her supposed father, don Beltran. Her rivals to the succession were first Alfonso, and upon his death Isabella, respectively half-brother and half-sister of the wretched King. Isabella, after grave difficulties and against the King's will, had married Ferdinand of Aragon, son of King John.

But even here there was trouble, for Ferdinand and Isabella were themselves living outside the law and in opposition to the rules of the Church for they had been married on the strength of a papal bull exempting them from the canonical impediment which prevents marriage between close relations.[3] And this bull happened to be a forgery. Thus the marriage of the future Catholic monarchs, in whom Spain placed so much hope, was only concubinage. For a Catholic people, the situation was serious—all the more so because a daughter had been born of the marriage which was not a marriage, and she was consequently bastard.

Thus the Iberian Peninsula had five kingdoms, to say nothing of great feudal lords still very powerful and determined upon their own will; three religions were practised with equal fervor—Catholic, Mohammedan, and Jewish; Portugal and Aragon both had a mind to seize Castile; and the King of France was looking thoughtfully at the Northern Provinces. The South, still Arab, though already the Arabs were on the defensive, had not forgotten its ancient might to which all the monuments of Spain bore witness, while in the Center and the North the clergy was disunited and the people fearfully backward. And the defence of the largest territory, Castile and Leon, depended upon an impotent discredited king and immediate successors who had broken the most sacred law of the day and the one most important for a monarchy—the law of the family.

Cardinal Borgia left Rome for Spain on May 15, 1472. He remained a few days at Ostia, then was taken by two Venetian galleys with his retinue which was more numerous and distinguished than the retinue of a King. On the eighteenth or twentieth of the next month, he landed at Valencia and received the kind of reception usually reserved for kings in Spain. High functionaries of court and city came out to receive him with all the nobles from round about. Houses were adorned along the way. He was given a fine horse to ride, while members of the nobility on foot held a canopy over his head. The people followed him in long processions to the churches, chanting the Te Deum.[4]

His first discussions upon the political situation were with the Primate of Spain, Alfonso Carrillo, Archbishop of Toledo. Carrillo was at this time the champion of Spanish morality against a pervert sovereign, and was in consequence hostile to La Beltraneja and favorable to Isabella in the affair of the royal succession. Borgia listened to Carrillo's arguments upon the birth of the King's so-called daughter and took upon himself to bring about the reconciliation of Henry IV with Isabella and her husband, to the end of avoiding conflicts which would still further divide a Spain already so fiercely divided. With this in view, he had interviews with the most important personages of the country. Knowing that the King's will tended to follow that of the Marquess de Villena, a convert Jew, he went first to see him; and so strong was his persuasive power that he won him to Isabella's cause. He approached the King himself and by skillful diplomacy got him to agree to extend a friendly welcome to Isabella and Ferdinand. The reconciliation was sealed by a banquet, from which the King came out ill to death with a violent liver attack. Naturally, the popular voice talked of poison.

While this banquet was taking place and the King was dying, Cardinal Borgia (no, he was not at it!) was traveling over all Castile, and was acclaimed everywhere as the

74

man who, by his tact and skill, had made possible the preliminaries of reconciliation and peace.[5]

But there could be no solid foundation for the future until the unpleasant question of the marriage of Isabella and Ferdinand was solved. So he bent all his tremendous energies to obtaining an authentic bull to remedy the errors of the past. Paul II had been opposed to this measure of prudence but Sixtus IV followed the advice of his legate and consented to issue it.

This real love-match was to have a decisive influence upon the history of Spain. As time flowed on, it consolidated into one the two great kingdoms, expelled the Moors from the peninsula by absorbing the kingdom of Granada, broke the factions by means of which a nobility, greedy for wealth and power, had been able to keep a submissive and ignorant people divided.

Later, when the ill-fame of the Borgias was well on its way, the rumor spread that the Cardinal had taken part in the manufacture of the earlier forged bull. Not only has no proof of this ever been found, but there is not the very faintest hint of a suggestion of it. The one thing certain is that Rodrigo strongly reprobated the whole business of the marriage and condemned those who with culpable indulgence had tolerated it. In fact the Archbishop of Toledo, for all that he was the highest dignitary of the Spanish Church and had powerfully contributed to the success of Borgia's mission, was never raised to the cardinalate, although the Archbishop Gonzalez de Mendoza and another Spanish prelate, Auxias de Podio, received this high distinction. Profoundly wounded at being thus passed over, Carrillo withdrew within his vast domains of Alcala de Henares. The fact is that in the mind of Borgia, who proposed the nominations, the good name of the Church was

F

a more important consideration than the gratitude he personally felt to the Archbishop of Toledo.

An impartial historian, seeing the events of the time in the light of their ultimate consequences, must judge Borgia's work exactly as the peasants of Castile judged it as he passed among them. The necessary preliminaries for the greatness of Spain were accomplished by him.

In Aragon also he exercised his influence for good. The old King John II was a rough fighting man, cruel and obstinate; he was at the time occupied in smashing rebellion among his subjects. Barcelona was besieged and in an almost desperate situation. Rodrigo went to the scene of hostilities and offered to co-operate with Ferdinand to the end that he might one day occupy the throne of Castile; but he asked the King, who had intended to wreak fierce vengeance for the rebellion, to show mercy. And he succeeded. He acted as arbiter in the conflict and offered the people of Barcelona mild conditions of surrender. They began by refusing but very soon changed their minds and accepted, with gratitude.[6]

It is clear that Borgia's work in Spain was of the highest importance. It is worth glancing at what Cardinal Ammanati said in the letter of which we have already spoken, begging Rodrigo to return to Rome: "Since there is no human power capable of uniting Aragon and Castile or reconciling the factions of Castile itself, what need is there for you to attack obstacles which are immovable? All has been done that could be done, and that is much, to satisfy the public."

Ammanati was not a good prophet. His colleague Borgia smoothed the way for the reunion of Castile and Aragon by his prudent long-sighted action in virtually placing Isabella on the throne of Castile and removing every legal obstacle to her union with the future King of Aragon.

There is no documentary proof that the Cardinal Legate went to Portugal at all, for however brief a space, though there is reason to suppose that he was in contact with the Portuguese court through an emissary. But it is scarcely necessary to remark that certain quarters accuse him of having spent the period of this mission with the ladies of the Portuguese court.

To come now to the purely ecclesiastical order, Borgia summoned the famous Council of Segovia, at which were gathered the representatives of all the dioceses of Castile and Leon. At this Council, among other decisions, he condemned the nominations of "so many ignorant clerics" and set on foot measures to obviate the continuance of this abuse in the future. But the most remarkable part of his religious activities was the sermon he preached before the clergy of Valencia upon his arrival. It is a fine piece of oratory admirable for psychological insight and elegance of form. I think it well to reproduce the whole of it. Even if you are not in the habit of reading sermons, read this one— if only as a piquant contrast to the appalling reputation of its preacher:

> "At last, Venerable Brethren in Jesus Christ, the day has dawned so desired and long awaited but until now postponed by circumstances. We have come to find our bride, the Church of Valencia, illustrious throughout the world by its glorious priesthood. We proclaim that this people entrusted to our care is distinguished by its faith and its religious practice and that in these virtues it is surpassed by no town of Christendom. It is at last given us to look upon your venerable assembly which has truly merited the voca-

77

tion of the Lord, and this more than all else fills us with joy and honor and lawful pride. We give thanks for it to Almighty God who has so favored us, we bless his Holy Name and with Simon we sing like the prophet: 'Now thou dost dismiss thy servant, O Lord, according to thy word in peace, because my eyes have seen thy salvation'—a word which has brought peace and consolation to the desire of my soul. We give thanks also to our Holy Father Sixtus who, by appointing us upon a mission to these Western Kingdoms, has given us back, after long absence, to our country and our family. Since our earliest years, when long ago we were placed at the head of this venerable diocese, we always had a full awareness of our duty and of the general aspirations of our faithful, we always realized the stimulus given to religious life by the presence of a pastor and the means of salvation that the personal direction of the pastor brings to his flock. We were not unaware that the title of Bishop, which means overseer, requires direct action and cannot be carried out by deputies. This indeed we knew from the imperious voice of Holy Writ: 'Be attentive to the guarding of your sheep, take good account of your flock.'

"God, who reads all hearts, be my witness that I have always used my good will for the accomplishment of all these duties; but unhappily we have always been compelled to be absent. We had to obey our Supreme Father. The dignity of Cardinal attaches us by the most powerful bond to the Apostolic See, and once named member of its council we could not be absent save upon a special mission. In any event, the vast and laborious administration of the Roman Chancellery, instituted for the good of the whole Church and yielding in importance only to the work of the Sovereign Pontiff, cannot without grave difficulty be carried on in the absence of the authority which presides over it. Our first duty is to obey him to whom God has given supreme authority and towards whom we are bound to supreme respect. If then we have been prevented until now from being with you and have therefore had to delegate to another the fulfillment of our duties here, it was not by choice or the decision of our own will, but in obedience to circumstances. This system of delegation is employed by the rulers of many churches, by kings and princes and the highest authorities. Thus it is that the Roman Pontiffs, the most venerated of all authorities, appoint their delegates to individual dioceses that they may exercise power in their place; and thus it is that Jesus Christ, who is in Heaven, established the Vicars of his flock to spread abroad the means of salvation.

"But today when thanks to His munificence we are with you, my brethren, we must enter at this our first meeting upon certain special questions which charity does not permit us to pass over in silence. First, of course, I wish to thank you as is becoming for having awaited our arrival with such constancy; the conviction we have of this has a clear proof in the kindness of your dispositions towards us, as well as in the diligence with which you have accomplished your filial duty. You have shown affectionate respect to your absent Father, you have listened to the words of those he has placed over you, you have taken care of your Church and seen to it that nothing was wanting for the celebration of the offices in the house of God; we give you thanks likewise for the welcome you have given us upon our arrival, with such great and solemn honors; you have not only celebrated our episcopate and our mission as Legate, but have especially manifested your good will towards us by joyous personal demonstrations. The great attachment you have for us has increased our affection for you, if such a feeling may be said to be capable of increase. May God, who rewards all, grant us in his kindness the power one day to express our gratitude for your filial service.

"In spite of all this, we exhort you all here present, our well-beloved brethren—although you have no need of any stimulus for your labors—to persevere as you have begun in virtue and in religion, and to offer to God our Creator and to the Church of Valencia our Mother, a devotion that they merit ever more strongly. This assuredly is demanded by your priestly profession and by your past labors. For of you it has been written: 'You are a chosen generation, a true priesthood, a holy nation, a people of election.' Be constantly occupied in the adoration of the Most High, knowing that sanctity is at all times necessary in His house, and that by adoration of Him we live by the Altar and occupy our place of honor. Act always in such wise that our ministry may be for the service of the people and that, as the Apostle Paul says, we do not give occasion for murmuring, accomplishing our tasks without sloth, preserving a fervent spirit and serving the Lord. See that the actions of your life are as much as possible in harmony with your profession and observe such modesty that neither the heart nor the eyes of those who see you may be troubled. As we are consecrated to be models and examples, the sin of forgetting the high nobility of our priesthood makes us even guiltier than the actual fault committed and the mere transgression. Let us then act honorably and with care for our good repute: it is a primary necessity for the success of our ministry.

"Among other things, my dearly beloved Sons, I commend to you the observance of fraternal charity. Live in harmony in the house of the Lord. The Saviour has said: 'One commandment I give unto you, that you love one another.' If this unity aids the glory and the growth of the Church, the degradation of dissension brings it detriment and ignominy; 'where envying and contention is, there is inconstancy and every evil work' as the Apostle Saint James says . . . 'Remove every stone of stumbling and every rock of scandal' . . . and 'let your spirit be but one, abide in peace, may the God of peace and love be with you.'

"And since the freedom of the Church, granted by our Lord and carefully guarded by our ancestors, has increased in the people the veneration of the priesthood, we beg of you not only to be of one mind in guarding and defending it as the most precious thing, but also to spare yourselves neither pain nor peril for its preservation. If, by earthly ostentation and vanity, the Gentiles make war and in their evil rivalries expose themselves to massacre and destruction to preserve their liberty, with how much more reason should we priests do likewise, whose reward is God himself, for whom death is life, we who have been set as guardians of the Church and of whom it is spoken: 'Fight for justice unto death and God will overthrow your enemies!'

"But if this liberty which remains to us were lost, what more terrible ruin could there be for us? Should we not be stripped of all honor and all power? There is no doubt: if this were to happen, we should be despised and trampled under foot, we should be 'the blame of men and the proscription of the people.' Let us then all work together for the preservation of that independence. Work in union with your prelates who in their turn will march with you and will thus be leaders in your battles . . . The fruit of your victory, won by the aid of God, is liberty; the consequence of fleeing would be vile servitude for it is written: 'The

81

hand of the valiant will bring power, but the slothful man will be subject and will pay tribute.' Great is your excellence and the Church is above all nobility. With all your strength, try to win liberty for yourselves and us, identify yourselves with us in such manner that, in the Saviour's words, you 'render to Caesar the things that are Caesar's and to God the things that are God's.'

"Of these matters and others of the same kind we shall have to treat often in the future and at still greater length. Today we shall make only a brief allusion to politics. We have been sent, my Brethren, as you know to work for the redemption of the faithful who are suffering under the sword of a ferocious enemy. The Turk, after having subjugated Asia and a great part of Europe, has twice already descended upon Italy, destroying everything with fire and massacre. He is now on his way, menacing the centre of our religion, towards the sanctuary of the Apostles and Martyrs, the City of Rome; if he were thus able to crush the head, the rest of the Christian body would quickly perish. If it is the duty of any to rush to the help of Rome, if it is the duty of any to prepare for the defense of religion, it is the duty above all of our Order. We are the shepherds of this flock, we are set upon the watchtower, precisely that we may keep it safe. It is for others a duty to follow our example. We call upon your love for the Lord, and fervently, paternally pray you to aid us, with your counsels and by all other means in your power, in the task imposed upon us at this juncture. We know your zealous work in the house of Our Lord and the good will with which you serve him: be assured that nothing is more important in your priestly ministry, and that it brings you the greatest merits.

"Let it suffice for the moment that I have spoken

these few brief words. I shall explain to you later in detail how, having put your hand to the plough, you can aid us in our labor and how we shall be able to make use of your cooperation. Now, dearly beloved Brethren, united with you as the bishop of this diocese we bless you with all our heart, with all our soul, and with profound love in Jesus Christ, in the name of our Holy Father and Pontiff Sixtus IV; and we hope that God the almighty Father, from His high throne may ever have His eyes fixed upon the Diocese of Valencia, and that He may keep you in His Heavenly Grace, you His children for His Holy Worship. Amen."[7]

The sentimental note in Borgia's mission is to be found in the visit he paid to the town of his birth, Xativa. There he was received not only with all the honor due to his mission, but with overflowing affection. He returned to the house of his earliest years; walked through all the streets through which he had ridden on his pony as a child; received the people on the square which bore the name of Borgia because of the respect in which his ancestors had been held; went to see his relations and friends; prayed in the churches; showed a lively interest in all his one-time neighbors and promised to grant favors to the place of his birth. Given the strong emotional element in him, as it is shown by his conduct and by the opinion of those who were in contact with him, this visit must have been the most agreeable moment of his momentous journey.

At the end of September, 1473, the Cardinal Legate said farewell to Valencia and to Spain for the last time and returned to Rome. A storm sank one of the galleys—the one in which his suite were traveling—off the Italian coast. Nearly two hundred perished. The other galley, in which he was, was badly damaged and within an ace of destruction, but it somehow managed to make the port of Leghorn.

Borgia had good reason to be satisfied with what he had accomplished, but the actual object of his mission had had no success. Kings had had enough of Crusades. They wanted no more of them. The conflicts raging among themselves made it too dangerous to send large contingents of armed men abroad. John II had told the Cardinal bluntly: "I must keep an eye on the King of France and on my subjects." If the King of Castile had any desire to fight Mohammedans, he had plenty of them close at hand in Granada. Bessarion and the others came back with the same report. They all had to tell the Pope that the affair seemed hopeless. Let us repeat: the day of Crusades, of Crusades worthy of the name, was over. It was now the period in which the Grand Turk was to have his finger in European intrigues; he had begun to establish friendship and even alliance with Christian sovereigns, and if the nations still feared him as an enemy, they no longer hated him as the Infidel.

Some years after this Spanish mission, Sixtus IV needed to send from Rome a special delegate to deputize for him in the exercise of the highest powers the Papacy possessed in the temporal order. Sixtus IV would have acted in person, but the situation in Italy obliged him not to leave Rome. Of all the cardinals, he chose Rodrigo Borgia to be his direct representative. The matter was the coronation of the Queen of Naples, Juana of Aragon, who had just married King Ferrante. As on his earlier mission, Cardinal Borgia was invested with all powers, ecclesiastical and temporal, and he had a quasi-royal reception at Naples. In granting him this delegation, on August 7, 1477, the Pope declares that he laments to see him depart since he is thereby deprived "of his habitual prudence, integrity and zeal, and of the gravity of his character."

The Pope was surrounded by cardinals, some of them his relations whom he loved deeply and loaded with favors; among the members of the Sacred College there were not only men like Cardinal Caraffa, who was of a noble Neapolitan family, but likewise personages of royal or princely blood. Yet he chose Borgia for this second mission because it was in him that he had the greatest confidence. Not that Rodrigo's fine manners, elegance and air of dignity may not have played some part in the decision—to say nothing of his habit of spending his own money lavishly on such occasions!

Borgia was now considered as the friend of princes. He is so described in a letter of Cardinal Ammanati Piccolomini and by Jacopo De Volterra in his *Diarium Romanum*.

Once again he carried out his mission with all possible splendor and solemnity. He was then forty-five, a tall man, well-proportioned; he had a leonine head, an easy dignity of manner, and a low and resonant voice. He produced a powerful impression in Naples. The Neapolitans are a people who love luxury and ceremonial, and they saw in him the most authentic representative of their own aesthetic tastes. But King Ferrante saw enough of him to realize that, if one day this man became Pope, he would not be easy to handle.

Prior to these two great missions, Rodrigo had had in 1469 the mission of accompanying Maximilian, King of the Romans—for so the Emperor-elect was styled before his coronation as Emperor—from Viterbo to Rome. And in 1475, when the King of Naples was in Rome, Rodrigo and Giuliano della Rovere were appointed to take charge of the honors of his reception. Looking at all these things quite impartially it must surely seem that the man to whom they were granted could not have been an object of criticism, still less of universal contempt. It is a plain fact that rulers of states, of old as today, may sometimes admit, in their domestic affairs, officials who in spite of their intellectual ability are by no means spotless morally; but in international negotiations they use representatives who are irreproachable and of high bearing, morally as well as physically. And at the Renaissance, representation abroad was the object of closer attention even than it is today. You only have to look at a list of Papal Nuncios and of the men chosen by kings, princes and republics for addresses on great occasions. On that list are the names of the most virtuous men in Italy and the world.

Certain words in the letter of Cardinal Ammanati already quoted have been interpreted as an accusation against Borgia that he accepted these missions in order to accumulate wealth; and it has even been added that he wanted the wealth in order to purchase his election to the Papacy in some future Conclave. History proves the contrary. These missions were extremely expensive. To undertake them, Borgia had to accept very great sacrifices, especially for the Spanish one. In plain words he was obliged to pawn all his benefices, to auction them to the highest bidder for three years, in order to have in his hands the considerable sums indispensable for the journey. And as it was difficult to find a moneylender to take the risk in an affair of this sort—since the benefices might be lost either by the death of the holder or by the mere will of the Pope—Sixtus IV had to issue a special bull authorizing the loan and specifying that Rodrigo's benefices, if they passed to another for any reason whatever, should not give this other the right to receive the income until the money loaned upon them had been completely repaid.[8]

On his return from Spain, Borgia handed over all the sums he had collected for the Crusade. The Pope checked his accounts and completely approved them in a release in which he expressed his appreciation of Borgia's irreproachable virtue and absolute honesty. All this is to be found in authentic documents, for the edification of that section of posterity which prefers history to the fantasies of legend. The Pope went on to declare that Borgia had carried out his mission perfectly and that he had rendered his accounts in a manner clear and easy to check.[9] It seems to me that an opinion uttered some centuries later is not necessarily more valuable than that of the Pope under whom the events happened.

Sixtus IV continued to show his friendship for Cardinal Borgia and to confer favors upon him to the end of his Pontificate. Leaving Rome on account of a terrible epidemic which had broken out, he asked Rodrigo and certain other Cardinals to accompany him. On all important occasions he had him at his side, and declared his work most useful to the Church of Rome. In one of his last periods of physical well-being, but already close to death, Sixtus IV set out for Ostia with his two nephews, the Cardinals Giuliano and Girolamo della Rovere. He invited Borgia also. Jacopo de Volterra describes various scenes he witnessed upon this occasion. There was a great banquet at the house of Cardinal Giuliano at Ostia, and another next day at the Episcopal Palace of Porto given by Rodrigo, who was Bishop of that place. In that evening hour, the Pope and the three Cardinals, free from all official constraint, took their pleasure in walking along the shore, by the sea whose waves fell gently on the sand . . . The Pope was in his most pleasant mood, for in such a moment of mental rest even the most arrogant can feel a certain glow of kindliness. He spoke laughingly with Giuliano and Rodrigo, and these two showed a mutual affection inspired by a sincere sense of brotherhood.

In that hour of friendship the stormy Franciscan who then ruled Christendom could have had no foreshadowing of the historical quarrel, which was to echo across the centuries, between the two younger men, his nephew and his chosen friend. He was close to death and his eyes rested upon them in a vision of a peaceful, harmonious future. On the stage of life, the greatest actors often have the least notion of the part they are about to play.

CHAPTER VI

The Conclave

On July 25, 1492, Innocent VIII, after having been for some months between life and death, died. The cardinals prepared to defend their independence and guarantee the rights of the citizens against the attacks of the baronial factions and of the over-excited mob—attacks habitual at times when the Papal throne was vacant.

Likewise precautions were taken that the election of the new Pope should be free from the influence of the great powers of the day, all of whom wished to have the Pontiff who would best suit their designs. It was the duty of Borgia as Vice-Chancellor to speak in the name of the cardinals to the delegates of the Roman people—who took advantage of the uncertainty of the moment—to quieten them by outlining future solutions of claims which they were now presenting at a moment ill-suited for their discussion. The dignity of the Roman Courts always suffered serious diminution during these intervals between Popes. Every time a papal election was to be held, the cardinals were thronged about by every kind of self-seeking interest. Yet ambitions and covetings often found solutions which obviated the greatest evils in that balance of interests which human society always tends to create save when the balance is destroyed either by the intervention of some one powerful force or by the play of psychological passions in great bodies of people.

On this occasion, once the Pope had been buried and the usual ceremonies completed, the Conclave was able to meet in relative tranquillity.

The Sacred College was at that time composed of twenty-seven cardinals. Two of them were cardinals *in petto*—that is to say nominated but not enthroned; but the Conclave admitted them as it had done on other occasions. Four were absent. It is very important to note the names of the absentees: they constitute the first proof against the accusation of simony which was levelled at this Conclave and later accepted as unquestionable. Here they are:

1. Luis Juan del Mila y Borgia, Cardinal of Los Cuatro Coronados.

2. Pedro Gonzalez de Mendoza, Cardinal of Santa Croce.

3. Andreas Spinay, Cardinal of San Martino.

4. Pierre d'Aubusson, Cardinal of Saint Adrien.

These absentees were all foreigners, I mean non-Italians. Two were Spaniards, two Frenchmen. The first on the list was Rodrigo's cousin and the second had been in close contact with him when he was Legate in Spain and indeed owed him his elevation to the cardinalate.

On the other hand, save for Borgia and Costa, the Cardinals present at the Conclave were all Italians. Here is the list:

1. Rodrigo Borgia, Vice-Chancellor, Cardinal of Porto.
2. Giovanni Michele, Cardinal of Preneste, of a noble Venetian family. A nephew of Paul II. The Venetian ambassadors speak of him with respect, and chronicles of the period describe him as a man of intelligence and unblemished morals.
3. Oliverio Carafa (or Caraffa), Cardinal of Sabina. Of

a noble family of Naples. An irreproachable priest. Enormously rich. Was considered *papabile* on more than one occasion.

4. Giorgio Costa, Cardinal of Albano, commonly known as Cardinal of Lisbon. The richest of all the cardinals. Much respected for piety and learning.

5. Antonietto Pallavicini, Cardinal of Santa Anastasia. In later Conclaves he is often mentioned as a candidate for the papacy.

6. Girolamo Basso della Rovere, Cardinal of San Chrysogono, better known as Cardinal Recanati, nephew of Sixtus IV. Played an important part during various pontificates. A man of energy and learning. Was spoken of with unvarying respect.

7. Domenico della Rovere, Cardinal of San Clemente. Another nephew of Sixtus IV. Used the income from his benefices upon the building of churches.

8. Giuliano della Rovere, Cardinal of Saint Peter in Chains. Later Pope Julius II.

9. Paolo Fregoso, Cardinal of Saint Sixtus. The "rebel Cardinal," as he was called. A fighting man. Commanded the pontifical regiment at the taking of Otranto. Was Doge of Genoa. Of a rich and powerful Ligurian family.

10. Giovanni dei Conti, Cardinal of San Vitale. Of a noble Roman family. Deeply respected. Already very old at the time of the Conclave.

11. Giangiacomo Sclafenati, Cardinal of San Stefano. Rich and honoured.

12. Ardicino della Porta, Cardinal of Saint John and Saint Paul. During the pontificate of Innocent VIII resigned his cardinalate and all his benefices to enter

a monastery. He was compelled to return to the Sacred College by the order of Innocent VIII himself.

13. Lorenzo Cibo, Cardinal of Santa Cecilia. Nephew of the previous Pope, Innocent VIII. All the authors agree that he deserved high respect.

14. Francesco Piccolomini, Cardinal of Saint Eustace. Nephew of Pope Pius II. He was later Pope Pius III and occupied the See of Peter with great honor in the short space that lay between the reigns of Alexander VI and Julius II.

15. Raffaele Sansoni-Riario, Cardinal of San Giorgio. A rich man, deeply versed in canon law. A relation of Sixtus IV.

16. Giovanni Colonna, Cardinal of Saint Mary of Aquin. He belonged to the rich and noble Colonna family.

17. Gianbattista Orsini, Cardinal of Santa Maria Novella. He belonged to the great Orsini family, who were the rivals for control of Rome with the Colonnas.

18. Giovanni Savelli, Cardinal of San Nicolo a Carcere Tulliani. He also belonged to a noble, rich and powerful Roman family. He received from successive popes and from the Sacred College financial and administrative missions which demanded proved honor.

19. Giovanni dei Medici, son of Lorenzo the Magnificent. He was later Leo X.

20. Gianbattista Zeno, nephew of Paul II. Of a noble family of Venice. Spent his fortune in the building of churches and other works.

21. Ascanio Maria Sforza-Visconti, Cardinal of Saint Vitus. Brother of Ludovico il Moro, who was later Duke of

Milan. Not inferior to any of his colleagues in power and fortune.

The two cardinals in petto were Maffeo Gherardo, cardinal of Saint Nereus, who was Patriarch of Venice and was at least eighty-two at the time of the Conclave; and Federigo Sanseverino, brother of the famous *condottiere* Captain Fracassa, and son of another *condottiere* of noble family.

Such were the electors. It seemed worth while to set out their names, as a reminder that almost all of them represented the richest, most illustrious, most powerful families of the Italy of that day, and to show that it would not have been easy to purchase so much distinction: for if honor is not to be measured either by wealth or birth, it still remains true that it would have taken a great deal of time and a great deal of money to purchase the consciences of such wealthy and powerful men, assuming that their consciences were for sale. The purchase of votes, which has been treated by certain unthinking authors as an indisputable fact, could not have been undertaken by any one person no matter how rich—and the Borgia fortune was not enormous.

A great State, or two great States, might have been able to draw upon resources or influence mighty enough to purchase these cardinals and induce them to place upon the throne of Saint Peter a colleague without honor or prestige —though there is no example in all the history of the church of the cardinals so acting. But a man like Rodrigo Borgia, who had often had to pawn his benefices to raise money, simply cannot in decent logic be thought of as able to purchase a Costa, a Colonna, a Medici, an Orsini, a Sforza, to say nothing of the proud Venetian cardinals who might indeed have done some purchasing on their own account if purchasing had been possible. The simony of Conclaves, spoken of by certain authors of the period, can only mean something quite different from what we understand by the word. It must not be forgotten that slander and exaggeration are the typical faults of the Italy of that day as of the Renaissance period generally.

According to contemporary stories, it seems to have been, if not proven, at least widely held, that France had deposited in Rome two hundred thousand ducats and Genoa one hundred thousand ducats to support the candidacy of della Rovere.

If we attach as much weight to this story as contemporaries attach, it must at least be admitted that the money did not do him much good. Cardinal della Rovere never really looked like being elected.

The fact is that the purchase of votes was quite impossible in a Conclave unless it had been prepared, wholly or largely, a long time before; and in that case it would be hard to explain the already-quoted Roman proverb: he who goes into a Conclave as Pope, comes out as Cardinal. In the narrow space in which the cardinals had to live during the election, all packed close together, each watching the others with that shrewdness one always finds in men leading a common life, and with that easy lack of ceremony which results from a common existence devoted to one single activity, it would not have been easy to carry out arrangements which had in the nature of the case to be strictly confidential. The onlookers would have been fairly quick with their suspicions. It is possible to imagine one cardinal approaching another by a whisper, a sign, an allusion; but in a period which was characterized by the violation of every undertaking and even of the sworn word, something stronger would have been required to bind the conspirators than such surreptitious promises. So simony, no matter how much it might have been desired, both by the buyer and the seller, could not be practised at the last minute, in the course of balloting which took place under the watchful eyes of all.

It remains that many chroniclers and some diplomats have spoken of simony. But they did the same for practically every conclave, especially for the conclaves which elected Sixtus IV, Innocent VIII, Julius II and Leo X. And it must be remembered that in this troubled time, not only chroniclers but even ambassadors suffered from the mania for finding scandal everywhere and vastly preferred a sensational rumor to the best-founded piece of necessarily plainer fact. A too ready acceptance of such sources of information is a proof either of a charming naïveté in the reader or else of a lack of critical intelligence; for the chronicles and diplomatic correspondence of the period swarm with errors.

Yet we must not too deeply blame those chroniclers, nor the light-minded diplomats who made it their business to please their own ruler by retailing slander about a candidate he did not like, or sought to amuse him by the story of an intrigue or the relation of some pleasing biting epigram. After all they were courtiers with their way to make.

If we remember that a cardinal like Ammanati, who was actually present at the Conclave which elected Sixtus IV, informs posterity that that Pope was elected "ex artibus et corruptelis"—by the wire-pulling and bribery—of Cardinal Borgia, when it is proved historically that Borgia opposed his election at every ballot and only at the last moment went over to the great majority, along with the other candidate Estoutevelle and Barbo, we need not be astonished at the error of men outside the Conclave. These alterations of the most evident truth always happen when a country is losing its traditional balance and readily believes the worst; for peoples also can suffer from a neurasthenia which is a variety of persecution mania.

But we must understand what contemporaries meant by simony. If it consists in a tacit understanding between a candidate who is bound to give up his palace and his many benefices once he is elected, and a number of persons who are anxious to have these profitable places and desire, therefore, to earn the gratitude of the new Pope by helping to elect him, then we are safe to make any guess we please: for this is the domain of psychology not of history. In the great reform of the church prepared by Alexander VI himself, and later in the Bull of Julius II dated 14 January, 1505, something is said about obviating abuses in the Conclaves: but given the highly emphatic style of these two documents, which is the general style of the Roman Curia especially at that time, we do not find in them that general opinion believed that votes were bought and sold. There are proportions in evil as well as in good, and we must preserve them if our judgement is to be just.

I have listed the names and titles of the electors. We must now consider the candidates. Before the Conclave there were three names upon men's lips—Caraffa, Costa and Ardicino della Porta.[1] Then came talk of Zeno and of Piccolomini. But the most effective canvassing was done in support of Giuliano della Rovere, who was backed by the French party, by Genoa and by the military envoys of the King of Naples, who were at the gates of Rome.[2] Borgia was scarcely mentioned: only the orator of Florence at Rome mentions his name as a very vague possibility. The electors began by scattering their votes as usual, and after the early ballots it was Caraffa and Costa who seemed to have the best chances. But as the voting went on it turned into a conflict between della Rovere and Sforza, the latter strongly supported by Borgia.

Cardinal Ascanio Sforza, vigorous, elegant, wide-minded, was very popular with his colleagues and he would probably have been elected if his brother Ludovico Moro had not cast over the Conclave the shadow of his personal ambition. When he found that he could not be elected, Ascanio gave his support to the colleague who had so loyally supported him and had only given up the struggle when the conviction could no longer be resisted that it was hopeless.

But it must be added that if Ascanio Sforza could not be elected even with the help of Borgia, still less could Borgia be elected with the help of Sforza alone. After all, Borgia was a foreigner, and what was worse a Spaniard; and the only foreigner besides himself at the Conclave was the Portuguese Costa. The other four were absent, as has been mentioned. Besides, Borgia was considered as an enemy not only by the French, but also by the King of Naples, by Venice, by Florence. He had a conception of the Church's supremacy which was little likely to appeal to temporal rulers. It is impossible that the King of France should have been unaware of earlier debates in the Consistory and of Borgia's stand against him. There had indeed been an incident between Borgia and the French Cardinal La Balue in the course of which the two cardinals insulted each other like fishwives.[3]

Zurita said that the King of Naples regarded the election of Borgia as a catastrophe, for if a weak man like Innocent

VIII had done him so much harm, what would happen with Borgia, who was strong, intelligent and clever.

All these reasons prevented Borgia from offering himself as a candidate as he had done in the preceding Conclave. So little propitious did he judge the moment, that in spite of the long last illness of Innocent VIII which would have given him all the time necessary to make plans, the two Spanish cardinals, one his cousin and the other his friend, did not even try to get to Rome.

How then and why was Borgia elected? The theory of large scale bribery would be a neat answer if it were possible. But if gold had been a consideration, then it would have weighted the scales for Giuliano della Rovere, who was supported by great States, necessarily richer than any private person.

We have not much direct information about this Conclave. Most of the authors who have left accounts of it say that Borgia was elected unanimously.[4] But there appeared later another version which modern historians have accepted. According to this version, after a stiff struggle, fourteen cardinals voted for Borgia (including Borgia himself). Thus one vote only was needed to give the necessary majority, and as they could not get that of della Rovere, or Caraffa, or Piccolomini, or Costa, or Medici, they had to fall back on the aged Venetian patriarch Gherardo, whose vote assured the triumph of Borgia.[5]

Whatever may have been the results of the successive ballots, which we are in no position to discuss, it is certain that the future Alexander VI was by his position and his qualities a strong candidate. At the time of his election he was sixty, and not a single document of the period has come down to us which speaks of his relations with Vannozza or Giulia Farnese. His enemies were numerous enough and they accused him of pride, faithlessness, cunning, but not of mistresses and children. The Florentine orator, speaking of Cardinal Ardicino della Porta, said that he could not be elected Pope because he had a son—legitimate by the way. But he does not make the faintest allusion to any bastard children, real or supposed, of Rodrigo Borgia.

When the Conclave realized that the winner was likely to be either an Ascanio Sforza, who stood for his brother Ludovico and all the evil that that man had done for Italy or a Giuliano della Rovere who was under obligation to France and Naples and indeed any foreign state that would support his candidature, it concentrated its votes upon the man most deeply versed in the affairs of the Church, the most independent in temperament, the man who during his long labors in Rome had shown the greatest ability. For the moment they forgot that he was a foreigner and a Spaniard; and his uncle Calixtus' memory was no longer seen as darkened with accusations of nepotism now that practically all the electors were themselves products of the same weakness. At the moment of final decision the cardinals realized that neither Sforza nor della Rovere would serve the interests of the Church, given their political connections; and that personalities of the second rank like Costa or Caraffa or Ardicino would be worse than useless.

Rodrigo Borgia's qualities made him the man needed at that moment of history. If the Church of Rome has been able to survive so many storms in the course of the centuries, it is largely by that special faculty she has of divining the hour of danger and choosing the man who must be put at the head of Christendom to save it. Thus at one moment she names a fanatic who defies the danger, at another the skillful politician who evades it. At one period appears a man of the world who can rival princes in worldly pomp; at another a pastor who defends with unshaken constancy all the dogmas, even those upon which science and human knowledge have bent their attacks. It is in this external adaptability, united with absolute inflexibility upon fundamentals, that a principal cause is to be found of Rome's greatness over twenty centuries.

Rodrigo Borgia received the supreme investiture possessed of all the qualities needed at that moment to preside over the destinies of the Church. With kings already secure upon their thrones he could treat at least as an equal; the turbulent Italian princes he could handle with all the energy necessary; and over the cardinals of the great families, more interested in the welfare of their relations than of the Church, he had the rights that flowed from his long tenure of the cardinalate and the memory of the protection he had given them in the early stages of their careers.[6] He knew by long experience exactly where were the defects of the organization of which he was a part, as is proved by the documents containing his project for a sweeping reform of the Church, a project later carried out by the Council of Trent. And he had learned to his own cost that a Pope must not be dependent upon the powerful princely houses which, with unvarying treachery, sold themselves to foreign rulers.

Further, of all the cardinals, he was the hardest worker, the one best versed in administrative and financial questions. His training for the highest office was better than that of any of his colleagues. He had been a cardinal for thirty-six years. He was Vice-Chancellor and had been so under five Popes. He had carried out missions of the very highest importance. There is no need to appeal to simony to explain his election.

I have already shown that simoniacal practices were difficult in the Conclaves. We must now examine this particular case in the light of the documents of the period. It is argued that the cardinals who voted for Borgia received considerable ecclesiastical benefices: thus Cardinal Ascanio Sforza was appointed Vice-Chancellor and was given the Castle of Nepi, which had been Borgia's dwelling in Rome and was later known as the Palazzo Cesarini; the Church of Santa Maria della Via Lata was given to Cardinal Fregoso; the Abbey of Subiaco to Cardinal Colonna; another cardinal was made Bishop of Porto. And so on. And so on. But all this would have had to happen in any case, simony or no simony, for the simple reason that a cardinal when he is elected Pope automatically vacates all his benefices. When he became Alexander VI, Rodrigo Borgia was obliged to distribute the many benefices he had accumulated in his long career. He had no choice in the matter.

No one has tried to produce evidence that these benefices were the price of votes, nor that they were offered in advance. Not one document of the period bears any hint of such a thing. It has been said that Alexander VI favored his supporters. It may be so: but in that event the vote must have been unanimous since every one of the cardinals received favors from him at the very beginning of his Pontificate. The cardinals who have been described as hostile to him in the Conclave received benefices like the others. Consider young Medici who was eighteen and to whom is attributed the phrase: "We have fallen into the mouth of the wolf. Let us flee or he will swallow us all." He received a nomination at the first Consistory held after the election. In that same Consistory, another of his so-called opponents, Basso della Rovere, was given the diocese of Palestrina and other benefices. Zeno was laden with favors during the first six months of the new Pontificate. Canonries and prebends in Spain and France were offered to Caraffa.

As to the man who is named as leader of the campaign against Borgia in the Conclave, Giuliano della Rovere, he received favors innumerable. To begin with he was given the Benedictine Abbey of the Diocese of Rieux and the Monastery of Saint Hubert in the Ardennes on the very day of the Coronation, 26 August 1492. At the Consistory of August 31 he was given the Camaldolese Abbey of San Bartolommeo at Arezzo, and he was confirmed as Legate at Avignon. In January, February and March of 1493, Alexander VI gave him a canonry, a rectorship, another abbey, a pension of fifty gold ducats, another canonry, another prebend and various benefices valued at nine hundred gold florins a year.

Alexander thought of everybody, even the absent, granting benefices and pensions to Cardinals Mila, Spinay, and Mendoza. If the fact of this distribution (after the election) is to be taken as a cause instead of an effect, then it would seem that all the cardinals had sold themselves, and nobody from that day to this has dared to say that.

Naturally Cardinal Ascanio Sforza was one of the most favored. It is true that he had been one of the cardinals who had had a first rate chance of election himself; and he was the brother of Ludovico Moro, a prince who seriously threatened the peace of Italy. Yet it was to him that Borgia made a gift of his house, which he had built with so much care and love. In the document in which he makes this donation, he sets out the motive for his action—the simple fact that the new Vice-Chancellor had no home of his own in Rome. He did not add, what every one perfectly well knew, that the Vice-Chancellor who has an enormous staff of officials under his charge must have a palace especially constructed for his complex and continuous duties, with voluminous archives and rooms capable of receiving great throngs of people from every corner of Europe. The construction of a new building would have required much time, years perhaps. In any event the palace was not made the personal property of Ascanio Sforza but simply the place of the Chancellery, and so it remained after the death of the cardinal and on to the day when Leo X presented it to the Cesarini.

Still on the matter of Cardinal Sforza, Infessura, followed by practically all later authors, tells us of four mules laden with gold which were seen going through the streets of Rome from Borgia's house to Sforza's; and this of course is represented as part of the price promised to Ascanio for his vote. This is merely one of Infessura's many inventions. It will not stand a moment's scrutiny.[7] We know that the private property of any cardinal elected Pope was considered fair spoil by the public, so much so that the populace had, or at any rate exercised, the right to make for his private palace and pillage it as soon as the election was known. It may have happened that some cardinal, thinking that he was *papabile* and wanting to save his fortune from public plunder, loaded some of it on mules and had it taken away. But Infessura places this incident before the Conclave, that is at a time when Sforza was a candidate and Borgia was not. Sforza's house was therefore in greater danger than Borgia's. It is worth remarking that whereas Infessura gives the story as a rumor, a simple "on dit," later historians have erased the "on dit"; for any hint of doubt

103

would diminish the dramatic character of the story of the Borgias.

Two other matters have been brought forward in support of the accusation of simony. One of these concerns the aged Cardinal Gherardo, patriarch of Venice; and the other tells of the purchase of the flower of the Roman aristocracy in the person of the Cardinals Orsini, Colonna and Savelli. But these two accusations stand examination as little as the other.

I have already said that according to one of the versions of what happened at the Conclave, when one vote was needed to elect Borgia, they obtained Gherardo's. The story is that the old man, almost decrepit, was easily bought, or allowed himself to be sold by his attendants. A historian of the importance of Ranke accepts the story on the evidence of Bruchard's *Diarium*.[3] And the majority of historians before and after Ranke have done likewise.

If the Borgia reputation had not cast its sinister light on this Conclave, sane criticism would have made historians see that the story was fantastic. In all Conclaves, when a majority begins to take shape for one of the candidates, those who are not obstinately committed to another go over to the majority. This is the whole ground of the system of "accession." That being so, it is absolute certainty that, when matters had come to an impasse in which only one vote was needed, Cardinal Maffeo Gherardo would have given his to the candidate who only needed one. And if he had not done so, his attendants fearing for his health, given his age and the confined quarters and the food which grew less with every day, would have put strong pressure on him. But the reconstitution of past history is often done upon false data and not by any calm

104

and rational interpretation of the facts. So it happened with the story of the simony of the aged Patriarch and his attendants. Today, the certain fact, proven historically, is that Bruchard was not at Rome at the time of the Conclave, and that the story in his *Diarium* is an interpolation—for every phrase in it has been taken from Infessura, whose veracity no modern author would care to guarantee.

Bruchard's *Diarium* in so far as it concerns Alexander VI, begins on December 2, 1492. Thuasne has shown that the account of the Conclave and the first acts of the new Pontiff, as well as the withdrawal of Giuliano della Rovere, were lacking in Bruchard's *Diarium* and that to fill the gap the copyists interpolated the corresponding section from Infessura's.[9] But Thuasne has not examined Bruchard's work critically; he has simply acted as a good editor, content to warn the public of obvious errors. The famous *Diarium* of the Vatican Master of Ceremonies awaits a more thoroughgoing analysis. For the moment it is sufficient to note that the work covers a long period—from 21 December 1483 when Sixtus IV was Pope to the year 1506 when Julius II still reigned—and that there are no political details in any part of the book save the part that treats of Borgia; everywhere else he deals only with matters of ceremonial. And given the habit of interpolation, there is something faintly suspicious in this.

Anyhow Infessura says that Cardinal Gherardo sold himself to Borgia and that the Venetians on his return stripped him of his benefices and refused him all respect and authority. Ah well! the Venetians were not able thus to punish their Patriarch, however anxious they may have been to do so, for the good reason that the poor old man never got back to Venice. He died at Terni, shortly after the Conclave, on his way home.

It is probable that this legend may have arisen from the fact that the Holy See had decreed that a sum of seven hundred ducats should be allocated for the traveling expenses of this cardinal after the Conclave. The money was not paid out till he was dead, was indeed used to pay for his funeral. It was the Holy See, and not the Pope personally, which gave the money. The gift was not exceptional but normal in such cases. And Venice, far from considering its Patriarch as a reprobate, paid great honors to his remains and raised a statue to his memory.

The other story was that three cardinals had been bought—Savelli for twenty-five thousand ducats, Orsini for twenty thousand and Colonna for a beggarly fifteen thousand. When one tries to track down the source of this story, nothing whatever can be found at Rome. In spite of the high local fertility in the matter of libelous pamphlets, the first to publish the rumor was a diplomat then resident at Florence, at the court of Pietro de Medici, a certain Manfredo Manfredi. He wrote to his ruler, the Duchess of Este, so that he was writing from one court hostile to Borgia to another court equally hostile. In the circumstances we can only feel that he admirably fulfilled his noble mission: which was, not to tell the truth, for that may be a very dull matter, but to please his employer, a thing essential under personal governments. It is inconceivable that the only three cardinals capable of being bought for cash down were the three Romans. Still more inconceivable that they should have known about it in Florence and not in Rome. It is worth noting that Manfredi does not guarantee the truth of the story. He merely says that he had it from a good source.

I think it has now been proved that no single one of

these accusations of simony will stand examination. But it is also true that certain unspecified affirmations of contemporaries have been accepted by subsequent writers as true evidence. There is for example Peter Martyr whose writings are regarded as a good historical source. This author, Italian, by birth, passed the greater part of his life in Spain. He was living in Spain at the time of the Conclave, and he mentions that Alexander VI bought his election.[10] It may be worth noting that the letter in which he thus accuses the Conclave of simony is dated 19 July, 1492, whereas Alexander's election took place between 10 and 11 August following. I do not mean that Peter Martyr prophesied both the election and its corrupt proceedings, but simply that his book has been worked over, touched up, corrected and added to according to ideas born later from the clash of interests between Alexander—who was determined to control the Barons, to be master of his own representatives, to establish a strong State in Italy against foreign invasions—and his adversaries, by which I mean all the powers of that day.

The truth is that all that has come down to us as actually written at the time and not subsequently altered affirms that Alexander VI was elected unanimously. Hartmann Schedel, a German author who was at Rome during the Conclave, writes that the cardinals, after the difficulties arising from the earlier ballots, agreed that Borgia should be chosen and that "in consequence, he was considered *by all his colleagues* as worthy of the Pontificate." This piece of evidence probably survives because Schedel hastened to publish his *Chronicarum Liber* at Nuremberg a year later, when the contrary current had not yet begun to flow strongly.[11] Michele Fermo, who published his *Conclavi*

Alexandri Sexti Pontificis Maximi in 1493 at Rome speaks of the unanimity of the election, and attributes it to the virtues of the candidate. Sigismundo dei Conti, whose narrative was only dragged out from under the dust of centuries in 1883, confirms the statement that Alexander VI was elected with the agreement of the whole conclave. And this is also stated by Giovanni Stella.[12]

The ambassadors Valori and Manfredo Manfredi also had to tell their princes that Borgia was elected unanimously; and when the Ambassadors Extraordinary came to felicitate the new Pope, they all declared that they were particularly happy at the unanimity with which his former colleagues had chosen him Head of the Church.

The Pope himself on several occasions mentioned his pleasure at this rare and exceptional favor. Writing to Ascanio Sforza in the difficult hours of the arrival of Charles VIII, he rebukes him for his attitude, and says this of Giuliano della Rovere: "Whereas he might have hoped much from us, because of the dear memory of his uncle, our predecessor Sixtus IV, yet after having with great magnanimity given us his vote and the votes of his friends in the Conclave, he later grew angry, and this precisely because he saw that you had penetrated very deep into our affection." And sometime earlier he wrote to the representatives of Terni: ". . . by the will of God, whose designs are unfathomable, they [the Cardinals] elected me on August 11 unanimously . . ."

And this unanimity should of itself suffice to destroy the credit of all the rumors of simony and at least to render suspect the great mass of stories later written concerning the matrimonial life of Cardinal Borgia and the depths of his immorality.

CHAPTER VII

The First Moments

I T IS TOLD that when he found himself actually chosen, Rodrigo Borgia manifested the liveliest desire to get into the magnificent pontifical robes as quickly as possible. He could not wait. It is said that he cried with delighted enthusiasm: "I am the Pope, the Pontiff, the Vicar of Christ!"[1] This was indeed the nature of the man. And it is in moments of high joy, physical or moral, that character shows itself truly. If Rodrigo did not actually say the words, yet they can be attributed to him with real probability. Eneas Silvius wept sorrowfully when he was elected; and a later Pius, Pius X, some centuries later, likewise burst into tears. Whereas Leo X, son of Lorenzo the Magnificent, cried out: "God has given me the Papacy and I am going to make the most of it."

Borgia had voted many a time for other popes; had many a time ceremonially kissed the feet of former colleagues. As the oldest member of the Sacred College, he had placed the triple crown on their heads. And after all that long waiting, it was his turn at last. In such spontaneous enthusiasm, unconcealed and overflowing, we see the whole man —the jovial sanguine man that he was to remain until a few days before his death. His eagerness to see himself clad in the purple and gold reflected the taste for pomp and magnificence that we find in him throughout his cardinalate in all public ceremonies, civil and religious.

109

So it seems to me quite in character that he should have manifested his feelings thus loudly. All the same none of those who were actually at the Conclave and witnessed the events that followed it has left us any hint of such a scene. To find it we must go to that narrative, anonymous and bristling with errors and lies, which I have already described as a fortunate historical document. But the nameless malevolent slanderer has for once said something which if not certainly true is at least lifelike.

The new Pope adopted the name of Alexander VI. Why? Is it that he meant to take up a warlike attitude, with the name of the great King of Macedon, the Invincible? So it has been said; but the only evidence for it is that the poets of that day did not fail to draw attention to the earlier Alexander in praising the later. What poets of any day would have overlooked that? On the contrary, all Borgia's policy as it developed recalls that of another Alexander, Alexander III, who united himself with the Italian Communes, and so obliged the Emperor Frederick Barbarossa to respect the Church of Rome. We shall see this latest Alexander enter into union, not now with the Communes, but with the new States.

This Papal election caused immediate manifestations of almost measureless enthusiasm. Papal elections, of course, normally provoked joy in the populace and floods of official rhetoric. But the authors of that time and later have noted that this time it went beyond the normal.[2]

Rome was en fête for several days. A spectator—a classical scholar perhaps—cried out on the night of the election: "Marc Antony himself was not received so magnificently by Cleopatra." Night was as bright as day. The people in thousands carried torches in their hands. Houses were covered with tapestry and ablaze with lights. Tri-

umphal arches, erected by groups of the people or by rich
individuals, seemed to spring up every few yards along
the principal streets. Inscriptions outdid themselves in
eulogy.

Coronation day, August 26, a Sunday, was a day of suf-
focating heat. But all Rome was present at the great procession in which not only the Roman nobility and the
people took part but all the princes of the States of the
Church. From the Vatican the procession made its way
toward St. Peter's, Alexander VI coming immediately after
the cardinals. At St. Peter's the canons were admitted to the
ceremony of the kissing of the feet, and the cardinals likewise, as he sat upon the golden chair. After mass, and a
prayer in which he called upon God's aid, he was crowned
by the Cardinal Deacon Francesco Piccolomini, later Pope
Pius III. From there he made his way slowly under the
eyes of the enchanted multitude to the Church of St. John
Lateran, passing the Castle of St. Angelo, near which the
Jews gathered to pay him homage. At St. John Lateran the
procession dispersed. The new Pope returned at night to
the Vatican amidst the shouting of the people through a
city illumined as Rome had never been illumined before.
And we are told that crushed with fatigue, and in spite of
several fainting fits he had had in the course of a day so
crammed with ceremonies, he immediately settled down to
deal with certain affairs that required immediate attention.

There were great celebrations also in many cities of the
peninsula. In Florence and in Milan the people joined with
their Lords in enthusiastic celebration of the election. In
all the cities over which the Church exercised its sovereignty the manifestations were as tremendous, and the
Prince-Vicars entered into the joy of the people with a
special ardour in order to disguise the anxiety they felt

111

about their own futures and to impress upon the new Pope their fidelity and their personal devotion.

It seems to me that this first great burst of enthusiasm, so much beyond the normal, was due to the feeling that the new Pope would have a policy of his own, and that this policy would be fully equal to the difficult times that everyone realized Italy must pass through. The historian Nardi, who understood the psychology of the period, states the situation thus: "Everywhere and especially in Rome, people were seized with a lively emotion, as if God had chosen this prince as the instrument of his special designs."[3]

As the celebrations in Rome drew to their end and the echo of the shouting died away, the official voice of the representatives of foreign states began to be heard. All sovereigns sent missions to felicitate the new Pope. The King of France dealt with the matter in person, as we shall see, though the circumstances were rather peculiar. The cities of Italy were the first to send their emissaries to offer homage. It was the custom at that time, upon occasions of this sort, to send more or less numerous embassies, composed of noble and eminent personages, among whom it was the custom to include a Latinist, an orator of renown. The discourses with which this orator was charged were prepared well in advance and made no mention of politics; very seldom did one find any allusion to the events of the day or the interests of the two parties. These speeches had to pass the severest test of the critical scholarship of the day. The importance of the mission was measured by the quality of those who composed it. And it was the small states—which only obtained consideration and respect abroad when they were represented by great men—who sent the best delegations, best that is both by the illustrious

112

names and the high culture of their members and by the splendor of their robes and their general magnificence.

Upon this occasion Pietro de Medici led the Florentine embassy in person. The Marquis of Mantua sent his brother Giovanni de Gonzaga. The town of Siena was represented by Angelo Ambrogini, the famous Politian. At the very beginning Venice showed the Pope how great was its pleasure at the news of his election: "On account of the God-like virtues and gifts with which they saw him endowed and adorned, he seemed to have been chosen and preordained by Divine Providence as Pastor of the flock, and Vicar in the Lordship of the Most Holy Roman Church."[4] The King of Naples, Ferrante, hastened to send the most friendly messages and an embassy led by his son, the Duke of Montferrat, rendered homage to Alexander VI.

The speeches uttered in the course of the various receptions all breathe the highest respect, as the custom was; but beyond that they reflect a quite special and extraordinary admiration for the person of the Pontiff, and all express the hope that under his rule the Church should recover its former greatness. Politian declares him superior to all other men.[5] Jason del Maino eloquently congratulates the cardinals upon having chosen such a Pope, in whom lie so many hopes for the Church, and in a highly colored outburst he declares that the Pope has no need of advisers: "You have nothing to learn from others during your Pontificate. Against you alone no accusation of ignorance can be made. You know the needs of the Holy See and of religion, you know what a Roman Pontiff must do, what is permitted to him and what is useful. In your great wisdom you have no need of any man's counsel. Consult yourself alone, obey yourself, follow your inclinations, take

113

yourself for a model . . . you will never fall into error if you rely upon your own judgment."[6] The orators from Naples offer him, in their sovereign's name, to take up arms to defend him and to defend the Church. The Emperor, through the mouth of his emissary, Ludovico Bruno, congratulates himself upon so happy a choice.

These special missions followed one another in a long series over a whole year. Meanwhile the Pope was working to organize the town and to establish a system for the administration of justice, to bring about some improvement of morals, to bring the Barons under control, and to maintain intact the territories of St. Peter. It was this work, vigorously carried on by a man of strong will and deep understanding of the situation, a resolute masculine man, which aroused the first difficulties. Alexander VI proceeded to a pretty harsh handling of delinquents high and low; and right at the beginning found himself at grips with the King of Naples, Ferrante, who had already been a thorn in the side of previous Popes.

At this period the family interests of rulers were of more importance than the interests of the peoples they ruled. Indeed it was often difficult to distinguish one from the other, to decide if this or that given action, a war even, arose from some wretched family question or from necessities of state. The King of Naples, a bastard son of the King of Aragon, had at once a violent nature and an insatiable ambition. There was no crime he did not commit against his subjects. His kingdom was always in a state of ferment and a large part of his nobility had fled for refuge to foreign courts, particularly the court of France. Bound by family ties to various of Europe's rulers, Ferrante's policy was to use these personal links to give him a decisive

114

influence in the affairs of Italy. But as the world is subject to an eternal dualism, the very things that brought him authority and prestige also brought him problems and misfortunes.

His granddaughter Isabella, daughter of Alfonso, heir to the throne and later King of Naples, had married the Duke of Milan, Gian Galeazzo Sforza. He had been under the regency of his uncle Ludovico Moro who was showing no haste to hand over control of the duchy. Further, one of Ferrante's illegitimate daughters, Beatrice, had married Mathias Corvinus King of Hungary; and when Mathias died, leaving no children, she had contracted to marry King Ladislas of Bohemia, promising him the throne of Hungary. Beatrice kept her word and made him King of Hungary. But Ladislas, having become King, refused to carry out his promise of marriage and asked the Pope, the ultimate judge of all such canonical questions, to annul the promise on the ground of defective form. Ferrante thus saw his plans collapsing.

To defend these two members of his family and preserve intact his own sphere of political influence, he asked the Pope to use his authority to insure—first, that at Milan the Duke Gian Galeazzo, no longer a minor, should take over the government and Ludovico Moro who continued to govern but was now no better than a usurper should be expelled; second, that Ladislas should be compelled to enter into the marriage he had promised. Neither affair interested Alexander VI particularly, and he was in no haste to give judgment, still less to take any action. The question of the Duchy of Milan was not in his competence and there was no reason why he should interfere, especially as Cardinal Ascanio Sforza, his Vice-Chancellor and the principal factor in his election, was Ludovico's brother. In the matter

115

of Ladislas, there was one important consideration he could not overlook—this monarch was on the furthest continental frontier of Christianity, defending Europe against the Turk.

Not to have to return to the subject of the marriage, let us note now that it was definitely settled in 1499, some seven years later. The Pope could never discover any juridical proofs of a promise made by Ladislas to Beatrice; but a canonical reason which had more weight with the Pope was based on the more important fact that Ladislas was already married to Barbara of Brandenburg! This Hungarian was no delicately scrupulous man in matrimonial affairs. After the Pope had declared his promise to Beatrice of Aragon null, he asked him to do the same for his marriage to Barbara. And as Barbara had no objection, the Pope consented. With the usual "on dit" some authors have written that the court of Rome had received money for these proceedings. As far as the Pope was concerned he named a tribunal in 1493 to decide the matter. How good the canonical grounds for the second nullity were, I do not know. But it is certain that the court of Rome was very much afraid of losing the good will of Ladislas; and what we find in the pontifical registers is a note not of sums received by the Pope, but rather of sums paid out by the Pope to the King.

But at this moment Alexander was not so much concerned about the family affairs of the King of Naples nor the political aspirations bound up with them. He was very much concerned about the advances made by that sovereign into his own territory. The shrewd Aragonese wanted a footing in the lands of the Church in order to establish contact between his own kingdom and the domain of the

Medicis of Florence, his friends and allies. Alexander VI, whose plan was to reconstruct the Papal States on a solid foundation, could not allow Ferrante to carry through his design to become master of the destinies of Italy by strengthening his alliance with Florence and ruling over Milan and Lombardy through his granddaughter, who governed the inept and sickly Gian Galeazzo. Part of Ferrante's plan at the same time was to neutralize, by his projected relationship with the King of Hungary, any action by Venice in Italy. Ferrante's policy thus threatened to destroy the equilibrium which had so long preserved the peace, and to put the Papacy and the whole peninsula at his mercy.

It was this ambitious project which caused the first difficulties for the new Pope. In its development, Ferrante did not employ overt violence. Slow, hesitant, treacherous, incalculable, it was his habit to make grave difficulties out of totally unimportant affairs. Lying was not for him a means of attaining some important end, it was simply a habit. "Insidious simulation, hypocrisy, an unquenchable thirst for vengeance which could yet wait for the slow ripening of its fruits"[7] made up his very existence. Thus there was one virtue in his perfidy: he knew how to wait. In the affair of the occupation of the territories of the Church it was precisely thus that he proceeded. But Alexander VI knew him and watched him. While these great projects were simply a matter of matrimonial arrangements and such like the Pope spoke to Ferrante's ambassadors in vague generalities; but the moment there appeared a concrete case of damage threatening the Church, Alexander VI was done with speeches and prepared to fight.

Franceschetto Cibo, son of Pope Innocent VIII, had upon his father's death left Rome and made his way to

Florence. There he was very cordially received, since his wife was a Medici, daughter of Lorenzo the Magnificent and sister of the future Leo X, then a Cardinal. Fearing to lose the properties the deceased Pope had given him in ecclesiastical territory—a loss which frequently happened on the election of a new Pope—he negotiated with Virginio Orsini the sale of the castles of Cervetri, Monterano and Viano, and of the hamlet of Rota for twenty-five thousand ducats, and that of the Castle of Anguilara and the possessions adjoining it for fifteen thousand ducats. Though he belonged to the Roman nobility, Virginio Orsini was in the pay of the King of Naples and was one of the great lords of his kingdom and the head of the army. The Pope realized that Orsini was simply a man of straw, and that these fiefs of the Church were, in this indirect fashion, passing to the King of Naples. Making use of his right, he declared the contract of sale null; and since he did not wish to have his just cause depend upon nothing but its justice, he prepared to defend it with a large number of armed men. With that perfect balance of judgement he was always to show, at the same time that he was calling upon the King of Naples to submit to impartial judges the question whether Franceschetto could transfer or sell these fiefs of the Church, he entered into alliance with the Republic of Venice and the Duchy of Milan, the two greatest powers in Italy for wealth and prestige.

King Ferrante, perceiving that he had lost on the political field and that he was about to lose on the legal, decided to transfer his effort to a third field and circumvent the Pope by a different means. He knew the weak spot in Alexander VI, and he thought he could realize his plans by proposing to the Pope a family alliance, a new bond of relationship which would serve him better than those he had made for himself in Hungary and Milan. He offered to

Jofre de Borgia, generally considered as the Pope's son, the hand of his granddaughter Sancia, daughter of the Duke of Calabria; and at the same time he suggested to Alexander VI that he enter into a political alliance with the Kingdom of Naples, though he was careful not to suggest that the Pope should abandon the alliances which now bound him to Milan and Venice. Borgia refused both propositions. He realized that if he accepted them he would be effectively separated from Venice and Milan, for the second alliance would necessarily neutralize the effects of the first; so that he would be detached from both these states and would be reduced virtually to the condition of Ferrante's vassal.

Even yet the old King would not give up. He saw that the Pope was becoming far too independent. He felt that the thing to do was to discredit him. A discredited Pope loses a great part of his strength. Thus he decided to use the weapon of calumny, writing against Alexander VI to various princes. Notably he wrote on June 7, 1493,[8] to his relations the sovereigns of Castile. This letter constitutes the first attack of its kind against Borgia. Thus the initiator of what was to be an unending campaign of calumnies was the most immoral and the most discredited man of the age.

The letter to the sovereigns of Castile would in ordinary life be quite sufficient to establish the bad faith of its author; but history seems to be written on different principles, and the letter constitutes one of the most effective elements of accusation in the whole Borgia story. King Ferrante told his illustrious Spanish relations that the Pope meant to take away his *condottieri* and that to this end he had offered large sums and land to the Orsini and Colonna families; that at the same time he had asked Virginio Orsini not to yield on the affair of Cervetri, Anguilara and other

119

possessions while at the same time he was making this affair a *casus belli*; finally that he meant to appoint thirteen cardinals with the sole object of making money, for he was charging a minimum of twenty thousand ducats for the office. Immorality, said Ferrante, ruled in Rome, disorder in all Italy. The Pope had but one interest: to procure the elevation of his children by all possible means. And, to bring upon the world another war, he was offering the Kingdom of Naples to the duke of Lorraine. The Pope was quite capable of appealing to the Turks, so that they might attack Ferrante from the South. The letter continued on this tone, relating a tissue of intrigues and invented perfidies; and to crown all the writer claimed that in the affair of the lands, he had proposed a formal legal enquiry, and that the Pope had refused and had offered instead a matrimonial alliance. These final details would be sufficient in themselves to give the letter a historical value certainly not unfavorable to Alexander VI, for it is proved by documents unquestionably authentic that it was Ferrante who had refused the legal enquiry and who had proposed the marriage of Jofre and Sancia.

None the less his letter produced its effect on the minds of Ferdinand and Isabella, as it did later on the minds of authors who have written on Alexander VI. When the ambassador Diego Lopez de Haro was sent to Rome to offer homage to Alexander VI he was charged to put pressure upon the Pope in order to bring him to an arrangement with the King of Naples. It is clear that Infessura alters the facts, according to his custom, when he says that the Spanish ambassador roundly rebuked the Pope for his conduct; but that he did try to bring the Pope to a compromise with the King of Naples is beyond doubt. Lopez de Haro, after the solemn ceremony of homage, asked the Pope, in the course of a series of conversations he had with him, to settle his difficulties with Ferrante and with Virginio Orsini, and to discontinue the preparations for war which were evident in the city of Rome. Under this pressure, the Pope offered the ambassador that he would reach a settlement but without modifying his preliminary demands for a legal solution of the affair. Ferrante could not refuse since in his complete distortion of the truth he had declared that the proposal for a judicial examination had come from him: so he had to agree to a peaceable settlement with the Pope on this matter. To prove the goodness of his will, he wrote a second letter in which he thanked the Spanish sovereigns for their intervention.[9]

But it must be noted that in this matter Ferdinand and Isabella were not the instruments of Ferrante but that on the contrary they were using Ferrante as an instrument in their own plans. The sovereigns of Castile had a more serious question to occupy their minds than the handful of acres claimed by Virginio Orsini, and Ferrante's complaint was used by them merely as a pretext. A totally different affair was to be broached in Rome. Those Jews who had apparently been converted to Christianity and were known as Marranos, were under violent persecution in the Iberian Peninsula. The tribunals of the Inquisition condemned them to very heavy penalties. They had acquired enormous power under the reign of the previous king, the wretched Henry IV of Castile. Convert Jews, sincere or not, had penetrated into the court, into the government and even into the ranks of higher clergy—all this in addition to their already great power in the realm of finance, public and private. There were Marranos in the highest aristocracy, there were even Bishops who preached the law

121

of Christ in public and in secret prayed according to the Jewish religion they had never really abandoned. Spain had thus witnessed the growth within itself of a very numerous ethnic group, which was not of the same origin, or the same race, or the same faith as the Spanish people. Civil power, a certain amount of religious power, and practically all financial power were concentrated in the hands of this group. There was a reaction, commingled as usual of self-interest and idealism. Men of sincere faith believed that it was necessary to unify the moral consciousness of the people, and that the people who governed and grew rich by governing were not Spaniards. But the great majority had no nobler thought than to take the place of the fallen tribe in the enjoyment of their goods and their positions. The State did not oppose the demands of public opinion, because the State meant the two sovereigns, and these, engaged in an enormous and expensive enterprise of national reconstruction, needed all the money accumulated by the Jews. The persecution took an organized and legal form, which did not prevent sporadic outbreaks of violence by a people athirst for blood and loot.

Rome had not the same needs as Spain, had not suffered from any such rise of a foreign element. Further, although it was the center of Catholicism it had long-rooted traditions of tolerance. While the popes tried to keep the children of Israel separate from the rest of the population, they did not persecute them. The Jew in Italy was not powerful or aggressive. The Christian, doubtless the heir in this of ancient Rome, was in general tolerant. Alexander VI in particular, a wide-minded man lacking the prejudices of some of the other popes, regarded the Jews as fellow creatures who had committed the error of practising a religion not entirely based on true doctrine. On the day of his coronation, receiving their formal homage, he had replied: "Hebrews, we admire and respect your Holy Law since it was given your ancestors by the most High God through the hands of Moses; but we are opposed to the false observance and interpretation you have of it, because the Apostolic Faith teaches that the Redeemer whom you await in vain has already come, and that he is our Lord Jesus Christ, who with the Father and the Holy Spirit is the Everlasting God."

The Spanish sovereigns, already at war upon the Jews, would not let anybody else tolerate them, even outside Spain. Through Lopez de Haro, they demanded that this state of things should cease in Rome, especially in regard to the Jews who had come there from Spain. This was the true mission of the Spanish ambassador in Rome. Alexander VI, as was his custom, replied in the most courteous terms but he refused point blank to do what the Spanish sovereigns wanted. He showered favors and honors on the ambassador, spoke to him of the great love in which he held his sovereigns and his country, and pointed out to him that the Jews did not represent any danger to the Eternal City. He always had this courteous skillful manner; and this, added to his superior intelligence, gave rise to the legend of his Machiavellianism. Men always attribute to trickery the defeats they suffer on the intellectual plane.

The Pope kept the promise made to Lopez de Haro in regard to the first part, the official part, of his mission. He prepared to come to an immediate settlement with Virginio Orsini and the King of Naples. But time had flowed by; and the settlement of the question of the lands, though due to the formal initiative of Spain, actually arose from

I

profounder causes. A storm was blowing up in the North which alarmed the King of Naples as much as it alarmed the Pope. Charles VIII of France was raising an army to conquer the realm of Naples, alleging his prior rights as inheritor of the house of Anjou. Ferrante realized what this preparation for war meant for the future of his family, and the Pope knew equally that it was better to have south of Rome a troublesome but not powerful State rather than one of the greatest powers of Europe. Thus the moment the two opponents, Rome and Naples, had precise information as to what was preparing in France, they abandoned their own refusal to compromise.

None the less, the Pope obtained that Cervetri and Anguilara and the other castles and domains should not be alienated by the contract of sale entered into at Florence in violation of feudal law; but that, by means of a new purchase, Virginio Orsini should receive them from the Holy See, paying the full price of forty thousand ducats, not to Franceschetto Cibo but to the Papal treasury. It seems further that in preliminary conversations the Pope obtained a promise from Virginio Orsini to transfer these properties to his son, which Orsini in fact did a few months later. Thus Alexander VI compromised only in form; for as to the substance he maintained his juridical thesis; and from the practical point of view he prevented these properties from passing definitively to the Crown of Naples.

Thus this grave conflict, which might have caused a war and which did cause such damage to the Pope's memory, was settled in the best possible way. And as every arrangement of this kind was supposed to be followed by a marriage, discussions were renewed as to a family pact between the Pope and the King of Naples. The Spanish ambassador took the initiative. This was the first time that there was any mention of the possibility of Cesar Borgia giving up the ecclesiastical state.[10] The King of Naples had expressed a desire to marry his daughter Lucretia to Cesar. But as the Pope categorically refused, they had to return to the original idea, the King's own idea, of marrying his granddaughter Sancia to Jofre de Borgia.

As absolute sovereign, even if elected, of the territories of the Church, the Pope furnished Jofre with adequate resources, but he refused to give him the Duchy of Benevento which the King urgently solicited. The King likewise gave a large dowry to his granddaughter. Jofre was made Prince of Squillace and Count of Cariati. To unify the interests of the Church and Naples, he was named *condottiere* of both States, each paying the half of the *condotta*. On August 16, 1493, Jofre and Sancia were officially married in Rome, Sancia having given proxy to her uncle Frederick, second son of King Ferrante. But the Pope would not allow Jofre to go to Naples, and it was only after Ferrante's death that the marriage was consummated.

Obviously a family union made thus at the cost of the goods of the Church would be inconceivable in our day. But in a period when the Pope was a sovereign like any other and the public patrimony was his personal patrimony, arrangements of this sort were held normal. Other popes, before and after Alexander VI, did the same in similar circumstances. We must not forget what Lorenzo the Magnificent said in his letter to Innocent VIII: The one thing a Pope can do for his relations is to provide them with goods while he is alive.[11]

But Alexander VI had another grave difficulty from the very beginning of his Pontificate.

Alexander the Sixth

Early in 1493, began the enmity, not always at full violence but always existent, between Alexander VI and Cardinal Giuliano della Rovere, later Julius II. It is impossible to arrive at an impartial judgment upon the two most famous Popes of the Renaissance save after a careful examination of the facts. Cardinal della Rovere had for long been a considerable personage, perhaps the most important member of the Sacred College. The election of Alexander VI was a rude blow to his ambition. During the dispute with Virginio Orsini and the King of Naples he took sides with them against the interests of the Church. The Pope had loaded him with benefices and shown him special regard. But Giuliano, whose violence of temper knew no moral or material curb, provoked such a situation that the Pope had no choice but to denounce him in full consistory. This was equivalent to an accusation of treason: for it clearly appeared that a prince of the Church had a secret understanding with a foreign ruler to obtain property belonging to the Church's suzerainty. Alexander's intellectual superiority, the lucidity of his statement, and the power of his dialectic were too much for the Cardinal's cause. He passed from intrigue to action.

He had approved the contract between Virginio Orsini and Franceschetto Cibo, at a time when it was unknown to the Pope. He had kept the King of Naples' representative in his own house while he was in Rome. And he had been Ferrante's chief adviser throughout the conflict. So when Alexander VI seemed determined to yield nothing of the rights of the Church and to go to war if necessary, della Rovere hastened to Ostia, of which he was Bishop, shut himself up in the fortress which commanded the mouth of the Tiber, and threatened the maritime communications of Rome. It seems probable that he did this in accord with the plans of the captains of Ferrante's entourage, who loudly demanded an attack upon Rome with the object of reducing Borgia to helplessness, or achieving some worse thing still. But the King of Naples, calculating the consequences of so grave an act, decided not to risk it. His ally, Giuliano, returned to Rome and was reconciled with the Pope who pardoned him on this first occasion as later upon others. On July 24, 1493, Virginio Orsini and the Cardinal dined at the Vatican. Della Rovere was one of the sponsors of the arrangement that was entered into: he represented the interests of the Orsini, while Cardinal Giovanni Borgia represented those of the Church. Alexander VI was deeply pained at the attitude of his one-time colleague and attributed it to jealousy at the favor he had shown Ascanio Sforza.

But Giuliano was temperamentally insubordinate. Made Cardinal during the Pontificate of his uncle Sixtus IV, he kept comparatively quiet, partly because of the double respect he owed him as Pope and Uncle, still more because the Pope had a character more violent even than his own. Under Innocent VIII, he was in control in the Vatican to the great unhappiness of the Pope, a quiet man. And now he could not bear to suffer the authority of a real chief. He protested because the Pope was defending the interests of the Church; he was irritated by the nomination of new cardinals; he would not accept resolutions of the Consistory, and he fortified Ostia for eventual use against Rome. Shortly after the reconciliation he went to France to urge on preparations for the war against the very King of Naples whom he had supported against Alexander.

Political difficulties did not leave the Pope unmindful of family affections. Little Lucretia was now rapidly growing up, was indeed already of an age to be promised in marriage according to the customs of the time. There are contradictory documents. It is affirmed that Lucretia, before and after the accession of Alexander to the Papal throne, was betrothed according to some, married according to others, to different nobles such as Juan de Centellas, Gaspar de Procida son of the Count of Aversa, and later to the Count of Prada.[12] But it seems fairly clear that there was no marriage and that the promises, if they were given, were not kept. The three men mentioned were probably only suitors. All three were Spaniards. But if Cardinal Borgia would have been satisfied with any one of them as a husband for Lucretia, Alexander VI naturally looked higher. Other candidates were excluded in the interests of Giovanni Sforza, Lord of Pesaro, relation of Ludovico il Moro. According to the most careful investigation it seems that he was Lucretia's first husband. The contract was entered into on February 2, 1493 and the marriage celebrated on June 12 following. This marriage united the family of Borgia with the family of Sforza to the greater triumph of Cardinal Ascanio and the greater annoyance of the King of Naples. Lucretia received a dowry of thirty-one thousand ducats, part of which came from a legacy of her brother, the first Duke of Gandia. The Pope generously made up the full sum.

As was the custom in the time of Innocent VIII, the marriage was celebrated at the Vatican. The religious ceremonies and civil celebrations were equally brilliant but without the pomp that was later displayed on such occasions. A long sermon and an even longer comedy were the principal attractions: to say nothing of a banquet for members of the family. Apart from the banquet the diplomatic corps accredited to Rome were present at every

128

point of the celebrations. Boccaccio, the envoy of Mantua, tells all about them in a dispatch to his government. He mentions that the comedy was suitable; and he names as the chief persons at the banquet—among the men the Pope, Ascanio Sforza, two other Cardinals, the Count of Pitigliano, Captain-general of the Papal forces, and certain others, making eight in all; and among the women, Adriana del Mila, widow of an Orsini and a relation of the Pope, Pitigliano's wife and Giulia Farnese. There were some sixteen people present. A phrase in this dispatch, written the day after the banquet, has served to make this marriage figure among the orgies of the Vatican. But Boccaccio simply adds to what has just been said that from eight to nine in the evening, there was a distribution of presents; then that, after a ball at which the ladies danced with one another, there was a comedy with music and songs. He finishes with the phrase: "Thus passed the evening: if well or ill, I leave Your Excellency to judge." This last phrase, in spite of its vague and suggestive form, was simply a respectful expression towards the high personage to whom the ambassador was writing. In all the diplomatic correspondence of the period—I have noted it especially in Venetian documents—this formula is commonly employed, politely leaving the recipient judge of the question. But in any event, since Boccaccio describes perfectly normal happenings which might have taken place in the house of any noble family of the period, and since it was the custom in the Vatican to give such banquets at which ladies were present, what significance can there be in a final, entirely formal phrase which cannot in any way affect the harmlessness of the account already given?[13]

The Pope made Cesar Borgia a Cardinal on September 20, 1493. On August 31 of the previous year he had done

129

the same for his cousin, Giovanni. Apparently he wished in the first moments to have a man of first rate ability in the Consistory, and Giovanni was such a man if we may judge from the dispatch sent by the ambassador Manfredi from Florence to Mantua, in which he is spoken of as "an excellent man, versed in affairs." Giovanni's was a single appointment. But along with Cesar, Alexander VI named eleven other cardinals, three of them boys in their teens. These were Ippolito d'Este, son of Ercole de Ferrara, who was only fifteen; Alexander Farnese, who was to be Pope Paul III; and Cesar Borgia, who was all of sixteen. If these three nominations, plus that of Giulio Cesarini, can be attributed to the nepotism of the Pope, the others were the result of profound political experience. We find Henry VII of England's Chancellor, John Morton; the eloquent Bernardino Lopez Carvajal; Raymond Péraud, the abbot of St. Denis; Domenico Grimani, son of the Doge of Venice; the King of Poland's son; and two or three others. To judge justly of these nominations, we must remember that the Church was then divided into two branches: one purely religious, and the other entirely political. The Bishops, having the care of souls, governed the first, while the Cardinals added temporal activity to such religious functions as they might have.

As to the extreme youth of three of Alexander's nominees, it may be said in extenuation first that other Popes did likewise, and second that many such young men, early made cardinals, later became great Popes.

Alexander VI, whose industry and application to work had been proved during his long years as Vice-Chancellor, showed remarkable skill in that while handling the Church's external relations and attending to the interests of his family, he ruled the internal affairs of the Church

with great strength and insight. Immediately after his enthronement, he named four doctors reputed for their
knowledge of jurisprudence as members of a species of
Supreme Tribunal, and enacted laws to remove judicial
abuses in the lower courts. He reformed the management
of prisons. He set apart one day of the week to hear in
person the claims of those who thought they had suffered
injustice. Later he reformed the constitution of Rome, or
to speak more exactly, he granted the Romans the right to
reform it. In an important document of the second year of
his Papacy, we find his whole theory upon internal government. It is the theory later put into practice, under his
direction, by Cesar Borgia in the Romagna, which made
him so popular that that region remained loyal to him
even after the Pope's death and his own fall.

Alexander "considering that the town which gave Law
to the world, should be prepared to give laws to itself,"[14]
called upon the heads of the people to outline the Constitution they wished, annulled previous constitutions granted
by the Popes, and proclaimed in advance that the new
constitution must be definitively approved by the citizens
of Rome. He allowed that in the course of time experience
might demand modifications; he did not give the Holy See
any authority to modify the popular constitution, but he
allowed the people the right to decree new measures and
reform old measures at any time.[15] The Pope's language
seems to belong rather to the nineteenth century than to
the fifteenth.

This reform, known as "Reformationes Alexandri VI,"
was approved and it is the most far-sighted and complete
document upon public law in the whole history of Papal
Rome, embracing the administration of the state, the relation of the citizens among themselves, and criminal justice.

131

Borgia went further. He set up a popular assembly which was to meet at least once a month "to choose the means necessary for good government and the prosperity of the Holy Roman Church and for the protection of the city and its inhabitants."

In the later months of 1493, the Pope decided to visit the territories which made up the patrimony of the Church. On October 26 he left Rome to visit Ascanio Sforza at Nepi. Spending long days on horseback he went to Ronciglione, Viterbo, and Toscanella. At Corneto in spite of his weariness after so much journeying, he went fishing with a small group of courtiers. Later he made his way to Civita-Vecchia. But he returned to Corneto. In spite of the almost endless alternation of public affairs and religious ceremonies, he still found time for fishing and for long and tiring hunting parties. At sixty-one he was strong and vigorous, and indeed so remained until the end, as the Venetian ambassador reported to his government a few days before the Pope's death. After Corneto he visited the rest of his territories and returned to Rome on December 19. Here he was acclaimed by the whole populace with an enthusiasm it had not shown for any of his predecessors for centuries past.

In this first part of his pontificate, Alexander VI made a decision of the highest importance: he divided between the kingdoms of Portugal and Spain the zone of the great new discoveries then being made. This decision, swift and opportune, prevented grave conflicts at the time and the still graver conflicts which otherwise would have arisen later.

The charge has been made that Alexander VI, called upon to reconcile the conflicting claims of Portugal and

132

Spain, simply took a map and drew a line from North to South as his fancy struck him, deciding that countries discovered to the east of this line should belong to Portugal, those to the west to Spain. There is no foundation for this stupid legend and no need to discuss it. The truth is very different. It shows all the care and skill and moderation the Pope brought to the solution of great questions.

When Christopher Columbus returned from his first voyage and gave a marvelous account of what he had found beyond the seas, the King of Portugal claimed that by a treaty of 1479, Spain had agreed that new territories discovered or to be discovered should belong to him. In fact, according to the treaty of Alcacoba, all the islands of the West except the Canaries belonged to Portugal. The King of Portugal, in order to support his diplomatic representations to his neighbors' court by positive arguments, prepared a fleet which was to follow Columbus next time he set out, and when he had led them to the new lands he had discovered, occupy them forcibly. Spain rejected the Portuguese argument on the ground that Columbus' discoveries had created a new situation not envisaged by the treaty. To prevent war, it appealed to the intervention of Alexander VI.

The Pope studied the question, and without entering into any long discussion with Portugal made use in Spain's favor of a formula of "donation of discovered lands," which he had previously used in favor of Portugal when that country had asked that its oceanic acquisitions would be legally recognized. From Martin V to Sixtus IV, Rome had granted to Portugal all the lands its navigators had occupied in the course of their long voyages. Following precisely the same principle the Pope promulgated in Spain's favor a series of three bulls dated May 3, 1493. The first

133

granted to the Kings of Spain the islands and mainland territories already discovered or which might be discovered on later explorations on condition that they should not already belong to any other Christian ruler. To justify this concession the Sovereign Pontiff stated that the new discoveries extended the sphere of European civilization and enlarged the domain of Christendom by spreading the Catholic faith in those distant countries. The second bull granted to Spain the same territorial rights, over the lands discovered by its subjects and representatives, as had been granted to Portugal by previous Popes. The third imposed upon Spain the obligation of teaching the Catholic faith and good morals to the inhabitants of the new territories. That Alexander VI should have signed three bulls on the same question on the same day, and not one single bull covering all aspects of the problem, is to be explained by the Vatican tradition by which each individual point is treated in a different bull.

None of the three is the famous bull known as *Inter Cetera Divina*.[16] This bull was dated May 4 of the same year, but was probably later. It speaks of the line of demarcation drawn from north to south and passing a hundred leagues east of Cape Verde. Why was this bull promulgated, and what was the reason of this particular demarcation of zones?

At this distance of centuries, lacking direct information we can only guess that the Pope wished to remove the possibility that Spain might claim a sort of exclusive monopoly over all lands which might be discovered in any part of the world.

The authority the Pope had for such a donation has been diversely judged. What right did Alexander VI have to concede to either country lands which did not even belong to Christendom, and still more what right could he possibly claim to allot lands not yet discovered?

The phrases used in the four bulls seem to breathe the theocratic theory of the Pope's supreme authority over all the powers of the earth. Yet by the last years of the fifteenth century, this theory was almost forgotten. In any case, the actual content of the bulls does not read like a claim to revive it. A close examination of the documents rather leads us to suppose that the Pope was making use of a different, purely spiritual, right. The conversion of the new territories to Christianity is presented as the central point and the determining cause of the concession or donation. The winning of souls is, in the spirit of the Vatican, a higher ground than any other. A Catholic expansion destined to set thousands of consciences on the way of salvation was something that no one would have disputed in theory at the end of the fifteenth century. Not that everybody thought along those lines in reality, for even so early absolute monarchies had arisen and the nations held themselves free from the tutelage of the Vicar of Christ. But there remained external formulas, for such things are always the last to disappear in the evolution of history. The contrast between the form of things and their substance, that is between the words used and the real intention of the mind, is always to be found when an era is approaching its end.

As I have indicated the bull *Inter Cetera Divina* largely reproduces the third bull of the day before; of the sixteen hundred words it contains, four-fifths deal with the obligation of converting the new peoples to the Catholic faith and of establishing to that end an adequate ecclesiastical organization. The Pope obviously realized that he could not impose duties of the ecclesiastical order upon a state

135

in a given territory, unless that state were in a position to exercise a continuous and unmenaced sovereignty. It was in virtue of this principle that he conceded such a sovereignty to Spain and threatened with excommunication *latae sententiae* whoever should dispute these possessions by force of arms.

> "Spontaneously . . . by a pure effect of our liberality, in the full consciousness and plenitude of our apostolic authority, we grant in perpetuity and make donation to you and your heirs, the kings of Castile and Leon, of all the islands and mainlands discovered and to be discovered to the West and the South. In consequence drawing a line from the north pole to the south pole passing a hundred leagues from Cape Verde and the Azores, all the islands and mainlands discovered and to be discovered to the west or south, shall be yours on condition that they have not already belonged to any other Christian prince since last Christmas . . . Of these lands and islands we declare you lords with full and complete power, authority and jurisdiction . . . We forbid all persons, whatever be their dignity, even be it imperial or royal, under pain of excommunication *latae sententiae*, to enter these islands and mainlands discovered or to be discovered, whether with the intention of trade or other reasons without your authorization or that of your heirs or successors."

Such are the terms of the bull.

Portugal was not satisfied with this solution, which limited its field of action at a moment when it was the naval power most capable of carrying out such enterprises. It continued to invoke the treaty of 1479. It was a grave error on its part to base its claims upon a treaty which did not envisage the distant lands discovered by Columbus, and was no longer in effect since, then as now, the authority of a treaty depends upon the rule *rebus sic stantibus*, that is on the condition that the facts are not fundamentally altered either by time, or by natural or unforeseen causes.

It charged its ambassadors to protest in Rome and in Spain; but it did not venture to put into effect its intention of occupying these new territories, for it did not wish to fall under the ban of Papal excommunication. Alexander VI stood firm. On September 25, 1493 he issued a new bull which has been called "a Bull for the extension of the apostolic concession and the donation of the Indies." In it he extends in favor of the Spanish Kings and their successors the sovereign rights already conceded, to any land which should be discovered by the subjects of the Kings of Spain to the east, west and south of the Indies. By this time the King of Portugal realized that it was necessary to arrive at a peaceable settlement. In the following year, after direct negotiations between the two neighboring courts, Portugal accepted the bull of Pope Alexander VI as having created rights for Spain, and Spain conceded Portugal's rights to occupy new territory, only changing the line of demarcation from the hundred leagues at which it had been fixed to two hundred and seventy leagues west of Cape Verde. This new treaty was signed on June 7, 1494, at Tordesillas, and by that name it is known. The two high contracting parties likewise agreed conjointly to solicit the Pope's approval for the change in the line of demarcation. The Pope gave his approval and the question was thus definitively settled.

This last phase of the diplomatic negotiations has given

rise to the view that Alexander VI was really acting as mediator or arbiter between Spain and Portugal. On various occasions the Popes did fill precisely that role; and Alexander VI in particular several times settled thus amicably difficulties both in the national and the international sphere. But in this instance, one fact stands against the view: the Pope, in making donation to Spain of new territory discovered or to be discovered, was using a right founded upon tradition—that is to say the right had been established on the occasion of the discoveries made by the Portuguese. And this counter-argument was supported by another: in two bulls—the last of May 3 and the celebrated bull of May 4—the Pope insists on the fact that this donation and concession is spontaneous, born of his pure liberality, and that in granting it he is making use of the plenitude of his apostolic authority.

Sound criticism makes it clear that Alexander VI was assuredly not acting in the conviction that as supreme sovereign of the world, having the right to delegate temporal power to the Emperor and to Kings, he was applying this right to the lands which should later constitute the two Americas. If certain theologians still defended such a doctrine, the popes, who had no taste for empty theorizing, held it no longer; and the practical realist Alexander was less likely than any other to believe in a theory so completely abandoned.

Nor can we suppose that the Pope wished to perform an act of temporal sovereignty for spiritual ends. It is true that the actual form of the bulls seems to emphasize this aspect, but I think it must be dismissed; for in reading the documents of the period we see that people were not filled with rejoicing at the thought that men of the new lands would be converted to Christianity: nobody was thinking

138

of anything save the gold and the goods to be got from the new territories. The Pope himself alludes to this when he says in the bull of May 4 that in these lands "have been found gold, aromatic spices and other things as abundant as they are precious, of diverse sorts and in diverse quantities."

The authority Alexander VI possessed for the delimitation of the colonizing activity of Spain and Portugal, is explained simply by the facts, provided we do not, like many historians, submit them to the torture of our imagination. In face of the differences that had arisen between Portugal and Spain, differences capable of causing war, the Pope, appealed to by Spain, intervened in the conflict and settled it in reliance upon precedents. These precedents consisted in this, that the recognition of the ultimate possession of newly discovered lands had always been given the form of a donation. Alexander simply preserved this form; but he did not seek to impose his will; on the contrary he accepted the agreements concluded between the two parties, since after all it was their affair. As the recognition of ownership was the action of the Pope, he must obviously attach to it as a condition the propagation and preservation of the Catholic faith.

The line of demarcation thus traced did not imply any special favor toward Spain: for at that time, immediately following the first voyage of Christopher Columbus, the true importance was not grasped of all the lands to the west of Cape Verde.

Thus from the first difficulties provoked in Europe by the discovery of America, Alexander VI drew prestige for the Church. He maintained the peace and gave proof that his colleagues in the Consistory had done well when they elected him unanimously.

K

CHAPTER VIII

The Question of Vannozza

W HILE Borgia was only a cardinal, we find no trace in documents or memoirs or chronicles that he had as mistress either the famous Vannozza Cataneis, or the not less celebrated and certainly more beautiful Giulia Farnese. It is only after he was installed in the chair of Peter that these two personages, who play so great though vague a part in the Borgia tragedy, make their appearance. And it was only after his death that the pamphleteers, and hard on their heels the historians, assigned to the two women an essential role in the life of Alexander VI. It might be argued that the mistresses and offspring of a Pope are naturally of interest to history whereas those of a cardinal have no particular reason to emerge from obscurity. But this observation loses force when we remember how frequently there is mention of the families, legitimate and illegitimate, of such Cardinals as Ardicino de la Porta and d'Estouteville.

This seems a good moment to go into the whole question of Alexander's relations with women, and to disentangle such facts as we can find from the mass of contradictions, lacunae, and exaggerations which has gathered about them. And if at the end of all things it is not possible to arrive at absolute certainty about his love affairs, at least we can find sufficient historic proof to enable us to separate what we know from what we do not know.

The Question of Vannozza

The first thing to be said is that it is extraordinarily difficult to affirm anything whatsoever with absolute certainty. For on the one hand his contemporaries seem clearly to have formed a solid opinion—this by the way rather as to the children of Alexander than as to their mother or mothers; and on the other hand there are facts and documents which make it impossible to accept that opinion as it stands. Any man who wishes to arrive at the truth by the kind of logical methods that would be followed, for instance, in a court of law and who will not yield to the temptation simply to repeat uncritically what others have said, must often find himself thoroughly perplexed at the stream of improbabilities and impossibilities he constantly meets in accounts hitherto regarded as accurate.

Thus if he accepts the common opinion, he finds himself called upon to believe that Vannozza Cataneis bore a son to the Pope at the same time as she was bearing another to one of her legal husbands; that Vannozza had a son by the Pope before she reached the age of puberty; that she had kept houses of ill-fame in Rome and that she was buried with the highest honors in the Church of Santa Maria del Popolo, the parish church of the Roman nobility, in the presence of a representative of Pope Leo X; and as a final contradiction that towards the end of her life she was poor and rich at the same time. In the matter of the children, which will be examined in another chapter, the contradictions are not less striking. The greatest of them is that whereas Alexander lived in Rome from the age of seventeen or eighteen, apart from that short intense period when he was Papal Legate in Spain, Borgia had not one but many children born in Spain, and these not at a time anywhere near the period when he was legate there.

Most of the biographers of Alexander VI have given us

141

a pile of absurdities not even agreeing with one another. Each according to his whim commits his own particular errors. Fundamentally they all suffer from ignorance, an ignorance so total and so overwhelming that even in the matter of Vannozza of whom we shall speak first, they err about her name, age, social condition, nationality, marriages, and children. It may be worth while to give an idea of all that has been said about her. It will make it easier later to get at the scraps of truth which can be certainly known.

Bruchard mentions Vannozza only twice, and makes no allusion to the Pope in her connection. The anonymous document mentioned at the beginning of this book, upon which historians have drawn so abundantly, presents her as a Spaniard. It relates how Rodrigo Borgia, while he was living in Spain, fell in love with a widow and made her his mistress. But the widow had two children and as time went on, he was intimate with them too and so lived in a sort of harem. The widow was the famous Vannozza, whom the anonymous author calls Virginia Vannotti. He adds that this was Rodrigo's first voyage to Spain and he places it in 1490, in which year he makes Pope Calixtus III die. The enormity of these absurdities puts them outside the range of discussion.

Litta, a serious author, regards Vannozza as the daughter of Ranuccio Farnese, but one of his continuators denies this and says that her name was not, as was thought, an affectionate diminutive of Giovanozza or Gianotta, but that it comes from the plebeian Roman family name Vannozza; and another of his continuators, one Odorici, falls into the same error. Salazar, who has left us a large collection of documents, follows Litta and Odorici in confusing Vannozza Cataneis with Giulia Farnese. In a *Life of Padre*

Affo, published by this same Litta, there is a genealogical tree of the Farnese family, which includes Vannozza. Moroni calls her Lucretia Vannozza and Tommaso Tommasi says that her first name was Catherine and her family name Vannotti.[1]

If there is no agreement as to her name, there is still less as to her social condition. While Litta elevates her to the nobility, Moroni makes her a prostitute, and a notorious one. This statement of Moroni has had a pretty successful career. Most of the authors of what we may call the intermediate period so describe her. Mariana thinks that she was a girl who had abandoned her poor but honest family.

As to her marriages, Infessura says that she took as her first husband a certain Domenico de Arignano whom later writers call Arimano or Carinano. But in a document regarded as authentic we find that she later married Giorgio della Croce, not as a widow but as a maiden, which destroys the hypothesis of a marriage with Arignano. By this Giorgio della Croce she had a son named Octaviano just about the time when Jofre de Borgia, later Prince of Squillace, was born. All the authors suppose that after Giorgio's death, in the very year of her widowhood, 1486, she married Carlo Canale. By 1486, she was no longer young and she had already had many children including the first Duke of Gandia who was born at the latest in 1461 or 1462 a quarter century earlier: which did not prevent her bearing another family for her new husband. And she must have been older still if we adopt the opinion of Thuasne who gives her still another husband and still more children before the first of the three marriages already mentioned.[2]

Pastor has it that Vannozza was born of Roman parents and that she was the Pope's mistress from 1460. He allows her three husbands, the first in 1474, Domenico de Arignano, then Giorgio della Croce in 1480, and lastly Carlo Canale, a nobleman of Milan, in 1486. Gregorovius agrees with Pastor. It is true that in a moment of candour, he admits that nothing is known for certain about her; but on another occasion he lets fantasy have its way and describes her house and her way of life. The house was not notable for elegance but it was large enough to allow her to receive the cardinals who were her lover's colleagues and the Spaniards who came in great numbers to the capital of the Christian world. But the reader is haunted by the earlier admission that he is making a present of this house, which he describes with such care, to a person of whom he has admitted that he knows nothing for certain.

To put the final touch to this confusion, Portigliotti reproduces a so-called bull of Alexander VI, one of those numerous documents that were forged at that time and since, inside the Vatican and outside. In this bull, dated August 6, 1493, the Pope is made to declare that while he was bishop of Porto and Vice-Chancellor, he had a son Jofre by a widow.[3] So Jofre was born in 1481 or 1482; and Giorgio della Croce, who married Vannozza in 1480, died in 1486, that is to say some years after the birth of Jofre for he made his will on October 9, 1485. Whence we should have to conclude, if the bull were authentic, that Jofre could not be Vannozza's son, which in fact he certainly was.

But as one more proof of how confused all this is, note that Thuasne, publishing the *authentic* documents of the Duke of Osuna, includes one according to which Vannozza—here given the family name Pinctoris but the mother of the Duke of Gandia, of Cesar and Lucretia, therefore our Vannozza,—was married for the first time, that is before Arignano, to a certain Antonio de Brixia;

144

and that this union was blessed with several children, one of whom was Paolo de Brixia a canon and later tutor of Giovanni Borgia, second Duke of Gandia. If this document were true, Vannozza must have married Carlo Canale and borne him children at a very advanced age indeed. But we must not let this surprise us in the story of a lady so surprising. In a notarial document in the archives of the Roman Capitol dated 15 January 1517, Vannozza, wife of della Croce and Canale, undertakes not to revoke a gift she had made *inter vivos* either for reasons of ingratitude or in the event of her having further children. Vannozza Cataneis, mother of the two Dukes of Gandia, of Cesar, Lucretia and Jofre would then have been seventy-five. This is one of the very few things of which we can be historically certain.

All these contradictory statements indicate that the opinion commonly held of Alexander is not the result of popular feeling, which one is sometimes obliged to accept for lack of certain information, but a patchwork, pieced together through centuries, of fantastic deductions held to accord with the equally fantastic personality of the Borgia of legend. They have been added not because they were true, but only because they seemed to fit the picture.

I have not raised this whole question because I hold that Alexander VI might not have led an irregular life or been the lover of this woman, whether she was married, widowed or spinster. On the contrary it seems to me not probable that Rodrigo Borgia was consistently faithful to his obligations of chastity. If we remember that Pius II and Sixtus IV had children; that no fewer than sixteen children, eight boys and eight girls, were credited to Innocent VIII; and that Julius II had three daughters as all Rome knew, we are not bound to suppose that Alexander VI was an exception. Had he been, surely someone would have mentioned it. On the contrary, assuming that there was this illegal union with Vannozza, its duration for so many years—given the circumstances, the period, the general indulgence for affairs of this sort—does at least indicate a certain fidelity. According to Pastor their relations began in 1460 and lasted for twenty-five years. If this is so, then given the moral standards of the Renaissance, a family life of this sort, long and tranquil and blessed by so many children, seems to show a patriarchal Borgia, sinful certainly but utterly different from the personage of the legend.

I have shown all the falsehoods that there are in the stories. But I do not agree with Leonetti and De Roo that the fact that they are false obliges us to hold that Borgia was altogether pure and chaste. One has only to look at his portrait in the Vatican by Pinturicchio and to remember how little given that period was to self-control and renunciation, to realize at least the probability that he may often have violated his obligation of chastity. The pen-portraits left us by the writers of the period no more show him as ascetic than does Pinturicchio's painting. He was a man healthy in body and mind, of abundant strength and vigor. He took pleasure in the things of life: in the comedy which reproduced that life; in the carnival, the joyous expression of the spontaneous qualities of the soul; he had an exaggerated sensibility, leading him sometimes to explosions of mirth in which tears streamed from his eyes, sometimes to a sadness which utterly overwhelmed his soul. All of which at least suggests that his habits were not different from those of other men of his time.

But to return from this psychological theorizing to the plain historical question, what truth was there in the substance of the story? In my opinion, the reason historians have fallen into so many errors is that they have adapted the facts to the personality they had already invented, instead of creating the personality from the facts. And they have added to their confusions by the wretchedly unworthy habit of accepting documents without verifying them.

If we examine this question of Vannozza closely, we find that there must have been several of them, for it was one of the commonest names of the day. The Vannozza who married Arignano was certainly not the Vannozza who married della Croce and Canale. The rich woman who left a fortune to charitable and religious works could not be the poor woman whom the notarial document shows so concerned about her small debts. Jofre's mother could not be Octaviano's. The Roman prostitute could not be the woman described by Paolo Giovio as the *"proba mulier Benossia."*[4] The woman who kept hostelries could not be the mother of the Duke of Gandia, the Duchess of Ferrara and the Prince of Squillace. Perhaps there was a third Vannozza who married Paolo de Brixia. There may even have been four of them: the mother of the Borgias, who probably married Arignano as her second husband; the wife of della Croce and Canale; the prostitute; and Brixia's wife. The historians, making no effort to distinguish, have piled them all in together to make one woman, a sort of moral and physical monster, bearing children in a continuous stream at inconceivable ages, and still expecting more of them at seventy-five.

This theory that there has been a confusion of names seems to be confirmed by an inscription discovered by Belli, which speaks of a certain *"Vanogia Catanea, mother of Duke Borgia."* It refers to a donation she had made to

147

have masses said for her deceased husbands della Croce and Canale, and at her death for herself.[5] Belli believed that he had come upon an authentic proof. Mantagne, relying on Belli, infers from this that the wife of della Croce and Canale is beyond all possible doubt also the mother of Cesar, since there is no other Duke Borgia than Cesar.[6] Logically, Mantagne's inference is correct, but the fact upon which it is based is no fact. De Roo's researches have established that the document concerning the gift for masses, to which the inscription refers, does not contain the phrase quoted.[7]

The document is of 15 January, 1517; whereas, according to Mantagne himself the inscription was only carved in 1608. The inscription therefore depends upon the document. But the document does not mention *any* child, therefore does not mention Cesar. The carver, or whoever employed him, added the words "mother of Duke Borgia" simply to show his learning!

Let us now try to establish what can be historically known of this woman. It is not very much, as Gregorovious has observed. All that we know of Vannozza Cataneis has to do with the second Duke of Gandia, Cesar, Lucretia and Jofre. There can be no doubt that these were her children.

On the night of the assassination of the second Duke of Gandia he and Cesar had dined with her, and she was their mother. This was said by everybody at the time. Later there was a suggestion of proceeding against her for an indemnity on the ground that she had, so the accusation said, recruited soldiers for her son Cesar. She went with her daughter Lucretia to Pesaro, when Lucretia married Giovanni Sforza. And when Lucretia was duchess of Ferrara, the two were in correspondence by letter. Also there exists a correspondence between her and Cardinal Ippolito d'Este. Long after Alexander's death her son, the Prince of Squillace, sent her his son to care for as grandmothers normally do.

At her death in 1518 she was given a funeral as ceremonious as that of a cardinal. Pope Leo X was represented by his Chamberlain. An epitaph was carved on her tombstone: "Here lies Vanotia de Cathaneis, famous by reason of her noble children: Duke Cesar of Valence, Giovanni of Gandia, Jofre Squillace, and Lucretia of Ferrara; and distinguished for her virtue, eminent for her piety as for her age and her prudence, one who merited well of the Lateran Hospice."[8] It was Geronimo Pico, executor of the will, who had this inscription made.

Marin Sanudo cites a dispatch from the Venetian ambassador in which, speaking of Vannozza's death, he says that the mother of the Duke of Valence and the Duchess of Ferrara is dead, adding the date and other details. The ambassador's dispatch (or Sanudo's copy) is erroneous on several points, which is not surprising since Sanudo contains errors innumerable; but what is important here is that the ambassador, or the copyist, slips in an allusion which seems to suggest that the dead woman was the mistress of Alexander VI.

This tiny handful of data does not make it possible to reconstruct her biography; but it suffices to tell us that there was a real Vannozza, who was the mother of the famous Borgias. Her liaison with Alexander VI would be clear and indisputable, if it could be proven that he was the father of the Duke of Gandia, Cesar, Lucretia and Jofre. But that is merely an hypothesis. And the difficulties multiply when we follow up the discovery that the children attributed to Vannozza by irrefutable documents—that is

149

the four children already named—had at least one other brother and sister, indubitably a full brother and sister, as is established by other documents indisputably genuine which have been subjected to the strictest tests.

De Roo after a very close examination arrives at conclusions diametrically opposed to the received opinion. According to him a certain Guillermo Raimundo Llançol y de Borja was born of doña Juana de Borja and don Pedro Guillen Llançol, and as eldest son inherited the properties of Gandia which had not then been erected into a Duchy. De Roo admits that this name does not figure on the family genealogical tree drawn up by Fidel Fita in 1564, but he considers his existence proved by Imkof in his *Genealogiae XX illustrium in Hispania Familiarum*. This author affirms that Guillermo Raimundo was the eldest son of Pedro Guillen.[9] This Guillermo Raimundo—who must not be confused with his nephew, the Papal Condottiere who died in Rome—married Violante, commonly called Vanotia, daughter of Seras, or Gerard, Lord of Castelvert and doña Damieta, herself the daughter of Juan del Mila and Catalina de Borja. Juan Luis del Mila, the Cardinal, was also born of this marriage.

Thus, according to de Roo both dukes of Gandia, Jeronima, Cesar, Lucretia and Jofre were the children of Guillermo Raimundo Llançol y de Borja and Violante called Vannozza. He bases this upon three arguments: first, although the Duchy of Gandia was actually granted while Borgia was Pope, the lands of the Duchy belonged previously to Llanzol Borgia; second, the bull of Innocent VIII, granting an ecclesiastical benefice to the first Duke of Gandia, says specifically that he was the nephew of a cardinal —and this could not have been Rodrigo Borgia since he was either the Duke of Gandia's father or else a distant

150

relation, so that it must have been del Mila; third, these children were Spaniards and the only Vannozza was this wife of Raimundo Llanzol de Borja. All these arguments go to make a neat hypothesis. But there remains the fact that Vannozza's children were all considered as Alexander's. That is the principal point.

But it is worth adding that Vannozza signed her letters as Borgia; a woman does not take the family name of her lover unless she means it to be understood that there has been a marriage, which could not be the case if her lover was a cardinal. These letters were addressed not only to her daughter but to important personages. If she was the wife of Llanzol Borgia, she used the name Borgia, though it was only her second name, because it was the more illustrious of the two, and because outside Spain, in countries where it is not the custom to bear the father's name followed by the mother's, where there are two family names, the second is held to be more important than the first.

There is another point. How does it happen that for centuries the name of Llanzol has been given, and is indeed still given by some, to Rodrigo Borgia?

How did the name of Llanzol y Borja reach Rome, if not through that branch of the family to which a Vannozza belonged? The Pope, from the moment that he was Pope, no longer had a name. He was Alexander VI. But those who were considered as his sons and were found under his protection were, if we accept de Roo's theory, really named Llanzol y Borja. Thus the name was transferred from the children, to whom it properly belonged, to the Pope because he was thought to be their father.

There is another quite strong argument for de Roo's theory. If Pedro Luis, first Duke of Gandia, was really the brother of the four well-known Borgias, which would make

151

Vannozza his mother too, then she must have been a Spaniard. Documents of the Court of Spain speak both of the nobility of Pedro Luis' parents and of their Spanish origin.

De Roo states further that Guillermo Raimundo Llançol y Borja died in 1481; because if we admit that Jofre's mother was a widow, he must have been born after his father's death. Vannozza would then have married Arignano, which may be the Italianized form of the name of Arenos, who were related to the Borgias. And finally, de Roo holds that upon her second marriage Vannozza—following the custom of the time which still persists in certain parts of southern Italy and Spain—gave her children to various members of her family, one of whom was the famous Cardinal Borgia, the richest of all. This theory of the second marriage would explain why Vannozza was never seen at the Vatican. Cardinal Borgia would probably not have approved the marriage, since Arignano was not of sufficiently high birth, and this would cause a breach between the two relations. This fact must be noted, that although the children obviously loved their mother devotedly, it does not seem that she assisted their elevation on the great stage of the Vatican. And the authors who regard her as the Pope's concubine cannot explain her non-appearance at the Vatican by reasons of shame or respect for public opinion, since the same authors tell us that Alexander's second mistress used to be present at ceremonies there.

In all this question there is thus more darkness than light. Whether Vannozza was the mistress of Cardinal Borgia from 1460 to 1483 or 1485 cannot be settled by any direct information about her. It can only be answered affirmatively if it can be proved that her children were also the children of Alexander VI.

CHAPTER IX

Giulia the Beautiful

Another long liaison is credited to Cardinal Borgia, and this one is supposed to have continued after he had become Pope. The person whose fortune it was to be the delight of his maturity—he was sixty when he was elected —was, it seems, Giulia Farnese, better known as Giulia the Beautiful. The Farnese family belonged to a noble Etrurian line, which had belonged for centuries to the Guelf party and from whom came renowned *condottieri*, whose services were sought by many of the great powers of Italy —Venice, Florence and the Papacy. Giulia's mother was a Caetani, and so a member of an old and noble Roman house.

In all modern writers, for they copy one another faithfully, we find the story of the liaison. If it were true, it would be a most striking proof of the monstrousness of the age and of the persons concerned. Cardinal Rodrigo Borgia, the story goes, first knew this lovely creature before her fifteenth year, at the house of his relative Adriana del Mila, niece of Cardinal Luis Juan del Mila. After her arrival from Spain, Adriana had married Ludovico, of the celebrated family of the Orsini, Lord of Bassamello. From this marriage was born a son called Orso or Orsino, who married Giulia, at the instigation of Cardinal Borgia himself who had made her his mistress either before or immediately after the marriage. The civil ceremony took place at Borgia's house; the Caetani and some of the Orsini, in particular Cardinal Giovanni Battista Orsini, were at the wedding. These high figures in Roman society, we are to suppose, lent themselves to this obscene farce to win the favors of a man who, remember, was not yet pope but only cardinal. The mother of the young husband, Adriana del Mila, had handed over a girl of fifteen to the lust of this man of fifty-eight, and apparently was in the habit of lending her house for their meetings. In this same house, witness of so much viciousness, lived also Lucretia who, whether she was Rodrigo's daughter or not, was certainly the object of all his tenderness and care. He had entrusted her to Adriana to act as her mother, guide and teacher. To continue: in spite of his age, Borgia had children by Giulia—children whom the authors are quite certain were his, although she was married to a young man at the time and lived with him in Rome or on their estates nearby.

There is the story. And assuredly cases of this sort have been known, for the lack of moral sense has as vast a sphere as virtue. Yet no one would dare in conscience to affirm such appalling perversions without irrefutable proofs. The only trouble is that the tribunal of history is less exacting than the tribunal of conscience.

The whole thing has its origin in popular suspicions, ever ready to form against the powerful, rhymes recited behind the hand, a whole obscure tradition of hatred, all helped of course by the unflagging imagination of the authors of the succeeding age. The legend of Alexander's relations with Giulia is not founded upon any serious information. In plain language it has no foundation at all. Like the story of the liaison with Vannozza, it is so ringed round with confusion and alterations of known fact that we are morally obliged to affirm this: not only are there no

valid proofs leading us to accept the story, but there are
negative proofs which force us to believe that it is simply
one more evil invention among all the calumnies which
have been heaped upon the devoted head of the Borgia
Pope.

Some authors of the first period, having heard that the
Pope had had a mistress, confuse Vannozza with Giulia.
This seems incredible, but so it is. The woman who gave
birth to Pedro Luis—probably as early as 1458, but certainly not later than 1462, is treated as identical with the
child who was fifteen in 1489. And the odd thing is that
so gross an error is not the act of careless authors. One of
them for example, Litta, was an honorable investigator
who wrote upon the great families of Italy.

The story of this particular amour has its foundation
in Infessura, Sanazzaro and Matarazzo, who all speak of
Giulia as the Pope's concubine. Such writers as Gregorovius and von Pastor add, as decisive proof, a letter of Alexander VI himself, and two others of a young priest, one
Lorenzo Pucci, brother-in-law of Giulia's sister. In reality
those who by direct examination know the works of Infessura, Matarazzo and Sanazzaro know that these works
are totally unreliable and that the greater part of what they
contain is false. Sanazzaro was a satirist, who served his
rulers and amused his readers at the expense of Alexander
VI. He lived in Naples and hated the Pope. He was in the
service of the Aragonese rulers, and was swift to desert
them when they were driven out of the kingdom.

Matarazzo, or the person who wrote under that name,
lived at Perugia where the academicians of the day, embittered by a servility they could not escape, wrote to tell
him, as amusingly as might be, any intrigues or inventions
of intrigues they happened to have heard of. The rheto-

nicians of that time were fundamentally rebellious, forced
to wear a submissive air and to flatter princes. It happened with them as it happens with school-teachers today
who—theoretically respected but in practice ill-paid and
not highly, or not at all, regarded—have grown bitter and
gone thronging into the camp of revolution.

Stefano Infessura was a man of a different sort. He was
a sincere patriot, one of the last representatives of that
Rome which had had republican ideals and dreamed of
the greatness of the long past. A friend of the Porcari family, he found noble splendid words to tell the sacrifice of
Stefano Porcari. He belonged to the popular party. Popes
as such were his enemies, and he used the same language
against all of them. His slanders against Alexander VI are
of the same breed as those he used to blacken the memory
of Sixtus IV and Innocent VIII. His method was to invent
facts or maltreat facts to prove the infamy of the popes.
Truth did not interest him. No historian attaches any value
to the writings of the first two; and Infessura's *Journal of
the City of Rome* is no longer considered by anyone as re-
liable. Which does not prevent his writings being used as
a source. Von Pastor several times repeats that one cannot
rely upon them. So does Gregorovius. And Oreste Tommasini sets out his opinion of him in these elegant terms:
"the academy inoculated him with an unfortunate passion
for epigrams, put at the service of hatred and ridiculous
intrigues." But it remains a fact that these learned men
accept his lies and inaccuracies as readily as any others,
when they concern the Borgias.

It must be noted too that when we quote Infessura, it is
in full awareness that there exists no original text of his
journal and that in their numerous copies, the editors have
been guilty of incredible ravages. His work has been al-

tered, hacked about and rewritten at the whim of copyists and translators. The differences between different copies are enormous. They contain not only modifications of the same story but radical changes. Even in the political ends aimed at, contradiction exists among the copies: some seem to favor the Colonna, others the Orsini. The very language is different: some manuscripts are in Latin, others in Italian, others in the popular speech bespattered with provincialisms. So that it may well be that Infessura himself was not as extravagantly inaccurate as he appears to us today.

In the matter of Giulia Farnese, we find in the extant manuscripts differences ruinous to the value of the allegations attributed to Infessura. For example one manuscript, speaking of the nomination of Alexander Farnese to the cardinalate, alludes to Giulia and describes her as the Pope's concubine. But in the same place, another manuscript after having named her, simply adds wife of Lord Orsini. Similarly, in the paragraphs recounting the nomination of cardinals made by Alexander VI on September 20, 1493, all the manuscripts have so many alterations and interpolations that the whole of these pages of the *Journal* must be dismissed as valueless.

On the second occasion on which Infessura names Giulia, similar differences are to be noted. In certain manuscripts, in the passage giving the order of places at the banquet, we read: "Then Giulia Bella, his [Alexander's] concubine"; in others, we have "Giulia the Beautiful named Farnese," and in others again "Giulia Bella" simply.[1]

Pastor and Gregorovius claim to find in a letter of Alexander VI the admission of this liaison. But the most painstaking investigators are often the worst critics and can be guilty of incredible errors of critical judgement. Von Pastor, habitually prudent enough, often allows himself illog-

157

ical deductions. As for Gregorovius, he will go through the most patient researches to discover the truth, and then, in setting out the results of his researches, quite calmly alter it. He was a conscientious student but he lacked historical sense and sometimes even, when fancy ran away with him, plain common sense. He might pass for the forerunner of those novelized biographies which have done so much harm to our view of history. Lacking a just vision of life, breathing only the stale atmosphere of archives, a man may make exact researches but he cannot write history. That is why the great historians of antiquity were statesmen or generals commanding armies.

Anyhow here is the letter to which von Pastor and Gregorovius refer. It is addressed to Lucretia Borgia and contains this passage:

"Madonna Adriana and Giulia have arrived at Capo di Monte where they found her [Giulia's] brother dead. This death has caused deep grief to Cardinal Farnese as to Giulia and both were so cast down that they caught the fever. We have sent Pietro Carianca to visit them, and we have provided doctors and all things necessary. Let us pray God and the glorious Madonna that they may very quickly recover. Messire Joanni and you have truly not shown great respect or consideration for us in the matter of this journey of Madonna Adriana and Giulia, in that you let them go without our permission: you should have remembered that such a journey, undertaken so suddenly and without our consent, could not but cause us extreme pain. You will say that they decided upon it because Cardinal Farnese had wished it and arranged it; but you should have asked yourself if it was to the Pope's taste.

The thing is done now, but another time we shall look
to it better and shall consider in what hands we place
our affairs."

That is all. Literally all. It is the typical letter of an old
parish-priest, a little touchy about the consideration owed
to him. Lucretia and her husband had not shown sufficient
respect or regard for the Pope. The cardinal, it seems, had
wished the journey; but they should have considered what
the Pope might wish. He ends by saying: "We shall look
to it better." This phrase is still at use in Rome in ecclesiastical circles.

Consider what the letter really says. The Pope complains
that Madame Adriana and Giulia had set out upon a journey without his consent, and he makes a veiled threat to
entrust his affairs to other hands for the future. But it is
only if we already hold that Giulia is the Pope's mistress
and not allowed to leave his side that we can possibly consider these phrases as the expression of a lover's resent-
ment. In which event the letter would not be a proof but
simply confirmation of a proof already existing: and this
we do not possess. On the other hand, we may ask why
does the Pope put together "Madonna Adriana and Giulia,"
saying that both had set out without his permission? It
would be more logical to suppose that the complaint is
aimed directly at "Madonna" Adriana because it was to
her that he had "entrusted his affairs" and she who had
failed in her duty by going on a journey without his authorization. Note also that the name Giulia comes second and
that the letter is not to Giulia but to Lucretia. What then
does the phrase "our affairs" refer to?

That obviously is the key to the interpretation of the letter. Adriana del Mila who had thus set off on a pleasure

trip—which had turned out so badly—without the Pope's authorization, was an employee at the Vatican. She held a highly confidential post in the service of Alexander himself. She was a kind of majordomo, like the glorified old housekeeper of an old parish-priest who had grown difficult with age, irritable and touchy, an old man who knew nothing about his household affairs, nor where small objects of daily use were kept, nor how to get along in his own house. We find Adriana del Mila continuously in the Vatican to the end of Alexander's life, and receiving a salary for her services. The letter in question was actually written for the Pope by Bishop Juan Lopez, later a cardinal and the most respectable of men—as were almost all who belonged to the Pope's entourage. What base conspiracy could account for the letter as it has been interpreted: that an ageing lover should complain to his own daughter, real or supposed, that the mother of his concubine's husband had taken his concubine away from him for a few days, and that this letter should have been dictated to a high dignitary of the church, a man of irreproachable character?

As a pointed phrase may be as effective in history as in daily life, it is worth noting one such phrase which did more than anything to defame Giulia. It is said that the Roman populace had nicknamed her "The Bride of Christ" —a phrase hallowed by St. Paul's use of it to describe the Church herself. This expression crops up in every book about the Borgias. What was its origin, as applied to Giulia? Stefano de Castrocaro, in a letter written from his country, is the first to mention the nickname and says he heard it in Rome; but he hastens to add that he cannot guarantee its truth. Jokes of this sort are habitual in the correspondence of the Renaissance period. Stefano's aim in writing the letter was to accuse the Pope of showing favoritism to

160

the young Farnese (Giulia's brother) by making him a cardinal. In this piece of slander directed against the new cardinal's sister he was probably simply the echo of one of the unsuccessful candidates for the same high office.

The protection the Pope was accused of having extended to Giulia's family will not stand examination. Giulia was the daughter of Giovanna Caetani, who in turn was the daughter of Ranuccio Caetani, the head of that powerful house. Her uncles, among others the Protonotary Giacomo Caetani, were present at her marriage, her father being dead and she under their guardianship. On the husband's side, the most notable relation was Cardinal Gianbattista Orsini, who likewise was present at the ceremony. Later, at the very time when the liaison was supposed to be in full force, Alexander VI turned against the Caetani, deprived them of their great fief of Sermoneta, and the Protonotary Giacomo died a prisoner in the Castle of Saint Angelo. The same misadventure befell Cardinal Gianbattista Orsini, while the rest of the family was completely stripped of its possessions. It is true that Giulia's brother, Alexander Farnese, later Pope Paul III, was made a cardinal while still only a boy. But quite apart from the probable importunity of Madonna Adriana—the person who was closest to the Pope and who as a woman may well have been expert in the art of asking—it is obvious that Alexander Farnese would sooner or later have become cardinal no matter who was Pope, from the simple fact that he had belonged to the highest ecclesiastical hierarchy from his childhood and to a noble Roman family. It was Innocent VIII, not Borgia, who had named the young Farnese a Protonotary Apostolic; and while it is true that protonotaries did not always become cardinals, yet men who had held the first office from early youth had a first-rate chance

161

of winning the second. In the list of the cardinals of that day, we find as a general rule a certain number from the Roman nobility. It was the custom, and the city regarded it practically as a right. Thus at this period a Colonna, a Savelli, a Conti, an Orsini were cardinals. Alexander VI added a Farnese, a descendant of a family which had been Guelf for five hundred years and which, remarkable to relate, had never been in conflict with any Pope.

When, following up the hint of Stefano de Castrocaro's bitter jest, the Roman populace nicknamed Farnese himself "The Cardinal of the Skirt," it had in mind the fact that he had been a member of the Pope's entourage, an entourage presided over by Adriana del Mila; and even if the catch-phrase meant anything more, which seems unlikely, there is no reason to assume the truth of a sarcastic jest which was unjust on two grounds: first by reason of the lack of any proof of immoral relationship, second by reason of the personal qualities of Farnese himself who was later to become Sovereign Pontiff by unanimous election.

Among the numerous satires then going about against all absolute governments, there exists a dialogue entitled: *Dialogue between Death and the Pope Sick with Fever*. It was in circulation in the year 1500. In it, Giulia reminds the Pope that she has borne him three or four children. The anonymous author could not have believed, as later writers have supposed, that one of these children was Cesar because he must have known Giulia and Cesar at least by sight and seen that they were more or less of an age. But he could not have known a great deal about Giulia, for she had only one child, a daughter, Laura, who was later to marry Nicola della Rovere, nephew of Julius II, when Julius was Pope. The marriage took place with great pomp at the Vatican in November, 1505.[2] Now Julius

162

II would not have consented to the marriage if he had had the least suspicion that Alexander was the girl's father; and even if he had been prepared to overlook so grave a matter, he would certainly not have married the two young people in his own palace at a moment when Alexander VI was never spoken of save as a Marrano—a baptized *Jew*.

We now come to the letter of Lorenzo Pucci. He was the brother-in-law of Isabella Farnese, Giulia's sister. There exists a letter written by him to his brother, Puccio Pucci, in which he claims to have said to Cardinal Farnese that Laura resembled Alexander VI and might easily have been his daughter. This young man was a protégé of Cardinal Farnese and probably liked writing amusing things to his correspondents simply because they were amusing, as was the custom. The epistolary cynicism of the period has led some of the most learned and able scholars of later periods into many errors.[3] It cannot for a moment be supposed that this young priest, who was always soliciting favors from the members of his family, would have gone out of his way thus gratuitously to mortify, indeed to insult them. But to show that his phrase was no more than a joke, we need but recall that the child was then a year old and the Pope well over sixty. Giulia's beauty had caused Rome to have certain doubts about her virtue, for beauty in a woman tends to provoke precisely such doubts. But the people best informed at the time had no notion that so horrible a drama was being acted in the highest society of Rome.

Even after the death of Alexander VI and her own husband, Giulia remained on the best terms with her mother-in-law, Adriana del Mila. Lucretia, at the very height of her own career, wrote to her to the end. Cardinal Farnese and all her relations retained their esteem and friendship for her. There is no trace of any contemporary criticism or allusion to the supposed illicit relations—not even after Alexander's death in the midst of all the hatreds he had left festering in the small Italian courts. It is only some forty years later that a Venetian ambassador made himself the echo of rumors he described as current in Rome. At Bonarzo, an Orsini property, stands the chapel which Orsino Orsini had built to the memory of his pious and virtuous wife.

If the relations of Vannozza and Rodrigo must continue to undergo the test of criticism, that test is decisive against the guilt of Giulia Farnese. If Alexander VI had had this Roman aristocrat for his mistress, his public policy had aroused so much hatred that an abundant literature would have soon sprung up to tell of this horror in his private life. But modern authors are compelled to admit that very little has been written about this second mistress, as little indeed as about the first.[4] If then nothing was written upon a theme calculated to pique the curiosity and delight the malice of everybody and to blacken the character of a man so much in the public eye, to whom the most improbable crimes were attributed, it is because there was nothing to write. We have there a very strong negative proof based upon the triviality of the evidence brought forward in support of the story of a liaison between the loveliest woman in Rome, in the flower of her youth, and an elderly Cardinal who later became Alexander VI.[5]

CHAPTER X

The Pope's Children

Aᴛ ᴛʜɪs point in Alexander's story, we enter a veritable labyrinth. Every effort to find a clear way through it is immeasurably hindered by the complications of human life and the malice of men. Alexander's children are few or numerous, according to the fancy of the historian and the period at which he is writing.

Some authors credit him with four, the four named in the funeral inscription of Vannozza. Others make it five, six, seven; or, if they add those he is supposed to have had by Giulia, leave us the impression that he had whole tribes of children. For although history only allows Giulia one child, the imagination of the chroniclers rather inclines to four, though some will not accept so penurious a limit. And in addition to all these, we must not forget the *Infans romanus*, a child sometimes credited to Alexander VI, sometimes to Cesar. And if we are to trust Infessura, we must add still another, the Cardinal de Monreale. But, as we have said, the various versions of Infessura's *Journal* do not agree. In the most malevolent version we read: "The Cardinal de Monreale is the son of the said Pope Alexander," whereas in another version the word "son" disappears and is replaced by "nephew."[1]

Labyrinth or not, we must now examine the question.

Giovanni, Cesar, Lucretia and Jofre were always in relation with one another, and both by their own actions and by the most ancient documents concerning them, we know that they were full brothers and sister, children of the same father and the same mother. Therefore if one of them is the child of Alexander VI, then all four must be. But these four do not stand alone. They had another brother and another sister, whose existence is established by documents surer and more valuable than an inscription.

There was in Spain a young man of great force and courage who had a swiftly successful military career.[2] While still a youth, we find him in the Cortes of Aragon, Valencia and Catalonia. At Ronda, he fought heroically and remained with the King throughout the campaign against the Moors. This youth, named Grandee of Spain and later Duke by the King, was Pedro Luis de Borja. He is indisputably the full brother of Giovanni, Cesar, Lucretia and Jofre. Modern authors, considering this impossible because they have invented their own idea of the mother, have made no serious effort at research. In this they are badly wrong. For their claim that the thing is impossible is only true if there were but one Vannozza, whereas there was certainly more than one. If we reconstitute Cesar's mother as she actually was, she might well have been the mother of Pedro Luis also.

The King, rewarding the valor of Pedro Luis, issued a royal ordinance in which, granting him the title of Grandee of Spain, he extended this privilege to his successors, who are named as Cesar, Giovanni and . . . , because they are the brothers german of Pedro Luis.[3] This royal ordinance, of which the text has reached us as we have shown it, gap and all, was promulgated on May 18, 1485, seven years before the conclave at which Rodrigo Borgia was elected Pope. Jofre, whose name was not in the document, was then only a child, and it may be supposed that in the official copy sent to Pedro Luis, the gap left in the original was filled in with his name.

At the end of the same year 1485, the King by another ordinance makes Pedro Luis a duke. In this ordinance, he again alludes to his heirs although he does not mention their names. But with more precision than in the previous one, he speaks of the noble birth of the person thus rewarded.[4] And when later, an inventory was made of the property of Doña Maria Enriquez, Duchess of Gandia, it is specified that she had been betrothed to Pedro Luis and married to Giovanni, the two men being described as brothers german.[5]

Of this Pedro Luis, first Duke of Gandia, there was no talk in Italy. In that country he was totally unknown, though in Spain he was a personage of considerable importance. He was betrothed to a cousin of King Ferdinand, Doña Maria Enriquez; on a question of property he withstood the sovereign himself and was sustained in his cause by Pope Innocent VIII; in war and in peace he held important posts. Before he was made a duke, he signed a financial agreement with the King and with Queen Isabella's famous favorites, Beatriz de Bobadilla and her husband the converted Jew don Andres de Cabrera, Marquis of Moya. Apparently he possessed a huge fortune and he inherited the lands of Gandia and others adjacent. The price he paid—he, not Rodrigo Borgia as had been said—for his duchy was not great; the King required as part of the price that he should pay a certain sum to the Marquis of Moya and his successors and should accept certain rights of the crown and of the town of Valencia over his domains. In the light of the theory that Cardinal Borgia had en-

riched this illegitimate son and had purchased for him the
dukedom and the domains of Gandia, it is interesting to
discover that in 1483, the Cardinal himself borrowed from
Pedro Luis de Borgia the sum of five thousand seven hundred and seventy livres, and that he paid the debt by the
transfer of a charge he held on the barony of Lombay.[6]
Pedro Luis died young, before Rodrigo became Pope.

Whose son was Pedro Luis?

Certainly he was of the same father and same mother
as the other four, for since it is established by authentic
documents that he was full brother of Giovanni and Cesar,
he must also be the full brother of Lucretia and Jofre. But
on no Spanish document, even when he is being made
Grandee and Duke, do we find the name of his father and
mother. On one of them we read: *"Precipue nobilibus ac
clarissimis parentibus,"* and that is all. This omission might
look suspicious. But it was not a strict usage to cite the
names of parents. It was often no more than indicated in
a general fashion that the ancestors or relations were noble
and illustrious. And in this case, if the father was, as de
Roo urges, Guillermo Llançol y de Borja, he had been
dead some three or four years in 1485.

It is urged that certain papal bulls make Pedro Luis
the son of Rodrigo de Borgia. But if these documents are
closely examined as to form and content, they are found
to contain errors and alterations which make their authenticity suspect. It would take too long to analyze them in
detail but a few main points will suffice. False documents
of this sort were forged at that time literally in hundreds.
This wholesale falsification, which was both a literary
mania and a business, was a source of much anxiety for the
popes and was the object of severe penalties. In the special
case of Pedro Luis the copies of the bulls which have been

found, signed by Popes Sixtus IV and Innocent VIII and describing him as the son of Rodrigo Borgia, are either not registered in the archives of the Vatican—and further wholly or partly lack any seal—or else, if the originals are listed there, they are not in the proper registers, but in a register which contains many blank leaves, and listed in such a way that they cannot be held to satisfy the requirements for authenticity.

Further, in the *Spanish* documents—that is on the copies of bulls discovered in Spain and not registered at the Vatican—the Latin is of the kind that was written in Spain. The name of Borgia is written in the Spanish form Boria, dates are inaccurate (like that of the election of Sixtus IV and that of the period in which Rodrigo became Vice-Chancellor); whereas on the *Vatican* documents if the form is correct there are grave errors of fact: they credit Pedro Luis with the intention of entering a convent at a time when he was actually fighting against the Moors, they describe him as *caballero* when he was already a grandee of Spain—that being the highest civil dignity of the realm —and to crown all, they say he is *domicellus romanus*, whereas the Spanish documents describe him as a Valencian. In both groups, there is no doubt whatever about the object in view—to establish that Rodrigo was father of this particular Borgia. The trick is obvious in the futile, insistent repetition of the relationship. Almost the oddest point of all is that one of these apparently papal documents bears the character of a Spanish civil ordinance, authorizing Pedro Luis to possess duchies, baronies, and so on—which was not the Pope's business at all but the King's. Finally, these bulls are not in agreement with other bulls, absolutely en règle, written in good ecclesiastical Latin, and listed on authentic registers. In these Rodrigo

Borgia is described as a relation, not the father, of Pedro Luis.

On this matter of Pedro Luis there exists another document of which account must be taken. It purports to be a will, apparently made in Rome. In this also Rodrigo's paternity is affirmed. Pedro Luis is given the name of Borxia, though everywhere else it is Borja. He restores his property to his father Rodrigo Borgia, under certain conditions and entrusts to him the guardianship of his brother Giovanni. This is surely a unique instance of a notary consenting to register a will in which the testator grants his own father the guardianship of one of that father's other children. A finishing touch is that he leaves Lucretia ten thousand Valencian florins for her dowry, and we know from other information that by her brother's real will Lucretia received eleven thousand. This document written in Rome makes Pedro Luis *"Habitador civitatis Valentiae,"* which contradicts the document which styles him *"domicellus romanus."*

Pedro Luis' birth must have taken place in 1458 or a little later, in Spain according to the view accepted even by authors unfavorable to Borgia. His death was in 1491, or a little earlier, also in Spain. The Vannozza who was mother of Cesar and the others lived seventy-six years, four months and thirteen days as her epitaph attests. As she died on November 26, 1518, she must have been born in July, 1443. Thus she must have been something over fifteen when Pedro Luis was born, and it is not only possible, but was normal at the period, that she should have had her first child at that age.

That is the sum of what is historically known about Pedro Luis. We now come to another sister of the Borgias,

a full sister. On a contract of promise of marriage, dated
24 January 1482, discovered by Gregorovius in the files
of the notary Beneimbene of Rome, appears a certain
Geronima Borgia. The document treats of a promise of
marriage between her and the youthful Giovanni Andrea
Cesarini. This document describes her as sister german
of Pedro Luis and Giovanni. The others are not mentioned, presumably because they were still children,
though Giovanni was a child too, but the eldest of the four.
Cardinal Rodrigo Borgia is named first in this notarial act,
along with the Roman noble, Gabriele de Cesarini, father
of the young man. Gregorovius and his continuators have
seen in this nuptial contract the admission that Rodrigo
was father of Geronima; and if this was so it would be an
admission covering the other five. But the actual reading
of the document leads to a different conclusion. Cardinal
Borgia was present at the ceremony not as father but as
representing Geronima's brothers. It cannot be said that he
did this through a natural desire to conceal his sin, since
it is also claimed that in numerous bulls he made clear his
right over his numerous progeny. In this document he
states his intentions precisely. He says that he acts under
the influence of paternal affection for the "*generosam puel-
lam virginem*" Geronima, who is leaving her family, and
that he means to treat her as if she were his daughter; and
that consequently, for the honor of his house and family,
he engages himself to this marriage and to a dowry.[7] The
dowry is four thousand gold ducats, not a great deal for
a father of the standing of Cardinal Borgia. He acts as
the protector of this family, certainly, but he does not
make that protection the ideal of his existence, as he was
later to do.

Gregorovius regards the expressions "*paterna caritate et*

M   171 *affectione*" and "*veluti filia recognoscere et tractare*" as an admission of paternity. It seems to me on the contrary, that paternal charity comes from the heart rather of one who has affection for another who needs it, being an orphan; a man's own child does not live on its father's charity. And "to treat as a daughter" seems quite clearly to mean that she was not his daughter, because a man does not speak of treating as a daughter one who is a daughter. If Cardinal Borgia was Geronima's father, he clearly did not on this occasion mean to declare the fact before a notary but to use expressions which would conceal it.

Before coming to the complicated question of Borgia's relation to the famous four usually treated as his, the curious reader might at this point read the Appendix (page 416) dealing with the origin of certain other children with whom he has been credited. These are Isabella, the little known Rodrigo (born when the Pope was seventy-two), and Giovanni—not to be confused with the second Duke of Gandia—who has entered history under the name of *Infans romanus*. A few words must be said of Giovanni here, though the main treatment is left to the Appendix. Upon him the biographers have fairly let themselves go. For with him, the drama becomes Borgian in the fullest sense. Here is promiscuity run wild. Consider: a son claimed by both Alexander and Cesar Borgia, with a third claim entered on behalf of the second Duke of Gandia, Cesar's brother.[8] After all, was not Cesar pointed at as his brother's murderer; and what could the cause of the murder have been save the incestuous love of both brothers for their sister Lucretia? So that Lucretia was the mother of this second Giovanni, while his father was either her father or one of her two brothers. It seems a pity to have to say that all this is sheer invention, embroidered solely for its own beauty upon the Borgia theme.

As a matter of fact no one now takes seriously the accusation of incest. It originated in the sordid conflict between Giovanni Sforza and the Borgias, when the Pope, wishing to annul Giovanni's marriage with Lucretia, declared him impotent. Sforza replied with an abominable phrase, reflecting upon the aged pontiff's *intentions* towards Lucretia. But, grave as the subject was, the offended husband did not allege any actual fact. His outburst was meant to be an insult, not a calumny. What is more, the only information we have as to Giovanni's phrase is in the text of a dispatch from Constabili to Duke Ercole of Ferrara.[9] Marco Attilio Alessio heard of the rumor later, and it is as a rumor that he mentions it. In fact, it was Matarazzo (or the chronicler known by that name) who really created the fable when, going far beyond Sforza—who after all merely accused the Pope of evil intentions not of evil action—he affirmed that Sforza had surprised Lucretia committing incest with her two brothers, and that this was why he, Sforza, had killed the Duke of Gandia. The Neapolitans, Pontano and Sanazzaro, rushed to back up Matarazzo with verses upon the incest. The Venetian ambassador Capello, for all his hostility to the Pope, reports the thing only as a rumor; but Sanudo develops it at length and leisure. Thus we see how a simple burst of anger by Sforza—a man who, enraged as men tend to be at being called impotent, hurled at his accuser the accusation of wanting his wife—has given birth to the horrible fable of triple incest.

But the most important question is that of the paternity of the four children whose names are engraved upon Van-

173

nozza's burial stone. At Rome the name of "the Pope's children" was generally reserved for these four.

It is true that the Pope calls all Christians his children, but in the present instance we cannot solve the problem by any argument so simple. The Pope's letters to Lucretia, for example, seem to run counter to the thesis that he was her father, for he often uses the expression: "daughter in Jesus Christ." Leonetti affirms that he has carefully examined all the important documents and that in none of them are they described as sons or children, but always as nephews or relations of the Pope.[10] Leonetti furnishes proofs of this statement but it remains the fact that in everyday life the word "children" was constantly used. It is true that Portigliotti, who was hostile to the Pope, writes: "For the Borgias as for all the great ecclesiastical families, terms of relationship had then a great elasticity, and were treated as interchangeable in a truly extraordinary fashion."[11] But we still feel that some explanation is needed for the unanimity with which these four personages, living so close to the Pope, were treated as his children.

They all attained high positions. The first Duke of Gandia was betrothed and the second married to Maria Enriquez, King Ferdinand's cousin; Cesar Borgia married the daughter of the King of Navarre; Lucretia married the powerful Duke of Ferrara; Jofre married the daughter of the King of Naples. But these great marriages are no argument against their bastardy. We must remember that a prince as important as Lorenzo the Magnificent gave his daughter in wedlock to an illegitimate son of Innocent VIII.

But if they were currently regarded as the Pope's children, it is also true that there is no authentic document which admits this paternity. And there are non-ecclesiastical documents which deny it; and a certain number of facts which are on the face of them irreconcilable with it.

It is of the highest importance to know where these four were born. Of Pedro Luis—who was certainly Alexander's child if the others were, since he was their full brother— there is no doubt. He was born in Spain. The majority of the writers on the subject agree in this view. Cesar Borgia himself declares that he was born in Spain, adding that "he and his brothers and sisters were born in Spain."[12] And again the majority of authors affirm this of Cesar. There is only the already mentioned anonymous manuscript on the life of Alexander VI which denies it. Cesar Borgia entered the ecclesiastical state, and since all the benefices he received were Spanish he was obliged to live in Spain unless he could secure a Papal dispensation, in which event he must have an accredited representative.

All that we know of Cesar's birth and early life in Spain leads to the conviction that Rodrigo had him come to Italy solely that he might make better studies there, sending him to the College of La Sapienza at Perugia. Rodrigo acted with Cesar as Calixtus had acted with him—after having protected him and given him considerable benefices and prebends in Spain, he brought him to Italy, for his studies and to prepare him for a more fruitful ecclesiastical career. And Cesar received exactly the same papal dispensation as Rodrigo to continue to pocket the income from the Spanish benefices although he no longer resided in Spain.[13] The importance of this dispensation is great, especially if we consider its date, 1489, when Cesar was about fourteen.

As to the second Duke of Gandia, whom we believe to be Cesar's elder brother, Gregorovious thinks he lived in Spain and came to Italy in 1490. Bruchard states more precisely that he was born in Valencia. There is no contem-

175

porary information as to the birthplace of Jofre and Lucretia. Gregorovious holds that they were Spaniards who came to Italy in extreme youth. We know that all four spoke Spanish as their mother-tongue and Bembo admires Lucretia's good pronunciation of Italian which implies that it was not her native speech.

If it were established absolutely that these four children were born in Spain we should have to look elsewhere than Alexander VI for their father, because it is not thinkable that Rodrigo Borgia's concubine was continually going backwards and forwards at that period, as one might today. The official documents still existent upon this vexing question are contradictory and not very helpful.

In a document of Ferdinand and Isabella which is found in the Salazar collection, there is an allusion to the father of Giovanni Borgia, second Duke of Gandia, in this form: *"que Ill* (illustrious) *quon* (quondam, deceased) . . . *de Borgia, genitor vestro . . . promiserimus"* (which we have promised to the illustrious deceased . . . de Borgia, your father). This would be decisive against the Papal paternity since Alexander survived Giovanni: but possibly the royal scribe made an error, and the word *quondam*, deceased, really referred not to Giovanni's father but to his brother Pedro Luis, first Duke of Gandia. But even upon that we have our doubts. In fact this declaration of the sovereigns, saying that they have made a promise to the father, cannot refer to Pedro Luis either, for in the same document Ferdinand and Isabella confirm to the second Duke of Gandia his rights over the fiefs he held in Italy— fiefs of which he had received the investiture after his brother's death, and this not from the Spanish sovereigns but from the King of Naples. Thus the reference to the "deceased father" is either an error or refers to something

The Pope's Children

we can no longer explain. But the phrase could certainly not apply to Alexander VI who was alive at the date of the document.

But there exists still another document which must belong to around 1501, in which the Holy See makes certain proposals to Louis XII of France. In it there is mention of the Duke of Gandia, Cesar, Lucretia and her sons Rodrigo and Jofre, as "nephews and relations" of Alexander VI. And this document was certainly included later in a dossier bearing the title: "Proposals Made by Pope Alexander VI to Louis XII King of France Concerning the Lordships, Titles and Offices held by his Nephews in the Part of the Kingdom of Naples which remains in the power of the King."[14] Names and descriptions are accurate, for in the Memorandum other questions also are treated. And since, outside Italy, the attitude of governments was for the moment impartial, we think account may be had of two other documents in the dossier, not Italian. The first is a letter written from Germany to Cesar Borgia, then Cardinal of Valencia, on 29 August 1495, and bearing this subscription: *"Ad Velentinum nepotem Suae Sanctitatis"*[15]—To the Cardinal of Valencia, nephew of his Holiness. And in a legal proceeding before the Parliament of Paris, in which one of the parties was Claude de Bourbon, grandson of Cesar Borgia, this prince spoke of Alexander as *"dudit Pappe Alexandre, son oncle"* and of Cesar as *"Cesar de Bourgia, nepveu du Pappe Alexandre Sixciesme."*[16]

The Italian documents are of course innumerable; and in all of these whose authenticity is unquestionable, our four personages are invariably called the Pope's nephews. Fumi relates that the Cardinal of Valencia was named "Protector" of Orvieto and that the council of that city received the news from his envoy who declared that the

Cardinal of Valencia, nephew of the Pope, was ready to accept the office.[17] When the Venetian senate admitted Cesar into the Venetian nobility it described him as "nephew of Pope Alexander VI."[18] In the two marriage contracts of Lucretia drawn up by the notary Camillo Beneimbene, one with Giovanni Sforza and the other with Alfonso of Aragon, the second calls her the Pope's niece while the first describes her as sister of the Duke of Gandia and a person whom the Pope loved deeply. The two Kings of Naples, Ferrante and Alfonso, say that Cesar and Jofre are nephews of the Pope.

In one of the Consistorial Acts which concerns the nomination of Cesar Borgia as cardinal, it is said that "at that time Pope Alexander named Cardinal Cesar Borgia his son, *thus giving proof that he was not his son but simply someone who had been brought up in his house.*" It seems that the Pope had ordered an investigation to find out who was Cesar's father and that he named as investigators Cardinals Gianbattista Orsini and Antonietto Pallavicini. Infessura says that these two dignitaries discovered and affirmed that Cesar was the legitimate son of Domenico de Arignano. Whether he is telling the truth or not—probably not— what emerges as certain is that all the cardinals accepted Cesar's nomination, not finding the impediment of bastardy. And at that period the Consistory was not entirely favorable to the Pope.

It is upon Cesar that we find still existent the greater part of the documents and opinions which treat of the question, because he was the most important of those who were called the Pope's children. Peter Martyr,[19] speaking of Cesar's death, said that he was regarded in Spain as the nephew of a brother of the Pope, and Zurita says that "the people considered Cesar Borgia as the Pope's son" but himself denies it.[20] Certainly ambassadors call him "nephew." Clemente de Vebron copies from a dispatch of Florimondo Brognolo the formula: "Cesar, nephew of a brother of our Lord the Pope."[21] About Cesar we have one rather original suggestion. Corvo says that a writer called Varillas gives as father to Cesar Borgia no less a person than Cardinal Giuliano della Rovere. Corvo considers that this theory deserves consideration, for it explains the hostility which always existed between Alexander VI and Julius II.[22] Boccaccio, ambassador of Ferrara in 1492 at a period when nobody thought of creating a family alliance between the court of Rome and the Duke of Ferrara, wrote: "The first husband of the said niece [Lucretia], had arrived in Rome and was sent away to Naples without having been seen by anyone."[23] Brognolo gives Lucretia the same relationship to the Pope he had given Cesar, and he confirms Cesar's relationship in another dispatch of May 19, 1493.[24]

There would be no point in reciting all the cases in which these four are described simply as of Alexander's family. It may be that Ercole d' Este's ambassador, writing from Rome to a friend, gave the ideal name to the relationship when he said: "Virginio Orsini has been to Naples and has taken with him a nephew, son of our Lord the Pope." A nephew who was regarded as a son or a son who was regarded as a nephew—one or the other: but given the double interpretation that either word might bear we are not much further forward.

For Giovanni, second Duke of Gandia, as for his sister and two brothers, we have bulls of legitimation and notarial acts stating the paternity of Alexander VI. Thuasne and L'Espinois regard these documents as of high value, and according to von Pastor they settle the case against

Borgia beyond appeal.[25] De Roo rejects them ruthlessly. The bulls of the Archives of Osuna either are not listed on the Vatican registers or else have been considerably altered —and this only where they touch on the illegitimacy. And these same bulls of Osuna, which at first seemed so impressive, are not in agreement with other bulls found in the Vatican. In these latter, there is no allusion to illegitimacy, though the canonical practice always was to note, upon every bull granting a benefice, a brief indication of legitimation if legitimation there had been. There does exist in the Vatican a bull on the legitimation of Cesar, but it is listed on a suspect register, with blank leaves and lacking the correct numeration. It is plain beyond question that this bull is false; it is sufficient to examine its Latin orthography which is not of the period. For the Vatican scribes of that day never used the Roman diphthong, and this is used in the bull in question.

There are other errors still, to prove that the documents of the Archives of Osuna have been altered. On one such document, in Spanish and attributed to the King of Spain, Cesar's name is spelled in the Italian mode, Borgia; and on another, in Italian, it is in the Spanish form, Boria. And there are in addition numerous contradictions and errors. These concern Cesar's age, making him older than Giovanni, they err about his studies, and so on. Everything supports the idea that these documents were due simply to the ill-will of those who made them, and that the object of making them was to strengthen the legend against Alexander.

For myself, though I find it impossible to come to any definitive conclusion, I think that there are two powerful arguments which must be overcome by those who accept

Alexander's paternity. First, that Pedro Luis, full brother of all the others, was certainly born in Spain, as were most if not all of his younger brothers and sisters. And if so it is difficult to see how they could be the Pope's children even if all the documents were in accord with one another and had the same probative value; and even if the opinion of the day was more unanimous than it was. Second, that this large family, born of Vannozza and supposedly of Rodrigo at intervals between 1458 or 1459 and 1481 or 1482, was not known at the time when it was being born and so regularly added to, but was heard of only after Rodrigo Borgia had become Pope.

CHAPTER XI

Beginnings of Invasion

T<small>HE</small> settlement of the difficulties between the Holy See and the Kingdom of Naples—a settlement begun upon the news that Charles VIII was preparing for the conquest of Naples and confirmed, in the manner of princes, by the marriage of Jofre and Sancia—was aided still more by the death of King Ferrante. Learning of his death, Bruchard drops his habitual reserve and writes in his journal that the King died: "Sine cruce, sine luce, sine Deo"—cross-less, lightless, Godless.

But from the point of view of a larger policy, it seems that Ferrante died either too late or too soon. That is to say he died at a moment when he might have been able to do something with his genius for intrigue and draw real profit from his close relations with the Court of Spain. Perhaps the old fox would have turned the situation to his own good by an alliance with Ludovico Sforza and Venice, abandoning the wretched Gian Galeazzo Sforza to Ludovico, and making certain concessions to Venice in the southern Adriatic.

With the entry of Charles VIII, began that stream of great evils Italy suffered from foreign domination over a space of four hundred years. It was the French claims upon Naples that caused the intervention of Spain; for if the bastard branch of the Aragon family had been solidly

182

established in the peaceful possession of the Kingdom, it would have been difficult for Spain to find a pretext for invading Italy. And the Spanish domination necessarily meant the later domination of Austria, for the house of Austria substituted itself for Spain and directly or indirectly laid a yoke which remained upon the peninsula for four centuries, apart from the brief Napoleonic interlude.

But if Charles VIII's adventure was disastrous for Italy, it also delayed the formation of modern France.[1] Everything that can be said about this improvised invasion shows it as an offense against reality and logic. The young King, a stupid man and inexperienced, totally reversed the policy of his father. Louis XI had added to France the Roussillon and the Cerdagne, the cities of the Somme and Normandy, the Duchy of Burgundy, the Artois and Franche-Comté, Anjou, Le Bar and Provence. His design was to "extend the kingdom on one side to the Alps where is Savoy, and on the other to the Rhine where is the territory of Burgundy."[2]

Charles VIII s plan on the other hand—leaving aside the aspirations he may or may not have had, concerning Jerusalem and Cyprus and the crusade which their capture would have involved—was to conquer the distant Kingdom of Naples in the name of the House of Anjou whose rights he had inherited. Now the House of Anjou had lost this Kingdom at the time of Ranier who was expelled by Alfonso I of Aragon; but Ranier himself had only won the kingdom in the first place by driving out the House of Suabia. The King of France, claiming that Anjou's rights were inviolable—apparently he regarded the usurpation upon which they were founded as sacred—and that the occupation by Aragon was illegal, made preparations to win back the Kingdom. To avoid having an enemy in his

183

rear, he signed the Treaty of Etaples, by which he paid a large sum to Henry VIII of England; restored the Roussillon and Cerdagne to the adjacent kingdom of Aragon; and the Artois and Franche-Comté to Maximilian.

Italy was a rich and populous country, and Naples one of the most brilliant of its states. But against this, its distance, and the possibility of popular risings of which the French already had grim experience, were arguments to be considered; and in any case a conquest of this sort was too dearly bought at the price of their nascent national unity. The conquest of a civilized country is seldom a paying and always a precarious business.

It is worth while to study the personage who determined this enormously important act. Zaccaria Contarini has left us a portrait of the King in his "Report upon France," written in 1492: "His Majesty the King of France is twenty-two years of age; he is small and ill-made, ugly of countenance, with large, colorless eyes; he is short-sighted; his nose is aquiline and both longer and thicker than is natural; he has lips likewise thick, always hanging open; his hands twitch with spasmodic movements very ugly to see, and his speech comes hesitantly. My opinion may be erroneous, but it seems to me certain that physically and morally he does not amount to a great deal."[3]

The probability is that Charles VIII's interest in the expedition against Naples was no more than a youthful whim. The Court of France was swarming with Neapolitan noblemen, headed by the Prince of Salerno, who had had to flee from Naples and the ferocity of Ferrante: for that King had set about the establishment of an absolute monarchy as quickly as possible at the cost of his aristocracy, who did not easily resign themselves to being thus stripped of their traditional feudal rights. All these men, of high

184

lineage and noble appearance and fine language, gathered close about the young French King. Meanwhile the high dignitaries of the French State were corrupt, lacking in intelligence, and had no idea beyond the increase of their own fortunes: so that they were readily tempted by the idea of all that could be made out of the Italian adventure—for they knew that the Italian States were rich, since they had often sold themselves to these same States. The Court of France of Louis XI had been a great corrupter of other powers; and the gulf between the man who corrupts and the man who is corrupted is quickly bridged, for those who do not respect the honor of others will seldom defend their own very obstinately.

But the Italians of Italy had even more to do with persuading the King to this disastrous enterprise than the Italians who had fled for refuge to France. The great instigator was Ludovico il Moro. Later, as we shall see, there was to be Giuliano della Rovere, who is presented in the history of Italy alongside Dante and Machiavelli as one of a great patriotic trilogy. But many others were guilty; all the princes and almost all the peoples of the peninsula in some way co-operated for the common ruin. Venice, rejoicing in its prudence, remained imprudently neutral. Only Alexander VI—who was not an Italian—remained immovable in his opposition. Clearly the Italians were the artisans of their own ruin; but the phenomenon is of all times and not exceptional; no conquest has ever been made without some degree of co-operation from the people conquered. The same rule holds in private life; violence is often the outcome of a situation in which the victim co-operates with his aggressor, by action or omission, for his own overthrow.

Ludovico, the principal agent of the catastrophe, was

185

simply looking for the solution of a personal problem—
the investiture of the duchy. The Duchess of Milan was the
daughter of Alfonso II of Naples. She was an energetic,
ambitious woman, and in any case her claim was legitimate
—that her husband, who was the rightful heir to the State,
should govern it. Ludovico, who had begun by being
regent, had now virtually usurped the power, since he
would not hand it over to his nephew, Gian Galeazzo,
now that he had attained his majority. While Naples remained in the hands of the House of Aragon, Ludovico's
desire to make the Duchy definitively his own seemed
unrealizable.

As early as 1491, France and Milan had agreed that
Ludovico should receive the investiture of his turbulent
city, under French suzerainty. From that time on, the
astute Ludovico had never ceased to act in Italy as representative of the rights and policy of the King of France,
and in France as the interpreter of Italian feeling. Having
thus prepared the psychological terrain, he sent an Ambassador Extraordinary to Charles VIII in 1493 to invite
him officially to undertake the conquest of Naples. His
error lay in believing that an intervention on such a scale
could be limited to Naples. He made an effort to obtain
the consent of Venice for the French project, sending as
ambassador the vivid and intelligent Beatrice d'Este, his
wife, who was not yet twenty. She made a public pro-
nouncement before the Venetian Senate; and she assured
the Senators in private conversation that the King of
France would send Peron de Basche on a mission to the
courts of Italy, including Venice and the Pope, in order to
win their support and make certain that nothing should
stand in the way of victory.

It is fascinating to see how Alexander grows in great-

186

ness at this crisis. It is always under pressure that great men are seen to be great. In this difficult hour the Pope showed himself altogether equal to the task the cardinals had entrusted to him. In a world of traitors—traitors to him and traitors to Italy—he continued his unwearying struggle against the importunity of the French invaders, the Italian courts great and small, the ablest and most powerful of the Cardinals, and public opinion, represented above all by the most popular man of the day, the Friar Girolamo Savonarola.

About the middle of the year 1493, the Pope, who was already aware of what Charles VIII was planning, thought to remove the threat by urging upon Charles and upon the Emperor Maximilian[4] the necessity of a Crusade against the Turk. Both the memory of his uncle Calixtus III who had promoted the crusade so tenaciously, and the Turkish advance along the Mediterranean coasts, may well have had their influence in this matter on Alexander's mind; but his attitude was probably inspired still more by the desire to turn the warlike French thrust towards other lands and other seas than those of Italy. Charles VIII accepted the idea and promised to discuss the matter with Maximilian; but at the same time, he sent Peron de Basche into Italy to inform the States of the North, Florence and the Pope of his true intentions.

We have just seen that Venice had already learned the object of this mission through Ludovico's wife: the Doge had answered her that he could neither express nor form an opinion until he had heard the view of the Pope and the Senate of the Republic. He told the whole story to Alexander VI. So when Peron de Basche arrived in Rome, the Pope was prepared. To the demand for the investiture of the realm of Naples in favor of Charles VIII, presented

N

by the envoy at the first interview as an ultimatum, he replied with the most perfect calm—employing the tactics customary with him in moments of difficulty—that he meant to transfer the whole question from the political to the juridical sphere. The envoy, who had expected a definite answer one way or the other, thus found himself faced with an obstacle he had not expected. The Pope had decided not to oppose the claims of the French King but simply to judge them. Charles VIII might put forward his claims, and these would be examined by a tribunal of the Holy See which was the suzerain of the Kingdom of Naples. The Pope imposed only one condition, namely, that recourse should not be had to arms. Thus he made it perfectly clear to the envoy that he would certainly refuse the investiture if there were an invasion. Basche, like a good envoy, did not like taking back to his master a reply that depended upon a hypothesis; and he carried on the dispute with violence, even threatening the Pope that Charles VIII would summon a General Council to depose him. But at the end of all things he had to return to France, having attained nothing save a promise that the claim would be juridically examined.

Four months later—in December, 1493—the King sent a new embassy, headed by Guillaume Briçonnet, whom the Pope had just appointed Bishop of Saint Malo. Alexander VI got on better with this envoy, who was in every way a better man than his predecessor.[5] He did not hasten to give a definitive reply, pointing out that he desired to learn the opinion of the Venetians to whom he had written. He temporized as long as possible. And during the time of waiting he was able to impress upon the mind of the ambassador, whose influence with the King was great, the conviction that the enterprise would involve dangers for

Christendom and for the monarch himself. Probably, he dangled before Briçonnet's eyes the Cardinal's hat. The warmth of Alexander's eloquence and the prospect of a brilliant ecclesiastical career completely won Briçonnet. On his return to France, he put before the court all the doubts that had been sown in his own mind and these seemed to produce a great impression.

But the French king was a weak man, and he had now fallen into the hands of a tempestuous and aggressive counsellor, a man whose violence allowed no obstacle. This was Cardinal Giuliano della Rovere, the future Julius II, who owes all his fame in history to his ungovernable temper. Once he realized that the Pope meant to oppose Charles' design, he believed that his hour had come. He slipped out of Rome and came by sea to France, where he was received at the court with great honors. If a General Council could be got together to depose Alexander VI, there could be no better preliminary to his own elevation to the Pontificate. It was because of him that Briçonnet failed. The two parties which surrounded the King and strove chaotically for control of his will came to an agreement and the invasion of Italy was decided upon.

The Pope intensified his policy of defence, since the policy of prevention had proved ineffective. In May 1494 he had bound himself by contract with Alfonso II, Ferrante's successor; and now he made ready to sign a military agreement. To cut the Gordian knot, and let the French sovereign realize that he had decided irrevocably to oppose his claims, he assembled the Consistory and, after a long and troublesome discussion, he announced that he would solemnly crown Alfonso. The French party among the cardinals, headed by Ascanio Sforza, resisted obstinately; but the Pope overruled their protestations. The French ambassadors in Rome again brandished threats of a General Council and deposition. But the Pope, untroubled, continued to insist upon legality.[6]

His decision was in no way shaken by a new embassy from France, more distinguished and more aggressive than the last, led by d'Aubigny. The Pope was threatened that the Council would be summoned and himself deposed forthwith, if he did not accord the investiture to Charles VIII. The Pope simply replied that he could not modify his attitude. If the King's claims were based upon legal right, they would be examined; if they were based solely upon might, they would be rejected. And he added that meanwhile it was not within his own rights to refuse to the house of Aragon rights of investiture which they had received in the past from the hands of so many of his predecessors. Since no compromise was possible on these two points, relations were broken between the Pope and the French mission. But though the Pope resisted with so much energy, his entourage did not resist at all, not even certain cardinals who until then had been faithful to him. And his *condottieri* to a man sold themselves to the French.

D'Aubigny made use of his time at Rome to buy up the Colonnas, Trajan and Paolo Savelli, and others besides. Upon the citadel of Ostia the banner of France already flew beside the banner of Giuliano della Rovere. Upon the territory of the Church the Pope's soldiers, yesterday in the pay of the Vatican, were now receiving French money, that is to say money given to France by the Italian princes. The work of erosion and treason produced its effects even in those closest to the Pope. He could not understand how they had all lost all sense of their own true interest. At times, he tried to re-establish moral discipline, at times he tried to persuade by argument. But the

190

influence of the moment lowered even his own great energy, though he never ceased to maintain that his juridical thesis was in the strictest tradition of the Church.

By now France realized the state of Italy and the isolation of Alexander VI. On August 11, 1494, after a meeting of the Royal Council at which were Giuliano and the ambassadors of Milan, the French army started for Italy. It crossed the Alps on September 2, by the fifth was at Turin, and the ninth at Asti, where Ludovico received the King according to the King's tastes, that is to say with the loveliest of the noble women of Milan. Charles VIII continued to Pavia, where he visited Gian Galeazzo, who was ill, then to Piacenza, where he learned of his death. The death had been long expected and was attributed by many—according to the custom of the time but upon no better ground—to poison, administered of course by Ludovico. At Piacenza appeared Alexander's Legate, Cardinal Giovanni Borgia, whom the King refused to receive, because he had officiated at the coronation of Alfonso II.

From Piacenza, Charles VIII advanced toward the south, while his troops deployed down both sides of the Appenines, as if on maneuvers. If the French army had received the very slightest resistance, the expedition would have fallen into utter disaster long before it reached Tuscany. But in face of the foreign invasion, everybody was paralyzed with terror. Charles made his way across the plains of Lombardy, upon whose throne Ludovico Sforza could now sit unchallenged; the King of Naples already had too many troubles of his own to dispute the succession. Venice was at last awake, and considering the interest it had at the entry of the Adriatic, realized that this invasion would put its coasts in the hands of too strong a power. The smaller princes and the peoples, who previously had

191

looked upon the foreign king as a liberator, were now subjected to the depredations of his soldiers, who were French, Swiss, and Germans. But there was no military resistance and the armies of Naples made no serious effort to resist the Italian troops who marched in the van of Charles' forces.

The Papal army had had to organize the Church's territory to defend the person of the Pope and the city of Rome, threatened by the former *condottieri* and the Vicars of the Church itself who had occupied the Roman campagna and seized the coasts in the name of the King of France. Thus the line of defence constituted by the entry into Tuscany was no longer useful. And, gravest of all in the circumstances, Florence openly "turned French," whether out of hatred for Pietro de Medici and his family, or under the influence of Friar Girolamo Savonarola, an agitator who mingled politics and religion, thus giving to mere party interest the passionate spiritual dynamic of asceticism. The Friar appointed himself ambassador to Charles VIII, and with his habitual absurdity spoke of him as God's envoy, the new Cyrus, and the reformer of the church.

A cynical statement of Ludovico Sforza sheds a flood of light on the situation. It is strange and impressive to see one country in one age produce a man like the tormented, visionary, epileptic friar and the subtle, opportunist, penetrating mind of a Ludovico. The Venetians sent two ambassadors to Ludovico to point out to him how dangerous the situation was and how, to defend his own state *which he held by so just a title*, he must make decisions that would prevent future evils. Ludovico, with all the frankness of a man who admits he has committed a fault but for strong and ineluctable reasons, gave them an answer which shows how far the realistic spirit of the Renaissance could go. On December 3, 1494 he told the ambassadors that he had indeed seen the dangers of a foreign invasion and that to prevent it in good time he had sent his wife to Venice; but the Venetians would not listen to her. This, presumably, is his version of the fact that the Venetians had at the time refused to recognize him as legitimate Duke of Milan, which would have detached him from the French intrigue. But this is only the preamble. Upon the substance of the question, I must reproduce his speech as it has been transmitted to us by the ambassadors of Venice. For it explains all that had already happened, and further how the King, who had come to conquer Naples with the universal complicity of Italy, managed to win universal hostility before he actually got to the conquest itself. Here is the text:

"This king of France is young and of poor judgement; he is not advised as he ought to be. His advisors are in two groups: the one governed by mons. Phillipe and his partisans my enemies; and the other by mons. de Saint Malo and Beauchario [sic] and his companions absolutely opposed in all things to the first. In their determination to overcome each other they have no care for the interests of the Kingdom. And each group is concerned with gaining money, with no care for anything else. All of them together would not make half of one competent man. I remember that when we were at Asti, the King gathered his Councillors to consult them upon various subjects. One began to dice and another to eat. One occupied himself in one way, one in another. When one, giving his attention to the matter for an instant, came to a decision and ordered that certain instructions be given, there was instantly another to cancel what the first had done. The King is haughty and ambitious beyond all imagining, and he has esteem for no one; sometimes, when he and I were sitting together, he left me alone in the room, like an animal, and went off to dinner. He came here with only fifteen hundred lances and three or four thousand Swiss, and he brought only thirty-four thousand crowns. It is true that I had agreed to provision him. But one day when he came to ask me for more, as I had seen that his officials thought of nothing save getting hold of all they could and not administering it, I said to him: 'If you want me to give you money, I must know and verify the distribution of what you have already received and what you are to ask of me in the future.' But the administrators, not willing to render accounts for fear of showing their own thieving, bothered me with no further requests."

Having thus drawn the picture, he goes on to explain his own state of mind:

"As to the Sarzana enterprise, I wish your lordships to know that it was I who advised it, to distract him from marching on the Kingdom of Naples. I thought thus to make him waste time upon the siege; for as this city is strongly fortified it seemed that three hundred men defending it would have been sufficient to make him lose two months attacking, and even then without success. But God willed, doubtless because of the sins of him who intervened in the matter,[7] that in so important a place there was no garrison, nor enough provisions for one night, so that that happened which had to happen."

194

He openly declares that he wanted his ally to lose the war, for that ally had not responded to his friendship, which he proves by the statement that Sarzana had been offered to Genoa (which belonged to Ludovico) but that the King had broken his word and reserved the place for himself personally.

> "How should we have confidence in him? He has been guilty of so many cruelties and has behaved with such insolence in all those of our territories through which he has passed, that the moment cannot come quickly enough of his leaving our territory. They are evil men and we must do all possible not to have them in our country."

Ludovico admits that he has already begun to act against the King. First, he has disarmed all the fleet of Genoa which was at the disposal of France, and has withdrawn and demobilized the forces he had in the Romagna. He has informed the Pope of his new state of mind, urging him to persevere in his efforts on behalf of King Alfonso; and at the same time he has told his brother Cardinal Ascanio that he must be reconciled with the Pope and in no way permit the rebellious *condottieri* to molest the Sovereign Pontiff or the King of Naples. By secret emissary he has encouraged Alfonso II to hold out two months, since Charles VIII has not the money for so long an enterprise. He has ordered Gajazzo, his representative with the King's armies, to maintain the independence of Florence and to tell the King plainly that if he wants to have Ludovico for a friend he must not touch the State of Florence because, "as I am already accused of having brought him into Italy for the affair of Naples, where he claimed to have so many

195

rights, I do not wish it to be said that I have been the cause of his destroying the States of Italy."

At the end of his speech, he told the ambassadors that he had kept Maximilian informed of all that he was doing.

The last part of his statement, following a reply from the ambassadors, concerned what was to be done for the future. He advised that all princes should tell Charles VIII to abstain from causing the least damage to the Pope who was head of Christendom, and that they should not let themselves be deceived by his declaration that he was going to Rome as a friend—"because it is not suitable that a friend should force himself upon another against his will"—or that he was going to Rome to reform the Church, a thing that was not within his competence, since in any event "he himself needed more reforms than the Church did."

He urged that the Pope should not grant the King passage through his territory: so that, being unable to provision his army, he would have to withdraw. He did not think any diplomatic action by the Pope was opportune at that moment, for according to information he had received, Cardinal della Rovere was more powerful in the diplomatic field than the Pope, since he had corrupted the Papal legate himself. And he ended by saying that if these remedies were not sufficient, others would have to be invented. And in fact, in the very course of that discussion, the said remedies were judged insufficient and the foundations laid of the future Holy League which ultimately forced Charles VIII to return precipitately to France.[8]

Meanwhile the King, ignorant of Ludovico's new perfidy, continued on his way.[9] He entered Florence, from which city he issued a manifesto announcing the Crusade —for which he had made no preparation whatever nor had any intention of making any. But he added that he was going to conquer Naples as a preventive measure, and he asked the "most Holy Father in Jesus Christ, Alexander VI, Pope of the Providence of God, to grant us the same courtesy that he has granted to our enemies, that is to say free passage through his territories, and the necessary provisioning, to be paid for by us."

This manifesto was the only public act of Charles VIII in Italy which showed any skill, but its insincerity was so obvious that no one attached any credit to it. On the other hand, he refused to receive the ambassadors who approached him with a new suggestion, according to which the House of Anjou—which meant the Kings of France—was to receive an annual tribute from the Aragonese Kings of Naples, as an act of vassalage or something of the kind. The King continued his march.

CHAPTER XII

Charles VIII in Rome

CHARLES VIII entered the Pontifical States against the Pope's will, and without taking any account of his new proposals; and he marched upon Rome after having occupied the fortified places he found on his way. In the Church's territories he encountered no resistance, for all the Pope's representatives had already declared in his favor. The Orsini family was the last to treat with him; but it did so finally and in a manner to cast much light upon the moral principles of the head of the family, Virginio, whom we have already met as General of the Neapolitan army, one of the most important units of which he was now commanding. The go-between in the pact between the Orsini and the French King was a cardinal, none other than the ambassador the Pope had sent to Charles VIII. When treachery has seeped in everywhere, destroying even the best instruments of political and military action, the head of a state is conquered before he has ever joined battle. Those who make pretence of continuing to serve him are worse than the open rebels. And what is most painful to the human conscience in all ages is that it is nearly always the traitors, open or concealed, who succeed and survive. Personal success is not the result of virtue, but of the greater or less degree of harmony between the individual temperament and the character of the period. Consider now the

198

action of Virginio, chief of one of the armies of the King of Naples.

The Orsini family placed under the authority of the French King all its castles, fortresses and divers fiefs. Virginio's children and his other relations, in fact the whole house of Orsini, entered with their men-at-arms the King of France's service. The fortresses of Campagnano and other places were to be delivered to Cardinal Pérault, as agent for the said King, and not returned to the Orsini till Charles VIII should have departed from the Papal States. But Virginio Orsini remained in the service of the King of Naples. How effectively, we may easily imagine. In fact, he personally received the French King at Bracciano, and at his entry upon Neapolitan territory left him free passage and went himself to Nola.

In face of this general collapse, the Pope had hesitated between leaving Rome and staying there. In the communications he had received from various states, he found contradictory counsels. The Spanish sovereigns urged him to remain in Rome, while Venice suggested that he withdraw into the strongest place in the Papal States and in last extremity they offered him asylum in their own city. In the Vatican all was ready for flight, but in the end the Pope decided to remain in Rome.

Towards the end of December, as the vanguard of the Royal armies was in sight of the city, the Pope received an embassy from the King, consisting of the Seneschal de Beaucaire, the Grand Marshal de Gie and the President of the Parliament of Paris, Ganay. It was a very distinguished embassy to send to a prince defeated and besieged in his capital. Still more distinguished to send to a Pope who was to be subjected to a Council and deposed. Charles VIII and his advisors, although Ludovico il Moro

199

regarded the whole lot of them as not equal to half of one competent man, realized perfectly well that they had before them not the Borgia Pope of legend, but Alexander VI, the head of Christendom, loved by peoples and respected by sovereigns.[1] He received the embassy, accepted its declarations that the King had no desire to infringe the rights of the Pope, and granted what was asked—free passage through the territories of the Church and the dismissal from Rome of the Duke of Calabria, son of the King of Naples.

It has been said that the Pope capitulated through fear; and his accusers, without examining the circumstances, have considered his action as a proof of complicity with the French invaders. But actually, Alexander VI was merely legalizing a situation that actually existed, for the King already moved freely over the Church's territories, and the Duke of Calabria could not in any case remain longer in Rome—he had to withdraw as best he might, if he wished to avoid being captured with all his men. No resistance was possible. But even this formal submission Alexander VI accomplished in his own fashion, that is to say with the dignity and solemnity he put into all the acts of his public life. He celebrated a solemn High Mass, assembled the College of Cardinals, invited the Duke of Calabria to be present at the meeting, and before the whole assembly stated his decision to allow the Duke to leave Rome. He decorated him with the insignia of a Knight of Jerusalem, and gave him the investiture of his Duchy of Calabria, together with the Apostolic Benediction. Before leaving Rome, the Duke repeated the invitation of King Alfonso that the Pope should leave the threatened city and withdraw to the Kingdom of Naples.

But whatever might be the dignity of these official forms,

Rome and Naples were defeated. There was no possibility of further resistance. In the same session at which he took leave of the Duke of Calabria, he declared his acceptance of Charles' demands, even the demand concerning entry into Rome. Still he limited the occupation of the city to the left bank of the Tiber. Among the last minute demands of the King figured also pardon for all the rebellious cardinals and the recognition that the fortress of Ostia, which had been the first to fly the French standard, belonged to Giuliano della Rovere. Even this the Pope had to swallow. He could not have liked it. Charles VIII had informed the successive embassies from the Pope, when he refused to receive them in the course of his advance, that he meant to treat with him directly. Now he was about to do so. But in this field, he was beaten.

Alexander VI remained in his palace. The French, observing the pact, camped on the left bank of the Tiber, without approaching the Vatican or the Castle of Saint Angelo. The King's entry into Rome on the last day of 1494 was made in the midst of a great popular demonstration. The Roman crowd filled the streets all enthusiastic at the novelty of the event. According to Bruchard, "From the palace of Cardinal Costa to San Marco, there was illumination of torches and fires at eleven in the evening and everybody was shouting: 'France! France! Colonna! Colonna! St. Peter in Chains! St. Peter in Chains!'"

It was the triumph of violence and treachery, sanctioned as usual by popular applause. Colonna and Giuliano della Rovere, cardinal of St. Peter in Chains, had their earned share of the short-lived glory. A few days later, the populace changed its mind, threatened to rise in arms against the invader; and Giuliano and Colonna felt that they were in danger of their lives.

201

While the King on horseback—he was, according to an eyewitness Tebaldini, "the ugliest of men, small, humpbacked and repugnant from every point of view"—followed by Giuliano, Ascanio and other cardinals was entering by the Porta del Popolo, the Sovereign Pontiff in his chapel at the Vatican was chanting vespers as was his custom. So at least says Bruchard.

Diplomatic contact between the two sovereigns was established the same day, for Alexander VI realized that it was necessary and sent a group of distinguished citizens to receive the King in the name of the city. Charles VIII took no notice of them whatsoever, and conversed the whole way with the gossiping Bruchard, hearing from his lips a stream of trivialities about the Pope and Cardinal Cesar. On January 4, 1495, Alexander VI succeeded in having the King receive a deputation of four cardinals— Pallavicini, San Giorgio, Bernardino Carvajal and Riario. These, knowing that Charles VIII was being maneuvered by the rebellious cardinals, thought it best to undermine them in their turn. They began by talking of the Pope: "Let slanderous tongues say what they like, Alexander VI was assuredly holier today than when he was elevated to the supreme pontificate, or at least as holy. He was neither a hypocrite nor a nobody, but one who had for thirty-seven years filled a high position which obliged him to make public not only his acts but also his words; and those who today are his detractors were then his leading supporters, so much so that he did not lose the vote of a single Cardinal."[2]

After having received this second mission courteously, the King in turn named his delegates, the Count de Brasse, Montpensier and the President Ganay. Now that the army was actually in Rome, the royal proposals were more exacting than those sent from Bracciano. What Charles VIII now wanted was the delivery of the Castle of Saint Angelo, the appointment of Cardinal Cesar Borgia as Legate—but a Legate who could not resign or have his legateship withdrawn by the Pope—the delivery of other papal strongholds, the restoration to all their rights and privileges of the Cardinals and Barons who had turned traitor—and the handing over to Jem, the brother of the Sultan of Turkey and a prisoner in Rome.

Some explanation is necessary of this last demand. This Prince Jem, who now enters our story for the first time, was one of the sensational personages of his own day. Jem was very popular in Europe. Betrayed by men of a faith—the Christian faith—in which he did not believe, persecuted by his own brother who offered a large sum in gold for his body, he must have taken with him into the tomb a profound contempt for the human race. His face expressed the proud and disdainful disillusionment of those who have been pierced to the very depths of their soul, and for whom death is a liberation in that it breaks the bond which unites them to fellow-creatures whom they despise. He was the son of the great Sultan Mahomet II. Upon his father's death he fought against his brother the Sultan Bajazet, was defeated and took refuge in Rhodes under the protection of the sworn word of the Grand Master of the Order of St. John of Jerusalem, Pierre d'Aubusson. But the Knights of Rhodes, bribed by Bajazet, sent Jem as prisoner to France. The Sultan was cunning and knew the cupidity of Christian princes. He attached an annual sum of forty thousand ducats to the person of the prisoner, considering that this sum would suffice to guarantee his remaining in captivity. Jem thus came to represent a magnificent income for the various Christian

o

and see P. 206

princes who disputed for his possession. After some difficulties, the King of France sent him off one fine day to
Pope Innocent VIII. Innocent VIII passed him on to Alexander VI. And now Charles VIII wanted him back.

Having summoned the consistory, the Pope rejected the
King's conditions and took no notice of the ultimatum
which accompanied them. Once again, in face of overwhelming force, he appealed to juridical principles. He
replied that he could not send Cardinal Cesar Borgia as
legate, because Papal legates are not appointed by Kings—
they are appointed to Kings by Popes, and this after careful discussion with the Sacred College; Prince Jem was in
a safe place—the Castle of Saint Angelo—but he was disposed to deliver him up, to serve against the Sultan his
brother, when the French King should set out on the
promised Crusade, not before; and as to the Castle of Saint
Angelo, he held it in the name of the Christian princes
and he would die rather than give it up.

When we remember that not so long afterwards Pope
Leo X, threatened by another King who was still a long
way from Rome, was all panic-stricken and said to the
Venetian ambassador: "We shall see what the most Christian King will do, we shall place ourselves in his hands and
shall ask him for mercy";[3] when we remember that the
rulers of Rome were neither animated by burning religious
zeal as in the first ages of Christianity, nor warlike by
nature but on the contrary rendered timorous by the very
exercise of their office—there is something admirable in
Alexander VI's refusal to yield to the demands of force,
when the cannons were pointed at him and his city in the
grip of the soldiery.

Having sent his refusal of the King's ultimatum, Alexander VI shut himself up with three thousand soldiers in

204

the Castle of Saint Angelo and made ready for its defence. The King aimed his cannons at the Castle, but did not fire them, probably because the Pope had spread the rumor that it was his intention to present himself upon the walls at the first cannon shot, robed in his pontifical vestments and bearing the Sacred Host in his hands.

But Alexander was of too practical an intelligence to rely solely upon the effectiveness of such gestures. He realized perfectly well that between a Pope and a King it was better to have emissaries of peace than cannon balls. He sent a special envoy. In the King's camp, opinions differed. The rebel cardinals were all for the summoning of a General Council to depose the Pope; but Charles VIII and his entourage wanted a Pope who would confer upon the King of France the investiture of the Kingdom of Naples: they did not want a long interregnum, probably full of unpredictable happenings which would postpone the realization of this wish. On his side, if Alexander had any strong intention of resistance, he must have abandoned it on the night between January 9 and January 10; for an outer wall of the Castle collapsed completely, proving how feeble a defence it constituted against the heavy artillery of Charles VIII, which had produced so great an impression throughout Italy.

So the negotiations unexpectedly produced an agreement. Actually, the solution was reached because the solution was to the interest of everybody. Even Cardinals Sforza and della Rovere, aspirants to the Papacy, saw danger in a Council. For after these few short days of the occupation, rapine and assassination and violence were widespread in Rome and food was running short. At such a moment, the summoning of a Council might well have cost them their lives. The populace would certainly have

205

treated them as responsible for the evils they were suffering. It was in fact Cardinal della Rovere himself who told the King that a popular rising was possible. He knew that the people who on December 31 had cried his own title: "St. Peter in Chains! St. Peter in Chains!" might very well be crying "Borgia! Borgia!" by January 10.

The Colonnas did not want a continuance of the pandemonium which was destroying the city they regarded as theirs and which looked like tearing from their heads their age-old halo as chiefs of the popular party, a halo they had gained at the cost of dangers innumerable and contests without end. In the French camp Alexander VI was not entirely without admirers and friends. The various embassies of earlier years had brought him into contact with some of the highest personages of the French court, and they had felt the fascination of his personality and the superiority of his mind.

The articles of the agreement may be grouped under three heads.

The first concerns the guarantees given the King for the continuation of his march—free passage for his armies over the Church's territory, but they must pay for the provisions they took; handing over to the King of Prince Jem, but he was to be handed back after the campaign of Naples and meanwhile the forty thousand ducats paid by the Sultan were to go to the Pope; Cesar Borgia would accompany the King, for a period limited to four months; certain fortresses were to remain in the King's power as guarantees, and certain pontifical governors were to be named by him.

The second concerns the Pope. The King was to make in person an act of obedience to the Pope and promise at all times to respect his temporal and spiritual rights, fur-

ther engaging to defend them against all who might invade
his territory; if the Sultan were to declare war upon the
Pope, the King would defend him; the King undertook to
make no demands upon the Castle of Saint Angelo; when
the King left Rome the keys of the gates and the bridges
of the city were to be returned to the Pope; after four
months, the King would have settled the matter of the
forty thousand ducats which Giovanni della Rovere,
brother of Giuliano, had appropriated to himself, a sum
which arose from the annual payment for Prince Jem.

The third head concerned the rebellious cardinals, cities
and Vicars. They were given a general amnesty.[4]

As we see, the Pope had saved the essential. There is no
word of investiture, and it was the King who was to make
the act of obedience. In exchange, the Pope yielded upon
Cesar Borgia and Prince Jem, but provisionally—upon
Cesar for four months and upon Jem while Charles VIII
remained in Italy.

On January 16, Pope and King met for the first time.
Alexander VI arranged that they should come upon him at
prayer. Egidio of Viterbo gives us a dramatic account of
the scene, which we may believe if we please. He says that
at sight of the Pope upon his knees in devout converse with
God, the King and his train were so deeply impressed that
they felt their hearts swell with great love and began forthwith to venerate the man whom up to then they had detested. Charles remained at the Vatican. On the nineteenth,
the day fixed for the ceremony of his obeisance, when all
were assembled, the King—who had already asked and
obtained two days previously a modification of the article
concerning Prince Jem—now solicited three further favors: the confirmation of all the privileges granted to himself and his followers, the investiture of the Kingdom of

Naples, and the recognition of what had already been mutually agreed upon the subject of Jem.

The Pope granted the first and the third of these demands; for the second, he invoked the necessity of a closer examination. The Pontiff's solemn and eloquent discourse so moved the King that he rose, not to insist upon the investiture but to repeat the formula prepared by Bruchard: "Holy Father, I have come to make obeisance and reverence to Your Holiness, in the same manner as the Kings of France, my predecessors." On a sign from the King, Ganay the President began to speak, declaring that his sovereign had wished to make in person, and not through ambassadors, his act of respect to the Holy See and him who occupied it, and that he recognized in Alexander VI the legitimate Pontiff, the true Vicar of Christ and successor of the Apostles Peter and Paul.

The next day, in the course of a solemn Mass said by the Pope himself, at which were present more than twenty thousand soldiers drawn up in the great Square of St. Peter's and an immense crowd of the people, the King acted as server at the point of the Mass where the priest washes his hands—he held the dish, poured the water and handed the Pope the towel. The Pope on his side granted all the favors the King asked for his suite, and named not only Briçonnet but also Philip of Luxembourg as cardinals.

On January 28, to the great satisfaction of the populace, Charles left Rome, imagining that he was leaving behind a friend and perhaps an ally. The Pope had ridden by his side through the streets of Rome and in all the conversations they had together had made him conscious of the power of his mind and personality. The investiture was not granted. Jem and Cesar accompanied the long royal

208

train but Jem died at Naples and Cesar escaped from the Camp at Velletri, only thirty-six miles from Rome.

Given the circumstances, no more brilliant diplomatic victory is imaginable. The Pope was at the mercy of a conquering King, his town occupied, all the Lords of the country against him, his representatives in open revolt, the majority of his cardinals in the councils of the enemy. Yet he did not grant the invader that investiture which was the sole object of the occupation of Rome; and he saw him depart as a friend, having already obtained a declaration of obedience and the absolute recognition of his own election as Pope. Yet the biographers have tried to distort the meaning of these perfectly plain facts, by subtle deductions meant to bring them into line with the judgement of contemporary chroniclers with their absurd accusations that the Pope was acting in complicity with Charles VIII.

One of the wildest of the accusations leveled against Alexander is that he summoned Charles VIII to the conquest of Naples. Later writers have watered down the accusation a little by saying that he concurred in the summons. Nothing could be more remote from the truth. From the time the French preparation for war began there was not a single moment in which the Pope was not in clear-cut opposition. Towards the end of 1492, shortly after his own election, he had called upon Charles VIII to join with Maximilian in preparation for a Crusade, but not for the conquest of Naples. More honest than the historians, Maximilian has left us this phrase in justification of the Pope: "Our Holy Father called upon the King of France to make war upon Infidels, not upon Christians."[5]

From the beginning of 1493, preparations were made in France, where the opposition of Alexander was well known,

209

for an attack upon him. The first notion was to summon a General Council, and when this failed they planned to declare the independence of the Gallican Church, and suspend all contributions to the Holy See. When Mateo Pirovano had an interview with Beaucaire and the General of Languedoc, they said to Pirovano in reference to the Pope: "As to him, it will be sufficient for the French troops merely to appear to make him keep quiet"; and they added that the King had two means of making the Pope repent his present attitude. "And when I asked," continues Pirovano, "what were these means, the General answered me that one was the Council, a thing for which, he subtly insinuated, it would not be difficult to obtain the agreement of the Emperor and King of the Romans (Maximilian); and that the other was not to give obedience and to hold back the incomes of the benefices, which bring great sums to Rome."[6] A little later, Carlo de Barbiano, Count of Belgiojoso, told Ludovico Moro of a conversation he had personally had with Charles VIII at Amboise, on September 28, in which the King had told him that he did not lack means to constrain the Pope. Further, all the numerous embassies sent by the King to Alexander report the Pope's opinion and say that it was opposed to the attack upon Naples and the entry of the French into Italy.

Thus we see once more with what irresponsibility and malevolence the history of the Pope has been written. For the sole proof of the accusation that he encouraged the invasion, is a bull in which he authorizes the King's troops to march through the Papal States. The bull is indisputably authentic, but it shows the date of February 1, 1494, at which time Alexander VI was in negotiation with the King of Naples. So that it appears to establish his duplicity. But the truth is that the copy of the bull or brief is indeed

dated February 1, 1494, but, according to the Florentine
mode, in the old style; in the modern calendar, the date
would be February 1, 1495, for the old-style year began in
the month of March—on the twenty-sixth to be precise—
in honor of the Feast of the Annunciation. Hence Alexander's bull does not date from the period when he was
treating with the King of Naples but from a period when
the French were in Rome and when, in consequence, the
authorization of free passage for the troops dealt not with
their entering the Church's territories but with their leaving them.[7]

When the historian knows the facts as they have been
handed down to posterity and has absorbed the spirit of
the period he seeks to revive, it is easy to judge the degree
of truthfulness of the various pieces of evidence, provided
he uses his critical sense and keeps the truth as his sole
interest. A student might have been for the moment put
off the track by error as to the date of the bull, but to
put himself right again he had only to ask certain obvious
questions.

Why did Charles VIII not make use of this bull if there
were a bull, in order to oblige the Pope to grant him the
investiture? And why did not Ludovico Sforza throw his
own responsibility upon the Pope? And why did not the
third party interested, the King of Naples, ever complain
of Alexander's deceit? Because the truth is precisely the
contrary of what so many historians have said. If the
French King never, either in France or Italy or Rome itself, made use of so convenient an argument, it was because it did not exist. And one proof of this is given us
later, in 1496, by Ludovico himself when he said to the
Venetian ambassador Francesco Foscari, that mutual suspicions between Milan and Venice must be avoided, be-

cause, with such suspicions, "it will be impossible to achieve any good, or attempt to save Italy as the present time demands. When shall we again have the fortune to find a Pope who watches over us so constantly as the Pope we now have?" And the ambassador in his dispatch mentions that Ludovico compared this firm attitude of Alexander VI with the vacillation of Sixtus IV and Innocent VIII. From the King of Naples we have not a single word of complaint; on the contrary suspicious and treacherous as Ferrante himself was, we find him some months before his death, when told that the Pope might come to an understanding with the French King, laughing at the news.

The policy of Alexander VI was always the same, and this is clearly shown when in the last years of his pontificate he conversed with the ambassador Giustiniani. His dispatches have come down to us intact, and they make it impossible for the fancy of modern writers to take the place of the facts. The Pope had every right to utter the cry "The Barbarians to the Gates." But he was not given to melodrama.

CHAPTER XIII

The Holy League

ALEXANDER VI realized perfectly that when Charles VIII marched off to Naples, he was on his way to no lasting conquest. He proceeded to prepare for his overthrow. Information reached him from all sides through the intermediary of the Vatican diplomacy, seldom brilliant, but so diligent. And it gave him a clear vision of the state of things in Italy and in Europe. Ludovico Moro, who had so urged the French King to come to Italy, was now pressing Venice to an alliance; and as formerly he had represented Charles VIII, so now he represented another foreign sovereign—Maximilian, the Emperor-elect. Venice was at last awakening, influenced by the emissaries of Maximilian, who, led by the Bishop of Frundiperg, offered the Doge a formal project of alliance. The only Italian states still favorable to France were—Savoy, for territorial reasons; Montferrat through hostility for Ludovico Moro; Ferrara, through fear of Venice; and Florence partly because of the ambitious eye the Venetians were casting upon Pisa, partly because of the Francophile policy they maintained through good success and ill.

But even more than the Italian States, the rulers of Castile and Aragon declared themselves against Charles VIII —because of the insolences to which he had subjected the Pope and the peoples of Italy so they alleged. The attitude

213

of Spain gave pleasure to the Pope. In fact, on the very day of the French King's departure, a Spanish embassy arrived to have discussions with him. As the interview could not now take place in the Eternal City, the embassy went after the royal cortege and it was at Velletri that it presented to Charles VIII its letters of credence and the proposals of its sovereigns. Antonio de Fonseca, one of the envoys, rebuked him in the presence of the French nobility for his attitude to the Pope, whom Spain, he said, was obliged to defend. He described as monstrous the demand to have Cesar Borgia as legate and the fact that he was virtually a prisoner. Finally he declared that the conquest of the Kingdom of Naples against the will of the Pope, who was the suzerain of that country, constituted a usurpation. The King replied mildly with an attempt to justify himself, claimed that the Pope had concluded an agreement with him without having suffered any constraint and that as to the justice of his rights over Naples, he would have the matter legally judged by the Pope and would accept his decision, after he had conquered it. But he concluded by saying that in any event he had now gone too far to withdraw and that discussion was useless.

Upon this final declaration which, since it placed the *fait accompli* above the law, rendered all further examination of the matter useless, Antonio de Fonseca took in his hands the treaty of Barcelona between the Kings of Spain and France, and tore it in pieces which he flung at the feet of Charles VIII, solemnly declaring that before the throne of God his sovereigns were absolved from further observing the treaty.[1] Fonseca's line of argument seems to have been dictated by the Pope himself, for it uses precisely the reasons that Alexander VI had appealed to continuously

214

from the moment that the question of Naples was raised by the French.

Velletri must have lived through days of extreme agitation, for shortly after this impressive scene, Cesar Borgia disappeared from the royal camp and escaped from the town in disguise.[2] The young cardinal, who was a man of great vigor, had disguised himself as a groom and made his way with all speed, some say to Rome which he left immediately on the Pope's advice, some say to Rignano and Spoleto. The Pope made a pretense of condemning Cesar's conduct, and sent the Bishop of Nepi to the King to tell him how deeply he deplored it; and the King sent Philippe de Bresse to Rome to protest against the breach of the pact. But all this is secondary in importance. What really mattered at that moment was that Charles VIII, deceived by the ease of his victory and his advance towards his new Kingdom, did not bother about the grave events preparing behind his back. He thought them unimportant.

King Alfonso II, upon whose military qualities so many hopes had been founded, did not fight. He abdicated, and fled with all his wealth to Sicily, where he died before the end of the year. Meanwhile, the two columns of which the invading army was composed advanced, one under the personal direction of the King by the good but fortified road of Ceprano, San Germano, Capua, Aversa and Naples; the other, led by Fabricio Colonna, Antonello Savelli and Robert Lenoncourt, made its way through the mountains of the Abruzzi. In the course of the advance, any resistance was sternly punished, while submission invited abuses by the soldiery. They entered this country, which they meant to make their own, with destruction and slaughter. Terror ran before them to Naples. The new King, Ferrante II, who had succeeded Alfonso, also ab-

215

dicated. He retired to Ischia, an island at the entry of the
Bay of Naples some three or four miles from one of the
shores of the Bay.

The Neapolitan army was pretty well demoralized by
the terror of the citizens and the treachery of its own
leaders. San Germano was abandoned, Capua was surrendered by Trivulce who entered the French King's service. Virginio Orsini took himself off to Nola. Charles VIII
arrived at Naples without opposition. But as he entered
the town, he suffered a catastrophe much worse than the
flight of Cesar. This was the death of Prince Jem. He
had fallen ill during the last stage of the journey, in front
of Capua. He had continued his journey, but in spite of
all the cares that were lavished upon him he died on February 25. Historians have accused the Pope of poisoning
him. This accusation began by the usual "on dit" of contemporaries, for Sanudo related that the Pope was suspected of having given the prisoner a delayed-action
poison. But Sanudo does not think it true, for the simple
reason that the death deprived Alexander VI of forty
thousand ducats, and was of no advantage to him at all.
Commines repeats the "on dit." But Guicciardini, a few
years after the Pope's death, gives the story as certain fact.

That men belonging to an age which spoke of miracle
when the wall of St. Angelo collapsed, and told of sick
people whom the Pope had cured in the presence of King
Charles simply by blessing them, and held it necessary to
consult astrologers before entering a town, should have
believed in this tale of a poison that would act at a fixed
date in the future, is not perhaps surprising. But it is a
little too much that it should still be believed today when
science has pruned these extravagances.

The King of France, who received Prince Jem from

the Pope on January 27, took him off on horseback through the Roman compagna, with all the fatigues and unpleasantnesses of the month of February, through marshy lands and under ceaseless rain. Prince Jem, who had been leading the life of a prisoner, was ill-fitted for the life of an army on the march. Thus it was that in front of Capua, practically in sight of Naples, he went down with a cold, with complications in the eyes and stomach.[3] But he had to go on, still on horseback, towards Naples. A month after the King had received him, he died. The famous Borgia poison, which allowed its victim to remain in perfect health in the midst of so hard a life, and only showed itself later, has not yet been discovered by science. I emphasize the incident because it is the first time that the Borgia poison appears on the scene.

But the death of Jem was nothing like so grave a matter as the situation of the French in their new kingdom, arising from the behaviour of the soldiery and the sheer incompetence of the men about the King. The Neapolitan nobility were made little of and kept at a distance, and the populace likewise. The conquerors, realizing that the vanquished could defend neither their persons nor their goods nor their liberties, treated them with total contempt. The King placed the crown upon his own head in the cathedral, amidst applause but no love; and Giovanni Pontano, the learned writer who had served the cruel and cunning Ferrante with such affectionate devotion, uttered a noble and elegant speech in which he lauded with the same affection and the same devotion the glory of Charles VIII, and hotly condemned the crimes of the House of Aragon.[4] Pontano was the intellectual expression of the collective baseness. But a rot had begun to set in among the invaders. Charles VIII had started upon this campaign at a time when his amours in Lyons might easily have turned him from it; and now once more he began to give himself to carnivals and women.[5] The members of his suite left nothing to the Neapolitans. Insatiably they laid their hands upon everything—money, titles, honors, power, and even pleasures; nothing was left for anyone else.

But in the midst of this intoxication and joy abounding, came news from the French ambassadors warning the King that he must think of his security. Commines urged him to make haste, lest he find obstacles to his return to France. And in fact a Spanish squadron was already cruising in the Tyrrhenian Sea commanded by Gonzalvo of Cordoba, later named the Great Captain; while upon land, the smallest army in Montferrat would have sufficed to render their return if not impossible, at least extremely awkward. So wrote the Duke of Orleans to the Duke of Bourbon.[6]

But what really woke the King of France up was not the warnings of his agents and best advisers, but the formation of the League between the Pope, Maximilian, the Spanish rulers, the Duke of Milan, and Venice. It was called the Holy League and by the Pope's will was announced on Easter Sunday, April 12, 1495. There were great manifestations all over Italy. Poets showered praises especially upon the Pope and the Most Serene Republic, and the vulgarest insults upon Charles VIII and the French. At Venice they were singing:

> Questo e papa Alessandro che corregie
> l'error del mondo con divine leggie—[7]

which we may roughly translate: This is Pope Alexander who corrects the world's error with divine laws.

There were celebrations everywhere, as if everyone felt

the breath of liberty blowing over Italy. The same scenes which had marked the triumphal arrival of Charles VIII were repeated, but against him.

Yet the prudent Lords of Venice, while preparing for war and sending soldiers and money to Rome, still dreamed of settling the conflict peaceably and proposed to the King an honorable way out. For so it considered the offer it made to Commines that the King might depart upon the galleys of Venice. The text of the treaty constituting the League said nothing of an alliance with a view to war, but only of the conditions of common defence. It was plainly a defensive treaty. But when defence is armed, and is superior in arms to the enemy, it is already an offensive. Between offensive and defensive there is only the most transparent of veils.

In face of events so grave, Charles VIII left Naples on May 20, leaving the Duke of Montpensier behind him, and manifesting no intention save of an interview with the Pope, to whom he had already communicated this desire. Did he in this difficult hour wish to discuss the situation with the man whose pleasant manners and skill in solving problems he had already experienced? Or was it his design to avenge the Pope's part in the formation of the League by an act of violence—by deposing him as he had suggested in his wrath upon the first news of the storm that was threatening? Neither of these theories seems to me sound. On his side, the Pope hesitated between following the advice given him by Maximilian and Venice to quit Rome, and remaining to receive the King. He postponed his decision, and made preparations both for the interview and for leaving Rome. Finally, remembering all that Rome had suffered some months earlier and the dangers he him-

219

P

self had run, he left the Eternal City on May 27, with twenty cardinals and seven thousand men-at-arms.

The King found no obstacle to his entry into Rome. There on June 1, he was received by Cardinal Pallavicini, representing the Sovereign Pontiff. This time the invaders observed discipline, which may suggest that good behaviour sometimes depends upon the punishment likely to follow its absence. This army was no longer so sure that its strength set it above the moral law.

On June 3, Charles VIII, who still was anxious to see the Pope, left Rome in quest of him, though whether as friend or enemy we do not know. Alexander VI, approached by one emissary after another, finally agreed and proposed Orvieto as the place of meeting. But the French ambassador observed that the King could not come away from the road that led to France, and suggested Viterbo instead of Orvieto. The Pope took this as a refusal and set out in haste for Perugia, with the intention of going on to Ancona. This proved to the French that Alexander was in reality determined not to meet them. Charles VIII was now keenly anxious to continue north, and for excellent reasons. So he decided to bother the Sovereign Pontiff no more. Alexander returned speedily to Rome where he was received by enormous crowds with indescribable enthusiasm.

In the north of Italy, there was already war although war had not been declared. The troops of Ludovico and of Venice were already in daily contact in the Duchy of Milan with those of the Duke of Orleans. The French reaction was so vigorous that they passed to the offensive and even occupied Novara. Charles VIII arrived at Pontremoli on July 3, knowing that the enemy was awaiting him. On July 5 he found himself in the difficult chain of mountains which defends the western part of central Italy against the north. His intention was to reach Asti. This involved crossing the Taro, a river stream which flows down from the Ligurian mountains to join the river Po. Its crossing is a simple enough operation in the dry season, but a little rain was enough to transform the stream into a dangerous torrent. Ill-led, the army of the Holy League committed the strategical error of awaiting the enemy as he came out from the mountains. If Charles had been attacked in the mountain passes, he would either have perished or been captured with all his troops. But he was not attacked until Fornovo, near the plain. Thus a way was open for retreat or flight. The battle was fierce. On the first day the Venetians and the Lombards made many prisoners. The Marquis of Mantua, leader of the Venetian forces, had had from Venice the strictest orders to make the King prisoner, and he nearly succeeded. But nightfall and the resistance of a group of Frenchmen who surrounded the King and withdrew into a wood, foiled all his efforts. The next day there was a truce, which the Marquis of Mantua made the mistake of accepting. On July 7, the King struck camp very early in the morning, and profiting by the confusion of the battle which was ill managed by the Allies, went off in all haste in the direction of Borgo San Donnino. It may have been rather a flight than a march, but it brought him out of danger, in spite of the ceaseless attacks upon his rear guard of Count Gajazzo, who a few months before had accompanied him in all friendliness to Naples as representative of Ludovico Sforza. The rest of the French army, abandoned upon the field, fought courageously. The King, having reorganized his scanty forces, reached Asti and the other army which he had left there.

There exists a certain difference of opinion about this

battle of Fornovo. The Allies regarded it as a great victory, but the French treated it as of small importance and indeed so far as it went as a tactical triumph for themselves, since the King had in fact got through the ranks of the enemy and continued on his way. Commines, who was at the battle, has left an account of it in which patriotism, the enemy of history, causes him to lose all critical sense. The Journal of Bernardino Zambotti says that there were four thousand killed of the Allies and of the French some sixty men.[8] This incredible first-hour news must have been what everybody received at Ferrara since Duke Ercole had linked his fate with the French. A few days later, when more exact information was to hand, it was learned that in the narrow streets of the mighty city of Venice the people were crying: "To Ferrara! to Ferrara!" Thus the populace showed its desire for an invasion of the neighboring duchy, and the poet cried: "Marquis of Ferrara, of the house of Maganza, you will lose your States in spite of the King of France."[9]

In reality there was exaggeration in both camps. The King had, indeed, found his way through the enemy lines, but he arrived at Borgo San Donnino still harried by a column of the Allies. In Italy there was talk of a great victory, and there were grand celebrations in the principal towns. But in truth it was not a battle between Italians and Frenchmen. There were many Italians in the camp of Charles VIII and according to Commines, it was they who were most concerned to carry on the struggle.[10] There were also many Swiss and Germans with the King. On the other hand, there were in the coalition army a great number of Stradiots—Albanians and men from other parts of the Balkans—in the pay of Venice. By the agreement of both sides it was because of these Stradiots that the Allies

222

did not bring off a really notable victory; for instead of following the Knights who continued to attack the fleeing enemy, as the tactics of the period demanded, they went off to loot the royal convoy. In plain truth, they were practically all fighting for booty and had small mind for glory —still less for such nobler sentiments as honor or love of country. It did not escape so penetrating an observer as Machiavelli that there could be no guarantee for the States while their defence was in the hands of adventurers who speculated in treason. That was why he insisted upon the necessity of creating a citizen militia.

From Asti, Charles VIII went to Turin and before returning to France decided to save Novara, which, occupied by the French army, was now besieged by the forces of Venice and Milan. We may consider the King as stupid, short-sighted, disagreeable, haughty and treacherous; but we cannot deny him courage and persistence and a spirit of adventure which drove him to face all the perils and fatigues of an army in the field.

At Naples things went ill for the French who remained there. It was won back by Gonsalvo of Cordoba, with the aid of the Spanish squadron lying in the Bay. Montpensier, who was acting as Viceroy, was obliged to sign a truce. King Ferrante II was once more master of the greater part of his Kingdom.

Seeing that Charles VIII was still in Italy and even threatened to return southward, the Pope thought the moment had come to strike the enemy in his own country, raising his subjects against him by means of religious sanctions. This method had already produced very favorable results for the Papacy, but at this new moment of history its effect could only be to create difficulties.

In a bull of August 9, 1495, the Pope addressed himself

"to our very dear son in Jesus Christ, Charles, most Christian King of the French," and after stern reference to all the violences of the invasion and the offenses of his ecclesiastical dignity and the abuses suffered by him, he enjoined upon the King and "upon your Dukes, Barons, Counts and illustrious Captains, and upon all those who were in Italy in your pay fighting with you, and others who are your partisans and allies or who bring you help and counsel and favor you," to cease from their project of war in Italy. The effect was not as considerable in France as it would have been in an earlier time; but it made a deep impression upon the Queen who was very pious, upon Briçonnet, dazzled by the cardinalate, and upon the Parliament of Paris which had had sense enough to oppose so dangerous and unprofitable a venture. Among many of the nobles also there grew up a spirit opposed to the war, which had never been popular, and in the end this spirit worked upon Charles' will. He crossed the Alps and never returned into Italy. Death took him still quite young, in April, 1498.

The Pope had no absolute confidence in the success of his bull against Charles VIII. He sent another bull to Venice praising the city for its virtues, to the great satisfaction of Senate and people. And as a reward for its attitude and an encouragement for the future, he sent it the Golden Rose which in the previous year he had sent to Charles VIII himself in the hope of checking his plan of conquest. Further he addressed himself to the Spanish sovereigns, urging that they continue the war against France at the French frontier, and to Maximilian urging him to attack at his end. At the same time he ordered the Swiss to cease from the service of his enemy, threatening them with the most rigorous sanctions of religion. His activity was prodigious, and was dominated by two ideas—the independence of Italy and the liberty of the Holy See.

But in Italy there still remained a King's Party. Cardinal Giuliano della Rovere continued to work for Charles VIII to such a point that the Senate of Venice told Baldassare de Posterla, the envoy of Ludovico Moro, that he must be removed from the King's counsels. Trivulce, who commanded the debris of the French army still in Italy, worked with the cardinal to raise Genoa in favor of Charles VIII. Further, there was one more of the eternal volte faces of Ludovico Moro who compromised the integrity of the League by concluding a separate peace with the French King even before Charles had departed for France. Many considerations combine to explain if not to justify this policy of the Duke of Milan. He was not a traitor by nature, as tradition has it, but by necessity.

The dangerous situations in which he had found himself and the ambition that ruled him had developed in him an excessive astuteness—mingled of distrust, cleverness and dishonesty—which served his interests to a certain point but beyond that point was the cause of all his troubles. In the stormy period of the Renaissance, as indeed today, astuteness is a drug that must be used in moderation.

The central point of the trouble was that the Duchy of Milan was on one of those unhappy high roads on which so many great battles have taken place in the course of the ages. It was the vanguard of Italy as against the Empire and as against France, to say nothing of its Swiss neighbors who did not care whose pay they accepted and could fall easily upon Milan itself; to say nothing either of the imperialist Venetians who designed to advance and command the roads over the Alps. Further, the Emperor

225

claimed suzerainty over Milan; and one branch of the royal house of France—as it turned out the next King— claimed the possession of its estates, in the name of its former lords, the Visconti.

Ludovico, realizing that his alliances were of very doubtful value, would have preferred to act as arbiter in the balance of Europe. To turn an inferior situation into a situation of privilege is the work of a genius—and the genius must be favored by luck. He was not a genius, nor did he think himself one; but he had high confidence in his ability, which had no moral frontier to limit it. He made peace with Charles VIII with the same object as when he had first called him in and then fought against him—the object being security within his own territory. After all, if by a turn of fortune the King of France should once again be strong, what could Venice, or the Empire, or the Pope, or even Spain do for him? For all those others a retreat was possible, but he was right out in front. At the first shock, he must fall. Further, apart from Spain which had its own policy, the other three allies did not fill him with any great confidence. He regarded the Pope as having a moral force which he used upon great occasions but only in the Papal interests. The Venetians had two policies: the one which concerned Ludovico, the westward policy, they held as secondary; it was the eastern Mediterranean that interested them most. They had institutions admirable at normal times, but inadequate to hours of danger because of the opposing opinions of the deliberative bodies. Ludovico said one day to an ambassador: "Each of these lords knows more than I, but not all of them together." Maximilian, the Emperor, was a man full of high intentions, clever and intelligent, but volatile and uncertain; and he was not supported by his vassals, who gave him neither men nor money.

Ludovico's fundamental error was to have invited Charles VIII into Italy. But in his subsequent conduct he worked for "the vital interests of his State," a concept which the modern view of international law has consecrated as superior to the concepts of justice and honor and right action, and has indeed withdrawn from human judgement.

Here was the reality of the situation. Charles VIII has left Italy only because for the moment France wanted no new adventures. But in Italy itself all was ready for a return to the old bad habits. There remained the same spirit of treason, the same men who had allied themselves with the King and accompanied him as far as Naples. The Holy League had thus created nothing definitive. Another King would take up the work of Charles VIII; and after him another, who was to cause the ruin of France and Italy and so prepare the total triumph of the Emperor Charles V.

CHAPTER XIV

Alexander and Savonarola

Alexander realized that no good could come to him from abroad unless he could bring definitively under his control the vassals of the Church, the Vicars, all the men who surrounded the Holy See. He had long known the true nature of these barons and dukes, but the whole incident of Charles VIII's invasion had made him see them in a still more evil light. The territory of the Church was without defence, at the disposal of the first comer, since those whose duty it was to defend it would deliver it to the enemy for money or favors. Such families as the Colonna, the Orsini, the Savelli, the Conti and all the rest had declared themselves in those difficult hours on the side opposed to the Holy See. The most distant vicars had opened their gates to the invader and many had even given him active assistance. All this must be corrected. Charles VIII's descent upon Italy had been a huge lesson to Borgia from all points of view.

In Alexander the political sense and the juridical sense met in perfect balance. Because the first did not overbear the second, he was saved from falling into opportunism; and because the second was vivified by the first, his ideas were saved from stiffening into a dangerous rigidity. Thus Alexander saw that the actual state of things could be corrected only gradually, but must at all costs be corrected.

With the exuberance that went with his physical and intellectual powers, he set himself to the task the moment a relative international peace allowed. And the task filled all the remaining years of his pontificate. In those years he punished and reduced to impotence all who had betrayed him, expelled the tyrants from his territory, and effected the complete submission of all the princes dependent upon the Church. Julius II fortunately followed in his footsteps and thus prevented the collapse of so great a work.

But as this was the beginning of his struggle, so it was the beginning of the sinister reputation of the Borgias. Now is the moment when all these puissant lords, with their magnificent courts and poets and scholars—the poets being scholars and the scholars poets—now is the moment when these lords, seeing themselves in danger, set on foot that campaign to discredit the Pope and his relations which grew steadily more intense as they lost their hold upon all that they had so evilly acquired. His first effort was no more than a trial of strength, and did not go well for Alexander.

The Orsini were the first that the Pope decided to deal with. What had they done? Only what, by inveterate habit, they had all done. They had gone over to the enemy, through caprice or for pay. They had no idea of country or religion or duty or honor. The Orsini had been at the orders of the House of Aragon; Virginio, the head of the family, was one of the great personages of the Kingdom of Naples. We have seen his relations with Charles VIII. Now that the King was no longer in Italy, and Montpensier was fighting to save something of what had been won in Naples, Virginio and his people—with other Vicars of the Church, like the Vitelli and Bartolomeo de Alviano—put themselves at the service of Montpensier and in the pay of the French King against the King of Naples and the Pope himself, whom until then they had served.

The Holy League, war on the frontier of France and Spain, the effort of Venice, the favorable attitude of Maximilian, all would go for nothing if the Kingdom of Naples, Ostia, the Port of Rome, and a great part of the Papal territories remained in the occupation of an Italian army at the orders of these *condottieri* acting in the name of the King of France. At this period when distances were made worse by the difficulties of the roads, and when the sordid egoism of the combatants not only weakened the idea of duty to an ally, but left men utterly in the dark as to where their own self-interest lay, victories at the circumference were no compensation for defeats at the center.

The Pope, following his usual method, tried to obtain by persuasion what might have been obtained by force. When he failed to persuade the rebels, he excommunicated them. Then, adding temporal arms to spiritual, he sent against the great Orsini fiefs the Duke of Urbino and Giovanni Borgia, second Duke of Gandia, who had just arrived from Spain and whom the Pope—combining his incorrigible nepotism with the desire to have a man he could trust at the head of his army—had named Captain General of the Church. The Papal forces obtained the unconditional surrender of all the strongholds of the Orsini family except Bracciano which was their principal fief. To add to the Orsini misfortunes came the definitive overthrow of the French further south. Montpensier was forced to surrender, signing a treaty by which his Italian *condottieri* were delivered to the mercy of the King of Naples. Virginio Orsini was imprisoned in a fortress, where he died maddened by the news of so many disasters.

A small episode now emerges to remind us that we are

treating of the history of the Borgias. We might find it amusing if the matter were not tragic. It may arise from a fantastic tradition preserved for some time in the Orsini family. Virginio, it seemed, was dead because the Pope had ordered the King of Naples to poison him, reinforcing the order with threats. And we are told that the affair was revealed by a child holding a candle one day when the Pope was writing. Over the Pope's shoulder he read the paper and saw that the Pope was writing to the King of Naples to poison Virginio Orsini immediately, threatening that if he did not he would withhold the investiture of the kingdom.[1] Nobody nowadays believes the story, so we may return to history.

The pontifical army, which had won partial victories so far, suffered a serious defeat at Bracciano. In the first stage of the battle the Duke of Urbino and Giovanni Borgia, thinking the capture of the place both certain and easy, advanced without precaution. But Vitellozzo Vitelli and Bartolomeo de Alviano, who had been allowed to leave the Kingdom of Naples by the King's indulgence, attacked the besieging army in the flank and practically wiped it out, on January 24, 1497. The Duke of Urbino was made prisoner and the Duke of Gandia managed to escape, but with difficulty and slightly wounded in the face. In war, victories and defeats are not always easy to explain. A matter of no great moment in itself may sometimes determine the issue. But it is certain that the Duke of Gandia had no experience of military operations of this sort, and the Duke of Urbino, a man of ability in many fields, was never a real soldier although he had led armies. It may even be that he did not command the respect that soldiers should have for their leader because in his private life— the opinion is unanimous and well-founded—he had not

231

the faculties of a complete man. In the opposite camp the two leaders counted then and still more later among the ablest *condottieri* of Italy.

Thus his first encounter with the barons did not yield the result the Pope had wished. He would have liked to continue the war but the foreign peril was again threatening and he had no mind to see himself entangled in lesser difficulties at a moment when he was facing a problem so much graver. In the north of the peninsula, the League was virtually dissolved and Maximilian, who had entered Italy with few arms but many plans, had gone back to Germany displeased with his allies (December, 1496). But if the Pope had not won the war against the Orsini, he was able at least to win the peace. Thanks to his skill, he turned defeat into victory, and mingling in the discussion material interests and idealistic principles—an amalgam at which he showed sovereign skill—he obtained the acceptance of the following agreement: The Orsini might remain *condottieri* of the King of France but only on condition that they must not take up arms against the Pope; they must pay seventy-five thousand ducats into the Church's treasury as penalty for their rebellion; the Pope would obtain the liberation of the Orsini who were still in the prisons of the King of Naples, and the Orsini for their part would set free all the prisoners they had made except the Duke of Urbino, who must personally pay his own ransom. Finally the Pope would return the captured fortresses and lands, except the Castle of Isola. These permanently rebellious vassals had not been finally conquered, but they emerged from this first trial of strength chastened and to some degree humiliated. Alexander had simply postponed the final reckoning. Cesar Borgia was to resume the work later, furnished by the Pope with better means. For the moment, it was necessary to envisage problems of greater gravity.

In 1497, the Holy League suffered utter collapse. Maximilian had taken advantage of his journey to Italy to annex the town of Gorizia. He alleged some sort of rights, but these were in any event posterior to those of the Republic of Venice, which had possessed the town since 1424 as a dependency of the Patriarchate of Aquileia.[2] The Venetians, for their part, aspired to the possession of the Adriatic coast held by the Kingdom of Naples. So that a double conflict was on, between the Empire and Venice and between Venice and Naples. On January 17, 1497, the Spanish sovereigns signed a separate truce with France, without bothering about their allies, just as Ludovico had done. Further the question of Pisa was growing more acute, so that a resumption of hostilities seemed imminent among all the Allies in the north of Italy.

Amidst this battle of appetites, Alexander VI multiplied his efforts to maintain the alliance which had saved Italy. Against the ambitions of Venice in the Adriatic, he opposed his own rights as suzerain of the Kingdom of Naples, and he forced the King to stand firm and the Venetians to accept his view, at any rate in appearance. He sent Cardinal Bernardino Carvajal to Maximilian with full powers; which gave courage and confidence to that wavering sovereign who had not been able thus far to make up his mind even to go and be crowned in Rome and take legal possession of his title of Emperor.

In the previous year, the Pope had obtained the entry into the alliance of the King of England, sending him a cloak and a sword of honor, a gift which caused the liveliest satisfaction to Henry VII. Finally, early in 1498, when he had lost all trust in the effectiveness of the League, he tried by direct arrangement with Charles VIII to get him to abandon his intention of returning to Italy and renounce his claims.[3] And it seems that he might well have succeeded in this if death had not taken the King soon after.

His efforts to separate Florence from France were still greater, because Tuscany with its mountains and strongholds could defend the Papal states against any invasion from the north. As the Republic would not fall in with his desires, he thought of a restoration of the Medicis. These projects were the cause of the conflict between Savonarola and Alexander.

Savonarola, a fanatical friar, had always believed that Charles VIII was a new redeemer. As, being a prophet, he could not be wrong, he was obliged to persist in this attitude. In fact, he remained faithful to this odd folly until the day he was hanged and his body burned. By an irony of fate he died on the day following the attack of apoplexy which ended the mortal life of the young French King. Alexander, finding a paranoiac of this sort in his path, at first wished simply to steer clear of him. For a normal man, people of deranged mind cannot in any event be useful friends, even if they wish to be; and they are always dangerous enemies. But the more tolerance he showed, the more intractable Savonarola became.

In this revolutionary period, when all moral values had become fluid, the friar became a great personality. He made a mixture of politics and religion to dominate the ignorant masses; and in his madness, which was partly the consequence of so great and rapid a success, he believed or at any rate asserted that God directly inspired the conduct he was to follow and the miracles he performed, as well as those he was ready to perform in the future if they were called for. Imbued with all the superstitions of

234

an age in which they abounded, he foretold catastrophes or alternatively days of well-being. In his visionary moments, he prophesied that the Infidels would be converted to the religion of Christ, that Charles VIII would return to Italy, that this time he would be its great redeemer and that he would not leave of Rome a stone upon a stone. Like all unbalanced men, he combined blind conviction with a deep-lying cunning which allowed him to graduate his rages, and either withdraw when necessary, or else let himself go to the furthest excesses of his violence.

The phenomenon of Savonarola is of no importance in itself. In Asia, nothing is commoner. And if the phenomenon is rarer in Europe, it was assuredly not exceptional. Certainly Savonarola was not the greatest of ecclesiastical agitators, which is perhaps why he shouted the loudest and caused the greatest disturbance.

What made him important was the period through which Florence was passing. It had itself arrived, under the influence of this abnormal man, at a condition of collective neurasthenia, which might have been comprehensible in an age of mysticism or in a less cultured city, but is totally incomprehensible in the learned elegant city that Florence was, in an age such as the Renaissance, at a moment when its two greatest lights were Lorenzo the Magnificent and Leo X. What is graver still, the Italian princes, who were not by way of being saints, believed in his supernatural character. And cardinals like Caraffa and churchmen like Gioacchino Turriano, Master-General of the Dominicans, supported him, and did so at the very moment when he was claiming that God had entrusted his secrets to him and that the proposals he made were guaranteed by the word of the Lord: "As we have received from Him [God] His infallible promise, we guarantee the accomplishment of this with the most perfect certitude . . ."[4] He was further announcing that the dreaded Turks would be converted because "He [God] has had the goodness to reveal it to me . . ."[5]

Alexander VI had too much respect for God to allow a man so unbalanced to abuse his name thus impudently. In a letter dated October 15, 1495, he told him not to provoke disturbances in Florence and concluded:

> "In your public pronouncements you predict the future and affirm that all that you say comes from the eternal light and as an inspiration of the Holy Spirit, whereby you lead simple men away from the road of salvation and from obedience to the Holy Roman Church. You ought to have preached unity and peace, instead of these things which the populace calls prophecies and divinations. You should further consider that the conditions of the period do not permit the proclamation of such doctrines, for if by their own nature they are liable to cause discord even if complete peace were reigning, how much more are they bound to do so at a moment when there are already so many rancours and factions."

Yet he excuses Savonarola, adding his own conviction that he is preaching these things not in any evil spirit, but in simplicity and for the good of religion; though he observes that it is a proven fact that practices of this sort do not serve it. He ends by ordering Savonarola to refrain for the moment from preaching and invites him to come to Rome "where we shall receive you with a father's heart."[6]

To this letter, as to others from the Pope, Brother Girolamo gave either evasive or intolerably arrogant answers, for his vanity had been hurt.

Alexander and Savonarola

After a period of patience, the Pope named a commission of cardinals to study the question whether he should maintain the excommunication he had felt obliged to launch or reconsider it. In this commission was included Cardinal Caraffa who until then had supported Savonarola. The Commission declared unanimously for the continuance of the excommunication.

Very slowly and with great prudence, the Pope, who had no desire for a continuance of the conflict, pressed the Seigniory of Florence in 1498 to prevent the Friar from carrying on his priestly activities since, being an excommunicated man, he could no longer officiate. Finally his patience was worn out. To a letter of the Seigniory, which persisted in not putting an end to the folly because of the Friar's popularity, he replied in late February, 1498, with irritation: Either they should send the friar to him in Rome under guard, in which case he would treat him well, for he desired his conversion and not his punishment, or at least they should separate him from the faithful whom he was poisoning with his theories and put him as a decayed member in a place apart, well guarded. And as he did not intend that the Seigniory should continue to make mock of ecclesiastical authority—and, may I add, of common sense—by postponing a definite answer, he threatened Florence itself with general excommunication if it did not obey.

But at Florence the popular mind was already changing of its own motion. Savonarola's prophesies were not being fulfilled. Another religious rose against him, denied his supernatural inspiration, and challenged him to the ancient ordeal by fire. Savonarola lost his usual superb self-confidence and had another friar of his order take his place. At the last moment he imposed conditions for the ordeal, saying that "God had suggested them to him."

237

When the fagots were actually prepared for the reception of the two religious, Savonarola started a theological discussion upon the modifications he wished introduced into the ordeal: in especial he demanded that his deputy should carry the consecrated host in his hands when he entered the flames. The crowd, greedy for the macabre, protested impatiently against being kept waiting. While Savonarola's passive resistance was holding up the ceremony, a great shower of rain put out the fires, which maddened the crowd beyond all endurance. From that moment Savonarola's days were numbered. He had always flattered and excited the morbid instincts of the populace: the day he could no longer do that, his ascendancy was gone. Florence treated Savonarola as peoples treat their dictators: they follow them with blind submission, they overthrow them with one stroke.

The attack upon Savonarola was as impressive as the former apotheosis. His principal supporter, Francesco Valori, was assassinated along with others. He was forced to defend himself, and did not find it easy. The people who had believed in his divinity were now set upon stoning him. The Seigniory finally began legal process against him and he was condemned to death. But Savonarola being a religious, the question belonged to the ecclesiastical sphere. That the sentence might be executed, the Pope must first authorize his being degraded. The further question must be settled which the Pope had already raised in claiming to judge him himself. The Senate asked Alexander VI to authorize it to execute judgement. In the letter it wrote upon the subject, it is worth noting its fear that the Pope might decide to save the life of the man who had so insulted him; for there is insistence that the execution should take place in Florence to give a salutary example, and it is observed that it would be unsuitable for foreign elements to be involved in questions of this sort.[7]

The Pope desired neither the life nor the death of Brother Girolamo, but only that the law should be carried out. The whole business of the ordeal by fire had caused him grave displeasure; and on April 8, before he had heard of the way, at once comic and tragic, in which the ceremony of the day before had ended, he expressed vigorous disapproval.[8] In reply to the Seigniory's request, he appointed two prelates to examine the trial from the religious point of view: one of these two was Savonarola's former superior, the Gioacchino Turriano of whom we have already spoken. They carried out their mission and as they found no grounds for reprieve, Savonarola was executed.

The friar has left violent invectives against the Borgia Pope. Generally he did not actually name him in his sermons, but he did indirectly repeat all the accusations that slander had set in motion against him. Like all fanatics, he was concerned more with the external defects that every organization tends to develop in the course of ages than with the fundamental things for which it exists. He attacked luxury by appealing to the basest envy. He destroyed works of art in Florence, and desired the total destruction of Rome.

From the first moment, the Pope's attention had been drawn to this man because of the harm he did by presenting the invader Charles VIII as an apostolic figure. Then, heedless of the insults hurled at himself, he tried to put an end to an agitation which constituted a challenge at once to religion and to intelligence. It was without personal rancor that he proceeded against him, with no desire save that strict justice should be done.

239

CHAPTER XV

Assassination of the Duke of Gandia

In that difficult year of 1497, with the threat growing of another French invasion and the Holy League losing all cohesion, Alexander VI suffered grave family griefs which, given his sensitive temperament and his affection for the Borgia clan, plunged him in the deepest depression. A contemporary says that never had there been seen *"un uomo piu carnale"*—a man more attached to those of his own flesh and blood. In fact the manifestations of his joy or grief when his relations were in question, the terms in which he speaks of them, his anxiety when any danger seems to threaten them, and the explosions of his enthusiasm when they have done anything noteworthy—all are evidence of a certain abnormality—not a seriously blamable abnormality, but abnormal all the same. And he acts thus not only for Cesar, Lucretia, Giovanni and Jofre, his children real or supposed, but for more distant relations like his nephew the Cardinal of Monreale, or his brother the first Pedro Luis, or Adriana del Mila, or Alfonso d'Este who was Lucretia's last husband. The language he uses to express this natural love has the tone of devotional books and prayers, the exaggerations of the pulpit. Probably his long habituation to the formulae of religious documents combined with his ardent and impulsive temperament to produce these ways of speech.

240

Assassination of the Duke of Gandia

On June 14 of that year—the very day on which Ascanio Sforza received from the mouth of Alexander and Giovanni and Cesar the news that Lucretia could not continue conjugal life with Giovanni Sforza of Pesaro because of the latter's impotence—Giovanni Borgia, second Duke of Gandia, was assassinated cruelly and mysteriously. The Pope's desolation was immeasurable.

Of this murder not only has no author of that day or since accused Alexander, but on the contrary all are in agreement that no man was ever known to suffer such bitter grief in such a tragedy. We know that for three days he refused all food, that the halls of the Vatican resounded with his weeping, that he even wanted to abdicate. In speaking of this death, the various authors have not concealed their ghoulish satisfaction. They have cast over Alexander's anguish a veil of sarcasm more ferocious than the smile of Iago. The Borgias had been punished! It was the just action of the God of Sinai, it was the vengeance of implacable Nemesis. They go further and urge that, cruel as such a punishment was, it must not inspire compassion for Alexander but general repulsion. Whether as victims or executioners, the Borgias must not for a moment cease to be hated.

Up to the year 1497, this execrated family had been attacked only as simoniacal and nepotist; the accusation of poisoning Prince Jem, which no one seriously believed, had begun the work of spattering the family with blood; the Pope was credited with a certain eroticism, enviable perhaps in a man of sixty-five; Lucretia's character was already assailed before she was thirteen. But neither ancients nor moderns have been able to cite anything before the year 1497 in any way worthy of the Borgia legend.

241

But in that year it began, more appalling than the legend of the Atreides.

Cesar had killed his brother Giovanni, from base envy or some worse reason. Alexander, not withdrawing his love from Cesar, became an accomplice in his crime. That was the accusation.

Giovanni Borgia had arrived in Rome from his Duchy of Gandia a year before he died. The Pope had ordered him to Rome some time before, but the Spanish rulers had not given him authorization to leave their Kingdom.[1] Upon his arrival in the Eternal City, Alexander had employed him as *condottiere* of the Church, then Governor of the Patrimony, then Captain General. Some months after, he let him have his first experience of battle against the Orsini and their citadel of Ostia, which was still in the hands of the rebels and in the shadow of Cardinal Giuliano della Rovere. By now, the Pope was preparing to give him a great dukedom, that of Benevento. The young man's career in Rome could not have been swifter or more brilliant.

He had given no proof of great military qualities, he was vain, haughty in public but agreeable in conversation, a pleasant companion, a lover of pleasure, and personally courageous. He inspired friendship and respect. He was very different from Cesar, who was Italian by temperament, more severe, more taciturn, more calculating. This Duke of Gandia was a Borgia from head to foot, and a perfect type of Spaniard.

On June 14, Giovanni and Cesar went with their cousin, the Cardinal of Monreale, to dine with their mother Vannozza Catanei, on the Esquiline. The reason for this small celebration was the journey to Naples Cesar was to make a few days later as Legate for the coronation of the new King Frederick.[2] Of this family gathering, nothing has

242

come down to us. Naturally enough. After dinner, the two brothers and the cousin, with a few servants, came out in the twilight and mounted their horses to return to the Vatican. As they came by the palace of Cardinal Ascanio Sforza, at the entry to the bridge of the Castle of Saint Angelo, the Duke of Gandia stopped and said gaily that he had some matter to attend to there. This was taken to mean that he was expected upon some amorous adventure. The two cardinals urged him strongly not to leave them or at least to take some armed men with him. Rome was not very safe, particularly by night. The Duke agreed to take one man; and he had another person mount on the crupper of his own mule. This person had been present, masked, at dinner and had been seen in the Duke's anterooms some days before. Leaving his brother and his cousin, the Duke set off towards the Piazza of the Jews. Here he ordered his attendant to await him until midnight, then to return to the Vatican if he had not reappeared. The two cardinals were not happy at the thought that the Duke was thus risking himself alone in the streets of Rome; and they remained a moment on the bridge in the hope of seeing him return, especially as he had given them to understand that he might rejoin them very soon on their way back to the Vatican. But seeing that he did not return, they set off again with their small escort.

No one has ever known where the Duke went with the masked man when he left the servant. Upon the fate of the servant, different versions have come down to us. Bruchard says that he was gravely wounded and that he died without having been able to give any explanation. Scalona, orator of Mantua, says that he was slightly wounded, and that he came back a little later to the Vatican to seek armed help. At any event, he could not have said a great deal since clearly he was not an eyewitness of what happened. But Scalona's version is probably more accurate than Bruchard's, for otherwise we should not know as we certainly do, that the servant had been left in the Piazza of the Jews with the order to wait there for his master.[3]

What we know with certainty from the inquiry that followed, is that at midnight of that day a certain Giorgio Schiavone, who was watching in a boat to prevent the theft of some wood that he had floated down to Rome, saw two men approach along the road which ran from the Castle of Saint Angelo to the Church of Santa Maria del Popolo. These men examined the neighborhood, looking on all sides to see if anyone might be there; then there appeared two others and afterwards a third on horse-back who was carrying a corpse. The corpse was flung into the river and the five men, after having made sure that the body had sunk to the bottom by filling with stones the cloak in which it was wrapped and which at first floated on the water, departed. Schiavone's declaration caused the Tiber to be dragged in that region, and the body was discovered, deep in the mud. It was the body of the Duke of Gandia. Rarely have obsequies been accompanied by such great manifestations of grief.

The day following the dinner, when the Duke was found not to have returned to the Vatican, there was naturally an alarm, but it was at first supposed merely that his amorous adventure had lasted a little longer than he had expected. The Pope was informed of the Duke's absence by a servant from the Duke's own house and by another of Cardinal Cesar's household; but though he was surprised, he too attributed it to some intrigue with a woman. But in the afternoon he grew anxious and summoning the two cardinals begged them to tell him the whole truth; for he seemed to believe that the Duke's absence, with the manner in which it was told him, was a polite way of keeping something serious from him which everybody knew but he. The Cardinals could only relate what had happened; whereupon the Pope cried out that now the one thing necessary was to discover whether he were alive or dead: in the extremity of his wrath he asserted that if there had been an assassination, he knew who were its authors. He ordered an immediate inquiry and under the personal direction of the Governor of Rome an investigation was set on foot which yielded no result as to the identity of the murderer, but which caused the rapid recovery of the body of the murdered man as has just been related.

Before this irreparable loss, the Pope's grief was beyond measure. But after the natural nervous reaction, usually to be found in sensitive characters, he recovered his calm. On June 19, he entered the Consistory where the Cardinals, ambassadors, and other high dignitaries uttered their deeply moved condolences. At that moment, Alexander showed his whole self, as men do in great grief—full of dignity, serene in judgement, a profound believer yet human and thoroughly realistic in his outlook. And I can only express my own feeling that in this he must appear all the nobler if the Duke of Gandia was really his son.

In the deep silence which grief always imposes upon an assemblage of men he spoke in a firm voice saying that the Captain-General of the Church was dead and that a grief beyond measure had entered his soul so that no earthly good could henceforth bring him solace; and that probably God had willed to punish him for some sin. He added that neither the authors of the crime nor its instigators were known. He declared the innocence of certain people whose names were murmured, like Giovanni Sforza

245

and his brother Galeazzo, Duke of Urbino, and Cardinal Ascanio Sforza whom Alexander said he considered and always would consider as a brother. And he declared that there was no reason to mention the Prince of Squillace, Jofre de Borgia, the dead man's brother. And as Cardinal Ascanio had not come to the Consistory, fearing some violence on the part of the Spanish soldiery who were very much worked up, the Pope prayed the Ambassador of Spain to let the cardinal know that it would be agreeable to him to see him. He ended with the words: "May God pardon the guilty man!"

The investigation continued, without result. But what was not known at the time could easily be invented afterwards: his enemies decided that Cesar Borgia was the murderer.

Yet contemporaries did not at once think of Cesar; nor in the following years, when every infamy was attributed to the Borgias, was a single fact brought forward or the least indication to support the theory of his guilt. It is only by the middle of the sixteenth century—a half-century after—that we find definite statements, though still without any proof whatever.

At the period of the crime, a letter from Scalona to the Lord of Mantua enumerates the various suspects, according to the rumors in circulation. The rebels of the town of Viterbo, Cardinal Ascanio Sforza and the Duke of Urbino (whom we remember as having been forced to pay his own ransom) are on the list. Scalona does not say if Giovanni Borgia had accused the Duke of Urbino for the disaster of Bracciano, but there is every reason to believe that the responsibility had been laid upon him. The same ambassador says that others were spoken of: the Duke della Mirandola, whose lovely daughter had caught Gandia's eye; and Giovanni Sforza, the husband of Lucretia, whose marriage was at that time under discussion on the ground of his impotence. He mentions also an opinion held by some that Gandia had been assassinated because of some other affair of gallantry, but he adds that whoever did the murder or ordered it, had long teeth—that it was a person of considerable power. There seems to be nothing more in all this than the guesswork common after every murder.

The people most under suspicion were the Orsini, although the most active investigations were carried out against the Duke della Mirandola. So we are told by the Florentine ambassador, Alessandro Bracci. But if the police looked in one direction, the popular voice murmured in another: it accused Giovanni Sforza, Duke of Pesaro, and his brother, though neither of them was in Rome at the time.

Cardinal Ascanio, after a long interview with the Pope, wrote to Milan that the Duke of Urbino had been accused, and he makes allusion to the Orsini. It seems clear that Alexander VI had these last in mind and that at the beginning he mentioned them with some conviction. But in reality, he never had sufficient data in hand, and his later conduct proves that this conviction was not very solid. However that may be, it was the Orsini who were most strongly accused and for longest. The ambassador of Milan informed Ludovico Moro, and the ambassador of Florence informed his own Seigniory, that they were regarded as guilty. The famous chronicles of the various cities bear different opinions as to the identity of the criminal. But Cesar is never mentioned. He, after some days of mourning, set out all in black for Naples, with all the honors and all the powers of a legate to crown the new King, Frederick of Aragon. He was received with respect and the greatest cordiality.

The first time we find in a document even the theory that Cesar might be guilty—it is not an accusation—is at the end of February of the year following, that is 1498. It is in a dispatch sent to Duke Ercole from Venice by Alberto della Pigna, ambassador of Ferrara: "I have again heard it said that the cause of the Duke of Gandia's death was the Cardinal his brother." He had heard this at Venice, far from Rome, and he sent it on to Ferrara, near Venice, where it had not yet been heard. Clearly this new rumor had no more foundation than the others. The truth is that in an assassination one accuses whoever is supposed to have had a motive. Thus we find accused—the Orsini because they were declared enemies; Sforza because he had been insulted with the accusation of impotence; the Duke della Mirandola, because he had a daughter whose beauty had attracted the murdered man; the Duke of Urbino because of military rivalries and the question of responsibility in a defeat. A year later, when it began to be said that Cesar was going to abandon the ecclesiastical career for the career of arms, it was assumed that he was going to succeed to the Dukedom of Gandia. This was enough to set people murmuring: "Cesar wanted Gandia's dukedom, so he killed him." But in fact, Cesar did not succeed his brother, for the Dukedom of Gandia and his other possessions, in Rome and in Spain, passed as was natural and legal to his son, who was likewise called Giovanni. This third Duke of Gandia married a niece of King Ferdinand and was the father of St. Francis Borgia.

Cesar was only the administrator of the Roman part of the inheritance which was liquidated later in consultation with the representative of Gandia's widow, Doña Maria Enriquez. Cesar continued to enjoy the Pope's favor, but there was never any question of giving him the Dukedom

248

of Benevento, which had been meant for Gandia, nor the goods and fiefs which Gandia held in Naples. He was not named Captain-General of the Church until two years after his brother's death, and he owed all his fortune to the protection of the King of France—by which Gandia, as a vassal of the King of Spain, would not have profited.

Following upon this rumor picked up by Alberto della Pigna, there is a famous pamphlet, the *Letter to Silvio Savelli,* dated November 19, 1501. In this letter, it is said incidentally that everybody in Rome is in dread of the Pope's son, for having killed his brother, he has turned from a cardinal into an assassin. But we have already seen the value of this pamphlet, the work of a paid hack. Nor in the rest of the document is there anything that bears much relation to the truth.

It was only after the death of Alexander that people began to believe in the accusation. But the arguments brought forward are so clearly false that they strengthen the case for his innocence. Della Pigna, in support of his first communication of 1497, says on June 18, 1504 that the widow of Giovanni Borgia, Duke of Gandia, had had Cesar arrested in Spain to avenge the murder of her husband. The thing is utterly false. The widow was on the best terms with her brother-in-law, and King Ferdinand declared that Cesar was detained in the Castle of Medina del Campo because of accusations which the Great Captain had sent him from Naples. In fact Ferdinand had Cesar arrested upon the suggestion of Pope Julius II, who had asked this of him;[4] Gonzalvo de Cordoba arrested Cesar in Naples (in spite of the safe conduct which had been given him) upon the order of the King of Spain and sent him as a prisoner to Spain. Doña Maria Enriquez had had nothing to do with the matter.

Two Venetian ambassadors have alluded to the crime, attributing it to Cesar. They are Paolo Capello and Giustiniani. Neither of them was in Rome at the time of the murder, and they wrote their accusation years later when the Borgia Pope and Cesar were a nightmare for Venice's policy of conquest.[5] The two ambassadors attribute the crime to Cesar on the ground of his desire to be his brother's heir. But we have just seen that Cesar was not the heir, that he could not be the heir of a brother who had a son of his own, nor did he inherit the favors—as it were dynastic favors—which the Pope had reserved for Gandia.

Cesar did not give up his cardinal's hat until a year after his brother's death. He went to France where he remained another year. Upon his return the Pope began to grant him favors similar to those which Gandia had received at the time when he was himself in Rome, which was something less than a year. One can judge truly of facts only if account is taken of the order of their succession; otherwise one is subject to the same errors of perspective as in looking over too far-flung a horizon.

Our conclusion must be that Cesar had no connection whatever with the crime. This part of the tragedy of the Borgias has been revised in our own day. The latest accuser of importance is Leopold Ranke[6] who, relying upon an act of accusation made by Sebastiano Branca de Telini, says: "He had his brother, the Duke of Gandia, cast into the river; he had his brother-in-law killed, the son of the Duke of Calabria, the handsomest young man ever seen in Rome; and further he had Vitellozzo killed, the most valiant man of the time." Ranke believed all this. Yet the most summary reading of Branca de Telini's *Journal* shows that it would be impossible to cram more historical errors into a single work.[7]

CHAPTER XVI

Family Troubles and the Reform of the Church

W‍HILE the death of Giovanni Borgia plunged the Pope into such affliction that contemporaries tell us that he would neither eat nor drink for three days, the story of Lucretia's relations with her husband did nothing to console him. A few days before the crime, Lucretia had withdrawn into a convent, because the family had separated her from Giovanni Sforza.[1] The point of going to a convent was to preserve her from all the suspicions with which her husband might have wished to cloud her honor. On June 14, Lucretia's family announced to Ascanio Sforza, as Giovanni's relation, that the marriage had not been consummated, in spite of the time that had elapsed, because of the husband's impotence. Ascanio sent on the unpleasant news to Ludovico, his brother; and the Pope assembled the Consistory. He declared that he did not wish to decide the matter himself and he named a commission composed of the Cardinals Antonietto Pallavicini and Giovanni di San Giorgio, to try the cause canonically and if the evidence justified, to declare the marriage null. The Pope had previously tried to obtain the separation of the parties by friendly arrangement; and to avoid scandal had shown himself prepared to let Sforza keep Lucretia's dowry and give him other concessions.[2]

R

Giovanni Sforza fought his case as vigorously as possible. But on November 18 of that same year 1497, he officially admitted his impotence, though previously, in letters addressed to his relations in Milan, he had stated his intention of proving that the marriage had been consummated and that marital relations had been frequent. The commission of two cardinals declared the marriage null on December 19. Lucretia was once more a maiden.

An affair of this sort could not fail to provoke rumors and comments of the most unpleasing kind, considering that the family in question was the family of a reigning sovereign, above all of a Borgia. The withdrawal into the convent was not held sufficient, nor the commission of cardinals, nor even the husband's avowal. Matarazzo, source for so many later writers, tells us in his chronicle that Lucretia, at that moment seventeen years of age, was the most sought after public woman in Rome. A phrase of the offended husband set buzzing a story of incest. It was said that the Pope intended to make her his own mistress, and it apparently did not occur to anybody that he meant to marry her to another husband, the only problem lying in the difficulty of choosing amongst such a throng of suitors.

Finally the story went about that Lucretia had a son, prior to the middle of March, 1498, which would mean that his conception dated back to her time in the convent. And incredibly von Pastor believes in the story, because a certain Poggio, secretary of Bentivoglio, Lord of Bologna, says that rumors were current in Venice about it! Von Pastor was a diligent collector of information, but he often forgot to use his own good sense. It was at Rome and not in Venice that the news of this son born in a convent should have been spread, and at Rome it was unknown.

Capello speaks of incestuous relations between brother and sister at the time of this son's arrival, and he speaks of a mass of other things rejected by history, rejected indeed by Pastor. That illustrious writer should have remembered that shortly afterwards the Duke of Ferrara received Lucretia with honor, respect and affection when she arrived at his palace as wife of his eldest son: so that he obviously attached little importance to the rumors of which his envoy in Venice had passed on the echo. What impressed von Pastor was that there were three concordant rumors. But apparently it never occurred to him that they might have a common origin. Which was precisely what they had. It is not the first time that Lucretia had been credited with a child. Earlier still we are told of one of those midwife's jests to the effect that Lucretia looked as if she had begun pregnancy—at thirteen. Later historians did not overlook so suitable a rumor.

But who was the father of the child conceived in the convent? Every modern historian is obviously entitled to please himself. The first accused was one of her brothers, the Duke of Gandia; simply on the ground that he was murdered soon after.[3] Then it was Cesar's turn because Cesar was the convenient scapegoat for all crimes. Come to that, why not the Pope himself? But that was too repulsive a story to be swallowed without one single shred of proof. So the more responsible writers have felt. Someone else had to be found. There was a certain Pedro Calderon, better known as Perotto, employed at the Vatican very close to the person of Alexander VI, and friendly with the whole family. He was found dead in the Tiber—an accident by no means rare, not because we are dealing with Borgias, but because long before the Borgias and long after such incidents were grimly frequent. Obviously he

253

would do very well for the father. So indeed Poggio wrote from Venice. He had heard it said. The one thing nobody bothered about was whether such a child really existed. The story was so apt that only a pedant could wonder was it true.

According to the legend, the Perotto affair was no isolated crime, but a link in a chain of crimes. This Perotto, who had possessed Lucretia in such exceptional circumstances, was murdered by Cesar. But Cesar was not in this avenging his family honor, but his own criminal passion. Perotto haunted the ante-rooms of Alexander VI and was one of his most faithful assistants. Cesar met him in one of these immense rooms and pursued him dagger in hand. Perotto fled at full speed and stumbled into the arms of the aged Pontiff. There Cardinal Cesar found him; and he plunged his dagger again and again into the wretched quivering body. The blood spurted upwards, drenching the Pope's face and the robe of his office.

But Bruchard, who also haunted these same apartments, knew nothing of the crime. He simply says that Perotto fell into the Tiber against his will.[4] There is no trace in his *Journal* of this tragedy, which would surely have been sufficient to shake the imagination even of this stolid Vatican official. Nor is anything said in the dispatches of ambassadors, always on the watch for sensations to brighten their official reports. Nor in the chronicles, whose error is not normally in the direction of reticence. In the letter in question Poggio tells Ercole d'Este that Perotto was not in the Vatican but in prison.

The account I have given of this tragic matter is to be found only in the *Letter to Silvio Savelli*, an anonymous letter addressed to a man in exile who had had his goods confiscated, his power destroyed and his family ruined by

254

the Pope; a letter which, though it is called a letter, is not a private communication, but a pamphlet—meant to be passed round from hand to hand among the enemies of a Pope who had dealt so energetically with all the nobles of the Papal domains. The *Letter to Savelli* is not a historical document, it is a weapon of war.[5] But it was the most effective weapon that could be employed to accuse the Borgias. The ambassador Capello, who had not yet come to Rome, was later to reproduce this accusation which he had assuredly read in the anonymous pamphlet.

Upon this question of the death of Perotto, there is a triple contradiction. Bruchard says that he died in the Tiber, Poggio in prison, the *Letter to Savelli* in the Vatican. It is instructive to observe what later historians have done with these three versions. They have rolled them all into one. Perotto was arrested, and placed in prison, then taken to the Vatican where he was murdered in the arms of the Pope, finally flung into the Tiber to be fished out later by the same authorities who had had him flung in. This way of reconstructing the past seems a little forced. Clearly if History has destroyed the reputation of the Borgias, the Borgias have done a good deal of damage to History.

In any event nothing whatever is known of this pretended son of Lucreţia. He disappears from the Borgia clan, although that çlan always aided and protected all its members—especially, as it would seem, its bastard members.

But to return to our subject, there can be no doubt that the death of the Duke of Gandia, followed by Lucretia's matrimonial difficulties, deeply afflicted Alexander. In the Consistory of June 19, he used the language habitual in a member of the Roman church under the influence of the age-old, unchanging psychology of the Catholic clergy: "God has perhaps willed to punish certain of our sins, for

255

the Duke did not deserve a death so cruel." Such words would have been uttered by any priest, at any level of sanctity, as an expression of humility and resignation to the will of God. But modern authors have regarded them as a definite act of contrition and confession.

In the course of the same Consistory, the Pope announced that he was naming a Commission of six cardinals to reform the Church, a reform to which he declared he would himself be the first to submit.

At this period everybody was talking of the reform of the Church. Reforms, like revolutions, are necessary, when the law must be altered to cover a new state of fact. In the course of time, ecclesiastical relations had changed, but the institutions had not changed. A reform was necessary which should put the two things into harmony again. But reform is a process that must be carried through rapidly: so that at any period it is bound to encounter formidable resistance because of the horror men have of novelty. That is why it takes passion, itself an abnormal state, to bring about great transformations. They cannot be brought about in cold blood. So long as this state of passion has not been formed in the public mind, everybody admits the evil and theorizes about the changes that are necessary; but no one has the nerve to set these changes in motion, so great are the material obstacles and dangers in the way of progress.

The Church was ruled at that period, politically as well as spiritually, as an absolute monarchy. This was not in accord with tradition, but had come about gradually through a combination of diverse causes. By now the Pope was God's representative upon earth in both spheres and against him there was no appeal. To speak of a Council at that time was to be a dangerous revolutionary, for that was a remedy whose effects always tended to go beyond the needs of the organism to which it was applied. To demand the summoning of a General Council was analogous to the demand for the meeting of the Estates General before the French Revolution. And in fact, though convoked much later and after long preparation, the Council of Trent and its labors did involve a good many dangers for the Catholic Church.

Anyhow, the popes and the cardinals, and the theologians with them, thought that a reform of the Church was necessary; for the Church was no longer an organization solely for the saving of souls with a view to the obscure world that lies beyond: it was an instrument, an organ, acting upon the moral life of this present world, in the midst of new political and juridical systems—the new national states, in fact, which had gone far in the direction of absolute autonomy. In all reformations, the theoretical concept of reform has as its animating principle something more concrete, something emotional—the protest against the abuses of the regime to be changed: the result is that, in the mind of the great majority, the doctrinal part of the reform is forgotten and nothing remains save an increasingly passionate desire to be rid of the vice and corruption to be found in the institutions that exist. So it was now.

Reform had been spoken of before Alexander VI, and was to be spoken of after him. But it needed the passion of a Luther, and it needed the favoring political milieu he had to act in. It required more than a half century of agitation within the bosom of Catholicism to arrive at the internal reform of the Church, with the Council of Trent. Upon all this Alexander had an accurate view, because to a clear and balanced intelligence, he added a thorough

257

understanding of the workings of the Church. While he was still a cardinal, he had attempted a partial reform in Spain with the Council which assembled at Segovia and was later transferred to Madrid. Further, in the Conclave at which Paul II was elected, he had sworn to the preliminary declaration, subscribed by each of the cardinals, that in the event of his election he would set about the reform of the Church within three months. In the Conclaves which followed, he himself proffered to the others practically the same oath; and in the Conclave in which he was elected, the oath dealt with the obligation to summon a General Council for the reformation of all that concerned the Church.

This obligation imposed upon themselves by the candidates for the Papacy—naturally ineffective because of the number of mental restrictions with which purely moral duties are always hedged about—does at least show that at the very heart of Christendom the thought of reform was persistently present, and that the Borgia Pope had had to recognize it as a necessity. In the Consistory of June 19, 1497, Alexander VI was thus accomplishing an act of which he had often thought, and to which he held himself bound by his declaration signed at the Conclave: although canonically this did not constitute an obligation binding in conscience. As grief elevates men and frees them, if only for the moment, from their normal prejudices and timidities, Alexander rose superior to the difficulties which at a normal time would have prevented him from examining the question of reform in itself. And he set about the task without worrying over the obstacles there would be in practice. The cardinals he named to the commission were the most distinguished members of the Sacred College: Oliverio Caraffa, Giorgio Costa, Antonietto Pallavicini,

Giovanni di San Giorgio, Franscesco Piccolomini and Raffaele Riario. To this commission the Pope attached his own secretaries, the Bishops of Cosenza and Capaccio, with the idea of taking some part in their labors himself.

Many historians to the contrary, the labors of the commission were intense and prolonged. De Roo has discovered numerous copies of proposals and information gathered by it, preserved in the Vatican in two special volumes, one of three hundred and forty-six pages, the other of one hundred and thirty-two pages. It seems that as their investigation proceeded, the goals they envisaged grew larger; and that in the end a General Council was considered as absolutely necessary.

Cardinal Caraffa, one of the most active members of the Commission, proposed four papal bulls each embracing one question; but one finds in the documents cited projects already drawn up which indicate that they finally abandoned the idea of reform by papal action alone. But the Council was not called; and the justification for not calling it was furnished by the Pope's worst enemy Julius II when in 1511 he assembled the Council of the Lateran, with very much more modest objects, and declared: "The Council has been long postponed since the time of Pope Alexander, because of the calamities which then afflicted Italy and still afflict it."

In the moral order, Alexander's initiative does not lose importance simply because it did not bear immediate fruit. It has been said that the Pope could not bring about such a reform because of his own want of moral authority. But Alexander VI had so much authority right up to the time of his death, that the sovereigns of the age all sought his friendship and protection; again and again we find them

259

leaving treaties open for his signature. The higher clergy kept its veneration for him to the end.

This reform, in which he had taken the initiative, had fanatical partisans among such of the clergy as expected it to give birth to the golden age.[6] But in fact—and it is to this that Julius II alludes—the arrival in Italy of Louis XII, his conquest of Milan and Naples, the Turkish raids upon the coasts of Italy, the pacts of Ludovico il Moro and Frederick of Naples with the Sultan, the attitude of the barons and princes of the Papal territory, and finally the imperialism of Venice—all these combined to create a hopeless atmosphere for a Council with so vast a program. Apart from the practical consideration that while everybody talked of reform, most of the talk was not very seriously meant, those who know the history of the Council of Trent must see Alexander's justification, for they cannot but know the influence exercised upon this purely ecclesiastical act by temporal sovereigns and the dangers it caused the Church to run.

The excellence of Alexander's intentions is shown in the preface to the document, or rather documents, which were prepared. I publish it here integrally, as evidence of the ideas he held in the year 1497:

"Placed by divine providence as guardian of the Holy See, in order to accomplish the duties of our pastoral office by rooting up the evil which must be overcome and implanting the good which must be encouraged, we are consecrated with all our soul to the reform of morals. We observe with pain that the behaviour of Christians has gradually grown far removed from the perfect discipline of old, has broken with the salutary principles of the past and the decrees of holy councils and sovereign Pontiffs in restraint of sensuality and avarice, and has yielded place to such licence that it is impossible longer to tolerate it. The nature of mortals is inclined to evil, and their appetites are not always in harmony with reason, but, as the Apostle says, they bring the spirit into the captivity of sin and lead peoples beneath its yoke. Assuredly we have always wished that this licence should be curbed by new constitutions. In this sense we have often labored under Pius II, Paul II, Sixtus IV, Innocent VIII, our predecessors of happy memory, when we were in a lower place in the hierarchy, enjoying the honors of the cardinalate. At the beginning of our pontificate, likewise, we decided to consecrate our cares to this matter, giving it the first place in our labors; but involved as we were in other and greater difficulties through the arrival in Italy of our dear son in Jesus Christ Charles, the most Christian King of the French, with a very powerful army, we were prevented until this day from continuing in our enterprise. But now we have just entered upon the reform with our Roman Curia, which is as it were the knot of all nations professing Christianity, and which has the obligation to be a model of exemplary life. Wishing therefore to bring so holy a thing, so necessary and long desired a thing, to a good end, we have chosen within the College of our Venerable Brethren, the cardinals of the Holy Roman Church, the six most tried members, men who live especially in the fear of God, to wit Oliverio, Bishop of Sabina, and Giorgio, Bishop of Albano, Antonietto, titulary of St. Praxed, and John, titulary of Ss. Nereus and Achilles, Cardinal priest, as well as Francesco of S. Eustace, and

Raffaele of San Giorgio, Cardinal-deacons. They will aid us with their labor as also with their counsels and their prudence. After having considered all the constitutions of the past and carefully weighed the present situation, we have promulgated by our apostolic authority the constitutions and ordinances joined hereto to which we likewise accord the authority of a Constitution, ordering that they be observed inviolably. The other constitutions of our predecessors will remain in force. And following the steps of our Saviour, of whom we are the unworthy Vicar upon this earth on which He began to act and to teach, instructing us not only by example but also by the word, we submit ourselves to the Law, even though we have the supreme power of the sacred Canons and the right to make laws, and in spite of the fact that we have the most sublime dignity and the highest authority. Desiring to give example to others, we respect the reform for our own person and for all our officials; we are resolved to lead our life according to our dignity and our rank, an obligation we extend to all who inhabit our palace, to our servants, and all who are directly placed under our command, in particular those who live at this Court."

The practical regulations which follow upon this preamble are numerous and very diverse. It would be too long to reproduce them here. In the documents which have been discovered there are listed in the first place certain reforms which the reigning Pope has already put into practice, in spite of the contrary custom established in the past. It is ordered that indulgences are not to be sold; illegal exactions by officials of the treasury and the sale of lands or cities within the Patrimony of the Church are likewise forbidden. The number of cardinals must not exceed twenty-four and they must live a pure and holy life; their banquets should consist of a dish of pastry, one boiled meat and one roast meat, and fruit, and during these banquets there must be reading of scripture, nor must music be any longer allowed nor songs nor stage-shows. The cardinals must reside in Rome and their escort when they go about the City must not exceed twenty horsemen. They must be chosen from among theologians, and must belong proportionately to all countries. Only a small number was to be recruited from among princely and ducal families. The members of their suite must not have concubines, still less must those who hold benefices on pain of losing them.

The Pope himself must not go about in Rome accompanied by men-at-arms but only by his proper escort, and he must always wear the red cape; he cannot have living in his palace others than ecclesiastics, and must not transfer either his court or his residence outside Rome without the authorization of the Consistory. The cardinals and bishops must reform their respective churches. Each year the bishops must summon a diocesan synod, and the archbishops must summon a provincial council every three years. Convents must be better conducted. Every bishop, abbot, and parish priest must live in his proper residence, unless with papal permission. All simony is to be punished by excommunication. Bishops must be doctors of canon law. Education is necessary for the lower clergy as well as the higher. Every ecclesiastical nomination must be preceded by an examination of the candidate's morals. Benefices are not to be excessive. Priests of poor parishes are to be helped from the papal treasury. And so it goes on. There are certain additional regulations concerning

263

particular abuses, especially in Germany and England. It is finally declared that the Pope should summon a Council as soon as possible and draw up a constitution to prevent abuses in the Conclaves.

It is worth noting that there is no allusion throughout to the Pope's way of life, beyond the reference to the costume he must wear and the escort that is to accompany him in the city of Rome and the people he is to have living in the Vatican.[7]

The measures studied by this commission of cardinals under the direction of the Borgia Pope and the decisions arrived at present a striking analogy, if not sometimes an actual identity, with those which were suggested and approved by the Council of Trent more than fifty years later. The Pope who then resumed the enterprise was Alexander Farnese, "the Cardinal of the Skirt," according to the Roman jibe, Giulia's brother and Alexander's favorite disciple. He was still very young when these ideas were being worked out. When he was elected Pope, forty years after Alexander had raised him to the purple, he had no need to exhume those pages buried so deep in the Vatican archives. They returned of themselves to his mind and with a patience that overcame all difficulties, he assembled the famous Ecumenical Council which so many popes had desired. It was Alexander VI whose powerful foresight had prepared the work; his ideas, in spite of the spiritual agitation of his own moment, have survived the centuries. And the fact of survival is for ideas one certain measure of greatness.

264

CHAPTER XVII

Marriages of Cesar and Lucretia

Cesar Borgia emerged upon the great stage of the world in 1498, but it was not until 1499 that his activities seriously began. The only documents we still have bearing upon his early life treat of family relationships—like his inclusion in the grandeeship of his elder brother—and the ecclesiastical benefices with which the Popes so prodigally loaded him. A few laudatory words on his studies tell us that they were satisfactory.

It is not until 1498 that he is mentioned in connection with the death of the Duke of Gandia; while the fables concerning the assassination of Pedro Calderon, called Perotto, arose later still. Until this year, the dread Cesar Borgia is simply a young cardinal with no thought save pleasure. He is given to hunting, looks after his hounds, dresses like a temporal prince, is not much addicted to religious ceremonies. He was not quite twenty-three.

To expect of a younger son of a noble family any notable devotion to the ecclesiastical life would be to show complete ignorance of the period. And to condemn one who, lacking vocation, embraced that life—often enough before he was seven—is to show ignorance not only of that period but of all periods. Cesar was the third of three brothers—sons of the Pope or of Guillermo Raimundo Lanzol y Borgia, or of Arimanno, or of whom you please—

and in his family there were two cardinals, not counting the one now dead who had been pope. In such circumstances there could be no question about his career: he must be an ecclesiastic. For this meant riches instead of poverty, a respected and even illustrious situation instead of the obscure life of an unimportant soldier. Besides, when one is only six, it is the family which decides, not oneself. So one fine day, our child finds himself in clerical garb. To be an ecclesiastic at that time in no way implied the need of vocation—all the less if one were destined to a high place—for the Church had so many civil and even military functions that she could use all kinds of characters and dispositions. The great mass of writing about Cesar's lack of spiritual vocation simply proves a lack of historical sense in the writers. They have been misled by the fact that Cesar later invoked this as a reason for quitting the ecclesiastical life: he did so not on any psychological ground but merely as a ground canonically recognized.

Cesar has been slandered even more than Alexander VI. Yet in the course of his very brief historical career, few men have succeeded more in winning the esteem and affection not only of masses of people but of the few. His active life began, as I have said, in 1499. By 1504, it was over. In that space he conquered peoples who received him as a liberator and some of whom remained faithful to him even in his eclipse; the King of France, the most powerful ruler in the world, not only had an exceptional regard for him, but at times treated him with familiarity as an equal; friendly courts received him with joy; Venice offered him a place in its own nobility; his subordinates gave their life for him, even after his fall; Gonzalvo of Cordoba, the Great Captain, protected him against the persecution of Julius II, and did not cease to protect him until he received the definite order of his own King, Ferdinand; and many cardinals obeyed him at first and defended him later, in spite of the death of Alexander VI. He was the decisive factor in the election of Giuliano della Rovere, as he had been in that of Pius III a few days earlier.

Those who know the instability of human nature will realize all that is implied by this friendship of the powerful, the respect of men in high office, the fidelity of masses of people. It is clear that in face of this general esteem, which is a proven fact of history, we must not be blinded by the anonymous pamphlets, nor the slanderous rumors retailed in private letters, nor the interested statements of the ambassadors of enemies, nor the word of princes and courtiers overthrown by the iron hand of this man who seemed to have taken victory for his bride. It is a grave error, in an investigation made centuries after the event, to accept mean suspicions, whispers, all the creeping malevolence with which damaged interests expressed their spite, the abusive anecdotes in which mediocrity takes its revenge upon the object of its envy.

Indeed the tendency to make Cesar the author of so many imaginary crimes, and the obstinate determination to leave him no shred of moral character, shows how powerfully his personality affected all men's imaginations. On the one hand we have the *facts*, great numbers of them, closely linked, giving a picture of a man of high qualities, respected, loved, impressing men of great worth by his intelligence, giving repeated proofs of decision and courage. Against that, you have isolated innuendo, rumors passed from mouth to mouth, and the hired sarcasm of vanquished enemies. Sound sense can scarcely hesitate. If the history of great men is to be written not according to their achievements but according to the gossip that has

S

267

gathered around their name, then in all history no one will be left worthy of respect.

As early as 1497 it was being said that the Cardinal of Valencia meant to withdraw from the ecclesiastical state. Rumors began to multiply. The most serious of these rumors was that Cesar wanted to exchange with his brother Jofre: he would take Jofre's wife Sancia, while Jofre would take his cardinal's hat. Sanudo gives this as an *on dit* of Venice, and Ascanio Sforza as a rumor heard in Rome. In 1498, the rumor that Cesar meant to return to the lay state was growing stronger. But there is now no word about Sancia nor of the exchange between the brothers.

The Pope was opposed to Cesar's withdrawal from the ecclesiastical state. Early in his pontificate, he had refused Ferrante's proposal of a marriage between Cesar and his daughter, among other reasons because he did not approve of his returning to the lay state. But now that Giovanni was dead, and it was beginning to be clear that young Jofre would never amount to a great deal, Alexander VI, whose family ambitions were measureless, showed himself more favourable to Cesar's desires. It is very probable that he had earlier cherished the idea that Cesar would one day receive the tiara, succeeding him as he had succeeded his own uncle Calixtus III; and that now, seeing that the young man did not get on particularly well with his colleagues, he saw that this aspiration could not be realized. He may well have thought that he could secure him a greater future by making him prince of a vast territory than by letting him remain simply one cardinal among many. That this was his mind, we have no evidence; but at least it accords with his usual clearness of sight and his excessive nepotism.

There remained a question of form, for the act was exceptional and provoked strong religious scruples. Alexander VI was not the man to regard either consideration as unimportant. In a conversation he had on December 24, 1497, with Ascanio Sforza and the ambassadors of Milan and Naples, he spoke at length of the Cardinal of Valencia's desire to abandon the ecclesiastical state, adding that if this were to be, it must be with the least possible scandal. This last point Cesar undertook to handle, as also to meet all the Pope's scruples. He began by declaring that if he remained a cardinal, he would lose his soul, for he would commit acts contrary to his vows; and he urged the Consistory to ask the Pope in full session to accede to his desires.

Alexander VI was perfectly well aware of Cesar's maneuvers and the arguments he was using; and by the middle of the year, he was completely won over to his intentions. He saw that if Cesar was to leave the ecclesiastical state, there could be no better moment than the present when he was himself without powerful enemies. King Frederick of Naples, who had succeeded his nephew, needed the Pope's help against the threats of the Venetians with their claims upon the coast of the Adriatic, and against the constant danger from France, whose King, Louis XII, was the former Duke of Orleans. Venice and Florence wanted his friendship. Ludovico il Moro seemed well disposed. Cesar was giving up one promising career, but he should have little trouble in entering upon another. At that period the best bond of political interests was marriage, and the Pope began to look into that side of the question. Thus while planning to lift the hat from Cesar's head, he was planning also to assure him high worldly office and to marry him to a woman of high birth.

In the private Consistory of August 17, 1498, the Pope

269

not being present, Cesar declared that he had never had any taste for the ecclesiastical life, and that if he had led that life and attained so high a rank in it, it was by order and grace of the Pope; and that, in spite of the long passage of time, his inclination toward the lay state persisted. Therefore he begged his colleagues to ask the Pope to grant him as an extraordinary concession that he be allowed to return to the world and marry a wife. He offered, of course, to give up all the benefices and prerogatives the Church had conferred upon him. The cardinals unanimously agreed to defer the matter to the Pope's will.

But Alexander VI had already been informed of the King of Spain's strong opposition to the granting of this dispensation. The King, who obviously knew of the project of marriage, did not wish the elective monarchy of the Church to be contracting family alliances which might be opposed to his own interests. He had his own views upon Naples; and of course, any agreement between the Holy See and France was against the interests of Spain. With his usual diplomacy, Alexander VI took his time, doing his best to convince the opposing party but always prepared, if the worst came to the worst, to follow his own will.

In the later months of 1498, Cesar began to give up his benefices one by one and the Pope thought to win the King of Spain's good graces by offering to transfer them to Spaniards.

Upon Cesar's renunciation, of which the exact date is unknown to us, there is an apparent contradiction among the documents. While the King of France conferred a French title upon him in August 1498, it was only at the Consistory of November 26 following that he ceased to be Bishop of Valencia. The contradiction may arise from the fact that the Pope postponed the acceptance of the re-

nunciation until the grant of new civil favors and prerogatives had been arranged: unless the difference merely
arises from purely formal details of registration. What is
certain is that when Cesar made his first statement to the
Consistory, the King of France had already undertaken to
have him in his service and, by a document signed at
Etampes, had made him Count of Valence and Diois in
the Drôme, territories of the Church but claimed by
France. Further, the King had promised him in marriage
Charlotte, daughter of King Frederick of Naples, or one of
his own relations of the blood royal. On October 1—still
before his renunciation had been accepted by the Consistory—Cesar set out for France with a magnificent escort,
the expenses of which Louis XII had promised to pay.

Meanwhile, in this same year 1498, the Pope was considering the marriage of Lucretia. From the number of
suitors, it would seem that a marriage with her offered considerable advantage. One of them was the Duke of Gravina,
of the Orsini family. Then a marriage was very nearly
arranged with the Prince of Salerno, Roberto de Sanseverino. But Ludovico Moro protested against this marriage,
saying that it was against the interests of the Sforzas and
would certainly bring about the ruin of Italy. Such powerful opposition to what looked like the purely private acts
of the Pope's relations proved once more the idea that was
held of the authority of the Holy See. If the Pope acted
like a temporal sovereign in favor of his own family, the
princes of the period, by the very restrictions they sought
to impose upon him in the matter, implied that they considered this state of things entirely legitimate.

It was on other grounds than Ludovico's opposition that
the marriage with Roberto de Sanseverino fell through.

He had revolted against King Frederick, who proceeded to invade his domains and capture his principal strongholds, including Salerno itself. Sanseverino was forced to flee. But as Lucretia was still in the matrimonial market, King Frederick speedily proceeded to arrangements of his own. He replaced the prince of Salerno, in both the principality and the love of Lucretia, by the natural son of his dead brother King Alfonso II. This son was likewise called Alfonso. The new proposal was immediately accepted, all the more heartily as this Alfonso of Aragon was a notable person physically and morally, and had vast domains. These included not only those of Salerno which had just fallen into his lap, but also those he had already held, like the principality of Bisceglia and Corato, then called Quarata. He had been a pupil of the famous Brandolino Lippo and when he arrived in Rome his appearance and manner created an enormous impression. Besides all this, he was already well known to the Borgias, because his sister was Sancia, Jofre's wife.

It is not true, though it has been suggested, that these marriages were brought about solely because of the dowry furnished by the Pope; for Alexander, a past-master at contracts and skilled in the handling of money, invariably obtained better conditions than he gave. In Lucretia's case he gave a dowry of forty thousand ducats, but the King had to assure to his relative fiefs which brought him eight thousand ducats a year and others which would in the future produce a further four thousand. Certainly in all these contracts there was a reciprocity of interests, but as certainly the greatest consideration was the value put upon the connection with Borgia himself.

Lucretia's marriage was celebrated on June 21, 1498, in roughly the same forms as her first marriage with Giovanni

Sforza. At this time there is no malicious insinuation, as in the case of her third marriage still to come: because at the time the Orsini and the Colonna were not on bad terms with the Pope, while at Naples the writers in the service of the House of Aragon had nothing to write, since it was one of their own lords who was being married. Historians have described this ceremony as quiet, that is to say not scandalous. There was the same family banquet as at the previous wedding, the same dance, the same comedy, plus a masquerade. The Pope was in high spirits. Cattaneo's remark is worth noting, that the wife seemed to be very much in love with her husband. She was eighteen, he seventeen.

They continued to live in Rome. The Pope showed them great affection. He appointed Lucretia as governor of Spoleto and Foligno, and later of Nepi. But a year later his policy had swung away from Naples. International complications had obliged him to take a new line, and the Aragons—Alfonso and Sancia—with their spouses Lucretia and Jofre, no longer found the climate of Rome entirely agreeable. It is to be noted that while Alexander VI was always ready to use his political influence for the advantage of his family, he never thus used the higher interests of the Church and his States.

Meanwhile, Cesar, whom we left galloping towards France, had arrived there and been received with the highest honors. Cardinal Giuliano della Rovere wrote to the Pope, with whom he was for the moment on good terms, that Cesar had won the liking of everybody by his fine qualities. Louis XII immediately raised the County of Valence to the rank of a Duchy. Thus it came about by a simple coincidence of names that the Cardinal of Valencia in Spain became the Duke of Valence in France, commonly called Le Valentinois. The King further took this "nephew of the Pope" as *condottiere* of his Kingdom, decorated him with the order of St. Michael, and declared him French. So there was Cesar obliged "to act and think" as if he had been born in France.

Apart from such minor envies as were bound to be aroused by the affection the King lavished upon him, Cesar's relations with the French court remained excellent, for he was a courtly and agreeable person. While he remained in France, he gave himself to all athletic exercises, enjoyed the pleasures that were going, was agreeable to everybody, and had the great good-sense to lend the King money. But he suffered one serious check in the matter of his marriage. Charlotte of Naples refused to marry him, in spite of the French King's insistence. For a stronger influence still, that of her father, was brought to bear. It has been said that she felt a repugnance for the ex-cardinal and did not want to be known as "the cardinal's wife." But when we remember the success of that sort of young prelate in the field of gallantry, the theory will not stand. And Cesar was one of the finest looking men of his age. Charlotte's attitude came solely from obedience to her father, who wrote to the King of Spain that he would lose his crown, his daughter, and his life itself, rather than consent to the marriage. Did this mean contempt for the Borgias, because he regarded them as adventurers, or personal hatred for Cesar? It meant neither. While he was still a prince, this Frederick had been involved in his father's proposal to marry his daughter to Cesar, a proposal that the Pope had rejected. Further, the King of Spain had married his own cousin to Cesar's brother. The bastard branch of Aragon would scarcely regard as a parvenu a man who was related to two popes and connected by close family relationship with the legitimate branch of their own house.

Frederick's opposition was purely political—and provisional. The Kingdom of Naples was a fief of the Church, and was also claimed by the King of France, who alleged that he had the better right to the throne. Cesar, a protégé both of the Pope and the King, might well be the object of an agreement between the Vatican and France: they might agree to give Naples to Cesar and thus settle three problems in one act. Biagio Buonaccorsi, Machiavelli's assistant, gives in the *Journal* he wrote with such good sense and simplicity the true reason for Frederick's attitude. That sovereign was prepared to grant the hand of Charlotte of Aragon to the Duke of Valence, if the King of France and the Pope would conjointly guarantee him the peaceful possession of the Kingdom of Naples. The condition was refused, and the matrimonial negotiations were definitively broken off.[1]

In accordance with the promise Louis XII had made, Cesar might choose a wife from among the King's relations. So he chose another Charlotte, Charlotte d'Albret, sister of the King of Navarre. They were married on May 10, 1499. Cesar remained only a little time with his wife, but his relations with her were always excellent. The daughter, Louise, who was born of this union and whom Cesar never knew, was brought up with respect for her father's name, and her descendants sought neither to hide her origin nor to apologize for it. When Cesar died, in a daring military enterprise, under the orders of her brother the King of Navarre, Charlotte wore the strictest mourning; and her short life—for she died at thirty-six—was, in spite of her renowned beauty, by universal opinion completely chaste in the gayest and most corrupt surroundings imaginable.

Before the celebration of the marriage Louis XII had named a special embassy which included Cesar Borgia and was led by Cardinal della Rovere. Its purpose was to make an act of obedience to the Pope and a declaration that the King of France recognized him as the "true ruler of the Universal Church, the true Vicar of Christ on earth, to whom is owed sincere and complete filial submission."[2]

There is nothing strange in this combination in one embassy of Cardinal Giuliano and Cesar. As I have said, Alexander VI and the future Julius II were for the moment reconciled. In 1497, the two old friends, so intimate under Sixtus IV, had settled their differences. Alexander might easily have taken vengeance upon his terrible and implacable adversary of a few years earlier, now that the adversary no longer had the support of the King of France or the King of Naples. But in spite of his sinister reputation as a poisoner of cardinals, he always showed complete readiness to forgive the cardinals who had offended him most—especially Giuliano della Rovere, Ascanio Sforza, and Pérault. Giuliano had been in Rome in 1497 and had then gone back to France. Now, in the late July of 1499, he and Cesar took the road to Italy, but without haste. Cesar stayed more than a month in Lyons and did not reach Rome until November. He had spent a little more than a year in France: and he returned to Italy a Duke, married to a King's daughter, and chosen friend of the most powerful monarch of the day.

CHAPTER XVIII

The Pope and Louis XII

THE protection granted to Cesar Borgia by the King of France was the work of Alexander VI, who had seen all and arranged all. The preparation had been legal and psychological, for without the union of the two there is no enduring success. The Pope had specified what was to be given to Cesar: a dukedom, lands, an income, a wife, and even the costs of his very luxurious journey. These costs were enormous and Louis XII later protested against them, not unreasonably. As to the psychological preparation, the Pope saw to it that the arrival of his beloved nephew in France should more or less coincide with three things agreeable to the King—the announcement that the cardinal's hat had been conferred upon Georges d'Amboise; the notification that the marriage contracted by the King when he was Duke of Orleans with Jeanne de Valois had been declared null; and the promise of the necessary canonical authorization for the King's marriage with Anne of Brittany, the widow of Charles VIII.

These actions have been strongly criticized on the ground that the Pope was using not only his political but also his spiritual authority in the interests of his family. But these ecclesiastical decisions had been arrived at in all justice and according to the rules of the church; and if he used them to simplify things for Cesar, he did not use them

277

only for that. The nomination of Georges d'Amboise as Cardinal de Rohan was a political necessity. He was already a bishop and at that moment his influence was strong with the powerful French King. He was twice highly considered for the papacy—at the only two Conclaves at which he was present, for death overtook him during the pontificate of Julius II. As for the nullity of the royal marriage, it was not pronounced by the Pope, for he had appointed a special commission to investigate the question and had instructed it that it must not grant the decree of nullity unless the facts alleged were certain. The canonical process is to be found set out fully in the royal archives.[1] Seldom has any legal process been surrounded with stronger guarantees. Here is an outline of what happened.

Upon receipt of the King's petition, sent by special ambassador, the Pope named the Bishop of Albi and the Bishop of Ceuta to conduct the process and arrive at a joint decision. This was on July 30, 1498. Later, fearing that the commission might not have the necessary authority, since a King was in question, he added the Cardinal of Luxembourg.

The process began at Tours on August 30. The King, by his procurator Antonio Scanno, alleged that Louis XI had forced him under pain of death, when he was only Duke of Orleans, to marry Jeanne de Valois; that there had been no ecclesiastical dispensation either then or since for the canonical impediments arising from the consanguinity of the parties and from the fact that the wife's father was the husband's godfather; and finally that Jeanne was unable to consummate the marriage. The King added that he had fled from his own house in order to escape this compulsion but that he had been cast into prison for three years because of his disobedience. The Queen appeared in person before the tribunal but offered only a feeble resistance. Because of the importance of the case, the judges took as assessors another cardinal and five bishops, as well as the Presidents of the Commission of Enquiry of the Parliament of Paris, and numerous doctors of theology and law. The sentence was promulgated on December 18. The decision was unanimous for nullity. It was neither the first time nor the last time that the Church has declared a marriage null twenty-five years after its celebration. In canon law, an original defect in the contract of marriage is not legitimated by the passage of time.

With great speed Alexander granted the dispensation required by the King for his new marriage with the widow of Charles VIII. A dispensation was necessary because there was consanguinity in the fifth degree. The reason alleged for the dispensation, a sound and normal reason, was the interest of the State. It was a question of preserving for France great provinces which the new queen had brought as a dowry to her previous husband.

In the light of these facts, it seems that there is no ground for the accusations brought against this process from Machiavelli to our own day. Alexander acted with the greatest respect for forms, as if he had foreseen that later generations would be scrutinizing his conduct with special malevolence. It is untrue that Cesar in person brought the bull authorizing Louis' marriage with Anne of Brittany; and ludicrously untrue that Bishop Fernando of Almeida was assassinated by Cesar's orders for having revealed what the bull contained before the King had granted the favors he desired. The bull was sent direct to Georges d'Amboise, and Bishop Fernando did not die until two years later.[2] If Cesar had known the accusations that would be brought against him by Machiavelli during the conversations he later had with him in the Romagna, he might have said, in parody of a famous verse: "The dead men I have killed seem in very good health."[3]

The Pope had pushed Cesar forward in his lay career with as much speed and success as in the ecclesiastical; but he had not for that reason made any concessions in the canonical sphere. We shall see later that he did not subordinate the Church's interests in the political sphere either to the profit of his own family. On the contrary, at the very moment when he was receiving from Louis XII the most remarkable evidences of friendship and devotion, he was trying to take his mind off Italy.

In history as in life there are men who take the strong line, both in the ideas they express and the acts they perform. What they say and what they do is better admired from a distance. They are like over-dramatic actors who must not be seen too close. But there are other men, and Alexander is one of them, whose excellence increases as we see the detail of their work, and we realize gradually that their virtue consists in the precision of their ideas, in the fundamental consistency of their aims, in their power of adaptability, in a continuing skill which attains its successes without disorder and without noise. The Pope, interested as he might be in the favors the King of France was lavishing upon Cesar, never forgot how he had been betrayed by everybody at the time of Charles VIII's invasion; and now that he again found himself in the face of French ambition, he was working once more in the interests of Italy and the Holy See. It was only when necessity forced him to compromise with invasion because he could not withstand it, that he tried by skillful maneuvering to set up some sort of balance among foreign States, which would guarantee such liberty as was still left to the States of Italy. The policy unswervingly followed by him will appear more clearly still in the conversations of his last years with the representatives of Venice at a moment when that city was attacked upon all sides, politically and commercially, on land and on sea, and by its own errors seemed determined to be the principal architect of its own destruction.

The general opinion seems to be that for Cesar's sake Alexander VI went over to the French interest. We shall see in the event that this judgement upon the Pope's policy taken as a whole is as false as the inventions about his morals. Once anointed at Rheims, Louis XII added to his title of King of France, the titles of King of Naples and Duke of Milan. Alexander knew well enough what the purpose of the coronation was; and in sending an Embassy Extraordinary to congratulate the new sovereign, he instructed it to treat the Italian question in its fullness if the King should bring the matter up and persuade him that it would be more useful and honorable for him to go to war against the Turks than to trouble the peace of the neighboring peninsula.

The ambassadors, who were the Pope's direct and intimate collaborators, were to treat of three questions separately. First, with regard to the Kingdom of Naples, they must repeat the answer given by the Pope in the time of Charles VIII, namely that if the King of France claimed to have better rights than the Aragon dynasty, a tribunal of the Holy See would examine the question, and the Pope would promulgate its judgement in all impartiality.

In regard to the Duchy of Milan they must remind His Majesty that the Sforzas had ruled there for fifty years and his ancestors had had the goodness not to attack them, and that to do so now would be to waste the forces of Christianity in a sterile conflict. The Pope undertook to obtain from Ludovico proofs of respect and consideration for the King of France.

Finally, upon the matter of Pisa, the Pope's advice was to return it to Florence, and so safeguard the peace of Italy, since the city had been a cause of endless discords between the Republics of Venice and Florence and the Duchy of Milan.

This project of a *pax italica* which the Pope had not been able to gain from the powers of Italy itself, he now sought to gain from the good will of the King of France. But the King, although he seemed to listen to the Pope's advice and went so far as to give a promise about Naples —which he obviously thought too difficult to conquer— cherished great ambitions in his heart, and was preparing for the conquest of Milan, only waiting for the moment when international circumstances might make it possible.[4]

But while the Pope worked to keep Italy at peace and free from foreign domination, the Venetians were intriguing in the opposite sense, and sent envoys to invite invasion. They were at unadmitted war with Ludovico Moro, which might become open war from one moment to the next. Venice, under pretext of presenting its felicitations to the new King, sent him an embassy to propose and conclude an alliance with him.

The articles of the treaty were discussed in detail over a considerable time. The King wished to send them to the Pope, that he might know them in advance and approve of them; but when the Venetians had wind of this prospect, they instructed their ambassadors to prevent it at all costs for they knew the mind of Alexander about the maintenance of the *status quo*.[5]

Thus it was that unknown to the Pope the alliance was

282

agreed upon. It was signed on April 15, 1499. Consider the exceptional seriousness of its articles: (a) a defensive alliance against any other power except the Pope, who might join this alliance if he so desired; (b) an offensive alliance against the Duke of Milan, in order that the King of France might recover the Duchy, which rightly belonged to him as heir of the Visconti, expelled half a century earlier by the Sforza family; (c) cession of certain territories and rivers by France to Venice, once France has occupied Ludovico Moro's territory—in other words the cession to Venice of a part of the Duchy; (d) offensive alliance of the two countries in the event of an attack upon France by Maximilian; (e) right of France not to participate in the war if the Turk should attack the Venetians before the commencement of operations against Ludovico.

This treaty was communicated to Rome by Cardinal Giuliano della Rovere after it had been agreed upon but before it was made public. The Papal court was deeply stirred by the news. Alexander showed himself enraged[6] against the Republic of Venice and decided to send a special mission, entrusted to Cardinal Giovanni Borgia, to visit the cities of Italy and prepare the constitution of a new League against a second French invasion.[7]

Buonaccorsi, who was in the second Chancellery of Florence, which dealt with foreign affairs, relates that on June 12, the Pope's Legate had proposed this alliance and the city had refused the offer and decided to remain faithful to the King of France.[8] Cardinal Giovanni Borgia carried out his mission, but without success. It is to be noted that this activity on Alexander's part against the French aims took place at the same time as the favors shown to Cesar by Louis, Cesar's royal marriage, and the oath he took to serve France. Two conclusions seem to emerge

283

T

from this: one, that the interests of the Church and Italy took first place in the mind and heart of Alexander; the other, that Cesar had not the power over the Pope with which he has been credited.

But Ludovico Sforza's behaviour was more than the Pope's good will could tolerate. As soon as he learned of the Franco-Venetian alliance, the Duke betook himself to the Turks, inciting them to attack the Venetians.[9] For Alexander, and indeed for any Pope, alliance or friendship with the Grand Turk was not merely a political crime, it was a mortal sin. Ludovico's action forced the Pope to consider the question not now from the political but from the religious angle—although it was likewise true that even politically considered, the Turks were already effectively threatening the sea coasts adjacent to Italy, and that their occupation of any part whatever of the peninsula would evidently involve greater perils than an invasion by the French.

In these conditions, Alexander had to replace his policy of keeping foreign powers out of Italy by a new policy which consisted of organizing a stronger State for the Church, since henceforth countries of superior military strength were to be upon her borders, and seeking to ensure that in relation to Italy the great powers of Europe should cancel each other out.

Most authors have asserted that the Pope entered the Franco-Venetian League at the very beginning; some think it was only later; but in both cases they hold that the price of his adhesion to the treaty, which facilitated the entry of Louis XII into Italy, was the aid given by the King to Cesar in his conquest of the Romagna. But it is certain that the Pope never did enter this alliance; and that the help given to the Church and Cesar by the King of France was due partly to his desire to keep the friendship of the Holy See, partly to the money the King had borrowed from Cesar, and finally to the skill and power of persuasion shown by Cesar himself.

Louis XII, having concluded another treaty with Duke Philibert of Savoy, began sending men and munitions to Trivulce, who was maintaining a ceaseless pressure upon the frontiers of the Duchy of Milan. Then he sent organized forces under the orders of the Count de Ligny and M. d'Aubigny. He himself moved south with his court, and at Lyons made preparations to enter Italy. Meanwhile the armies of Venice entered the Duchy on the other side.

Ludovico, seeing that his forces could not resist the attack of his enemies, put his children and his wealth in a safe place. In fact he sent them to Germany, to his brother Cardinal Ascanio. Then he took counsel with the representatives of the people in the hope that the resistance of the towns would give him time to receive help from Maximilian and the King of Naples and to recruit Swiss and other mercenaries. Skilful as ever, he spoke to the people's deputies of his own errors, which yet had been forced upon him; of the overwhelming taxes which had no other ground than the necessities of the time; and of his decision to be henceforth a good ruler, exercising impartial justice, and ruling his subjects mildly. He recalled all that his ancestors and himself had done for Milan, and he assured them that the French would wage universal destruction in the Duchy and would treat all its people harshly as is the common way of conquerors. He ended with an exhortation to resistance, for, said he, the French are impetuous in attack but lack perseverance. The deputies, after much consultation among themselves, answered that the people had decided to open the gates of their towns to the French.

Ludovico redoubled his urging, whereupon they grew bolder and reminded him that he had been the first to lose faith in victory since he had sent his family and his wealth out of the Duchy. Abandoned by the people, with an army inadequate to circumstances so difficult, attacked at both ends of his territory, disaster was inevitable. He left Milan.

Louis XII entered the city on October 6, 1499, with great ceremony, accompanied by the cardinals Georges d'Amboise, Giuliano della Rovere, and Giovanni Borgia, by the Dukes of Savoy and Ferrara, Cesar Borgia, the Venetian ambassadors, the Marquis of Montferrat, and the Marquis of Mantua. The populace applauded enthusiastically, delighted at the ceremony which provided at once a spectacle for their gaze and a stimulant for their nerves. Cesar's retinue was the most admired, according to Baldassare de Castiglione, who was present.

Louis XII did not remain long in Milan. Cleverer than Charles VIII, he did not mean to go too far from his base, which was France. But at Milan, he made preparation for the conquest of Naples; and he was persuaded by Cesar to help him with sufficient forces for his operations in the Romagna. But once the King had gone, Ludovico reappeared at the gates of his city and with the help of the populace, who had been maltreated by Trivulce and the French, he won back his duchy as quickly as he had lost it. But the reconquest was brief. He who had never kept his word at last fell victim to treachery. At Novara, the Swiss whom he had in his pay came to an understanding with their fellow citizens of the French side, and decided to desert him. The Duke, with a thousand promises, begged them to be faithful to their pact and offered them all he had; but he could obtain no more than permission to mingle with the soldiery and escape in disguise. In spite of this he was denounced, made prisoner, and sent to France, where he ended his days at the Château de Loches, allowed reasonable liberty and treated with a good deal of respect. The French have always shown these marks of generosity to their vanquished foes.

Far from remaining inactive, the Pope profited by this favorable moment, to push on with his political reforms. He equipped his armies, confiscated the property of the Caetani—in spite of their close kinship with the Farnese, that is with Cardinal Alexander and Giulia—and imprisoned the protonotary Giacomo, on a charge of lèse-majesté, in the castle of Saint Angelo where he died shortly after, in July, 1500.[10] His reason for treating the Caetani so harshly was the discovery that they had prepared to support King Frederick of Naples, who on the model of Ludovico, had made an alliance with the Sultan Bajazet and actually offered him a harbor in the peninsula. But the charge of lèse-majesté was more to the mind of the Pope at that moment, when, free from the hostility of foreign kings, able to reckon upon their good will and the help of France, he was making ready finally to reduce the prince-vicars who were the shame of Italy and the ruin of the Roman State.

CHAPTER XIX

Assassination of Alfonso of Aragon

THE ancient custom established by Boniface VIII of celebrating every hundred years a year of jubilee, whereby sinners might cleanse their souls by pilgrimage to Rome, obliged Alexander to announce the year 1500 as such a year. The initial period of a century had been progressively reduced until Paul II finally fixed twenty-five years as the necessary interval between one jubilee and the next. A journey to Rome at that time was a fairly dangerous adventure. The Church's Vicars, governors of the cities and strongholds along the way, either turned brigand themselves or were in league with brigands. Bands of Corsicans and men from the other islands landed upon the Adriatic coasts of the peninsula and levied large tribute upon the goods of those believers who came for the profit of their souls to the Eternal City.

To compensate for all these obstacles and perils, the Pope on the advice of theologians added a plenary indulgence for the souls in purgatory to be gained by pilgrims who interceded for them.

But Alexander was of too practical a mind not to bother also about the mortal life of the pilgrims. Towards the end of 1498, he spoke in the Consistory of steps to be taken to facilitate their journeys and to see to the security of the ways of communication. To this end he proposed an organization similar to the Spanish Holy Brotherhood, consisting of a public body made up of one member for each hundred houses, with the power to execute summary justice. But this initiative, exceptional at the time, was very much not to the taste of the Vicars, who refused to cooperate. The small Italian lords, living like the richest princes, with expenses mounting beyond their resources as Machiavelli tells us, simply had to rely upon continual depredations to eke out their incomes. Therefore, this popular police force remained no more than a plan, a mere wish on the part of Alexander. But the Pope could not look on with indifference at the crimes thus committed and in February 1500 he published a bull fulminating against all this brigandage: "We order [under pain of excommunication] all [Vicars] that if a pilgrim is robbed, the lord of the territory on which the crime is committed must restore the stolen goods."

But neither the grave risks nor the horrible inconvenience of the voyage prevented the faithful from pouring into Rome from the remotest parts of Europe. Veritable waves of humanity broke ceaselessly at the feet of the Pontiff. Bruchard tells us that on Easter Sunday, the Pope blessed as many as two hundred thousand pilgrims on the dusty ground surrounding St. Peter's. All the pomp and solemnity of which Rome is past master was displayed for the delight of the faithful. Gold-clad cardinals moved through the streets and presided over the religious ceremonies in the principal churches. The Pope's soldiers, on horses magnificently caparisoned in velvet, rode at the head of processions of rejoicing pilgrims. As in all monarchies the near relations of the Sovereign had the charge of directing the cortèges, in sun or rain. Religious fervor was united with the splendor of power, in the image of the

289

supernatural power of the Being who was the center of men's adoration. Acts of high importance require a noble and even a magnificent setting, solemn splendor predisposes the mind for wonder, which is the gateway of obedience. The jubilee would not have been a Catholic act if it had not been accompanied by that display of power and grandeur demanded by the God of Sinai.

Naturally certain minds, the sort that have no personal need of external aid to strengthen their hold upon eternal truths, disliked such an emphasis of splendor, and they returned from Rome to their convents and hamlets in a state of agitation and uncertainty; but the great mass of the faithful were convinced, satisfied that they had been present at spectacles which shadowed forth the world to come and the happiness of that eternity which is to be the reward for present virtue and present suffering.

The Pope had to postpone the closing date of the jubilee, and extend its privileges to other cities and states which solicited them with the liveliest insistence. This favor was granted to Italy, Hungary, Germany, Sweden, Norway, France and other countries. By successive bulls, Alexander VI, then at the height of glory and universal veneration, settled not only the nature of the privileges but also the means of obtaining them and what was to be done with the money received. It was from this question of the money that the only difficulties of the jubilee arose. The Pope was accused of having handed over the sums received to Cesar and Lucretia; but in reality the greater part was set aside for the war against the Turks, and allotted in certain cases to princes and states fighting against them like Venice, Hungary Poland, and Portugal. A certain part of it was used in building churches and making roads. In Germany, where there was growing a robust spirit that was rather local than national, the princes showed lively opposition to the sending to Rome of the sums collected in their states. Here indeed we have the foreshadowing signs of the Reformation, which came upon Germany only twenty years or so later. The Pope, informed of the position, consented to the jubilee funds remaining in Germany, and ordered that they be paid over to the Emperor on condition that he engage himself to take part in the Crusade against the Turks. Maximilian agreed to this undertaking and received the money, but he speedily forgot the Crusade and did not restore the money.

For men of that moment, the year 1500 was the year of jubilee. For history its importance is very different. For history, it means the beginning of the conquest of the Romagna, the death of the Duke of Bisceglia, and the division of the Kingdom of Naples between Spain and France. The importance of events varies with the centuries, for history is an expression of the relation between the moment when the events took place, and the moment when the writer is relating them. For us this jubilee is simply one in the long series of jubilees that follow one another down the centuries; and it is of no great importance to us that Rome was then demanding national funds in the name of religion and the various nations were refusing to pay them. These were grave questions at that moment because they had their repercussions upon the fate of whole peoples. But what remains to this day colorful is Cesar's rapid conquest; what preserves the living accent of tragedy is the death of Lucretia's second husband; what set in motion consequences we are still feeling was the thrust of Spain into the mainland of Italy. Without these three events the year 1500 would not stand out notably in the story of the Borgia Pope.

291

On November 7 of the previous year, the King, returning to France, had put at Cesar's disposition four hundred
men-at-arms under Antoine de Bessey and three hundred
under Yves d'Alègre. Cesar sent these troops into the
Romagna, and himself hastened to Rome to put himself
at the head of the army which the Pope had prepared for
him. His speed was extraordinary. On November 13 he
entered Rome, and on November 21 he marched out with
a force of eight thousand men commanded by Orsini, Giovanni Battista del Conti, Vitellozzo Vitelli and Baglione.[1]
The Pope had sent on spiritual weapons in advance of
these temporal weapons; for in the month of October he
had issued a declaration stripping of all their rights the
Vicars—Catherine Sforza, who held Imola and Forli in
the name of her eldest son Octaviano, Malatesta of Rimini, Varano of Camerino, Manfredi of Faenza, Guidobaldo de Montefeltro, that Duke of Urbino who had let
himself be beaten before Bracciano, and Lucretia's first
husband Giovanni Sforza. The deprivation of their rights
was judicially pronounced by a pontifical tribunal. Alexander, formed by half a century in the Roman Curia, could
not act save with the most rigorous formalism. He put all
questions *ad punctum juris.*

The military campaign undertaken by Cesar was, to
the mind of the populace in the Papal States, a war of
liberation not of conquest. Like all absolute monarchs in
their battles with their great feudal lords, Alexander was
bound to the people by a community of interest. The
Vicars had no mind to respect sovereigns who were always
being changed, and indeed were elected by conclaves subjected to their own influence; and for their people they
were hateful tyrants, who regarded the fortune and honor
and peace of their subjects as things of which they might

dispose as they pleased. Few peoples have ever had worse governments than those of the Romagna and other provinces of central Italy. These petty rulers reached their place neither from the clash of battle nor from the love of their peoples nor from a long tradition—all three things which serve as a kind of filter and do to some degree purify even the most perverse—but from the success of some piece of domestic treachery or the capricious nepotism of some Pope. Their thirst for money and power rejected every moral and legal bond. They could not sleep quiet in their beds, because others were always avidly on the watch to steal from them the power and wealth they had themselves stolen; the small degree of moral equilibrium that remained to them they lost in the daily expectation of attack and under the pressure of threats which never relaxed.

The fact that the Pope had declared these tyrants deprived of all their rights gave back hope to their peoples, and inspired them morally so that all were waiting with impatience for the opportune moment to rise in open revolt.

The pontifical forces were directed first against Catherine Sforza, with whose name the pages of the history of that period are filled. She was a strong woman, warlike and cruel, yet profoundly feminine. She was so subtle that she succeeded in deceiving Machiavelli, so persuasive that she managed to get round Alexander VI, who in restoring her to liberty recommended her to the good graces of Florence; at once so forceful and so likeable that she obliged Cesar to treat her with all consideration when he had made her prisoner. She was a virago, fighting with a courage that would not admit defeat; she had had three husbands, many lovers, and children innumerable. The bloody repressions she carried out after the assassination of the princes Riario and Feo her husbands, remain a model of blind ferocity even for that ferocious day.

Countess Catherine, as she was called, when she found herself attacked by the Papal forces, left Imola in charge of Dionigio Naldi, her lover of the moment, and shut herself up in Forli to defend it in person. But Imola, in an irresistible popular movement, opened its gates to Cesar and after a few bloody clashes Forli likewise surrendered —but not the fortress, near the town, to which Catherine had retired. It had to be taken by storm. All the defenders were slain, and the Countess surrendered to a French captain of the troops of Burgundy. Cesar rewarded the Captain and took charge of Catherine. In the days that followed there was endless discussion—inevitable in any army composed of allies—as to who had made her prisoner. Finally Cesar took her off to Rome. There, placed at the disposal of the Pope, she was imprisoned in the Belvedere; she tried to escape and was moved to the Castle of Saint Angelo. Later, probably urged by the King of France, Alexander set her at liberty. On July 13, 1501, he commended her to Florence where she wished to reside, observing in his letter that he had treated her with kindness and that he was restoring her to freedom because such was his custom, in the spirit of the pastoral office he held. It is probable that this kindly conduct was inspired also by the remembrance of Sixtus IV, for Catherine had had among her husbands a nephew of that Pope, and Alexander always regarded Sixtus with gratitude and affection. He later gave another proof of benevolence by granting to the children of Girolamo Riario and Catherine a pension of two thousand five hundred florins a year.[2]

That Cesar returned to Rome after the capture of Florence was due neither to his desire to receive triumphal honors nor to the necessity of accompanying a prisoner as important as the Countess, but to his fear of the consequences of the recapture of his Duchy by Ludovico Sforza. He was particularly concerned as to what might happen if Maximilian also made up his mind to invade Italy. Further, the French troops who had been put under his orders had been called off to Lombardy to fight against Ludovico. The Pope, who had no mind to be caught up in a difficult enterprise at so unsure a moment, ordered Cesar to remain in Rome. But he dedicated the interval to the agreeable task of promoting Cesar and paying him magnificent honor. On March 19, of that year 1500, he named him Vicar of Imola and Forli, and on March 29 Gonfalonier of the Church. Nor was even that enough. In the same year he conferred upon him the order of the Golden Rose. Cesar spent these few months organizing a new army under the directions of the Pope, who on his part was gathering the necessary funds for a renewal of the war against the Vicars the moment the international sky cleared.

But a new blow was to strike Alexander at this hour of intense activity. Alfonso of Aragon and Lucretia had just settled down in Rome, close to the Vatican, on the further side of the Piazza of St. Peter. The young couple, to whom a son had been born, led the life normal to princes at that day. The husband, under the sounding name of Duke of Bisceglia, appeared in all processions and official ceremonies, flattered and admired and living in perfect harmony with the Holy Father and the rest of the Borgia family. By general opinion, Lucretia adored him. On July 15, 1500, as he left the Vatican to return to his house early in the evening, he was suddenly set upon by a large group of bravos, disguised as beggars. He was seriously wounded. His assailants fled up the steps of St. Peter's, their flight protected by a group of horsemen—some forty it is said. They escaped from the city by the Porta Pertusa.[3] His attendants raised the wounded man and carried him back into the Vatican.

As always in such circumstances, the first thought was to save the victim, in spite of the desperateness of his state, by summoning the most eminent physicians. And measures were taken against the renewal of the attack—for the first had been so audacious as to make a second not improbable —by reinforcing the guard. Cesar, in his position as Gonfalonier, took measures for the public order, with an edict that no one should bear arms in the neighborhood of the Vatican under pain of death.[4] A judicial inquiry was set on foot to discover the authors of the crime.

The papal doctors gave all possible care. The Colonnas, then in close friendship with the Duke of Bisceglia, sent an eminent surgeon and King Frederick sent his own doctors from Naples. At his bedside were his wife Lucretia and his sister Sancia. But in spite of all these cares, Biagio Buonaccorsi writes, he died of his wounds.[5]

A legend quickly began to take shape. The legend was improbable, vague, contradictory. Its only ground was the view that Cesar was guilty of any crime if he happened to be within reach when it was committed. The account of the crime in Bruchard's *Journal* makes no allusion to Cesar. It merely says that as the prince of Bisceglia had apparently made up his mind not to die of his wounds, he was strangled in bed. But this is clearly an interpolation by the copyist, made some years later when it was the common assertion that the Duke had been murdered by Cesar.

That the words *"in lecto suo fuit strangulatus"* are an in-

296

terpolation seems evident, since we are told further on that the Aragonese doctors were arrested, sent to the Castle of Saint Angelo, submitted to the Inquisition with the object of verifying what care they had taken of their patient, and set at liberty because they were innocent.[6] Bruchard also says that the wounded man had been most closely guarded and that, after his death, his body was carried into a chapel of St. Peter's, where Cardinal Borgia and the family watched in prayer.

The Venetian ambassador, Paolo Capello, relates that Bisceglia, recovering, tried to kill Cesar from the balcony of his apartment while Cesar was walking in the Vatican gardens; and that it was in revenge for this that Cesar murdered him.[7] The ambassador of Florence, Francesco Capello, reports as a rumor current that some of Cesar's men entered the room of the Duke, now convalescent, and he died of fright. Matarazzo, writing his chronicle at Perugia, tells us that Cesar killed his brother-in-law with his own hands. Brandolino Lippi, who had been Bisceglia's tutor, declares that both the author and the cause of the crime are unknown.

The writers of a later period have woven all these accusations into one complete scene. Cesar, when he saw that his bravos had bungled their job, decided to poison his brother-in-law since he would not die of wounds so grave; but Lucretia and Sancia dissuaded him and themselves undertook the preparation of his meals. But Cesar came back, in company with the Pope, and said to his victim: "What was not done at lunch, will be done at dinner." And in fact on August 18 he introduced Michelotto—the very man who was supposed to have played the part of the masked stranger in the tragedy of the Duke of Gandia— into Bisceglia's room and ordered him to strangle the Duke.

This Michelotto figures as the basest villain in all the villainous affairs of the Borgias, although in actual fact he was at the time a highly respected captain, serving Cesar at the head of an important body of soldiers; when his master died, he entered the service of the Republic of Florence.

In the great heat of the Roman summer, Alfonso had to be buried with all speed, and this increased the suspicion that the crime was the result of family quarrels and therefore the work of Cesar. But the most recent writers—Pastor, Creighton, and Alvisi, among others—who know through their researches in the Archives all the efforts made by the Vatican to discover the truth about the crime, agree with Bruchard in accepting Buonaccorsi's version according to which Bisceglia died of his wounds and hold it absolutely impossible that Cesar should have been the author of the crime.[8]

In any event what interest could he have had in ridding himself of this youth of barely nineteen? At that very moment he was enjoying his first great triumphs, doubly sweet for being the first. He must have felt that fortune was his own sister. Kings were thrusting him on his magnificent upward way. A few months later, he was made a member of the nobility of Venice. Why should he have cast so black a shadow upon all that had come to him so easily?

It is difficult after so long a time and upon so little evidence to risk a guess as to the author of the crime. Pastor suspects the Orsini because Bisceglia was in the close friendship of the Colonna family. It is possible. But it seems more probable that the author of the crime—a personage of considerable power to judge from the number of armed men that took part in it—was avenging one of those private offenses which evade the perspicacity alike of the public and the historian.

To send assassins into the very Piazza of St. Peter's to attack a relation of the Pope, a King's son, near the Vatican, to have forty horsemen at hand to ensure the escape of the criminals—all this proves that its author was determined upon an act of revenge which for psychological reasons he could not defer. Otherwise he would have awaited a more favorable opportunity, in a place further from the papal palace. In a word, other means would have been used to destroy an enemy who happened to be in the way, unless there was a lust for vengeance that could not wait.

Upon her husband's death Lucretia retired with her grief to the Castel of Nepi. There she would have preferred to remain much longer, but she had to come back to Rome that winter because there was already talk of a new marriage. Suitors were still numerous, in spite of the terrible reputation later historians suppose that her brother had of killing her husbands or threatening them with death if they would not agree to give her up on ignominious grounds.

A few days after the attack on Bisceglia, on July 25, the Pope went in solemn procession to Santa Maria del Popolo. Cesar marched at the head of the cortège with his men-at-arms, saluted with reverence by populace and pilgrims. For the populace knew nothing of the intrigues of the ambassadors, and its judgement of things was sane. Nor did it occur to King Frederick of Naples to accuse Cesar of his nephew's death, although the Borgias and the family of Aragon were very soon afterward in fierce opposition.

CHAPTER XX

The Division of the Kingdom
of Naples

THE jubilee was drawing to its close. The Pope had just reorganized his army to resume the war in the Romagna and in his other territories. The Kings of France and Spain had come to an agreement upon the question of Naples and Frederick offered the Grand Turk permanent cession of the town of Tarento, in the extreme east of his Kingdom, as price of an alliance which would defend him against those two great European powers. Italian policy was entering a new phase in these early years of the sixteenth century. We are very far from the system created by Cosimo de Medici and so well-maintained by Lorenzo the Magnificent, a system based upon the supremacy of the four great states—Venice, Naples, Milan and Florence —in perfect equilibrium.

The position now was that the Duchy of Milan depended directly upon France; and so in its international relations did Florence, a Republic democratic in tendency and invariably pacifist save when its trade and commerce had to be defended. Venice was anxious to break every link with Italy and have no friendship save with the King of France; but it wished to strengthen its hold upon the Adriatic and expand its territories upon the mainland with his aid and at the expense of Naples and the Papal States. Its ambition drove it into a quarrel with its powerful neighbors, the Este and the Gonzagas. Naples, the largest in extent of the four, was on the verge of collapse, for the family which ruled it was being betrayed by its own relations in Spain.

In such an age, when the great principles of international law were not very clearly known—they are not so very stable today—and when political respect for the head of Christendom looked like disappearing, Alexander VI was more than ever confirmed in the certainty that only a strong Papal State was capable of guaranteeing Rome's ecclesiastical authority, and that since the balance of Italy was gone he must rely upon the balance of European powers to safeguard the small shreds of independence Italy still enjoyed.

But new conflicts arose from this new situation, for peace and order are no sudden growth but the consequence of a long process of adaptation; and every new state of things, in politics as in economics, no matter how necessary it may be to the common good, must be a cause of strife if it comes too rapidly. In fact seldom have more problems appeared upon the political chessboard than in that dawn of the sixteenth century. There was conflict between Germany and France, quieted for the moment by a family pact and certain concessions. There was conflict between Spain and France, settled by a partition, which proved not durable, of the Kingdom of Naples. There was conflict between Venice and the Papacy, which Alexander VI while he lived kept from degenerating into open war, but which Julius II later envenomed to the ruin of the only two powers still left standing in Italy.

Alexander VI set about increasing the Church's temporal power by sending Cesar once more into the Ro-

301

magna. Having seen the rapid conquest a few months earlier of Imola and Forli, and having learned both from Rome and from the French that the Papal attack upon the Vicars was soon to be resumed, the Venetians sent Bartolommeo de Alviano, their principle *condottiere*, to Rimini and Faenza with a numerous body of soldiers to defend the Malatestas and the Manfredi, respective lords of the two cities. The Pope protested and so did Louis XII, so that the Venetians were obliged to withdraw their troops and their war-loving *condottiere*. Cesar was able to set about his task hindered by no great obstacle. But the attitude of Venice had shown the Pope where the real danger lay and what its remedy must be. He arrived at a solution, of that kind of canonical correctness which churchmen often introduce into politics. He resolved that Cesar should act in the interest of the Holy See but in the name of the King of France. Thus the Venetians would be definitely rendered neutral. Cesar, at the head of an army of ten thousand men, occupied towns and territories with his usual speed, but without having to do any great amount of fighting. The only serious opposition he found was in front of Faenza. Before his arrival Pesaro had expelled Giovanni Sforza and welcomed the armies of Rome as liberators. Rimini, so abominably governed by the Malatestas, followed the example. And so it was for all the small towns and strongholds on his way. But Faenza enjoyed a sound public life. After the death of Galeotto Manfredi, assassinated by his wife Francesca Bentivoglio, sixteen of the most important citizens governed the town as political guardians of Astore, son of the dead prince. And the city had no mind to change its government. Cesar attacked it during the winter but in vain, and he had to raise the siege because of the severity of the weather and the sallies of the besieged. It was only at the end of April, 1501, that he was able to enter, and this not by a victory properly so called but through the treachery of one of the garrison and the fact that they had no food left. Astore Manfredi and one of his natural brothers, by name Giovanni Battista, was sent to Rome and imprisoned in the Castle of Saint Angelo. Later they were found dead in the Tiber. They may have been killed for reasons of state, for Faenza still wanted its prince back. But we have no certain facts to go upon and the enigma of these two deaths has never been cleared up.

After the fall of Faenza, Cesar had two plans, and had to renounce both of them because of the King of France. One of his plans was to expel the Bentivoglios from Bologna and the other to restore the Medicis to the government of Florence. As the price of abandoning these plans, he obtained considerable help in money and men-at-arms from the Bentivoglio family, and from the Florentines the post of *condottiere* and a treaty of peace. Unable to go further east, Cesar turned to the west. He attacked Piombino, which was ruled by Jacopo d' Appiano, but he was unable to continue the operation in person and had to leave the troops under the orders of Vitellozzo Vitelli, who captured the town.[1] The King of France ordered Cesar to rejoin the French army, which in July, 1501, came down through the mountains of Tuscany upon the Kingdom of Naples.

Louis XII had prepared this operation with more care than Charles VIII, yet the issue was equally disastrous. The truth is that care, prudence, intelligent effort contribute to the success of human enterprises in a lesser proportion than is usually credited to them. The unexpected is

303

always liable to neutralize or destroy the wisest plans and to remedy the mistakes of the incompetent.

This attack upon Naples caused the greatest sorrow to Alexander. As scapegoat for all the ills of the period, he was naturally accused of this one also. And the greatest of his accusers is no less a person than Leopold Ranke, an incomparable historian but in this matter lacking the secret documentation of the period. It has been said that Alexander VI had summoned the Spaniards to Italy and had allied them with the French. But the political antecedents of this military campaign show him cleared of that responsibility. His participation in the Franco-Spanish alliance was no more than an acceptance of a *fait accompli* which he had done his uttermost to prevent. In a word, he bent before the inevitable, in the hope of limiting its disastrous effects as much as might be.

I have already said that in his first embassy to Louis XII he had recommended him either to leave the question of Naples as it stood or else to refer it to a juridical tribunal. Then he had proposed that the house of Aragon should remain rulers of Naples on condition of paying the King of France a tribute for such rights as the House of Anjou might have. Sanudo himself, reproducing Capello's account, makes Capello say that the Pope, when granting Louis XII the nullity of his marriage with Jeanne de France, had asked him not to meddle in the affairs of Naples save as the interests of the Holy See might require. But whether Capello said this or Sanudo said it for him, it remains inaccurate, since as we know the Pope had not personally declared the marriage null. But at least the episode shows what the opinion of the period held his mind to be.

At every opportunity, as for example when the King

of France was in Milan, the Pope repeated his urging that he should not interfere in the affairs of Naples. There is no single one of his actions which might be considered as a direct or indirect invitation—or even hint—to the Kings of Spain and France that they should occupy Naples, before these two rulers themselves agreed upon the matter in the treaty of Granada.

And the treaty of Granada was put through in secret behind his back. Zurita relates that the Spanish ambassador, Mosen Gralla, said one day to Georges d'Amboise, Cardinal de Rohan: "If we should come to an agreement with you in the affair of Naples, as you did with the Venetians over the Duchy of Milan, what would you think?" To which the Cardinal replied: "We should thus maintain peace between our two realms."

Whether this dialogue took place or not, we know that on September 2, 1499, at Granada, the two monarchies divided the Kingdom of Naples between them. The Pope did not know of the treaty, which was kept strictly secret, until it had been brought into being. Nor was King Frederick of Naples told of it—not, that is, until later, when he asked for Spanish troops to be sent to his Kingdom, to aid him! The secret had indeed been carefully kept.

The French, having secured Spain as an ally, now wished to secure Venice. In May, 1500, their ambassadors formally asked the Venetian Senate for a new pact of alliance. Given, they said, that many people—the Marquis of Mantua, for example, and the Duke of Ferrara—have the air of friends and are not; given further that the King of Naples who has already sent money to Ludovico il Moro for the reconquest of Milan, was now in negotiation with the Turks and was continually urging Maximilian against France; it would be useful to come to an agreement and

305

make war upon all the enemies of Venice and of France, especially King Frederick and the Grand Turk. Conquered territories would be shared. This alliance must be notified to the Holy Father, that he might be induced to invite other monarchs to the crusade against the Turks; and if they showed themselves hostile to the idea or negligent, he might remind them of their duty and publicly rebuke them for their conduct "thus putting God upon the side of the most Christian King of France and the Republic of Venice."[2]

The Venetian Senate accepted the proposed alliance, only adding as an essential condition the annexation of Ferrara and Mantua to the Republic.

Not content with his alliances with Spain and Venice, Louis XII thought well to settle the difficulties between himself and Maximilian. They concluded a truce, a preliminary to peace, in which the parties agreed that the Duchy of Milan should be given by imperial investiture to the King of France, but should return ultimately to Charles—grandson of Maximilian, who was later Charles V. In fact Charles was to receive it as a dowry with Claude, Louis's daughter, whom he should marry as soon as the two had reached the necessary age.

In these circumstances, with the French army already on the march southward and the Spanish army prepared to sail from Sicily, the ambassadors of France and Spain approached the Pope and asked him to recognize the treaty of Granada which divided the territory of Naples into two parts. One part was to be a kingdom, comprising the cities of Naples and Gaeta, with all the Campagna and the Abruzzi, whose sovereign should bear the title, King of Naples and Jerusalem; the other part was to be a duchy, including Calabria and Apulia. They further asked that the Pope should grant the investiture of the Kingdom to France and of the Duchy to Spain. It was clearly impossible for Alexander VI to reject this demand, which bore the sanction of the international law of the moment. And he had proofs that Frederick of Aragon was in negotiation with the Turk. Nonetheless he postponed the granting of the investiture, and even his acceptance of the proposal, and made a counter-proposition. In a word, he demanded that the essential point of the agreement between the two powers must be the Crusade, with the division of the Kingdom of Naples following as a consequence. In fact, the Treaty in its new form bore the name of League of Pope Alexander VI with the Kings of France and Spain against the Turks and their Allies and Accomplices. These Allies and Accomplices were the King of Naples and—in Alexander's view—the Savelli and the Colonnas.

The French troops entered Rome on their way to Naples. With them came Cesar with his own soldiers. But both bodies continued rapidly southward. The Holy Father thought he had realized the great dream of his existence, the dream he had inherited from his uncle Calixtus III, the dream for which Pope Pius II dying at Ancona had made his pathetic vows. In Alexander's mind, the Crusade was at last to begin.

D'Aubigny's Frenchmen and Cesar Borgia's Italians, who until then had treated the localities they passed through reasonably well, were guilty at the taking of Capua of one of the most appalling massacres in history. Sigismundo dei Conti claims that Cesar with other leaders made great efforts to prevent the violence, but failed because the army was exasperated by the considerable losses they had suffered in a counter-attack of the besieged. Guicciardini, who never misses an occasion to show us the Borgias in the worst possible light, says that Cesar had the women prisoners paraded before him and that he chose forty of the most beautiful for a harem. But Guicciardini is the only one to mention this; he gives it as a current rumor, though he did not write until some years afterwards and in Florence. We have eye-witnesses' accounts of the butchery and the raping and the rest of it, but no hint of any such action by Cesar.

In any event, Cesar terminated the Naples campaign at the very highest point of his reputation. The King of France sent him a special messenger with letters thanking him for his help in the enterprise, and saying that the King would know how to show his gratitude and treat him as a good friend and kinsman.[3] The Spanish sovereigns gave him the title of Duke of Andria, which had belonged to King Frederick when he was prince; and as these honors were always accompanied by large benefices, Cesar emerged from this short war well furnished with money. Thus while Guicciardini brings Cesar to Rome with a new and rather special crime, in fact he returned there with redoubled prestige.

Cesar was back in Rome on September 15. Alexander VI was not the man to let the occasion pass without dealing a mortal blow to his enemies, in this case the Savelli and the Colonnas. Encouraged by the treaty signed in Rome engaging the two kings to the Crusade and by the capture at Capua of the two chiefs of the Colonna family —one of them died as a result of his wounds—he had already, by a bull of August 20, excommunicated all who bore that name and confiscated all their goods. The bull is long and sets out the many revolts of the Savelli and Colonna families against the Church. Cardinal Giovanni

Colonna was included in the confiscation, but he was allowed to keep all his ecclesiastical benefices except the Abbey of Subiaco. Two days after Cesar's return, Alexander issued a further bull confiscating the property of other feudal houses, notably the house of Estouteville which had been allied with the house of Colonna. As in similar cases previously, these punishments aroused popular enthusiasm. A few days afterwards, Alexander VI visited some of the strongholds and cities of these ancient families, and was everywhere loudly acclaimed.

He had reserved to himself the free disposition of these and the Caetani properties. He used it. Having granted certain castles to the Orsini, his friends for the moment, he divided the rest into two parts. Of one part, he made the duchy of Sermoneta, which he gave to the little Rodrigo. Of the other he made the duchy of Nepi and Palestrina, which he gave to the little Giovanni. They were both of the Borgia house and objects of his liveliest affection.

The famous pamphlet known as the *Letter to Silvio Savelli*—Silvio being then in refuge at the court of Maximilian—is dated as of November, 1501. It is a reply to the bull of excommunication just mentioned. Just as the bull sets out in detail the crimes of the Colonnas and the Savelli, so the letter sets out in detail the crimes of the Borgias. Its author was a Neapolitan writer called Geronimo Mancione, if we may accept certain indications given by Agostino Nifo.[4] Thanks to this pamphlet, which was abundantly drawn upon by contemporaries and is still today drawn upon by the enemies of the Borgias, we know of Alexander's belief in liberty in personal relations. He had Mancione's work read to him, as he had all the insults read that were continually being printed against him. Sometimes

309

he laughed the great laugh of a cheerful corpulent man, sometimes he received them with a smile on his sensual lips. It never occurred to him that anybody could believe these fantastic things, which had their inspiration sometimes in the anger of an interested party, sometimes in the mere high spirits of some street-corner poet. He said to the ambassador of Ferrara one day: "Rome is a free city, where every one can say and write whatever he pleases; they say much evil of me, but I don't mind." And he criticized Cesar for refusing to show the same tolerance.[5]

But upon strictly ecclesiastical matters his view was different. In that sphere he saw any deviation as a crime. It was he indeed who first introduced censorship into the church. In a bull of June 1, 1501, after having praised printing, he declared that this instrument though so useful for propagating what was good, might yet produce great catastrophes by giving publicity to evil.[6] He observed that in many places, especially in the provinces of Cologne, Mainz, Trier and Magdeburg, books were being published against the Christian religion and that he, as representative of a God who came down upon earth to enlighten the human mind and scatter the darkness of error, was obliged strictly to prevent the continuance of these evil practices. Therefore, the printers of the four places named must henceforth obtain permission for their publications from their respective archbishops who must first examine them; further they must suppress any dangerous books already in circulation. This censorship, established for the four German States, was applied by certain bishops in other dioceses, and later, in 1515, Leo X extended it to the whole Christian world. In the comparison of the two attitudes, we see Alexander's unvarying system: rigid to excess in any matter that touches the Church as a spiritual or moral entity, but easy and tolerant upon temporal and purely personal questions.

In these years 1500 and 1501, Alexander VI was taking great interest in the Turkish question. With his usual energy, he addressed himself to the European princes to get them to undertake the Crusade they had promised; but these not only did not answer him, but entered into arrangements more or less openly with the Sultan. We have seen that the Duke of Milan had invited him to attack the possessions of Venice; and this the Turk did bloodily and destructively, burning towns, and massacring the inhabitants or carrying them off into slavery. The King of Naples, as we have seen, offered him a foothold in his own kingdom. The King of France, by the intermediary of his celebrated ambassador Commines, was in conversation for four hours with the Turkish representative in Venice. Florence sent the Sultan money; Maximilian himself, against his own interests, allowed the Turkish army passage through Carinthia, that it might attack the Venetians by land. The fact was that, with the powers of Europe so balanced, the Grand Turk might easily give victory to the scale in which he flung his weight: and the powers of Europe did not overlook the possibility.

. On March 11, 1500, the Pope gathered in the Consistory a kind of congress formed of all the ambassadors in Rome. In his opening discourse, he pointed out the danger of a Turkish invasion. He praised Venice which in defending itself was defending all Christendom. He declared that by sea he relied upon three powers principally—France, Spain and Venice—and by land upon Poland and Hungary. He ended by offering whatever ecclesiastical concessions might be asked to raise the necessary funds. But the ambassadors evaded his demands, each declaring that he had not the necessary powers and that his state would do what other states felt like doing. Alexander was irritated and in his closing speech deplored the attitude of the King of France and Maximilian, and denounced Frederick of Naples for having had relations with the Turks.

Yet he was not discouraged by the failure of the meeting. Realizing the avarice of the rulers, he began to gather the money himself. He compelled the cardinals to contribute large sums in proportion to their benefices. He did the same for the great prelates. He decreed fresh ecclesiastical taxes; he made new financial arrangements with Henry VIII of England,[7] which as it happened Henry never observed. He obtained from Maximilian and his great vassals the promise of an army of thirty thousand foot soldiers and a large body of cavalry. The King of France went so far as to promise a few galleys. But at the end of all things there was only the Spanish fleet under Gonzalvo of Cordoba to help the Venetians—and not for long—while the King of Hungary fought against the invading Turks. At this time the Pope conferred upon the Spanish rulers the title of Defenders of the Faith. But realizing at last that no promise was kept and no treaty observed, he limited his action to forming an alliance with Venice and with Hungary. He is supposed to have been greedy for money, but he gave King Ladislas all the ecclesiastical benefices of his country and in addition forty thousand ducats a year; and he also sent fifteen thousand ducats to his representative in Venice for the needs of the fleet. The alliance was weak and divided Christendom was saved only because the Turk, at the height of his warring ardor, was compelled to turn eastward and use all his immense forces against Persia.

312

CHAPTER XXI

Poison

So FAR Alexander VI had not been directly accused of any crime. Even his enemies observed his immense grief at his assassination of the Duke of Gandia; in the murder of Perotto, he played the part of victim rather than executioner; he took all possible measures to save the Duke of Bisceglia. As to Prince Jem, as we have seen, there was no real accusation at all. The festivals at which he was present were gay—even to the throwing of sweetmeats into the corsages of the ladies of the party—but there was nothing pornographic or repulsive about them. It is only now, in his seventieth year, that he takes his first steps upon the high road of infamy and discovers his vocation for crime. It was indeed at this period that the legend began to form: for it was now that the *Letter to Silvio Savelli* was published, and the hostility of the Venetians declared, and the tyrants overthrown who had occupied the church's vast territory. The historical crime-novel as we know it has taken three centuries to write. It makes curious reading.

On July 6, 1498, the Pope accused Pedro de Aranda, Bishop of Calahorra, of the crimes of heresy and simony. This Pedro was a Spaniard, to whom the Pope had shown such affection and confidence as to name him majordomo of the Vatican. A Jew by origin, he had apparently been converted to Christianity. It will be remembered that in

313

Spain many converted Jews occupied important positions. Queen Isabella had one as her confessor; and her chosen friend was Beatriz de Bobabilla who was married to the Jew Cabrera. The Marquis of Villena, who had considerable power with the previous King Henry IV, was a Jew. The editor of King Ferdinand's *Book of Reason* was of Jewish origin, as were the King's treasurer who was descended from a Rabbi, and his friends and chosen companions: Jaime de la Caballeria, Juan Cabrera and Sanchez de Paternoz. Many of the great Spanish houses had allied themselves in marriage with Hebrew families in order to re-gild their escutcheons.

Pedro de Aranda's career had surmounted the difficulties which might have arisen from the accusation brought against his father that he was a Marrano, that is that his conversion to Christianity was only a pretence. He had arrived as we have seen at the bishopric of Calahorra, and had also secured the entry of his natural son into the ecclesiastical career, using his influence in the curia to have the youth made a Protonotary of the Vatican and secretary to the Pope.

Sanudo, who copies the Venetian ambassador Capello, says that it was in order to get hold of his wealth that Alexander condemned Pedro and had him imprisoned in the Castle of Saint Angelo, where he died shortly after. The accusation was not made in 1498 when Aranda was arrested but later when the great flood of invective really began, that is in 1500. But we know the case gave rise to a long judicial process. The Pope denounced Pedro in full Consistory in 1498 and named a commission of inquiry composed of the Bishops Isvalies and Eggert Durkop and the theologian Pablo de Mondia. This commission reported directly to the Consistory. It condemned the Bishop of

314

Calahorra as a heretic—not believing in the Most Holy Trinity since he denied the Son and the Holy Ghost—and a follower of Jewish rites; as a simoniac, because he demanded money for every religious act; as rebellious against the Holy See, since he would not admit into his diocese priests legally ordained in Rome nor recognize the benefices which had been granted to them; as a forger because he had fabricated two documents, one in order to damage a third person, the other in the interests of his own son. The full report of the inquiry, together with the enumeration and classification of the witnesses, who numbered more than a hundred, is to be found in the Barberini Library in Rome.[1] Pedro seems to have been restless by nature, strong and aggressive and unruly, firm in his convictions and confident of impunity. The witnesses declared that he always omitted the names of the Son and Holy Ghost in public prayers, that he prayed face to the wall in the Hebrew language, and that he discussed the most abstruse problems of religion from the Jewish point of view. There was talk also of his keeping the Sabbath and having animals slaughtered in the Jewish fashion. He ate meat on Friday and Saturday, beat his priests until the blood ran, and was guilty of many other unpleasant actions. Faced with evidence of this sort, the most hard-headed jury would have had to find the man guilty. The commission issued its sentence, which involved the confiscation of his goods to the profit of the papal treasury. But if the Pope was greedy for money, it is to be noted that he used a part of the confiscated property for the maintenance of the prisoner, whom he authorized to keep two servants, and that he gave one of his houses in Rome to the Hospice of St. James to be used as a hospital.[2]

This accusation against Alexander came at the same time

as another concerning certain Marranos who were obliged
to go in procession through the streets of Rome, dressed
in yellow with a red cross on their breasts and a lighted
candle in their hands, as an act of contrition. Bruchard
agreed with Sanudo that this farce was probably put on to
make money. Four centuries later, the word "probably"
is dropped, and it is stated as a positive fact that the Marranos were punished for the sake of money. But the fact
remains that they were punished, which seems to suggest
that they preferred to undergo the penance rather than
pay the fine.

From theft to murder there is but one step. That step
we must now take. According to the legend, the Pope had
a taste for trying out his criminal talents especially upon
the members of the Consistory. Apparently it has never
occurred to his accusers to ask why men like Cardinal
Giuliano della Rovere, who was one day to succeed him,
and Cardinals Ascano Sforza, Colonna, Pérault and so
many others, who betrayed him time and again and were
rich and loaded with benefices, lived to such a ripe old age.
Alexander has stated his own defense before the bar of
history in the remark he made to the ambassador of Ferrara that his nature inclined him to pardon. One day, in
a conversation with Beltrando Constabili, he reminded him
that he had pardoned cardinals whom Charles VIII himself had described as traitors. "I should have the right to
inflict the death penalty upon the Vice-Chancellor [As-
canio Sforza] and upon the Cardinal of St. Peter in Chains
[Giuliano della Rovere], but I did not wish harm to anyone and I pardoned forty of the nobility."[3] Quite apart
from his faith, which was profoundly religious, he was a
churchman in the sense that he was imbued with that spe-

316

cial psychology which bases all its acts upon a long tradition; and in the light of that tradition he felt that as pastor of the flock his duty was to guide it indeed but likewise to pardon any sheep that strayed if pardon would bring it back into the right way. Again and again he insisted upon the fact that his high mission imposed upon him the duty of opening his arms to all.

But the universal opinion is that the Borgias' speciality was to be poisoners—and, odder still, poisoners of cardinals. According to this opinion, they even invented a special poison whose secret they carried with them to the grave, a poison called *cantarella*, whose base was cantharides, or arsenic, or some other chemical substance unknown. It was a white powder which sometimes had a repellent taste, sometimes no taste at all. A small dose dissolved in the wine of the chalice, or in water, or in soup, or sprinkled like salt—and the victim died just when the assassin wanted him to. On one occasion, this *cantarella* allowed Prince Jem to travel day after day on horseback in the depth of winter, and only got its man at Naples; on other occasions we find Cardinal Michiel and Cardinal de Monreale swept from the world of the living in a few hours. But the Borgias did not, like other famous poisoners, poison because they were mental cases. They acted not from sadism but from sordid self-interest. The mainspring of their tragedy was love of money.

We cannot set out these poisonings simply in chronological order; we must put them in groups in order to understand them and judge of the falsity of the stream of accusations in the light of the evidence which has reached us. Notice first that in all this period it would be difficult to find any more or less unexpected death, where the person was well known, which did not set ambassadors and chron-

317

iclers talking of poison. From the death of Henry IV, King of Castile (and indeed long before), to the death of Georges d'Amboise in the time of Julius II—nor was he the last—someone was sure to utter the accusation of poison. But when a Borgia is in question, the unsupported formula, "It is said that so-and-so was poisoned," constitutes absolute proof, whereas in other cases historians attach no importance to the suspicion unless it is reinforced by some kind of evidence.

In the particular matter of the poisoning of cardinals, there exists a special reason leading authors of later ages to accept the merest rumor, the vaguest and most improbable insinuation. It is that the Pope immediately took possession of the goods of the deceased cardinals. The moment he learned that they were dead, or even that they were ill, he prepared to take possession of their goods; and the moment they were dead, he took them. The argument is that if the Pope had so watchful an eye upon the sick man in the matter of his goods, then he had caused the death precisely with this in mind. But to argue thus is to show complete ignorance of the ecclesiastical laws of the day. By canon law, an ecclesiastic could not dispose of his goods unless he had received authorization from the Pope; otherwise his heritage passed to the Church.[4] It was discussed whether a distinction might be drawn between property that arose from ecclesiastical benefices and ordinary personal property; but the attempted distinction gave rise to such confusion that it had to be abandoned. Nevertheless, the Popes exercised their power with much discretion and often granted the authorization to make a will, with the reserve that the authorization might later be withdrawn.

In the time of Innocent VIII the administration of the

Church had grown so relaxed that the moment a rich prelate died, his subordinates and relations took anything they could lay their hands on, saying that he had given it to them before his death. Alexander VI put an end to this abuse, though he often spontaneously offered part of the dead man's goods to those who had been his companions in life. In sending his agents to the house where the dead man lay, the Pope was carrying out an act of authority similar to that still performed by judges under many legal codes when, on the demand of an interested party, they place seals upon the rooms, even before the dead body has been removed for burial. Julius II later regularized this practice.

The first Cardinal whose death was held due to the Borgia poison was himself a Borgia—Cardinal Giovanni Borgia, who died in January, 1500. And it was Cesar who was suspected, not the Pope. Only Guicciardini accuses the Pope also. Bruchard, or his copyist, or an interpolator, simply says that the high fever from which Giovanni suffered for two days was considered suspicious; and Sanudo adds more explicitly: "It is thought that he had been poisoned." He further declared that Cesar had him poisoned because of the affection the Pope bore this relation of his. It is probable that in the preparation of this part of his *Journal*, he used the dispatches of ambassadors and even treated their inferences as matters of fact. The Venetian ambassador wrote that Cardinal Borgia had been sent into eternity like all the others and that it was Cesar who had sent him. But there is one fact which runs counter to the legend of Alexander's greed for money: the dead cardinal's fortune might, according to civil law, have returned to the Borgia family, had the Pope consented; but instead it went by canon law into the papal treasury. Cardinal Giovanni's ill-

319

ness lasted only two days, and Cesar and the Pope were both far away. He had left Cesar a couple of weeks before his death to go to Rome and take part in the Jubilee. We learn from Pier Francesco Justolo, that Cesar was deeply grieved by his death.[5] And in fact the cardinal had been his companion and his most devoted friend. They regarded each other as brothers, to such a point that some supposed that this Borgia, Cardinal de Monreale, was a son of the Pope.

The most recent authors do not accept the accusation. But one is puzzled to know why in some instances they accept Bruchard's *Journal* and Sanudo's as unquestionably true, while in others they reject them out of hand.

Two Venetian cardinals are also supposed to have been poisoned—Zeno and Michiel.

Both men belonged to a noble family of Venice. Sons of two sisters of Pope Paul II, they had been raised to the purple by him. Colleagues of Rodrigo Borgia under three popes, they had supported his acts as Pope and served him honorably. On May 7 or 8, 1501, Zeno, Cardinal of Verona, died at Padua. The suspicion that he had been poisoned arises solely from the long conflict that followed between the Pope and the Seigniory of Venice concerning his goods. According to Bruchard, Alexander had given the cardinal authorization to dispose of what belonged to him by will, but had later withdrawn the authorization. The Seigniory, to whom the will left part of the fortune, would not admit the withdrawal of the authorization. The Pope threatened Venice that he would appeal to the Emperor and the Kings of France and Spain, sent the city a brief of excommunication, and laid his hands upon such small parts of Zeno's fortune as were outside Venice. Bembo[6] says that the Pope took possession of two hundred gold livres which the cardinal had hidden at Ancona. This happens to be true, though not in the form given to it by Bembo, a writer concerned with literary effect and not at all with the facts. Bruchard tells us that the dead cardinal had sent to a convent of nuns in Ancona twenty thousand ducats which they were to hold and deliver, upon his death, to a prelate whom he named. This prelate, however, died before the cardinal and when the Pope learned of the existence and the origin of the money he had it returned to the papal treasury.[7]

The greater part of the fortune was in the hands of the cardinal himself at Padua. Sanudo says[7a] that as soon as the Seigniory learned that Zeno had made a will and was on the point of death, it forbade his relations entry into the house, and sent the two Rectors of Padua and Ludovico della Torre with a hundred armed men to guard the goods which were in the house itself. Once the cardinal was dead, Venice took the whole sum, which Bruchard tells us came to over a hundred thousand ducats, though Sanudo says it was only a little more than sixty-four thousand.

Though this confiscation was entirely illegal the Seigniory took no notice either of the papal excommunication or of the difficulties in which it might be involved with foreign states. It kept the money, but throughout its conflict with the Pope it never claimed that the cardinal's death was due to poison. Zeno had died at Padua near Venice and a long way from Rome.

Similar difficulties arose upon the death of Cardinal Michael. He died shortly before Alexander VI, on April 11,

1503. The suspicion of poisoning arises from the fact that the cardinal died of a stomach illness which lasted two days. This time it was the Consistory which decided upon the appropriation of his goods. A few months later—note that Alexander was now dead and Cesar in prison—a certain Asquinio de Colloredo, a Venetian ecclesiastic who was the cardinal's confidential assistant, was tried and condemned as his murderer. Poison had been the means used. When the sentence was read out on March 16, 1504, though he had denied even under torture that he was guilty, he now admitted his share in the crime and declared further that he had been ordered to carry out this infamous act by the dead Pope, by Cesar who was at that moment a prisoner, and by certain Spanish cardinals then in refuge in Naples.[8]

When we remember what happens in troubled times, Colloredo's conduct is comprehensible. The instigator of any crime that happens to be discovered is always the dethroned sovereign. But in this instance, contemporaries— even the enemies of the Borgias—did not believe in their guilt: for no proceeding was set on foot against Cesar or against the Spanish cardinals although they were the opponents of the new Pope Julius II. If the accusation had had the least show of truth, Julius II would have seized upon it as a weapon against the family he detested. Colloredo was beheaded, and his declaration must obviously be regarded as a last desperate effort to save his own skin.

In all these poisonings of cardinals, there is one really curious fact. The victims were not the Pope's enemies but his friends. We have seen this for his nephew and for the two Venetians. And now we are to find him accused of poisoning his intimate friend, Cardinal Juan Lopez, whom he had defended even against the King of Spain.

Upon the death of Cardinal Lopez, we know literally nothing save what Bruchard tells us; and this contains no suggestion of murder, and incidentally proves the cardinal's devotion to the Pope up to the last. Bruchard relates that "on August 5, 1501, at the seventh hour, the Cardinal of Capua gave up his soul to God in the Apostolic Palace"; and that "before his death, he asked to be buried in the chapel of Calixtus, in the Basilica of St. Peter, and that he did not wish to make a will, leaving all his goods at the disposition of his Holiness."[9] But this account is not accepted by Burckhardt, author of *Kultur der Renaissance*, nor by Sismondi before him. They both list Cardinal Lopez among the poisoned victims of the Borgias. The Pope, at this moment of great heat in Rome, was at Frascati; and Bruchard, knowing Alexander's affection for the dead cardinal, not only told him of the death, but of the state of decomposition of the body on account of the heat. The Pope sent a special envoy with the message that all the cardinal's desires should be carried out and that he should be buried in St. Peter's in the Chapel of Calixtus as he had asked.

Cardinal Gian Battista Ferrari also died in the papal Palace. The Pope visited him and on leaving—probably because the doctors had told him that they had no hope of saving his life—he ordered an inventory to be made of his goods. Giustiniani, in a dispatch, writes the ritual "poison is suspected." Much later ecclesiastical authors wrote that in the time of Leo X a certain Sebastian Pinzon was accused of the death of Cardinal Ferrari and that, after denial under torture, he later admitted his guilt: he did not mention the name of Pope Alexander or make the slightest allusion to him.[10] But if torture forced Pinzon to declare himself guilty then it was a gross injustice. For Bruchard describes the whole affair of the cardinal's illness with the doctors who attended him and others who were summoned to consultation; and his account excludes all notion of poison—even so fantastic a poison as cantarella must have been! The cardinal was ill for seventeen days, refused to take any medicine, ate and drank heavily on certain days. Then he seemed to grow better, but a high fever came upon him. After July 16 there was a momentary improvement but he died four days later. The doctors who attended him, and who, as Bruchard tells us, were for the most part eminent, could not get him to take medicines before the seventeenth, and even then he swallowed only a tiny dose of what they administered.[11]

Like Bruchard, the ambassador Giustiniani lists the various phases of the illness. Only after he has announced the death does he remark—"by certain signs it is thought that the Cardinal died of poison."[12] In the Consistory, the Pope disposed of Ferrari's goods. He gave the Bishopric of Modena to the dead cardinal's brother because of the great affection there had been between them. Giustiniani, in his usual tone of hatred and biting criticism, says that Ferrari's large heritage would compensate the Pope for the damage done him by the loss of "this cardinal, who was so useful an instrument for gathering money, for it is the general opinion that His Holiness will not find others adequate to this function."

This Gian Battista Ferrari, because of his office of Treasurer, was pretty generally hated. Upon his death there was a shower of epigrams, all expressing the common detestation of the man whose job it was to collect money. Here is a typical one:

> Ne dicas; sit terra levis, nec spargite flores.
> Nummos, si requiem mihi dare vis, numera—

which may be roughly translated:

> "Say not 'May the earth be light' nor strew flowers.
> If you would give me rest, count your money."

Another equally piquant, and as hard on Ferrari as on the Borgias, ran:

> Bos bona, terra corpus, Styx animam—[13]

"The bull [gets] his goods, the earth his body, the river of death his soul"—the bull being part of the armorial bearings of the Borgias.

Cardinal Gian Battista Orsini is reckoned as the last of the Borgia poison victims. Alexander had had good relations with him in spite of his intermittent conflicts with the family to which he belonged. Nevertheless, the late happenings at Sinigaglia, where Cesar had in one stroke settled the fate of his condottieri, including the Orsini, obliged the Pope to have the cardinal arrested and placed in the Castle of Saint Angelo. But in his prison he was treated with the consideration customary for great personages and political prisoners. His family visited him, his food was sent in from outside, he had his private doctor, and part of the castle was more or less at his disposal. He fell ill. The illness followed its course, the foreign ambassadors and family being kept informed from day to day by the doctor already mentioned. On February 22, 1503, he died. The Pope paid him the honors due to his high dignity. On February 23, the representative of Florence wrote to the Seigniory: "Cardinal Orsini died yesterday and was buried within twenty-four hours in the Church of San Salvatore of the Orsini house. By order of the Pope, the body, accompanied by members of the family and cardinals of the curia, was carried through the streets uncoffined. . . . Monks celebrated the religious service and there were sixty or seventy lighted candles." The fact that the Pope ordered the body to be carried uncoffined through the streets of Rome must have arisen from his fear that there might be talk of poison. Pamphlets came into his hands, and he read them with the smile of a man who knew human weaknesses, and so knew that it is always the most perverse who accuse their enemies of perversity. But all the same he had no wish that simple people should be deceived. He had the doctors summoned who had cared for the Cardinal, made them give their diagnosis under oath and actually asked them if the death could be attributed to poison. All denied it. The Orsini house, which returned to power a few months later, when Alexander was dead, never uttered any accusation of this sort nor spoke of poison.

An English writer has made a statistical examination of the deaths of cardinals during the pontificates of Sixtus IV, Innocent VIII, Alexander VI and Julius II; and he concludes that proportionately there is no noticeable increase in the mortality of cardinals during the period of Alexander VI. And this author is in no way favorable to the Borgias.[14]

This story of the Borgia poison is clear proof that human naïveté is as great today as in primitive ages; it has merely changed form. But this naïveté goes so far, and is marked

by such a want of common sense, that we are driven to
conclude that if men write or read it is for entertainment
and not to transmit or acquire knowledge. While in the
legend the Borgia crimes are piled one upon the other, we
find in *history* that the family was profoundly respected
by contemporaries. At the beginning of the sixteenth century the moral sense had certain blind spots unknown to
other ages, but it did exist. The system of slander then
used is a proof that there was reprobation for evil and a
public sanction against those who committed it. The contempt the Pope showed for calumny, and the indignation
felt by Cesar at its spread, are equally proofs that calumny
could affect the public. So that if the Borgias were honored
and respected in their own day, it was because what was
then furtively whispered and is today held true, was considered as false or at the best doubtful, especially by those
who were acquainted with the facts and knew what passions were there to heat the atmosphere.

CHAPTER XXII

Lucretia's Third Marriage

LUCRETIA's marriage to Alfonso d'Este, eldest son and successor of Ercole, Duke of Ferrara, marked the moment of greatest splendor for the Borgias. She was entering into an old and honorable family related to all the great houses of Italy, into a court of high luxury and exquisite intellectuality. Her new husband gave up for her the Duchess of Angoulême of the French royal family, whom King Louis had offered him. His first wife, who died in early youth, was a Sforza, sister of the Empress of Germany, Maximilian's wife. The negotiations for the marriage between the house of Borgia and the house of Este were lengthy: for there were international problems involved and there was the desire of each side to secure the most advantageous matrimonial contract. Ercole d'Este, driven by cupidity and encouraged by the King of France, wished to gain as much as possible from this union with a house whose head was not only a rich and powerful monarch, but also the suzerain of his own State. He thought he ought to obtain rapid and positive advantages, and not mere hopes of advantage, because although the ruler in question was the head of all Christendom, yet he would take with him into the grave all his authority and all his power to enrich his family. Assuredly, a man so shrewd as the Duke had not overlooked what the Venetians were then saying—namely that the fortune of Cesar, Lucretia's brother, also depended upon the continuance of Alexander's life. And Alexander was now over seventy.

Further, there were international intrigues and the opposition of political interests. Venice, as we know, wished to annex Ferrara and Mantua, and Louis XII had offered his cooperation to this end. A family alliance with the Pope would render this plan unrealizable. And in another sense, Maximilian feared that the marriage would consolidate French domination in Italy, then represented by Cesar Borgia. For Florence a political alliance, the natural result of a family union, between the Papal States and Ferrara, would encircle its own territory in a ring of iron. Even such relations of the Este family as the Gonzagas saw in this alliance the definitive predominance of the Dukedom of the Romagna in that part of Italy, and hence the unconditional submission of all princes to the Holy See. For the barons dispossessed of their fiefs and their possessions, this marriage represented final destruction, banishment from power and poverty unrelieved. It has rarely happened that a union between ruling houses has provoked so many oppositions or affected international politics so deeply. The opinion of the powers was unanimous and hostile: the thing must be prevented at all costs. Ercole was begged by Maximilian on no account to agree. Venice and Florence worked to the same end with a persistence that forgot courtesy. The Gonzagas did not conceal their anger. The King of France wished to unite the Este family with his own. To prevent the marriage, there was set on foot a determined campaign of insults, anonymous pamphlets, and incredible accusations.

For his part, the Pope firmly believed that the alliance of the two houses would secure the future both of Lucretia

329

and Cesar after he was dead. And that future was with him a prime preoccupation. Lucretia was good and gracious, but she was a woman who could not have fended for herself alone. Cesar had good qualities but life had been too easy, and he had had no experience of failure. He was clever and intelligent, bold and decided, capable of waiting and making prudent preparations. But his life was not directed to one unvarying goal. He had not that consistency in his plans which is a guarantee of success. He liked distraction; he liked pleasure. He had habits which did not go with the habits of a man of action. Haughty by nature, he would not give himself the trouble of creating, by daily care, the sympathies and friendships and solid affections which aid a man in the hour of trial. He could be admirable when necessity was there to spur his powers; but he was not so in ordinary times. Men of his sort can win conquests but they cannot keep them. All this the Pope was sagacious enough to know. One day, incapable of keeping his deepest feelings within himself, he revealed his gloomy vision of the future to the Venetian ambassador: Cesar, he said, slept all day and stayed up all night; then he added, as if thinking aloud, "I do not know if he will be able to keep what he has acquired." For his part, Cesar attached as much importance to Lucretia's marriage as the Pope himself.

Once Alfonso of Aragon was dead, it was natural that there should be new suitors for Lucretia. In November, 1500, the Florentine ambassador, Francesco Capello, told the Seigniory that the Duke of Gravina, urged on by his uncle Cardinal Gian Battista Orsini, was on his way to Rome to ask the hand of the young widow; and Bruchard too speaks of this. There were other candidates, but less bold. It was even said that a Colonna might enter the Papal family.

But from the beginning Alexander VI had examined the situation and made up his mind. At another time, an Orsini might have been favorably considered. But today the Pope was engaged body and soul in the enterprise of winning back for the Holy See the territory that King Pepin had given it, which involved making Cesar the all-powerful grand Vicar of this territory. Lucretia must serve to this end as Cesar's soldiers had served and the soldiers of the King of France.

Cardinal Gian Battista Ferrari, devoted to the Pope, had been in the service of Duke Ercole. He was the man needed. So we find him on February 18, 1501 writing a letter to his former protector, setting out how useful would be a marriage between his son Alfonso and Lucretia Borgia. When the Duke of Ferrara received the Cardinal's letter he was already in negotiation with the King of France for the marriage of his eldest son with Louise, Duchess of Angoulême, niece of Louis XII; and it seemed to him impossible to enter upon another negotiation without dishonor for himself and offense for the King of France. But Alexander's view was that nothing need be difficult when time allowed intelligence to find the means of overcoming the difficulty. In fact he tried a most daring maneuver: he addressed himself directly to the King of France, asking his aid in the project, actually asking him to solicit a favorable decision from the Duke of Ferrara. At first, Louis XII not only refused to help, but declared himself opposed to the marriage. But finally, yielding to further pressure from the Pope, he approached Ercole and advised him to ask Lucretia's hand for his son. He told the Duke he was withdrawing the suggestion of the Duch-

Y

331

ess of Angoulême, but he warned him to be very exacting
in the matter of the dowry. Ercole yielded to the King's
request—on both points; and with that superb skill in play-
ing a double game which characterized the Renaissance,
he fended off the opposition of other States and his own
relations by saying that the King of France had forced the
marriage on him against his will. The preliminary negotiations were long. There were many people to be convinced
and many difficulties to be surmounted.

The Duke of Ferrara demanded as dowry two hundred
thousand ducats in cash, twenty thousand in jewels, the
abolition of the tribute of four thousand ducats the Duchy
had to pay every year to the Vatican, and the territories
of Pieva, Cento, and Porto Cesenatico. As a postscript he
further demanded benefices for his son the Cardinal Ippolito. Obviously all these demands were made in full
knowledge that the other party would not accept them as
they stood and that after interminable discussions they
would be beaten down to something more reasonable. This
way of negotiating marriage contracts still exists today in
many parts of Europe. For those who have experience
with such places, this affair of the Borgia marriage must
look like a scene from the life of today. There was absolutely endless discussion, all extremely vulgar in the eyes
of a posterity which in large part believes that marriages
are the result of a spontaneous choice dictated by love and
by love alone. But however things may be now, that was
not the custom then. On the contrary, there would be long
negotiations, broken off, taken up again; and the two most
interested parties, though not allowed to express their
opinion publicly, yet did on occasion help their respective parents by the attitude they adopted. Thus Lucretia,
whose sale-price was the matter in question, secretly

pressed her father to give the utmost possible; while she made herself as agreeable as she could to the other side so that in fixing the price they might reckon something for her goodness and her affection for the family she wished to enter. There was also the delicate matter of the intervention of helpful friends, there was the gossip retailed by servants, there were momentary obstinacies which looked eternally unconquerable. The contract was fought out vehemently and with the keenest arguments, in which the financial point of view was mingled with the moral in the subtlest dialectic.

But once the matter was settled and the consent of the heads of the two families obtained, all was changed. On every face friendly smiles took the place of unbending severity, as though to show that the contract was simply a necessary evil, something that form demanded, and that money was really a very vulgar business which meant nothing to such high-minded people; clearly the only thing that anybody was really concerned about was the union of the two families, the happiness of the two young people, and the prosperity of the children who should be born. Marriage was suddenly back on its proper level, which is the level of fine sentiments and mutual affection. Only if we understand the customs of the day will we understand the language of Ercole d'Este—though the Pope cried out that this great lord was behaving like a small shopkeeper —or make sense of Louis XII's hint to demand as much as possible. Otherwise this marriage must look like a sale of the goods and rights of the Church to the cupidity of Ercole d'Este.

The Pope replied to the Duke of Ferrara's demands by offering half the sum demanded; and for the rest he had recourse to the College of Cardinals, for the question was

333

an affair of state as well as a private matter. The cardinals accepted the papal decisions.

But if the matrimonial contract had required long preparations, the wedding required preparations as long. In the first place Ercole was insistent that the conditions of the contract should be carried out before the wedding: this, as I have said, because a Pope can only help his family while he lives and this Pope was very old. Then the marriage must be celebrated with the uttermost splendor; for both families wanted to show how great was the satisfaction they felt in the union. Ercole wished to send a cortège worthy of the nobility of his house and to receive a cortège worthy of the high position of Lucretia.

Thus it was not till the beginning of December, 1501, that the Cardinal Ippolito d'Este left Ferrara with his brothers Ferrante and Sigismond, many other personages of high birth and a train of five hundred people. On December 23 he entered Rome by the Porta del Popolo. The reception given him was enthusiastic and magnificent. Twenty-three cardinals, and all that was noble and of high respect in Rome, united with a multitude which applauded unendingly, attracted by the beauty of the ceremony, and deeply moved at the thought of Lucretia and all she had suffered. Cesar, in shining gold, was at the head of an army of four thousand men. Gian Battista Scabolini, one of those who speaks of the beauty of the cortège, says that Cesar rode a magnificent white horse which seemed to have wings and that "his robes and the furnishings of his horse were estimated at ten thousand ducats, since they seemed all of gold, pearls and other jewels."[1] The Pope received the Este representatives with deep emotion, surrounded by twelve cardinals.

From the correspondence that has come down to us, it

appears that Lucretia Borgia was considered a model of virtue. The ambassadors of Ferrara wrote: "The more we examine her and the more closely we study her way of life, the higher is our opinion of her goodness, her honor and her wisdom. We have likewise noted that she is not only pious but deeply devout." In a long and very intimate correspondence addressed to Isabella d'Este, wife of the Marquis of Mantua, by someone who signs himself Il Prete we find similar proofs of respect and praise. Il Prete could not alter the truth even to satisfy the rulers of Mantua, who, for political reasons, had not been and still were not enthusiastic about the marriage. For him, Lucretia was beautiful, courteous, honorable, in a word, perfect; he describes the smallest details of her life, her clothes, her daily routine.

On December 28, the halls of the Vatican were thronged. All the Cardinals who were in Rome were present; and there were any number of bishops and ambassadors and nobles to admire Lucretia's charms. By the Pope's desire, the representatives of the city were also present. Ferrante, brother of the bridegroom, took Lucretia's hand, and putting the wedding ring on her finger, pronounced the word: "The most illustrious lord Alfonso, your spouse, freely sends you this wedding ring; and I, most illustrious Lady Lucretia, present it to you in his name." She replied: "And I accept it fully and freely."

On January 5, 1502, Lucretia left Rome with an equally imposing cortège. Cesar had given her as an escort two hundred soldiers. She was followed by young women of the Roman nobility. The localities through which she passed were ecstatic in their ovations; princes and cities sent their gifts. Her husband came to meet her at Castel Bentivoglio, where he remained some hours with her, then went on ahead to Ferrara to receive her officially. According to details which are of no great importance historically, but are valuable for the light they shed upon the state of mind of the persons concerned, it seems to me that Alexander VI had greater affection for Lucretia than even for Cesar. He had absolute confidence in her and on two occasions left her in the Vatican to see to his correspondence and have an eye on all that happened. We never find on his lips any criticism or reproach of her. When he speaks of her he seems lost for words to describe her virtues and all her excellence. On that January day in 1502 he saw her for the last time.

There were immense celebrations in Ferrara. It seemed that Lucretia brought joy and happiness with her. That, it may be, is why the future—in spite of the death of the Pope and the fall of Cesar and the troubles of the age—treated her not unkindly.

But in the midst of all this rejoicing the sort of hostility that was a habit in Rome could not be entirely silent. There were two satires then current in the city. They were either written down by Bruchard or later interpolated in his *Journal.* Later writers have used them as a reason for vilifying Lucretia as she was vilified by her contemporary Matarazzo, who had never known her nor ever known anything directly of her, and who wrote with the sole object of dragging the Borgia family in the mud because so his master paid him. One of these satires has to do with a festival of harlots—fifty of them and unclothed—said to have been given by Cesar, in which obscenity reached a level excessive even for that age. And in this lunatic bacchanalia, rumor has it that the Pope and Lucretia both figured. If Bruchard's *Journal* is carefully examined we find that that meticulous Master of Ceremonies was not given to writing of indecency, and in fact abhorred it. I have already given the grounds for my doubt of the authenticity of all that is found in his *Journal*, but in the present instance it must be added that only a professional writer of pornography would have dreamed of describing a scene of this sort in such grimy detail.[2] Bruchard was not an eyewitness, and if he had written at all upon such a subject, he would have written in general terms. Besides if Cesar on this occasion had staged a show of such unbelievable obscenity, it would have meant that he was in the habit of giving others of the same sort, even if on a smaller scale; all the more since apparently the Pope himself and the fiancée of the eldest son of a great family found it quite normal to enjoy the fun. But in fact there exists no hint of any other such orgy anywhere in Bruchard. And the moment chosen by the pamphleteers was the precise moment when the ambassadors of the Este family were in Rome and were most particularly interested in Lucretia's morals and the kind of life she led.

The details of the orgy are unprintable here. Like Bruchard, Matarazzo describes it in his Chronicle but he got it from the same source as Bruchard or the interpolator. Matarazzo was far from Rome and some friend had told him of these pamphlets against the Borgias. The ambassador Francesco Pepi wrote to Florence that the Pope was until a late hour on the previous night in Cesar's apartments, but he says nothing of the obscene spectacle. He speaks only of "dancing and laughter." The probability is that Cesar had arranged some kind of festival, and that the slanderous part is all by way of addition. What we have for certain at this period is the witness of the men sent by Ercole d'Este: telling only of the virtue and good conduct and devotion of Lucretia.

337

The other story, which deals with animal abominations, is if anything filthier still. There would be no pleasure and no end served by describing it. As usual there are contradictory versions, and no evidence whatever.

But while the malicious humor of the Romans was thus finding consolation for its spite against the Spaniards who had risen so high and threatened the ruin of so many local great families, Lucretia was riding towards her new country. There she was received with open arms by the most cultivated court in Italy; and the greatest poets of the day wrote in her honor.

CHAPTER XXIII

The Capture of Urbino and Camerino

Alexander VI devoted the first half of the year 1502 to the task of organizing the possessions he had won for the Church. The properties of the Roman barons with their towns and strongholds, as well as the territories occupied to the north of Rome, he placed for the most part under the direct administration of the Holy See. Everywhere he lowered the taxes, settled certain local controversies which constantly gave rise to strife and bloodshed, and established a normal and legal regime of liberty and order as liberty and order were then understood. In every place the populace experienced the immensity of the relief from the brutal exactions of the princes who had governed them. In the Romagna, he established a Vicariate under the authority of the Duke of Valencia and Romagna. Giovanni Olivieri, Bishop of Isernia, had in the previous year organized the Duchy to the satisfaction of everybody.[1] Now in the year 1502, Don Ramiro de Lorca continued the work, without regard either to the friends or the enemies of the regime, with speed and justice. Alessandro del Monte, who succeeded Ramiro de Lorca, finally gave the province a system of government which may be regarded as more democratic than that of Florence and as well organized as that of Venice. Cesar, under the Pope's direction, was the ultimate judge of the work of his delegates, granted favors to the towns which asked for them, exempted the poorer territories from taxation, and carried out constructional works of military and civil necessity. What is of special importance is that he raised the citizen's dignity and sense of responsibility by charging him with public duties of which so far he had been deprived, save, exceptionally, as at Faenza during the minority of Astore Manfredi.

But peoples do not easily accomplish great strides forward in their political development. The times of which we speak were not propitious for the establishment of a new public order working peaceably. The difficulties arising at every moment from the clash of interests and the altered psychology of the new conditions were not suited to the fruitful application of good principles of government. The social element upon which it is necessary to act was not solid enough to take a definite form. Italy was then a vast experimental laboratory of institutions. In public life, experiments do not give clear and definitive results, precisely because good government is not this or that system but a state of harmony, resulting from a slow adaptation between the political organization and the needs of the individual. Thus in this period the systems of democracy and aristocracy, of liberty and tyranny, of monarchy and republic, all had general discontent as their common denominator. Yet in the brief period during which Cesar Borgia governed the Romagna, he gave that state a sense of the public good as a goal hitherto unknown; and in a general way the populace seemed satisfied with the new regime.

To these successes of what we may call internal papal policy, there correspond none in the international order. New difficulties were appearing on the horizon.

The war against the Turk, which the Pope had prepared

so laboriously, devoting his greatest resources to it, had been abandoned by the principal powers, Spain and France; while the Empire continued to do nothing, in spite of the promises given and the money received. Only Venice and Hungary, because they were directly attacked by the Turk, remained in agreement with the Pope. But Venice, in that kind of madness which falls upon a people on the point of ruin, were putting obstacles in the way of the Pope's action, although he was acting in their interest. Alexander VI was surprised to find that, having sent fifteen thousand two hundred gold ducats to the Bishop of Venosa at Venice for the equipment of new galleys, nothing had been done because of the ill-will of the Venetians themselves, who took advantage of the Bishop's unexpected death.[2] The Venetians feared the papal influence in the eastern Mediterranean, even in that hour of danger; and by their present action they were risking all their chances in the war.

In a dispatch of Antonio Giustiniani, ambassador of Venice, we have a symptom of the state of mind which mistrust among allies often produces and which leads to the defeat of both. After the capture of Santa Maura by the galleys of Venice and the Pope, each party was claiming for itself the credit of the victory; Alexander VI, maintaining in the Consistory the version of the event favorable to the Church, asked: *Quid juris*—as if it were a question for the future, who should keep the captured place. The Venetian cardinal Grimani replied sarcastically: "Holy Father, your Holiness can keep it in your own name and that of the Holy See by fortifying and strengthening and defending it." Giustiniani tells us that the Pope pretended not to notice.[3] But in fact Alexander had no choice but to pass over in silence and bitterness of soul this biting comment by a prince of the Church upon the Church's weakness. For it was quite obvious that the Holy See could not fortify or defend the place.

Graver still for the Pope were the differences that had arisen between France and Spain in the territory of Naples. The treaty of Granada had divided the territory into two parts, but had omitted some places from the division altogether. With the precipitation and carelessness common in treaties which deal with the allocation of future conquests, the Kings of Spain and France had forgotten certain provinces. When both sides wished to occupy these territories, the French and Spaniards found themselves fighting a war at first undeclared, but soon enough declared. It ended later, after the death of Alexander, with the definite expulsion of the French from the Kingdom. Alexander essayed to settle the difference, and the rulers agreed to accept his decision. But the treaty of Granada, by dividing a territory which had been for centuries united, had created one of those international situations which will not stand up to the test of facts, however honorable are the intentions of the contracting parties at the moment of agreement: for facts always revolt against arbitrary creations.

The Pope was called upon by the Spanish ambassador in public Consistory to intervene in the conflict. The orator stated that the Catholic Kings and His most Christian Majesty had concluded a peace (the one which had preceded the conquest of Naples) not only to their own interests, but for the good of Christianity; and that now there had arisen differences and discords between the two states, unknown to the sovereigns. And now their royal majesties asked the arbitration of His Holiness and the Sacred College to put an end to all the differences that might arise between the two kingdoms in this realm of Naples.[4] Alexander accepted this flattering charge and proposed the only solution possible in such cases, where there exists no pre-established right. What he proposed was the acceptance of the state of fact actually existing, in other words that each party should retain what it held at the moment of conflict. The war had broken out against the will of the respective governments, but peace could not issue from arbitration, however highly placed the arbitrator. The conflict continued, causing great sorrow and very grave difficulties to the Pope, who considered any solution not based upon the *status quo* as contrary to the interests of the Holy See.

These problems at the very gates of Rome and the imminence of the Turkish danger which he feared beyond all others, obliged Alexander to hurry forward the organization of a strong state under a family of warriors dependent upon the Church—a Vicar, a kind of sentinel, armed and ready, defending the temporal integrity of the Holy See. And he was confirmed in his purpose of uniting the forces of this great papal state with those of the Venetians and thereby preventing foreign domination in Italy. Unfortunately for this last purpose, Alexander's political thought could not find concrete realization in that tempest of passions. His first program, which had been to keep the foreigner out of Italy, had failed with the entry first of Charles VIII and later of Louis XII. This new program could not even be begun because of the continual refusal of the Venetians, who preferred small territorial gains, ephemeral and almost useless, to a tranquil prosperous life.

Because of these international uncertainties, Cesar was obliged to spend five long months in Rome, practically in idleness, the longest time he was continuously with Alexander since giving up the purple. On February 17, they left Rome together to spend a few days at Piombino, to which they went by galley from Civitavecchia. The Pope consecrated a church, and attended the worldlier festivals which Cesar found indispensable and the Pope not unenjoyable. They studied the defences of the place and other works. From Piombino they went to the Island of Elba where they examined the plans of the fortifications. The Pope who was then over seventy rode through the streets of the town on a mule and was received by the populace here as everywhere with much affection.[5]

But on their way back a storm endangered the galleys and the lives of the travelers. Cesar jumped into a small boat with a few sailors and managed to make the shore while the violence of the sea kept the galleys from entering the harbor. The cardinals passed a night of terror. Not so the Pope, who gave proof throughout of perfect intrepidity.[6] It was the second time Rodrigo Borgia had suffered the violence of the sea and each time he was near to losing his life. There were several other instances in his life of danger from natural causes. Once, as he was walking in the Vatican gardens, a piece of iron crashed from a great height and fell at his feet. Another time, a ceiling collapsed on his head. He emerged from both accidents unharmed.

Back in Rome, the Pope continued to study the international situation and worked at the preparation of a new army. Cesar also remained in the city, leading his usual life. He rose from bed very late and stayed up all night, frequenting places of pleasure, usually masked. But he was watching for the moment of action. Meanwhile the forces of the papacy were gathered and the *condottieri* received their payment and in addition rich properties in the Roman territory. Paolo and Giulio Orsini, the Duke of Gravina

344

and Vitellozzo Vitelli were the principal leaders of the new army. No one knew for what purpose these troops were meant, and as a result everybody was in a state of fear. But the likeliest enemies could be none others than such of the Vicars as still remained, especially those against whom the Pope had at various times issued decrees stripping them of the right of investiture. A few months later, Cesar, talking to Bishop Soderini at Urbino, admitted that his intention was to destroy, not this or that Vicar but every tyrant in Italy. Thus, when the Pope considered the great powers so neatly balanced that he could resume the work of sweeping the whole papal territory clean of the worst criminals who had ever ruled, it is not surprising that he sent Cesar to complete the program. It would be misleading to say that the Pope, in combatting tyrants, was animated by a lofty sense of abstract justice. His was a clear and realistic mind, and he would not have credited himself with that kind of mission. His object was to have done with those many Vicariates because the Church could not count upon them in case of necessity. That was why he had made no difference between the Manfredi family who were loved at Faenza and Catherine Sforza who was loathed at Imola. Similarly, he drew no distinction between the abominable Varano of Camerino, and Guido-baldo de Montefeltro, who was popular at Urbino for his just and honorable government.

On June 12, 1502, Cesar left Rome to join his army. Even so late, on the very eve of action, nothing was known as to the precise intentions of the Pope and Cesar. The latter's departure from Rome coincided with a rising in Arezzo against Florence and an invasion of Florence's territory by Vitellozzo Vitelli. So everybody believed that Florence, with which the Borgias had in any case never been on good terms, would be attacked. But everybody was wrong. The Papal army marched against Urbino. It is certain that the Pope and Cesar were privy to Vitellozzo's action. But it seems that they later dropped the plan, mindful of the danger it would have involved in face of the protection accorded by France to Florence, whose geographical situation simplified communication between France's possessions in Milan and Naples. On the other hand it seemed that the Pope did not know in advance of Cesar's sudden attack upon the Duke of Urbino, who lost all his estates in a few days. This lightning action against Urbino, which was scarcely an attack at all but little more than a military parade, has been presented by authors of the period as a mean trick on Cesar's part, criticized by the Pope himself. Guidobaldo was indeed surprised, for he was not expecting to be attacked. The very night on which he learned of Cesar's approach, he was at supper outside the town, totally unaware that he was at war with anyone. He had time only to flee. But Duke Guidobaldo was in contact with Cesar's enemies and had refused to carry out his duties as Vicar of the Church. Further Cesar accused the Lord of Urbino of having prepared a treacherous scheme to deprive him of all his artillery and then to attack him as he passed through his territory. Anyhow Cesar justified himself to the Pope in a long letter for having commenced an action of war unknown to the Pope and unauthorized by him.

According to the diaries and chronicles of the period, the affair is not very clear. It would seem that once more we have an instance of what can only be called double-crossing. The truth that has come down to us is that on the one hand, Cesar was working against the Duke at Urbino by means of emissaries before he knew that Guidobaldo was plotting with his enemies at Camerino; and that on the other hand Guidobaldo did not know of Cesar's designs against him when he was secretly helping his Varano neighbors, who were enemies of the Church. In short each was plotting against the other, neither aware of the justification for his own conduct provided by the conduct of the other.

The ease with which this conquest had been brought about helped to convince the Pope that Cesar had been in the right; and to his titles of Duke of Valence and Romagna he added the title of Duke of Urbino.

But if Urbino was taken in three days and with no trouble to anyone—that is without anyone killed—as Cesar informed Machiavelli,[7] the capture of Camerino was difficult and bloody. The Varanos governed their States with a strong hand. Giulio Cesare Varano, then seventy, had in his youth murdered his own brother Rodolfo. He was a dynamic character, and he had gathered about him a good number of men who, driven by Alexander and Cesar from the Papal States, had come to Camerino in all ferocity to fight their own battle. But the people and the local citizenry had no love for their ruling family and were not at all disposed to undergo the painful consequences of the capture of their city by an enemy whom they considered rather as a liberator. Nonetheless the war began with great violence, and to begin with, fortune seemed to smile on the Varano cause. Annibal, Giulio's son, with his cavalry was too much for the Duke of Gravina, Francesco Orsini. But Cesar Borgia, who was at some distance, reinforced the papal army with good artillery and a large number of infantry, and laid siege to the town. A popular rising forced the Varanos to ask for terms of peace. As often happens when such negotiations are publicly known, the populace did not await their conclusion but opened the gates of the city to the invader. The Duke of Gravina made captive all the members of the family except one—the youngest, Gianmaria, who was in Venice—and sent them to Cesar. A few months later the aged Giulio died in the fortress of La Pergola. His sons were killed some three months later when Cesar's troops were forced to beat a hasty retreat before the rebellious advance of Vitellozzo and the Duke of Gravina himself. Cesar, or his military leaders, fearing that the prisoners might be delivered by the rebels, had them killed.

It does not appear that Cesar Borgia intended to inflict the death penalty upon the Lord of Camerino. And the slaying of the sons seems to have been a supplementary measure taken by Michelotto without consulting Cesar. The historians have said much that is unprovable and improbable about these executions. They have stated that the Varanos had surrendered, that the terms of the surrender were not kept by Cesar, and that they were executed in breach of the sworn word. But the fact of their capture is well known and disproves the accusation of bad faith thus levelled against Cesar. They did not surrender and consequently could not impose conditions.

In Rome, the capture of Camerino was celebrated with great manifestations of joy. The Pope was well content.

CHAPTER XXIV

The Conspiracy of the Condottieri

Between the Pope and Cesar on the one hand and the leaders of the papal army on the other—the men who might have been loosely termed the great vassals of the court of Rome—there was a fundamental opposition of interests, which had to show itself sooner or later. Alexander chose to use men like Vitellozzo Vitelli and the Orsini and Oliverotto de Fermo to destroy people like the Varanos and Bentivoglios and the lords of Sinigaglia, who were very similar morally and politically to themselves; and these captains knew perfectly well that when they had exterminated the others, it would be their own turn to be exterminated. To all it was obvious that the Pope was following the policy of "I shall avenge me of my enemies with my enemies." Besides among these tyrants, *condottieri* and enemies of the Pope, there were many family links, not only because proximity forced them to it but because at that time, among lords great and small, every agreement was sealed by a marriage. So that the assailants were related to the men they assailed.

At the time of the attack on Urbino and Camerino, the captains had shown no enthusiasm. Behind scenes, the Church and its *condottieri* exchanged threats. But they continued to save appearances by remaining more or less in agreement outwardly: because the *condottieri* were re-

349

ceiving the money necessary for the upkeep of an army which otherwise they could not have had, an army which might serve at need against their present paymasters; and because the Church hoped that the authority of the Holy See and the fear it inspired would prevent the protesting leaders from forming a conspiracy, apart from which no serious difficulties were likely to arise. The *condottieri*, anxious to avoid a rupture whose consequences might well have been fatal to themselves and hoping that later some way might be found to harmonize the papal interests with their own, strongly urged Cesar to attack Florence, and encouraged the dislike he instinctively felt for that city of merchants. In this enterprise, Vitellozzo had a personal interest—he wanted to avenge the death of his brother whom the Republic had executed somewhat hastily when they believed that as chief of their army against Pisa he was betraying them.[1]

Meanwhile, with Vitellozzo invading Florence for his own satisfaction but with the consent of Cesar and the Pope, and with Cesar making his triumphal entry into Urbino and Camerino, Louis XII arrived in Italy once more and assumed the rôle of arbiter—which his material forces by no means justified—of the affairs of the Peninsula or at least of the north and center of Italy. France was then greatly respected. It was said not too extravagantly: "All Italians are Frenchmen." A policy of continuing friendliness and the use of force at the right moment would have given France that age-long domination of Italy which instead passed into the hands of Spain and then of Austria. But at this moment, the conduct of the French was marked by a series of inexplicable errors, all the more surprising since neither the King's advisers nor the King himself were fools. On July 7, 1502 Louis XII was at Asti. All the enemies of the Borgias sped to the camp of this great distributor of justice. Among them there were many who had not yet been made to suffer but who feared that they soon would be if fortune continued to smile upon Cesar's warfare and the Pope's policy. The King immediately resumed his rôle of protector of Florence, and Cesar yielded humbly. Vitellozzo was obliged to abandon Arezzo and all the Florentine territory under Cesar's threat to come personally to Civita Castellana, where he lived, to constrain him by force. But for the rest, the King remained faithful to his word not to intervene in the affair of the Vicars, except to aid the Pope.

All the same Cesar realized the danger he ran. The French court was packed with his enemies, who with the subtle skill of the Italians of that day used calumny when calumny might profitably be whispered in the ear of the powerful, and were skilled in the use of gold, which so powerfully shapes men's convictions. Cesar informed the King that he would come to see him in Milan and on July 25 he left Urbino incognito with a handful of men, stayed in Ferrara long enough to see his sister Lucretia who was ill, and on August 5 arrived in Milan.

There were many who believed, or at any rate spread the rumor, that the object of the King's coming to Italy was to punish Cesar; others thought that he meant to take him back to France. When he learned that Cesar was approaching, the King came to meet him with such evident pleasure and sympathy as left no doubt whatever about the friendliness of his intentions. "Welcome, my cousin and good kinsman," he said, and flung his arms around his neck, embracing him again and again. Then he brought him into the Château, to the apartments he had made ready for him. Cesar's enemies had by now realized that it

351

would be safer to leave the court. The Marquis of Mantua had no choice but to be reconciled with Cesar, and as pledge of friendship the marriage was announced of the two children, Louise, Cesar's daughter, and Francesco, the Marquis's son. It was Cesar Borgia's hour of triumph. Eyewitnesses were dumbfounded to see how Louis XII, who had always shown great kindness to Cesar, now showed him an affection so exaggerated as to make him the second personage of France, giving him precedence of all the princes of the blood royal who were there present. This behaviour of the King was all the more startling because everyone had expected the reverse, for the small Italian courts were a great whispering gallery where desire created rumors which passed for certain, though no one knew their origin; and it was accepted as indisputable that Cesar no longer had the King's protection.[2]

Contemporaries should have realized, if any contemporary were ever capable of understanding the history of his own time, that the King of France preferred the Pope to any dethroned princeling; but what they could not very well have known was that, before Cesar's arrival in Milan, Alexander VI had worked out an agreement with the King. The Pope had no liking for these journeys by foreign sovereigns and he was always in fear of a new conquest. He had complete contempt for the cardinals who surrounded the King and were always pushing him into intervention in the affairs of Italy. In his excitement, he could utter violent abuse of them: "These idiot cardinals [Giuliano della Rovere, Ascanio Sforza and Raffaele Riario] who surround the King of France have described Italy to him as a paradise, yet he has found hell here. We very much hope to see them discredited with the King, for the reward of the dishonest is always the hatred of those who begin by favoring them."[3]

But as on this occasion Alexander VI could not prevent the King's coming into Italy, he advised Cesar to postpone his journey to Milan, and he sent Monseigneur Trozo, in whose ability he had confidence, to explore the ground.[4] His political method was to prevent evils, but to accept them when they had happened and try to extract if not good at least some utility from them.

While Louis XII was in Italy, the Pope had been charged with the settlement of the conflict that divided France and Spain on the matter of Naples. The Spanish sovereigns, through the ambassador, offered him a "fine and useful present," urging strongly that he should take the side of Spain. The King of France offered no gift, but presented himself in person and gave pledges of his favor. The Pope inclined towards France, because France for the moment seemed concerned to maintain the *status quo*; and he offered Louis that he would send Cesar with ten thousand men to defend his rights in Naples, on condition that the King would support him in the territories of the Church.

The King found the Pope's proposals good and he signed a formal treaty with Cesar. Cesar was to aid France with ten thousand men if necessary, and on his side the King undertook to help with three hundred lances in the effort to win Bologna for the Church and to overthrow the Orsini, the Baglioni, and Vitellozzo.[5] This secret arrangement explains the reception given to Cesar, his journey by the King's side as far as Genoa, and the cordial and affectionate farewell which swept away all the hopes of the enemies of the Borgias.

This treaty also casts a new light upon Cesar's relations with his captains, upon the conspiracy which took place,

353

and the ease with which it was repressed. These Orsini and Vitellozzo, whom the King of France had undertaken to destroy, were at that moment the principal leaders of the Papal army; they were paid by the Holy See from whom they received new properties and new titles. If Cesar entered into a secret pact for their overthrow, the reason was that he already regarded them as enemies. And in fact, upon his return from the King's camp, the Captains began to conspire against him, in alliance with the very Vicars they had undertaken to fight. The hatred of these lords against Cesar was great. Bentivoglio said that he would kill him at the first opportunity, Oliverotto that he would kill him within the year. Vitellozzo swore that Cesar should not escape him. There was no exaggeration in the remark of Isabella d'Este that in so exceptional an epoch there was no point in forwarding the interest of the ally of the moment or brooding over the crimes of former enemies. The spirit of the time was to decide one's course from day to day by the rule of immediate interest. Machiavellianism was not the creation of Machiavelli any more than treachery was the monopoly of Cesar Borgia.

The Pope, once he was certain of the support of the King of France, began his attack—in the spiritual sphere— upon the Bentivoglio family of Bologna. In a brief of September 2, 1502, he summoned before his tribunal Giovanni Bentivoglio and his sons Annibal and Alessandro. In this brief he speaks of the necessity of peace for Bologna and shows how the violences of the Bentivoglios against the citizens have compromised it; in a tone of feeling he recalls the years he passed in the University there, which had brought him to so deep a love for the unhappy, ill-governed city. These explanations gave the lawyer in him both juridical and moral satisfaction. But in reality if Alexander

VI meant to bring Bologna within the States of the Church, it was in order to double its defensive strength. He did not mean to attach Bologna to the Dukedom of the Romagna, but to have it under the direct authority of the Holy See. This he told the King of France many times.

But for war against the Bentivoglios a good army was necessary. Cesar could count on roughly five thousand men directly under his orders. The Orsini, Vitellozzo Vitelli and Oliverotto da Fermo had some nine thousand men. Together and well supported by artillery they could hope for success, especially if the three hundred lances should arrive in time from the King of France. The moral effect produced by the soldiers of Louis XII would be even more effective than the material aid they brought. But the Duke quickly learned not only that he could not count upon the nine thousand men led by the *condottieri*, but that this part of the Papal army, paid by Rome, would in the event of war be on the Bentivoglio side and against him.

At La Magione near Perugia, a property of Cardinal Orsini, there met towards the end of September, Cardinal Orsini, Giulio, Paolo, and Francesco Orsini, Vitellozzo Vitelli, Gian Paolo Baglione of Perugia, Antonio de Venafro representing Pandolfo Petrucci, and Oliverotto da Fermo who had shortly before murdered his parents and the lords of Fermo his protectors at a family dinner, and seized possession of their States.

The meeting was secret. An offensive and defensive alliance was decided upon between the persons present and the Bentivoglios, with the object of restoring to the rule of their states all the princes expelled by the Pope. The immediate plan was to attack Cesar Borgia, who was at Imola, to defeat and destroy him. Venice and Florence supported the conspiracy but with a certain prudent reserve—espe-

355

cially Florence, which sent Machiavelli to Cesar. The conspirators of La Magione increased their numbers with the definite adhesion of Pandolfo Petrucci, tyrant of Siena, of the Duke of Urbino, of one of the Varanos—son of Rudolfo who had been assassinated by his brother Giuilo—and of other personages less notable. But though this conspiracy was arranged in September, the Orsini were still dealing with the Pope in October, drawing from the Holy See the money to pay their troops, thus deceiving Alexander who still believed in them. Only the extreme caution which was habitual to him prevented him from paying out the very large sum they asked for, which they were only awaiting in order to go into immediate and open revolt.

But the secret could not remain a secret much longer. Cesar was at first completely overwhelmed at the news, but quickly recovered his energy and immediately had an interview with the Pope in Rome. Both decided for war. With the money he received abundantly from Rome, Cesar began to organize a new army. And fortunately for him, the conspirators, who would have been sure of some success in the first moment, postponed their attack. In fact, the action against Cesar was undertaken not by the *condottieri* but by the populace of Urbino who still remembered their good lord Guidobaldo. The war—if we may so style these rather incoherent hostilities—was carried on without much vigour. Each one of the conspirators tried to find some way of getting into touch with the Pope, for they were all in especial dread of him. The only battle that took place was at Calmazzo, where Don Miguel Corella and Don Hugo de Moncada were beaten by the Orsini. Moncada was captured. Cesar, thus forced by circumstances, could but concentrate his forces in the province of Romagna, abandoning the rest of the territory; but in secret he organized a new army, with superb self-confidence. The conspirators, instead of converging upon the center and destroying the strong nucleus of the enemy, spread themselves over the whole extent of territory. They conquered cities instead of destroying armies, a common error of all ages.

In a short space, Cesar had ready a body of men, if not superior, at least equal to his adversaries, apart from the army of Bologna, which remained upon the defensive. At Rome, too, the Pope was taking up arms. And the King of France, sending the lances that he had offered Cesar, wrote to the Pope that he would come in person if necessary to fight against all his enemies.

The time the conspirators had lost was precious. By now they were fast breaking up. But neither the Pope nor Cesar had any intention of fighting them in the open field and thereby losing soldiers and money and incurring the risk which is never absent from a battle. The two Borgias knew the men they had against them, knew that every one of them, for all his oaths of alliance and fidelity, would leave his dearest friend to his fate if it meant any profit for himself. Alexander VI had not broken off relations with Cardinal Orsini who was the heart of the conspiracy; and Cesar was in secret but continuous contact with the Bentivoglios and Pandolfo Petrucci. The moral disintegration of the conspiracy was complete; each individual conspirator was secretly trying to make terms for the saving of his own skin, and finally an arrangement was reached of which the principal victim was the only decent man in this group of blackguards, namely Guidobaldo de Montefeltro, Duke of Urbino. He lost his State, for part of the new agreement was all that Cesar's previous conquests in the name of the Church were recognized.

357

There were two different pacts. In the first, the captains engaged to return to the service of the Pope, only they were not in future all to serve together but one at a time. Cesar and the rebels, including Pandolfo, signed this document. The second revoked the sentence depriving the Bentivoglios of their investiture, and they remained rulers of Bologna. The Pope and the Bentivoglios signed this pact. It was further agreed that the Bentivoglios should be *condottieri* of Cesar, paying him an annual tribute, and that a grandson of the lord of Bologna should marry a niece of the Bishop of Elne, later a Cardinal, a nephew of Alexander.

With peace thus concluded, Cesar immediately set about the attack upon Sinigaglia, which was governed by the *prefetessa*—Giovanna de Montefeltro, widow of Giovanni della Rovere—in the name of her son, Francesco Maria, who was also heir of Guidobaldo de Montefeltro, his uncle, and therefore of the Duchy of Urbino if Guidobaldo had still been its master. The former conspirators, instead of abiding by the clause of the treaty according to which one at a time was to serve in the papal army, all joined together in the new enterprise. Only lacking were Baglione, ill at Perugia, and Giovanni and Giulio Orsini who were with Cardinal Orsini in their Roman strongholds. It was Oliverotto da Fermo who bore the whole weight of the action, such as it was, for there was not a great deal to do. The *prefetessa* fled, leaving the castle in charge of Andrea Doria, who was later in the service of Genoa. The advance of the papal armies brought Oliverotto with some three thousand men close to Sinigaglia. The Orsini and Vitellozzo camped some five miles from the town, with a contingent superior in numbers to Oliverotto's. Cesar had spent Christmas at Cesena amusing himself in his own

way. On December 28, he was at Fano where he remained
till December 31; and on the morning of that day, taking
with him don Miguel Corella, he proceeded to Sinigaglia,
to which the captains had sent him an urgent summons, on
the pretext that Doria refused to deliver the fortress save
to Cesar in person.

The exact course of the tragedy that followed, and from
what side the treachery came, is not easy to determine
from the contradictory reports that have come down to us.
Cesar believed that the former conspirators had decided to
assassinate him on the night of his arrival in the town. In
his letters of the first day of January written from Sinigaglia
itself, almost immediately after the event, he addressed
himself to Isabella de Gonzaga, to the communes of Pesaro,
Atri, Venafro, Piombino and others, and of course to the
Pope, relating and explaining what had happened. According to his account the Orsini and their accomplices—after
having been pardoned for their first treachery when, being
in the Pope's pay, "they had revolted, turning our arms
against ourselves"—took part in a new conspiracy at Sinigaglia—"pretending that they had come with few men,
when in fact they brought all the soldiers they had been
able to collect, with whom and with the aid and agreement
of the captain of the enemy fortress, they combined to do
against our person that which, forewarned of the affair,
we have done against them."[6] Cesar considers that "the
world must be happy and content, especially Italy, which
sees thus suppressed and extinguished the public and
calamitous pest from which its populace suffered."[7]

Cesar's account is corroborated by the general opinion
of the period which regarded as traitors "the tyrants so
marvelously suppressed." So held the King of France, who
thought Cesar had acted like a Roman. Machiavelli, in his

first report to the Seigniory, later modified, speaks of the fresh treason of the captains. The Pope informed the Venetian ambassador that Ramiro de Lorca, executed a few days earlier by the Duke of Cesena for some cause not precisely known, had before his death revealed to the Duke the intentions of the former conspirators. The Duke of Mantua felicitated Cesar, and the other lords likewise. Posterity may see the act as infamous, but the pleasure it gave contemporaries was considerable.

Following the majority of the accounts, the order of events seems to have been something like this. Cesar, who had come from Cesena with over six thousand men, put them in order for their entry into the city, mingling infantry and cavalry and shortening the ranks. At the approach to the bridge over the river Misa, the Orsini and Vitellozzo Vitelli came forward to meet Cesar, who embraced them, and they joined his troop, riding alongside him. Vitellozzo, says one of the accounts, was unwilling to be separated from his soldiers because he felt he was going to certain death if he did so. But willing or unwilling, he certainly entered Sinigaglia with the Orsini alongside Cesar. Oliverotto was in the act of passing his troops in review; he, like Vitellozzo, was unwilling to be separated from them but, at the summons of don Miguel Corella, he joined the others. Cesar held friendly converse with them all the way up to the palace in which Cesar was to lodge. The two Orsini, Vitellozzo and Oliverotto started to take leave of the Duke, but he indicated that he wished to speak to them and invited them to dinner. So all went together up the stairway and met in a room. Here the Duke had them seized, having left the room himself "for a personal reason."

That all had been prepared is clear from what followed. Cesar's troops immediately hurled themselves upon those

360

encamped without, and scattered the soldiers of the former conspirators, killing a great number of them. The rest, unable to make head or tail of so sudden an attack, deprived of their chiefs, broke up and fled in all directions; some few managed to escape. The Duke's infantry, having accomplished this easy task, returned to Sinigaglia drunk with wine and blood. They continued to loot the city until Cesar on horseback put an end to their excesses by having some of them executed on the open street. Thus it was that he was found by Machiavelli, who was startled and almost stunned by what he had seen. The Duke greeted him, dismounted, and told him sternly all that had passed.

On which side was the treachery? Though we need not share the enthusiasm of Louis XII, it is clear that Cesar's action showed a certain boldness, to capture the generals of an army superior in numbers and then with lightning swiftness to destroy that army itself. It could not have escaped Cesar that the hesitation of any one of those who had to carry out the plan, the slightest accident, any suspicion by the enemy, would have brought the scheme crashing about his head and made him the victim and not the executioner. In deciding upon an act so daring, so thick with dangers, he must have been forced by strong necessity. And in fact the impression one gets from the documents of the period is that his enemies of yesterday, who were his friends of today, would inevitably have been his enemies again tomorrow, until one or other was destroyed. And that happened which was in the natural order.

That same night of December 31, at ten o'clock, after a very summary trial, Vitellozzo and Oliverotto were executed. The two Orsini remained under arrest to be brought to trial in Rome.[8] The next morning, the citadel surrendered.

At receipt of the news of Sinigaglia, Alexander had Cardinal Gian Battista Orsini arrested. Bruchard says that the Pope had let the cardinal and Bishop Jacopo de Santa Croce know that the citadel had fallen into the hands of Cesar's men, that they thereupon came on horseback to the Vatican to congratulate His Holiness but were arrested as they entered the Hall of Pappagallo.[9] But it is certain that the date of their arrest was January 3 when the Pope did not yet know of the surrender of the fortress: he knew only of the terrible incident of Cesar and the captains. Bruchard has another error in his account, due probably to interpolation by copyists, in that he says that the cardinal was imprisoned in the Torre di Nona.[10] In fact Cardinal Orsini was confined in the Borgia Tower, a commodious set of apartments in the Vatican, where he had his own servants.[11] The Orsini family, which was very numerous, rose in arms backed not only by its customary allies but even by its age-old enemies, the Colonnas. They threatened Rome and the Vatican, so that the Pope, with an urgency which revealed how grave was the danger, summoned Cesar and his army to come to the defence of Rome and of himself, for both were at the mercy of the enemy.

So great was Alexander's attachment to legal forms, that he submitted the whole matter to a regular process of judgement. Instead of being swept into an act of immediate violence against Cardinal Orsini and his accomplices, he ordered simply that they should be brought to trial.

The governor of Rome proceeded to sequestrate the palace and the goods of the cardinal and the other prisoners, in the only form then known—that is to say by occupying them, which meant expelling those who were there. Historians have included this sequestration and the manner of its accomplishment among the crimes of the Borgias.

Cardinal Gian Battista was almost blind and in a very bad physical condition. Given to all vices, a reckless gambler, he ordinarily spent whole nights in pleasure; his detention, the sequestration of his goods, what seemed like the utter destruction of his family, all combined to sap the small strength he had left; and he confessed his sins, while his health grew worse. As we have seen, he died in the Castle at Saint Angelo. On the other hand the Bishop of Santa Croce was set at liberty because there was no evidence of his guilt.

Cesar ignored the Pope's order to return to Rome and continued his triumphal march. At Cagli, the Bishop Gaspar Golfi urged the inhabitants to resistance, but they proceeded to open the gates of the city, and he was condemned to death and executed out of hand. Citta di Castello,[12] which had suffered the tyranny of the Vitelli, surrendered to Cesar, who accepted the surrender in the name of the Church and not as Vicar. Perugia rose, shouting in the manner of that day "Duke! Duke!" thus acclaiming Cesar as their new lord. But once more he accepted the surrender in the name of the Church. Fermo, Cisterna, and Montone were likewise occupied by his troops and submitted to the papal authority.

Now, with a rapidity surprising in a man who normally spent the hours of daylight in bed, and with a decision he was not to show after the death of Alexander, Cesar fell upon the territory of Siena. He had already broken what he called the arm of the conspiracy. Now he meant to destroy its brain. That brain was Pandolfo Petrucci, tyrant of Siena, skilled in the use of gold with the strong and the sword with the weak. Once already he had escaped the

action of the Pope and Cesar by sending money to Louis
XII as the price of his protection; and now that Cesar had
penetrated his territory and the people of Siena were in
revolt, twenty thousand more ducats started on their way
across the Alps. Pandolfo had to leave Siena on the night
of January 28, 1503, but in two months he was back. Cesar
had congratulated the Sienese upon having won their liberty and got rid of Petrucci. But now they were subjected
anew to his tyranny, more ferocious than ever. These two
months of Borgian liberty cost them dear. The repression
was horrible.

More clear-sighted than Cesar, Alexander, who had no
liking for ephemeral triumphs, was against the political
and military line that Cesar had followed against Petrucci.
Besides, while success followed success at the periphery of
the Papal states, at Rome enemies threatened the very life
of the city and the Pope. The situation was grave. As soon
as the Orsini had recovered from their first stunned surprise at the news of what had happened at Sinigaglia and
Rome, they began to attack the various papal strongholds
and advanced to the gates of the city. In face of the common enemy, the century-old quarrel of the Orsini and the
Colonnas was brought to a truce, and the two great houses
united. Giulio Orsini, of Ceri, the ancient family eyrie, cut
off all commerce with Rome, which was only eighteen
miles distant from his stronghold. A Colonna occupied
Palombara, and from the important position of Bracciano,
Fabio Orsini dominated the roads and gathered arms and
men. At the end of January the Orsini and their allies attacked the Ponte Nomentano leading into Rome.

The Pope demanded that Cesar bring back the army,
and for the first time we are aware of a definite resistance
on Cesar's part to the papal orders. It would even appear

that the Duke either feigned an illness that he had not or exaggerated an illness he had while he was at Acquapendente, as an excuse for not coming speedily to Rome. It is in this year 1503 that we see clearly revealed the difference in outlook and interest between the Pope and Cesar. Cesar desired to carve out for himself a strong state to the northeast of Rome as permanent Vicar of the Holy See and nothing more. Whereas the Pope, who likewise strongly desired the formation of such a state for his beloved Cesar, had also his general policy and wished to carry it as far as possible towards realization before he died. For Cesar, it was not the Roman barons who were the enemies, but the long-established tyrants of the Romagna; and the King of France was the supreme arbiter of Italy. For the Pope, both the Roman barons and the tyrants of central Italy had to disappear in order that the Church might be independent; and the King of France had to be treated with respect when it proved impossible, by force or cunning, to keep him at home.

The various dangers impressed the Pope, but did not intimidate him. On February 7, he outlawed all the Orsini except Giangiordano—to be more precise, he outlawed Giulio, Fabio, Francesco, Giovanni, Orgentino and Franciotto Orsini. Giangiordano was then in the service of the King of France in what had once been the Kingdom of Naples, which is why he escaped the Vatican thunders. We appreciate still more the energy of the aged Pope when we learn that four days before this bull of excommunication, he had received an unfriendly letter from Louis XII expressing his displeasure at the course of events in Italy and the activities of Cesar. Petrucci's money, and the insinuations of Venice and Florence, had produced their effect.

Alexander saw clearly that if he yielded to the will of this distant power—which assumed no responsibilities and decided what should be done with no knowledge of the necessities of the actual situation—he was signing his own ruin. At such a moment, any hint of weakness would have invited the presentation of claims and complaints without number to the French King, who seemed to assume the rôle of protector of the Vatican when their views agreed and of severe critic when their views differed. The Pope considered that Louis XII represented no serious danger. He ordered the policy of destruction to continue, without bothering further about the royal wishes.

But the war against the Orsini and their allies was carried on only sluggishly. Cesar was on good terms with Giangiordano who had come back from Naples to his fiefs, that is to the actual battleground. Bracciano was not attacked, for Cesar simply said that he could not go against the expressed will of the King of France and also that Giangiordano and he belonged to the order of Saint Michael, the members of which were forbidden to settle their differences by arms and bound to submit them to the King's decision. The Pope felt real desperation at hearing scruples of this sort from Cesar.

All the same, apart from Bracciano, all the rest of the territory was occupied by the papal armies, thanks to violent pressure from Alexander. The fortress of Ceri was conquered and dismantled. The barons were expelled from all their strongholds. The Pope compelled his own kinsmen to abandon the territories of the Church's patrimony. Francesco Colonna, who was married to a Borgia, was compensated; and the Duke of Nepi received Piombino; but both had to restore their goods and titles to the Holy See. As to Bracciano, Alexander would not agree to treat it as an exception. He offered Giangiordano Orsini a huge indemnity, consisting of the goods that the prince of Squillace possessed in the Kingdom of Naples. But Giangiordano refused. The King of France intervened and was named depository of Bracciano, until its ultimate destiny could be decided.

We are now at the eve of the Borgia Pope's death. His policy seemed to have won a complete triumph. The Roman barons—who had dominated the Holy See for centuries, or had governed its territory, supporting now one Pope, now another—had been destroyed or driven out or reduced to impotence; the tyrants of central Italy, save only the Bentivoglios and Pandolfo Petrucci, were dead or driven from their domains. Upon their ruins arose a strong State governed by civilized men, with wide municipal liberties, with its own militia, defended by an army of over ten thousand men.

But Rodrigo Borgia knew that only a close and sincere alliance with Venice could consolidate his work. The salvation of Italy could issue only from the union of Venice and the Papacy, and with the salvation of Italy, the independence of the Church and the perpetuation of the house of Borgia.

CHAPTER XXV

Rome and Venice

THE work of Alexander, bringing under the effective authority of the Holy See the territories which tradition rather than law had attributed to the Church, has been denied by writers of the quality of Ranke, Gregorovius, von Pastor and certain others.[1] In spite of the facts we have just been considering, the merit of having constituted the pontifical State is generally attributed to Julius II. Yet they might have been shown the error of this view both by the judgement of Julius II himself who, in speaking of his work of reconquest, always alluded to the occupation carried out under his predecessor Alexander; and by his repeated insistence after Alexander's death that Cesar Borgia yield up the towns and strongholds of the Romagna.

Upon these two Popes, Borgia and della Rovere, history has given two opposite judgements, equally false. It has accused the one of all vices and errors, it has pardoned the vices of the other and interpreted his errors to his glory. The reason is clear. Alexander was not the kind of historical personage who seizes the imagination of posterity; his labor was slow and coordinated; he had no regard save for real success; the prodigiousness of his efforts was concealed behind their results; he never looked upon himself as a genius inspired and inspiring, but simply as one who cooperated in the mighty organization, supreme and eternal, to which he belonged. Neither glory nor approbation seemed to him to matter; the opinion held of him by others did not interest him much.

Now history wants a hero to admire; and when it cannot find a genuine hero, then it admires the false appearance of one. Julius II was theatrical, vain, and what we now call colorful. He went to war without money or soldiers; with a high fever and in falling snow he entered in triumph a town already conquered by others; he acted the patriot and mouthed great words against the Barbarians,[2] this man who had figured in the train of every foreign sovereign who had entered Italy as an invader, who as cardinal and even as Pope joined with the Barbarians in continual alliances against Venice—the only Italian power that remained erect—who, to put the final touch upon disaster, invited the Spaniards to the invasion of northern Italy, thus preparing a century of misfortune for the peninsula. But how could historians fail to make much of the fine phrase of this gout-ridden, heavy-drinking man, when he said to the artist painting his portrait: "Don't put a book in my hand, give me a sword!" How could they fail to picture his entry into Perugia, with a vanguard composed of his cardinals? How could they feel other than burning enthusiasm at hearing him cry that by himself alone he would kick the French out of Italy? History loves large gestures and sounding phrases. Julius II saw the Vatican as a great stage for the rôle he had to play; Alexander's only concern was the work to be done.

But in spite of his efforts, the Borgia Pope was unable to consolidate his work of international policy. His program would have insured to Italy for future centuries a normal development like that of the other nations of Europe. But

369

all Italy worked for its own ruin. He was not responsible for this final want of success, any more than for the entry of the French and Spaniards into the Kingdom of Naples and the Duchy of Milan. The Italians of that day had lost all instinct of self-preservation. The mistaken policy of Venice was the prime cause of the evils Italy was to suffer, as Ludovico Sforza was of the evils Italy had suffered already. But lack of success cannot efface the splendid page written by Alexander. Fortunately it has come down to us intact, thanks to that mine of information still largely unexplored, the State Archives of Venice.

During the first half of 1502, the Pope was at the very height of glory. He was supported by Louis XII in his work of conquest in the Romagna and in the Patrimony of the Church. The Spanish sovereigns granted all that he asked. His family prospered, while he himself grew into old age with so little flagging of vigour that one of the ambassadors said that he found him younger every day. A man less dynamic than he would have chosen so favorable a situation to take his repose. With the gay humour that was naturally his, he might well have given himself to a life of pleasure, feeling that he had largely fulfilled his duties to the Holy See. But the old churchman, who had spent almost all his life in Italy and felt himself Italian in soul, realized only too well that the Kings who flattered him so were not good neighbors and that if his skill had so far prevented them from spreading their tentacles over all Italy, they would probably do so before long, threatening Rome and imposing their will upon the rest of the Peninsula. He knew that he had built a solid edifice, but that it was necessary to build strong walls for its defence. He knew that Venice was the one element that could be

370

counted on to oppose foreign powers; and though he knew its hostility and mistrust and personal hatred of himself, he set about winning it to his view in the hope of bringing it finally to alliance. And in this task, in spite of continual disappointments, he was still occupied when death overtook him.

From March 1502 he began to give form to his ideas about this alliance. Its basis must be a prudent anti-foreign policy. To treat with Venice was not easy. In international politics it inspired the same mistrust as do those states of today who would rule by utilizing for their own advantage the balance of other powers. The Venetians were then considered—as were the English centuries later—as cold, calculating, putting their power and wealth into the international scale as and when their own interests demanded, and relying ultimately upon vigilant isolation. They wanted to have influence everywhere, with the least effort and with no responsibility. The Pope knew them well and disliked their policy, not only because his own temperament found it repugnant, but because he could see clearly what it would mean for the future. In conversation with Alessandro Bracci, representative of Florence, he revealed his general opinion upon the Venetians. Bracci wrote to Soderini on May 15, 1503: "Finally, he [the Pope] wished to know your lordship's opinion of the Venetians, and what we should do in this complication and what side we should take." The complication referred to was the war between the Spaniards and the French in Naples, the new visit of Louis XII to Italy, and the attitude of Maximilian. Bracci goes on to say that he told the Pope: "The Gonfalonier of Florence knew well the nature of the Venetians and the way they proceed on such occasions, for experience of the past had taught him that they never moved save on condi-

371

tion of obtaining certain gains." The Pope replied: "They
are troublesome people and I have never been able to
placate them; they are your friends only when it suits
them, but one day they may make a mistake . . ."[3]

All the same, Alexander knew that there was no solution
for Rome and Italy without them. For two years he tried
to win them round. On March 20, 1502, he had a formal
proposal made through one of his secretaries to the ambassador of Venice. In the months before that he had
made certain vague approaches, without obtaining any reaction from the other party. He knew that these approaches
had been sent on to the Seigniory of Venice and that the
Seigniory had made no comment even to its own ambassador. This time there was nothing vague about his action.
From the ambassador Marin Zorzi we know what took
place and it seems well to reproduce his dispatch integrally:

"Today, March 20, 1502, Adriano, a papal secretary, who in spite of his unpleasing and sinister
appearance seems to be much valued by the Pope,
spoke to me with much circumlocution and for perhaps two hours wearied me to death with his talk:
'Don't you see, my Lord Ambassador, the ruin of
Italy? Don't you see that these two Kings of France
and Spain are in agreement to seize Italy? Though it
is said that the Emperor [the King of the Romans] is
coming to attack the Pontiff, what would you do in
Italy if the Pontiff fell? How can it be that your Senate, reputed to possess the highest wisdom in the
world, does not think of this? It will think of it perhaps when the damage is done! Could you not contract a secret alliance with the Pope in whatever form

372

is most suitable, so that if these sovereigns arrive for the common ill of you all, you should be united to defend your territories? This alliance would be directed neither against France nor against the King of the Romans, it would be established only to guarantee your and Italy's security. The King of France has decided to enter into alliance with the King of the Romans and the King of Spain, and has informed neither the Pope nor you! But could not you two— without offending him and with no derogation from the existent pacts which bind you,—have a secret understanding, a concordance of opinion [what would today be called parallel action] without publishing it or in any way making it known, so that if these people came, as they have done before, to attack one of you, you would find yourself well prepared and would not let them rob you of what is yours?'"

The Ambassador repeats that the papal secretary talked for a long time, urging his arguments. But that it was difficult for himself to reply since on the one hand he knew that what was said really came from the Pope, and on the other, he knew that the Seigniory wished to do nothing about these proposals since it had given no word of reply when he had communicated similar suggestions on previous occasions. In fact, Zorzi changed the subject and spoke of the Turkish question, adding that the Pope could prevent the intervention of the European sovereigns in Italy by persuading them to a crusade against the Infidel.[4]

But at this moment, Zorzi was replaced by Antonio Giustiniani. Of Giustiniani's labors there remains a long correspondence, much used by later writers to strengthen their accusations against Borgia. They have used these pages for stories to garnish their own, without seeing the political element in them—I mean all that these men of their period were aiming at in relation to their contemporaries and the future. It seems to me that anyone who reads these dispatches carefully in the light of what ultimately happened—discounting the malicious guesses and suspicions later disproved by the events themselves and making all allowance for the hostility shown to the Pope by an ambassador whose very mission was to mistrust him—must remain profoundly impressed by Alexander's personality, must indeed consider him as a statesman of the first order, a politician with firm and fixed principles. I think too that this record of daily contacts between the Pope and the ambassador shows the ambassador as a thoroughly slippery character, and Venice itself as guilty of mistake after mistake and always tending to go beyond even the elastic limits of international dignity.[5]

Giustiniani formed his opinions and interpreted facts by the very worst method one can employ when dealing with public affairs. His rule was simple. For him Alexander was a man who said one thing and meant another: so that one should always do the opposite of what the Pope suggested. This kind of mistrust, which many people make the rule of their own judgement particularly when they lack trust in themselves, has caused great evils in international life. It is the almost invariable rule of diplomats of small capacity. And as the human mind does not easily change once it has fixed the direction of its ideas, Giustiniani held to his line in spite of the constant proofs he had that his particular prejudice led him into error after error. I have made a careful and detailed study of this correspondence, especially examining the many occasions on which Giustiniani informs the Seigniory that the Pope has lied; and my conclusion is that it was the very reverse: the Pope did not lie and what is more Giustiniani knew that he did not. Before this evidence of persistence in known error, only one hypothesis is possible—that in thus slandering Alexander, he flattered the prejudice of the Seigniory which employed him. Giustiniani did not reach the level of the colleagues who came before and after him in the high diplomacy of Venice, but he did not differ much from the run of diplomats of his own day. I shall cite some examples of his malice and his errors.

When Cesar came to pay homage to the King of France at Milan and then went with him to Genoa, the ambassador insisted in all his dispatches that Cesar would not be allowed to leave the court and that the King would compel him to return to France. The Pope kept telling the ambassador that it could not be so, that Cesar would remain in Italy, and that he was at the French court entirely of his own will. The Pope was lying, said the ambassador to the Seigniory. But on September 2, Cesar bade farewell to the King and returned to the Romagna.

When the Pope had Cardinal Orsini and certain of his partisans arrested in Rome, Giustiniani said that they would all be executed. They were not: the Bishop of Santa Croce and Abbot Bernardino Alviano were set at liberty a few days afterwards.

After his flight from his capital, the Duke of Urbino took refuge at Pitigliano. The Pope informed the ambassador of this but the ambassador wrote to his masters that the fact was not sure, that the Pope was spreading the rumor so that he might attack the territory of Pitigliano and seize the money Venice had sent there as payment to the prince of that town who was its *condottiere*. But the Duke had taken refuge at Pitigliano and was there when the Pope said he was.

Bartolommeo Alviano's wife, surprised with her sister on the point of taking flight, was arrested by Cesar's troops, then set at liberty. The Pope told Giustiniani this, but the ambassador declared that, "he did not accord great faith to the news, but was sure that the truth was quite different."[6] But it was perfectly true that the two women had been set at liberty.

Trozo, a highly confidential secretary of the Pope, fled when it was discovered—so Soderini, the Florentine ambassador, tells us—that he was communicating the secrets of the pontifical court to France; Giustiniani, with a multiplicity of unverified information, declared that he did not believe in the story of the flight—either the Pope had sent him on a secret mission, or he had connived with the flight on some sinister plan, or had killed him. But Trozo had fled, he was arrested, and it is historically proven that the treachery of this very intelligent servant caused the Pope great pain.

Upon the death of the Cardinal de Monreale, the Pope's nephew, the ambassador asked for an audience; he was told that it would be granted him another day because of the grief in which the Pope was plunged. He communicated this insignificant fact to the Seigniory, adding, "The pain he is suffering must be the trouble of counting the money and making inventory of the jewels." But it is known that the Pope had a great affection for his relation and was so affected by his death that he never really recovered from his grief in the time that remained before his own death.

In January Alexander told the ambassador that Pandolfo Petrucci had left Siena; the ambassador remarks to the

Seigniory that the fact must be quite the contrary. But Petrucci *had* left Siena.

A month before his death, Alexander told Giustiniani that he needed the papal army in Rome because of the gravity of the situation; Giustiniani of course did not believe him but on the contrary said that the Pope wanted to invade Siena or some other town. But the Pope encamped his army in two groups, one close to Rome, the other further off; and he further granted permission for the Spaniards, the most loyal of his soldiers, to join the army of Gonzalvo of Cordoba in the Kingdom of Naples. He had no thought of attacking Siena.

I might multiply these examples, upon matters great and small. But it would be monotonous, for all the examples would prove the same thing—that the ambassador was never justified in doubting the Pope's word. In the whole of my investigation I did not find a single instance in which the ambassador's suspicion was well-founded.

Such being his state of mind, neither the ambassador himself nor the Seigniory of Venice could have a clear vision of things. And the Pope knew what the situation was; and tried to render it less grave, to clarify it, to explain it and himself. All without result. He maintained his friendly attitude to the ambassador but this was merely regarded as one more trick. Upon this sort of suspiciousness—sometimes called feminine—no effort can produce any impression.

From the moment Giustiniani came to Rome, the Pope resumed his negotiations for an alliance between the two States. In the month of May, the month in which the new ambassador entered upon his functions, he spoke to him generally upon the subject, as was normal in the first inter-

view. On June 30, when he learned of Louis XII's return
to Italy, he spoke with the Venetian of the danger threatened by this journey. The ambassador did not see it and
said: "Our Republic hoped for good from this arrival,
given the mutual friendship and alliance between France
and Venice." The Pope would not let him continue, and
cried: "God grant that it be so!" The Seigniory and its ambassador certainly showed great satisfaction and confidence in the relations between Louis XII and Venice. A
few years later Venice was crushed by Louis XII. At the
time when he was receiving the greatest proofs of respect
and approval from the French King, the Pope remained
suspicious. In a number of dispatches dated June and July,
the Venetian orator informed the Seigniory that the Pope's
mind was very much occupied with the news of the King's
coming into Italy.

On his side, Louis XII gave continual evidences of his
respect for the Pope. On the eve of his departure for Italy,
he declared that as peace had been established between
France and Spain, they had agreed to take His Holiness
and the Sacred College as arbiters in any difference that
might arise between them: and this not only in their own
interest, but in the interest of all Christendom.[7] Once in
Italy, we have seen his extraordinary amiability to Cesar.
When the Captains of the Holy See rebelled, he offered to
chastise them in person. And indeed it was he who made
it possible for the Pope to deliver Italy from all these
tyrants and establish a strong Papal state. But Borgia was
a statesman and his aim was that the Church (and his
family) might continue to live after his death by their own
right and their own strength and not by the favor of a
foreign King—a favor he had reason to think not lasting,

378

as events later confirmed. Alexander would have nothing of temporary solutions, however attractive. For he felt he could handle the present. It was the future he was afraid of. And the future could be secured only by the union of the Papacy and Venice, for between them they were rich enough to maintain the most powerful army in Europe.

On October 13, when the King of France was about to leave Italy, the Venetian ambassador wrote a long dispatch setting out the Papal theory on the necessity of this union. It is just as Adriano had stated it to the previous ambassador, Zorzi. But it is the personal peroration of Alexander that is interesting:

"His Holiness took me aside, because I was already standing and said to me, 'Is it possible, ambassador, that this Most Illustrious Seigniory should have its ears so blocked that it will not gratify us and do what we have so often demanded; and that it should choose not to trust us, who desire nothing other than a good and special understanding with it? We have already told you that though we are by nationality Spanish, and may seem in a certain manner favorable to France, we are in reality Italian. Our root is in Italy, it is there that we must live, there that our Duke [Cesar] must live. Our affairs are insecure without Venice. It mistrusts us, and this mistrust means that since we cannot base our action upon Venice, we are compelled to do things which otherwise we should not do.'"

The ambassador says that the Pope talked to him the whole morning about the foreign peril and the necessity for the union of the two States, and he adds that he made the usual reply—that is he evaded the issue by talking of

379

the good relations which existed with everybody. To which the Pope replied:

> "Ambassador, you are falling back into the usual generalities, which is the custom of you people when you want not to do a thing. But we have to come down to details. Please write all that we have said to the Most Illustrious Seigniory; then we two shall speak on some other occasion uninterrupted."

The Pope determinedly sought for this other occasion to return to the matter. Round about November 10, he invited Giustiniani to come to the Vatican. In the Hall of Papagallo, Monseigneur Trozo awaited him and said: "Magnificent Ambassador, I have been waiting more than half an hour for you. Enter, our master wishes to see you." The Pope began to speak again of the alliance, when the Cardinals of Santa Prassede, Santa Croce and Ferrara arrived. He told them to wait. Then the two French representatives arrived and the Pope, fearing that this long and secret interview might make them suspicious, said to Giustiniani: "What we have to say to you will take time, and we do not wish to arouse suspicions in those who are outside, for the thing must remain secret. Another day I shall appoint an hour for our meeting."

On November 14, he sent for him again and urged his view vehemently. In a dispatch to the Council of Ten, Giustiniani gives a long summary of what the Pope said.

It is of supreme interest.

> "Ambassador," said the Pope, "we have already given you to understand our desire to make alliance with the Most Illustrious Seigniory, and to make one single thing of us and it. Assuredly, we have spoken

in general terms, and your reply has been in terms more general still. We are convinced that you have told all this to the Seigniory because it was the duty of your office; and likewise that you have received no reply on this matter, the Seigniory having chosen not to make one, because they felt that our talk had been in the abstract, and further because of a certain mistrust they have of us. Today we are prepared to speak to you more openly since you represent that most excellent State, in order that you may expose our heart to its gaze and communicate our words, which are said with such an expression that they will reveal what we have in our mind."

"Then," continues the ambassador, "he made a long speech to prove the evil into which Italy had fallen for no reason save the mistrust that the Italian rulers had one of another. And from five these rulers have been reduced to two, the other three being in the power of a single one. And the Pope continued:

'The state of Milan is in the power of the King of France, so at this hour is Naples, and the Florentines are slaves. There remain only ourselves and Venice, and if we choose to persist in our mistrust—through your fault it must be said and not ours—we shall soon see the ruin of us both because, note well, these Ultramontanes (not to name anyone in particular) await with open mouth a chance to swallow the rest of Italy. And if the thing has so far been delayed, it is because they have not agreed upon the form; but it is not the will which has been wanting, and we can give you good proof of this, and you yourselves know it well. If we will open our eyes and think honestly, the signs

381

we have noted are terrifying. Speaking of ourselves first, we say that if the Lord God had not caused this discord between France and Spain in the Kingdom of Naples, we should find ourselves this year in agony. God intervened. But if our affairs had gone ill, it would have been the same for you, for you cannot think that you would have escaped; and though your power is great, you would not have much water to put out that fire. It is for all these reasons that it is good that we put away our mistrust and come to an understanding. Let the Seigniory not be suspicious that we speak thus to deceive them, or that we wish to put them into a difficulty, for that is not our intention. And if the Seigniory, which is so prudent, believes that in this union there is more gain for us than for Venice—though it is a matter of our common good—it will be thereby convinced that it is to our interest to be loyal, for if we cheat Venice, we shall cheat ourselves. Do you believe, ambassador, that we should wish to see the Seigniory so oppressed that in case of our own need we should be unable to find a state in Italy capable of coming to our aid, especially when it is a question of that Seigniory which has always been so devoted to the Holy See? We know full well that the favors of your Seigniory which is immortal are quite different from the favors others do, people from whom the more one expects, the less one gets: and what they give, costs so dear that it would be better not to have received it. One never gives them enough for the little they have done, and they always want one to remain under obligation to them although they never desire to be under obligation to others. Before doing a service to a friend, they twist

382

and turn so much that they reduce him to despair.[8]
You too have suffered: in this enterprise against the
Turks you have had a good experience of all this kind
of thing. . . . We know how this Seigniory acts and
how others act. We have arrived at an age where we
must think of leaving our posterity, in the assurance
that it will be able to preserve what we leave it, and
this is impossible without the concurrence of the
Seigniory; which should indeed convince them that
we do not wish to deceive them, for what we tell you,
we desire for the public good and the personal interest of our successor."

After this extraordinarily powerful dialectical exposition,
the Pope came to the part where he desired to take hold of
the mind of his listener and through it of the mind of the
distant Seigniory. He went on:

"We do not wish to throw ourselves at the head of
the Seigniory. Let it decide. Let it say to us 'Do thus,'
and if we do not do it, then let it not believe us. We
know that what has closed the ears of this Power is
that it does not trust us; but let it tell us what it
wishes and what we can do to inspire confidence, and
if we do not do it then let it have no confidence. We
have often performed actions which have caused it to
believe that we were interested in others rather than
it; but we have been obliged to this by itself which
did not wish an understanding with us. Now we place
our heart in its hands; may it not refuse the offering,
for in truth, if it does not consent, now that we have
so humbled ourselves before it as our words show, we
shall be driven to think that it is not certain that it

383

has as good a will towards us as it has always given us to understand."

In conclusion, he thus summarized his ideas:

"Let the Seigniory, which is very prudent, consider that if it is a thing useful for us to be allied with it—as in fact it is—and if further it regards us as a man who knows what his interest is, it will judge that we are truly opening our heart to it. If the alliance could be more to its prejudice than what we are doing now, let it make no alliance. But if otherwise, why not make it? Wherein can a good understanding and a close friendship with us damage it? What harm could come to it therefrom? Whom would it offend by making it? On the contrary, it would thus be doing what has always been its custom in acting like a good member of the Church and a defender of the Holy See, a thing for which it has gained glory and an immortal name."

The ambassador who had listened to all this without departing from the coldness of his attitude, described it to the Seigniory and he finished his dispatch with the words: "As he spoke, it seemed that his breast opened and that the words came from his heart and not from his mouth."[9]

But the Seigniory did not want an alliance with the Pope. On the contrary, the general opinion in Venice was that the republic's great enemy *was* the Pope since he had advanced to the very coasts of the Adriatic and had established himself there. It did not grasp that in any case a Papal Vicariate, which by its nature must be political and shaped for warfare on land, could not enter into competition with Venice in the commercial and maritime domain.

But the aspirations of Venice at this time included a territorial expansion within Italy, and it hoped to achieve its aspirations with the aid of the foreign invaders, who were in fact its own enemies. It is startling to see a government so skilled and cautious going wrong on such a point at such a period. The Pope's attitude, before Giustiniani and before the Seigniory, was in his own words an attitude of humiliation. And we might accuse Alexander of a lack of dignity if all that he had foretold had not happened. Had there been no League of Cambrai a few years later to distribute all the possessions of Venice, and had there been no sack of Rome and no degradation falling upon the Holy See, the supplications of this clear-minded statesman might have suggested a moment of weakness or lowered morale. But there are hours in which the sacrifice of a man's own dignity is the greatest of all heroism, a heroism which only the great egoists lack power to appreciate. This supplication to prevent an evil which folly and ill-will were in process of bringing to pass ennobled him who constrained himself to it: all the more when we remember that at this very moment, in full Consistory, he assumed the proud superiority that belongs to the Vicar of God upon earth.

Upon December 2 of that same year, seeing the Venetian ambassador among those whom he was to receive, he asked him to wait until he had received all the others for he desired to speak to him undisturbed. In the conversation that followed, after he had rapidly treated current affairs, he returned to his favorite subject, since he had received no reply from the ambassador to his burning words of November 14. Alexander found things going ill in Italy. In all the end of that year and the beginning of the next, the assertion of this truth was a leit-motiv in all

385

that he said. For the historians who say and repeat that Alexander was occupied solely with favoring and aggrandizing his family, this pessimistic note is not easy to explain, since his family was then at the height of power and glory.

Continuing the conversation, the Pope pointed out to the ambassador that though Italy's situation was dangerous, yet something could be done. And he was keenly desirous to find the means:

> "We should not want the French to come and destroy our country, for, I assure you, they bring fire with them, they respect neither enemies nor friends, and they regard all the wrong they do to Italy as a mere nothing."

As he had remained seated all day at the reception, the Pope rose and invited the ambassador to walk a little; the truth was that he wanted to be standing for the final words, because he knew that by his imposing appearance, the brilliant eyes whose brilliance the years had not dimmed, the solemnity of his gestures, he would impress his listener more powerfully:

> "See, ambassador, how each of these two Kings, of France and Spain, is striving to drive the other out of the Kingdom of Naples. It would be an evil affair for us and for you if the Spaniards possessed this Kingdom, but it would be still worse if it fell totally into the hands of France, because they would have us bottled up here, and would have us acting like choirboys. Nor would it be any better for you. For the love of God, let us have an end to our difference. Let us understand each other a little and busy ourselves a

386

little with the saving of Italy, for we have in a supreme degree obligations to those who come after us. You who are immortal—for the Seigniory never dies and has the future before it—should occupy yourselves still more; yet it would seem that you do not think so, if we may judge from certain of your attitudes, which are not very well-chosen.

"You know what people are saying? That you are too prudent, that you desire to see too far ahead. We have told you that it is good to listen to those who implore you. Abandon this 'too far,' which is often harmful."

And he concluded "We have often spoken to you thus and have never been afraid of repetition, that we may be clear in our conscience."

From the beginning of the following year the policies of Venice and the Pope, far from taking the turn Alexander wished, came into fresh collisions in all spheres. The Pope, after having proposed a formula for peace in Naples —a formula which had not been accepted by the two Powers—tried to follow a policy of balance of power by leaving the two opposing parties to destroy each other. For the Pope, the triumph of Spain was an evil, but the triumph of France a worse evil still, for that nation would have obtained absolute preponderance over the whole Peninsula—the very preponderance which, thanks to the errors of Julius II, Spain obtained shortly after by destruction of the power of Venice and the Republic of Florence, and by the sack of Rome and all that followed. The French and Spanish ambassadors positively laid siege to Alexander, each wanting him on his own side. And Alexander, whom we are asked to see as a man discredited and made

387

vile by every crime, refused to grant either party the moral support so urgently solicited. The ambassadors of both came often to the Vatican, but again and again had to leave without being received by the Pope, who found a thousand pretexts for not seeing them.

Venice also chose to remain neutral, but it sought to do so by means of secret alliances with each of the opposing parties. On March 22, 1503, Giustiniani informed the Seigniory, that he had seen the Pope who had suddenly and without preamble asked him: "Well, ambassador, how will things end with these Spaniards?" Giustiniani thought that the Pope was alluding to the alliance Venice was secretly negotiating with Spain; and he declares that, pretending not to understand, he replied vaguely: "Apropos of what?" The Pope replied: "Apropos of this alliance I am told you are trying to make with them." The ambassador smiled and declared that he was unaware that the Seigniory were negotiating a new alliance, and that they thought that Venice's good and long-standing friendship with the Spanish monarchs would suffice, together with the alliance which already bound it to the King of France. The Pope broke in: "It is impossible to have an understanding with two enemies like that at the same time!" But Giustiniani, seeking to conceal the truth, retorted by a play of words in which he confused the Pope's attitude of favoring neither side and Venice's plan of being secretly allied with both: "It should be possible to arrange, in so far as Venice is concerned, a situation of this sort, if one is in line with Your Holiness who has the friendship of both parties and is the enemy of neither." Giustiniani adds in his dispatch: "At these words he looked me straight in the face, shook his head and said: 'Tell the truth, on your honor, ambassador. What does the Most Illustrious Seigniory really mean to do?'" And the Pope concluded sadly: "It would be a good thing to think a little of the fate of Italy!"

The Pope was more afraid of a peace made by France and Spain at Italy's expense than of the war itself; and Giustiniani considered this as a proof of Alexander's cynicism and accused him of wanting to prolong the conflict. When there were rumors of peace, the Pontiff said in the Vatican on April 8: "See, ambassador, how these Ultramontanes come together without any intervention either on our part or on yours. . . . It would be useful for us also to be concerned about our own interests, and to have an understanding, at the expense of nobody but for the security and preservation of our States." And on April 11, when the rumors were growing stronger, the Pope returned to his favorite theme: "Ambassador, we must look to our interests. Let us unite our poor Italy; it would be united if the Most Illustrious Seigniory would deign to reply to what we have so often asked without its ever doing so."

Machiavelli, writing later about Alexander under the influence of the false reputation that had grown up about him, said that he had always deceived and always succeeded in his deceptions. Giustiniani had the same opinion when he said: "The better his words are, the more suspicion they must inspire in those who know his nature, which caresses those most to whom he means most harm."[10] Upon this period we have no more complete or informative documentation than the long correspondence of Giustiniani in which we can retrace the day by day relations of the Pope with Venice and occasionally with other countries. In the light of these pages written by a great enemy of the Pope, Alexander VI was not the one who deceived but the one who was deceived. And if con-

389

temporaries really believed that he possessed this faculty of lying and getting his lies believed, we must suppose that the Venetian was suffering from a kind of mirage, of the sort that often afflicts inferior minds, leading them to attribute to imagined causes failures actually due to their own incapacity. Alexander VI had qualities that do not go with the art of deception—he was indiscreet and spontaneous. "The Pope cannot keep anything to himself," was the view at the time. Further, he felt emotions so keenly that even when he was not speaking, his face showed what he was feeling.

Giustiniani and others have told us of these peculiarities of his character in many documents. In the communications he made to the Seigniory on May 18 and 20 of that year 1503, the ambassador said that the Pope was in ill-humor because he wished to remain neutral in the Franco-Spanish conflict, and that he spoke ill of the French and took no pleasure in the success of the Spaniards. On another occasion, Cardinal Grimani in full Consistory tried to intervene in a discussion upon an ecclesiastical question between Venice and Rome. Grimani was a Venetian, and the Pope knew that these cardinals were more attached to their family, their city and their state than to the Church. Unable any longer to contain himself—although he was then trying to negotiate an alliance with Venice—the Pope shut him up brusquely with the words: "I know what you want to say, but in this matter I do not want your opinion."[10a]

But if Venice did not want an alliance with the Pope, both Maximilian and the King of Spain wanted it keenly.[11] These were two powerful States. Alliances with them would for the moment be useful to Borgia, his family and the Holy See; but the Pope realized the disadvantages they would involve in the future, and he rejected them. He wanted an Italian alliance because he knew that any other would be equivalent to opening wider the gates to the conquerors, whose ultimate and supreme purpose was to subject the Holy See to their will. But Giustiniani, having finally received his answer, told the Pope that Venice did not accept his ideas. Alexander replied: "We have lost the great hope we had in that Seigniory; for previously, by the information of our legate, we had come to believe that the Most Illustrious Seigniory would have been unable to satisfy our desire and in consequence raise up the affairs of this poor torn Italy."

He saw clearly the difficulties threatening Venice and he added that perhaps the future would lead the Seigniory to understand where its true interests lay, though in his opinion it might then be too late. With his powerful political insight, he pointed out to the ambassador that after the war there would come peace and the two kings would regard Venice and Rome as enemies; in any event the conqueror would not rest satisfied with the Kingdom of Naples, he would want wider territories. When that time came they would seek, under the urge of necessity, to set a limit to the expansion of the conqueror: but it would no longer be possible.[12]

But Venice met all the friendly words and arguments of the Pope with an attitude which, if not inexplicable, was at least out of harmony with its traditional intelligence and nobility. While Rome was trusting Venice and seeking union with it, Venice was passing on the Pope's ideas and plans to the King of France. The Pope learned of this but took it calmly and admonished Venice paternally: "We could not have imagined that the Most Serene Seigniory

391

would have acted thus, since it is so prudent and circumspect and in its wisdom knows that a State like its own should value its good faith and so act that everyone could speak frankly to it . . . and it may consider today all the harm it risks doing to itself by this breach of faith." The ambassador denied the accusation, but the Pope would not accept his denial for his information was certain. And in fact we find in the Archives of Venice accounts of information passed on while "begging the Most Christian King and the Cardinal de Rouen most urgently to keep silence so that the work may be continued."[13]

But even after this proof of the Seigniory's moral faithlessness, the Pope continued to have confidence in its intelligence. One day he summoned Giustiniani to question him about a declaration made by the French ambassador, Monseigneur de Trans, a great friend of Cesar Borgia, to the effect that Venice had negotiated a new alliance with the King of France. The Venetian denied it and the Pope believed him because Trans had just been spreading the news that the Holy See was on the side of Spain. He cried out: "This Monsieur de Trans ought to be called Monsieur de Trame [plot]. He tells us that you are French and that His Majesty the King of France has promised you Sicily, while he tells you that we are Spanish."[14] Finally, on August 11, a few days before his death—and thus after his so-called poisoning—the Pope said to Giustiniani, speaking of the devastation wrought by the French troops on their march towards Naples:

"See, ambassador, how many evils result from the fact that we have not arrived at an understanding between ourselves and the Most Illustrious Seigniory. Rest assured that all this would have been over and

392

that everybody would have joined us and Venice, and that we should have been able to govern Italy in peace and restore it to its ancient liberty."

Two days later Alexander VI fell ill, and on the eighteenth he died.

Venice had founded its policy upon one single basis, and this happened to be the one matter in which its interests were in conflict with those of the Papacy. Like many another state in the course of history it had failed to realize that a country's policy must never depend upon one single line of interest, but must be the result of very complex efforts in view not of one particular goal to be attained but of the total well-being of the state. The Romagna was the point where Venice and Rome met and where their ambitions came into collision. It was the only such point. Pope Pius II had said that all the ills of Italy came from the Romagna. And at the moment we are considering, the Romagna was the cause of very great evils indeed. Romanin has affirmed and proved that the Seigniory had at this period a policy which bordered on lunacy.[15] Cesi, a Venetian scholar, has said truly: "In refusing to direct Italian policy according to the clear vision of Alexander VI, Venice prepared its own ruin."[16]

What ultimately happened—and this constitutes the one judgement upon human action from which there is no appeal—shows in all its grandeur the political effort of Pope Alexander. Into the wars which burst out after Alexander's death Venice was dragged in the worst possible conditions for itself. Julius II—a pope with an appalling temper which he never tried to check, with no definite policy, interested in the affairs of Italy only when he happened to feel like it—placed himself at the head of a coalition against

393

the one strong power left in Italy. Louis XII and Maximilian were parties to the Treaty of Blois, September 22, 1504, in which they agreed to form a coalition against Venice with the object of destroying its power and sharing between them its territories on the mainland. The Treaty of Blois was followed, on December 10, 1508, by the Treaty of Cambrai, which included a greater number of allies in the war against Venice.

The preamble of this ruthless document whose instigators were the Italians themselves, especially Julius II, ends thus: "We have found it not only useful and honorable, but likewise necessary, to call upon the whole world to carry out just vengeance in order to extinguish, like a common fire, the insatiable avidity of the Venetians and their thirst for domination."

In the articles that followed, all Venice's possessions, on the mainland and overseas, were divided up among the signatories. Ravenna and all that Venice had conquered in the Romagna, went to the Pope; Padua, Vicenza, Roveredo, the territory of Trevisa, and the whole of Istria, to the Emperor; Crema, Cremona, Brescia, Bergamo, and all the dependencies of the Duchy of Milan to the King of France. The King of Spain, who was also King of Naples, received Trani, Otranto, Brindisi, Gallipoli and all the other districts the Venetians held in the south of the peninsula. Dalmatia went to the King of Hungary and Cyprus to the Duke of Savoy. Venice was humbled and utterly crushed. It was mere chance that stopped Louis XII when, anticipating Napoleon, he meant to occupy the city and suppress its independence. It was likewise by chance, that the Sultan Bajazet, after the Peace of 1503, found himself involved in serious difficulties with Persia and so left Venice undisturbed.

CHAPTER XXVI

Death of Alexander VI

In spite of his great pessimism about the future, the actual situation in Europe was favorable to the Papacy in these last months of Rodrigo Borgia's life. The King of France, though he was the arbiter of Italian policy, wanted to have him as an ally. The King of Spain called upon Maximilian to grant Cesar the investiture of Tuscany with the title of King.[1] The towns of Siena, Pisa and Lucca were offered by the two adversaries, Spain and France, to the Holy See. On January 11, 1503, Priuli, with the exaggeration normal in the Journals of the period, wrote in his a phrase which reveals how favorable everything seemed for the Borgias: "Some wish to make him [Cesar] King of Italy, others wish to make him an emperor, because he succeeds in such wise that no one could have the courage to refuse him anything whatever."

At this moment, Alexander saw no limit to his family ambitions save his own conscience; and the only difficulty in the way of the expansion of the domains of the Holy See was that he saw with certainty that if he leaned to one side or other without being forced to it by events, he would be participating in the rupture of the existent equilibrium and thus in the consolidation of one or other foreign conquest. For it would be concentrated in a single hegemony, and this would lead to the absolute domination of the foreigner in Italy. He saw what Julius II could not see.

CC

Therefore he decided to wait till events should dictate the line he was to follow, and sought to draw what profit he might from the victory of others. His great enemy, Antonio Giustiniani, hated him from the very bottom of his soul as only an ecclesiastic or a diplomat can hate—this because they are obliged to feign, the one piety, the other courtesy. On July 4 Giustiniani addressed to the Seigniory a dispatch which in the precise circumstances of that moment constituted the greatest praise that could be given a statesman.

The Pope's brain, he affirmed, was very restless and continually aspired to great things and lofty enterprises; he had gold in abundance, and in addition he had now the favor of the Spaniards and, so it was said, would ally himself with them after their victory—that is, after the conquest of Gaeta; with his money and his armies, and given such arrangement as he might make with Maximilian, to whom he was ready to give the funds for the Crusade in Germany, there was nothing to which he might not aspire —even a grandeur higher than reason would counsel. Giustiniani added that this great enterprise might have for object the conquest of Florence, Bologna and Ferrara; and he said that all the princes of Italy feared him and wanted the King of France to send troops sufficient "to prevent the satisfaction of so many appetites." But gloomy and discouraged at the Pope's invincible skill, Giustiniani concluded his observation thus: This would not be an adequate remedy much longer, because following his usual method, Alexander would change his tactics and ally himself with the King of France so that the misfortune of the Italian lords would be greater than ever.[2]

Setting aside its psychological value, this dispatch reveals that the ambassador assumed that the Pope meant to continue to expel the small lords from their thrones, though in the previous year he had accomplished a good part of this program. The Venetian was right. Of all that has been said at the time and since upon the ambitions of Borgia, the one thing historically certain is the declaration made by the Pope himself in the Consistory of March 8, 1503, when he proposed the creation of new charges for the procuring of further funds. With his clear mind and his experience of finance, after fixing the necessary annual yield at forty thousand ducats, he declared: "This money will be for the needs and opportunities that may occur in the work of extirpating the evil thorns of this country and of acquiring all these States for the Church, that we may leave behind us the good renown of having done what our predecessors have tried to do, but without success."[3]

But Alexander, as usual, would not undertake an attack by way of arms without preparation in the political sphere. At this moment the political situation was not clear; therefore while the army continued to reorganize in its encampment, he compelled Cesar to remain in Rome and allowed him to continue his nocturnal life with its pleasures and gallantries. He waited until the struggle for Naples should be settled; and he meant that the winner, whoever he might be, would find him rich and powerful.

In the Consistory of May 31, he named nine new cardinals—five Spaniards, three Italians and a German. Giustiniani says that they were for the most part men of good repute but that they each had to pay a sum of money—up to twenty thousand ducats in some cases—and that the total the Pope received on this occasion was a hundred and twenty thousand ducats. He observed that if we add this sum to the sale of benefices already mentioned—whose product he calculates as sixty-four thousand ducats

—plus the heritage of Cardinal Michiel, the Pope must have a magnificent sum in his treasury. His conclusion is that a pope's resources depend upon his will. It is certain that Adriano de Corneto, a great Latinist and philosopher, did not pay the twenty thousand ducats; for we know that he did not have them. The election of cardinals was expensive because of certain traditional or legal largesses and more or less voluntary contributions to the Papal Treasury, but they do not constitute simony. The money went to the common treasury of the Church, sometimes for the Crusades and at other times, in Borgia's phrase, for the extirpation of evil thorns.

In this year 1503 Rome had a summer even hotter than usual. The lack of hygienic provision in the city and the proximity of the marshes all about gave rise to terrible epidemics. On July 7, a Florentine employed in Rome, Francesco Fortucci, wrote to his masters: "There are many sick with fever, and people are dying in great numbers." A few days later he repeats: "Many people are dying with fever and there are some cases of plague it is said." And on July 22, he begs permission to leave Rome, for the terror in which he is prevents him from carrying out his duties properly. Fortucci had reason to be terrified, for his chief, the ambassador Alessandro Bracci, had died of fever on the sixth and Antonio Zeno, who took his place, was gravely ill. In August the situation grew worse. Constabili and Zeno reported that life in Rome was then insupportable. The first informed Ferrara that everyone of importance was ill; and the second told Florence that with the number of the sick and the tremendous heat, the town was in a very evil plight. Nature, with its inescapable laws, was to put an end to the policy of Pope Alexander. It is the accidental element which is always liable to break the straight line of events. Rodrigo Borgia, after all, was seventy-two. Certainly he was vigorous, still rode on horseback, slept little, worked hard, made periodic visits to the domains he ruled, and bore all the fatigues of long religious cere- monies. But in advanced age, the body may sustain accus- tomed labors with the greatest vigor yet collapse very quickly before something abnormal.

During these last months, Alexander was not only in ill- humor, but seemed haunted by the gloomiest presenti- ments. He often revealed his state of mind in conversa- tions with ambassadors. "Many people are dying," he cried, "we should give a little more attention." His jovial tem- perament, his love of work, the satisfaction he found in visits in which discussion of high matters alternated with the lightest of gossip—all this did not run with the ap- palling heat and the epidemic which was decimating the ranks of his friends and collaborators.

On one of those August days, the Pope left the Vatican to sup at the country property of Cardinal Adriano de Corneto, a man whom the ambassador Zorzi had styled "Monseigneur Hadriano, a sinister man." It will be remem- bered that he had recently been raised to the purple. In his dispatch of August 13, Giustiniani says that the meal took place five or six days before the day on which he wrote; but it must have been even earlier still. Cesar Bor- gia had accompanied the Pope. Apart from the cardinal who was the host, there is no evidence that any other car- dinal was present; certainly no other fell ill. For in the Consistory of the day following the death of Alexander, the only absentee among his colleagues present in Rome was Adriano himself.

Because of the simultaneous illness of some or many of the people present at the meal, still more because of the death of the Pope, this supper has been regarded as the last scene of the Borgia tragedy. The great poisoner had to die by poison that his life might have an epilogue worthy of the terrible legend that hung about his name. Alexander VI died in the twilight of August 18, 1503, as a result of poison taken at the beginning of the month: so say all the stories that have come down to us, except the most recent, which, with a little more critical sense, reject as absurd the version or versions spread abroad. Voltaire was the first to deny the story—this not upon historical data but because of his profound insight into psychology.

Certainly the theory that the death was due to poison was immediately heard in Rome. This was natural enough, for all the great personages of the period were supposed to be victims of this method of elimination. But to add color to the story, the Pope's body, whether because of the great heat or of the nature of his illness, or because he was very corpulent, began to decompose immediately; his tongue hung out of his mouth and his skin grew black; which made all who were disposed to think he had been poisoned, think it. As Giustiniani describes the illness and the supper in early August without any mention of poison, the first author to assert publicly that Alexander was poisoned at the supper was Tommaso di Silvestre. He says on August 22, that Pope Alexander died on the previous Friday with certain other prelates and bishops, and that they had been poisoned at a banquet given by Cardinal Adriano.[4]

Then who was the poisoner?

How fantastic the accusation is appears when we enter upon the details. Giovio, Guicciardini and Bembo say that a servant poured the poison by mistake into the glasses of the Pope and Cesar. Guicciardini is more precise still: he says that Cesar had meant to poison Cardinal Adriano and had sent the wine prepared for this purpose to his house: he had sent it on ahead by a servant who was not in the secret. But Cesar was delayed en route and the Pope arrived first, very thirsty, and drank the fatal potion; Cesar arrived immediately afterwards and drank the same wine as his father. Bembo accuses the Pope himself of being the poisoner—he had wanted to assassinate his former secretary, who still as cardinal assisted him in handling the business of the Vatican. Peter Martyr of Anghiara is by way of having written in November of that year about the poisoning: but this author, an Italian living in Spain, regarded his letters as literary exercises and dated them at his whim. Matarazzo and Sanudo modified the details but without making any substantial change in the substance of the narrative. Sigismondo dei Conti, who showed himself favorable to Alexander while Alexander lived and hostile afterwards, says that Cesar was the unwitting cause of his father's death, but declares, like Guicciardini, that he cannot guarantee the truth of what he relates.

Priuli wrote in his Journal as early as August 16 that news had come to Rome that the Pope and Cesar, meaning to poison Cardinal Adriano, had prepared his death by putting poison in the sweetmeats which were usually passed round among the guests after a meal. But by the error of a servant, the Pope and Cesar themselves took one of these sweets, as did Adriano. Apart from Bembo, who accuses only the Pope, these authors and later authors like Mariana, Zurita and others usually accuse Cesar but not the Pope, while Giovio and Priuli accuse them both.

The divergence in these accounts appears also in regard to the person who actually served the poison. Some like Guicciardini say that the poisoned wine, having got to the

401

house before Cesar, was served to the Pope by a servant who knew nothing of the matter; others, that the Pope allotted the task to a servant who was in the conspiracy, but that another who knew nothing of it was the instrument of the crime. Some ingeniously suggest that the servant whose misison it was to pour the wine had been bribed and gave it to the poisoners instead of to their victims. Others accuse the Venetians of having paid a servant to poison the Pope and Cesar.

The confusion increases when we come to the consequences of the poisoning. Giucciardini says that the Pope was carried back to the Vatican in a dying condition and died next day, and that Cesar was thought to be dying too. Giovio makes the Pope die four days later. Mariana sends Cardinal Adriano to the tomb also. But the Pope in fact died some fifteen days after the meal, and Cardinal Adriano several years after, having led meanwhile a fairly troubled life.[5]

In the matter of the remedy used by Cesar to cure himself, the accounts are various and improbable. Some say that he got rid of the poison by taking a cold bath; others that he found safety in the belly of a mule which was cut open and within which he lay while its entrails were still palpitating.

Following the contemporary or almost contemporary writers, all the writers of the intermediate period have told similar stories and added the necessary explanation—I mean the motive for the crime. For the Borgia of legend there could be no other motive than money. So that it was necessary to plant rich cardinals round the fatal table. But in the matter of cardinals, there was only one, namely Adriano, and he was still poor. And in fact, the Cardinals who had escaped death so narrowly, gathered in the Pope's bedroom in the days which followed the supper, followed with perplexity the development of his illness, played cards by his bedside, and in general kept him company with great affection.

I have described the legend. Voltaire, as I have said, was one of the first—about the same time as Raynaldi—to observe the difficulty and unlikelihood of all these accounts. He has been followed since by many others, such as Villari, Reumont, Pastor, Creighton, Gregorovius, and Alvisi, to name only the chief. But none of these authors has thought it worth his while to undertake a serious revision of the accusations against Alexander himself, which have been accepted on the faith of documents of the same sort and of as little evidential value as those that make Alexander die of poison.

Alexander's death was perfectly normal, his illness explicable and its issue quite natural.

We have said that in the summer months, Rome was uninhabitable. The five Popes who were Alexander's immediate predecessors died during the months of July and August. Calixtus III died on August 6, 1458, Pius II on August 15, 1464 (not in Rome but at Ancona), Paul II on July 26, 1471, Sixtus IV on August 12, 1484, and Innocent VIII on July 25, 1492.

From the documents of the period we can easily arrive at a kind of bulletin of the Pope's state of health in the last month of his life. On July 8, he had a slight attack of dysentery, as he himself told the Venetian ambassador on July 11, when the ambassador found him lying on a bed fully dressed. "I was at the palace, and entering the pontifical apartments, I found His Holiness lying dressed on the bed. He seemed to me quite well but he told me that

403

for three days he had not felt well because of a colic, but that he hoped it was not serious."⁶

On the following day, the Pope reviewed troops from a balcony of the Vatican; and on July 14, he attended actively to business sitting on the throne of the pontifical Great Hall. All the same Giustiniani, who visited him that day, found him somewhat depressed. On July 26, he discussed with the Venetian the important matter of the alliance of Venice with France, and it was on that day that he made the pun on Trans and Trame already related.

He was very much affected by the death of the Cardinal de Monreale, his nephew, and refused to receive the ambassadors. Then, one day early in August, he went to sup with Cardinal Adriano de Corneto. On August 7, he made the remark to Giustiniani mentioned earlier about the number of the people dying every day and the need of attention. On August 8, died another of his nephews, who was Captain of the Vatican guard, and he watched the funeral cortège from one of his windows. He was much attached to this nephew and much grieved at his death.

The next day he went down with fever himself and the Bishop of Venosa, who was his doctor, though ill himself, came to visit him and decided to remain in the palace. But the next day Alexander assisted at the religious ceremony in celebration of the anniversary of his elevation to the pontificate, and later received the ambassadors, declaring to Giustiniani once more that Italy's misfortunes came from the separation between Venice and the Papacy. But obviously his mind was occupied with the thought of his own death. He was not gay as was his custom when assisting at public ceremonies, and he said gloomily: "This is a bad month for heavy people."

On August 12, the fever returned with vomiting in

which he expelled a good deal of bile. On August 13, he was bled; they took away nine ounces of blood according to some, while others say it was even more. This caused the fever to fall and some of the cardinals who had kept him company all day played at cards by his bedside. But though the fever was less, it had not disappeared and on the fourteenth he was bled again.

On this same day Constabili, ambassador of Ferrara at Rome, sent to the court of Este, where Lucretia was, the following dispatch which speaks of the whole course of the malady though, in the light of the information we have gathered, it shows that the ambassador was not fully informed on some matters.

"Yesterday morning I was informed from a good source that His Holiness ordered to be summoned the Bishop of Venosa who was ill in his own house and another doctor of the city, and that he has kept them both at the Vatican. I have also been informed that yesterday the Pope vomited, but he had a fever and that nine ounces of blood were taken from him. During the day His Holiness had with him certain cardinals who played cards while he rested. I have been informed that yesterday during the night he slept well but today he has had an attack like that of Saturday, an attack of a kind of which the people about the court will not speak and they refuse to give any information about his state. I have tried in all ways to find out what is happening but the more I try the less I learn. The doctors, apothecaries and barbers are kept there and not allowed to withdraw. Whence I conclude that the illness is serious. . . . It is not surprising that His Holiness is ill, since everybody at the

405

court is in the same state because of the bad quality of the air one breathes here."

On August 15, the fever was still present with a high temperature. The day after, Constabili says that the fever still continued and a day after that Giustiniani wrote to Venice: "The fever continues to torment him, and there is some danger. I have been told that the Bishop of Venosa says that the Pope's illness is very grave." On August 18, he sat up in his bed, in the presence of certain cardinals. He heard mass and the Bishop of Venosa came out of the room weeping and saying that the crisis was imminent. And in fact Pope Alexander died at nightfall.

Certain modern authors have presented this outline of the Pope's illness to eminent physicians asking them whether, with such symptoms, Alexander could have died of poison. Their response was absolutely that he could not. But there is not much doubt that the same doctors would have given the same negative answer if they could have been shown a similar series of bulletins for Prince Jem, for Cardinal Zeno or any other of the cardinals who figure on the Borgia crime-sheet.

Thus Alexander VI died of fever, perhaps with cardiac complications, since Giustiniani reports to the Seigniory that he died of heart disease. It is difficult to determine the character of this fever. It is probably one of those which were endemic at Rome, or it may have been one that came from the East as was often the case. It is certain that Cesar's illness and Adriano's were of the same nature as the Pope's, and that on the night of the supper the poisoner was a mosquito of the type that transmits the germ of malaria, yellow fever and the like; and this mosquito attacked practically everyone present.

Death of Alexander VI

During his last illness, the Pope apparently never mentioned the name of Cesar or Lucretia. And though Jofre was in Rome and not far away, there is no evidence that he saw him in his last moments. On the morning of August 18, the Pope asked to go to confession. The Bishop of Carinola, his confessor, also gave him Extreme Unction.

The Pope's funeral and all the subsequent religious ceremonies were carried out according to the ritual. Bruchard, who gives only a summary treatment of the illness, now lets himself go upon the smallest details, for he was the Vatican Master of Ceremonies and was in his glory.

The whole wretched legend according to which the Pope's dead body was dragged out by the feet, that at the moment of death he had a dialogue with the devil, that he was tossed unceremoniously into a mean grave, is one more creation of the enemies of Alexander VI who grew bold at that hour of recovered hope, in the prospect of regaining their former wealth and territories. Bruchard tells us that the body was washed, that he himself helped to place the rich vestments upon it, that the catafalque was covered splendidly, and that all the religious offices were celebrated. The obsequies lasted nine days and were carried out with all the traditional forms. The Cardinals who were in Rome were present as well as a great number of the regular and secular clergy.

All the time it was exposed the body was horrible to see, so Bruchard tells us with a certain complacence.[7] Giustiniani and Constabili also remark that the corpse was black and swollen and very ugly to look upon.[8]

It appears certain that Cesar, as soon as he learned of Alexander's death, took possession of his riches and the money he had, sending Miguel Corella into the pontifical apartments and to Cardinal Casanova. But Bruchard, who

407

tells us of this appropriation by violence, says that the Cardinals of Santa Prassede and Cozenza made an inventory of the Pope's goods, which Miguel Corella had not finished the evening before because he did not know where they were. To obtain the funds necessary for immediate needs, the cardinals had to borrow money, for the pontifical treasury was empty. But it must be remembered that Alexander had found it in the same state when he ascended the throne of St. Peter eleven years earlier.

Alexander's work stands out in full relief in the days that followed his death while the ritual nine masses were being celebrated for the repose of his soul. For if it had needed eleven years to give the Church its political independence by withdrawing it from the control of factions and to win it a territory of its own, it needed only a few days for the cardinals—in the service of the princely houses or bound in the interests of enemy states, blind to their duty, feeble and incompetent—to destroy all that Alexander had built up. The way in which particular interests turned against the Church, against the political and religious institution he had so loved, renders clearer in the eyes of posterity the exact significance of his policy.

A poet in the pay of one of his enemies wrote four insulting lines against him, but the last line, rightly interpreted, contains the whole truth:

> "Sevicia, insidia, rabies, furor, ira, libido
> Sanguinis atque auri spongia dura sitis,
> · Sextus Alexander, jaceo hic, jam libera gaude,
> Roma tibi quoniam mors mea vita fuit."[9]

Setting aside the qualities here attributed by the poet to Alexander—violence, treachery, lust, and the sponge-

like thirst for blood and gold—we may find in these few
verses the affirmation that Rome lives again satisfied and
that the death of this man was life to Rome. In fact Rome
up to the reign of Alexander belonged neither to its inhabitants nor to the Church but was the domain of noble
houses, restless and rebellious to all the rules of duty and
order, especially after the Schism of Avignon. This was the
Rome Alexander had destroyed, and now it lived again
with his death. The princes returned with their courts,
their soldiers, their poets, their populace ever ready to
applaud violence and cunning.

On August 19, Silvio Savelli, to whom was addressed
that famous letter which with other documents of the same
sort has served as a source for the history of the Borgias,
was back in his former palace and had set at liberty all the
prisoners so justly imprisoned there. Silvio Savelli had been
allowed to return to Rome while the Pope was alive and
had been received and pardoned, for Alexander had a
conception of liberty which was not that of the period. It
is probable that, like certain of the Colonnas and other
barons, he received a pension or some other aid from the
Papal treasury. On the twentieth, the political prisoners
began to emerge from the Castle of Saint Angelo and the
exiles to pour back into the city. Prospero Colonna, whom
the Sacred College had asked not to enter Rome, arrived on
the 22nd with a large troop of horse. An envoy from the
cardinals presented him the letter in which he was asked,
for the tranquillity of the coming Papal election, to stay
out of Rome; he did not read it but continued on his way.
That night there were celebrations at the Capitol. The
people cried: "Colonna! Colonna!" and five cardinals came
to pay him homage. The next day Fabio Orsini was back
with large troops of cavalry and infantry. There was much

409

shouting of the populace in his honor, homage of cardinals, numbers of people murdered in the streets, Spaniards especially, over a hundred houses burned by the fury of the factions. Rome relived the middle ages which Alexander VI had thought gone forever.

The possessions of the Holy See, built up with so much care, disappeared as by enchantment within a few days. Cesar Borgia, who was ill and who in any case had not Alexander's resolution, decided to join one of the factions and chose that of the Colonnas. To win their good graces, he sent them his countersign which would allow them to occupy the castles and strongholds Alexander had taken from them. But these people had no need of the countersign, any more than the Savelli or the Conti or the other barons. All who were charged with guarding the cities and castles and territories delivered them up without resistance.

On August 22, the Duke of Urbino took possession of his state. The Varanos entered Camerino on August 29. The *Prefetessa*—the mother of Francesco Maria della Rovere, grandnephew of the future Pope Julius II—entered Sinigaglia, and Gian Paolo Baglione took Perugia, which refused to open its gates, on September 9. Giovanni Sforza was back in Pesaro, the Appianos at Piombino. Later the Malatestas, with Venetian support, occupied Rimini,[10] but Dionisio Naldi expelled them in the name of the Church and of Cesar Borgia. The Malatestas then sold their seignorial rights to the Republic of Venice. A bastard member of the Manfredi family entered Faenza with the help of the Florentines. The Ordelaffi likewise received the aid of Florence in taking possession of Forli, a city of which they had been lords before Girolamo Riario and Catherine Sforza; and in fact they entered the town on October 22 while at Rome Cardinal Riario, uncle of the claimants, was

410

soliciting the help of Venice against the troops of the Church. The Venetians themselves entered the Romagna and occupied the papal territory.[11]

All this represented a direct assault upon the interests of the Church for, apart from a few towns and the Romagna, which had been set up as a Vicariate with a government over which the Church exercised indirect control, all the rest of the territory belonged directly to the Church. But the great vindicator of the Church's rights was gone, and all the old usurpers returned with new rage and cupidity. The citizens paid dearly for the few years of liberty they had enjoyed. In many of these small states the vengeance wreaked by the returned tyrants was terrible.

This movement of reconquest involved a whole political and moral revolution. The Roman poet might have added the name of Italy to the name of Rome when he said that Alexander's death was its life. In fact, but for his death, these princes who sold themselves on the very field of battle to the highest bidder, who placed themselves at the service of every foreign invader, who were all parricides or fratricides or at least plain murderers, would never have come back to life.[12]

But now at last they were victorious, and victory becomes in its turn a moral conquest. Alexander was condemned.

In his old age, Alexander VI, though by now thinking of death, continued to labor without making any precautionary provision for the future. A man of great foresight, capable of long views, he yet fell under the common rule which makes us work even on the edge of the grave, when we are about to disappear forever, as if we could continue our effort and enjoy its fruits. He had never thought of

411

who was to succeed him. Was this through respect for the princes of the Church? Was it through over-confidence in the men he had raised to the cardinalate? Was it because he knew that when he was dead no one would respect his will, because, to dominate assemblies by force, even assemblies of cardinals, one must constantly raise the whip and be prepared to scourge?

What is certain is that though he was nepotist in the very highest degree, he had taken no measures in favor of his own for the time when he should be no longer there to protect them. I think it not fantastic to hold that he took no steps because the idea was so deeply implanted in his mind that the Pope can provide for his family only while he lives and that once dead there is nothing he can do for them.

Of the relations who survived him, the most in view were Lucretia and Cesar, whom many contemporaries call his children and whom posterity has almost unanimously regarded as his. Lucretia, bound now by affection and no longer by interest to the Este, punctiliously fulfilled the obligations imposed by her situation at the court of Ferrara, first of all during the lifetime of Ercole and then as consort of her husband Alfonso. She did not suffer directly from the reaction which brought such trouble to others of the house of Borgia. On the contrary, she was able to be of use to certain of her kinsmen, for we find in refuge at Ferrara a good number of Borgias; and there still exist petitions addressed by her to King Ferdinand on behalf of Cesar when he was imprisoned in a Spanish castle. Much admired, she was celebrated by poets and held in great esteem by her husband's family. She died on June 24, 1519, in childbirth, at the age of forty-two. Two days before her death she wrote to Pope Leo X an admirable letter, which finishes thus: "I commend to your sacred favor, my husband and my children, who are all the servants of Your Holiness." Her husband wept bitter tears at her death.

Cesar had a hard fight before him. It was without success, and the death which ended it was courageous but not glorious. Upon the years that Cesar Borgia lived after Alexander, studies have not been made with the historical care necessary. The Venetian Archives contain a good deal of information, and there is something also to be found in the long summary of Giustiniani's dispatches made by Villari. It is clear that Venice had seldom feared anyone more than she feared Cesar Borgia, even when he was a prisoner at Rome, or at Naples or in Spain. And rarely has a State persecuted a member of another State so obstinately.[13]

After much wavering of fortune, at first under Pius III, who did not live quite a month after his election, then under Julius II, who was elected thanks to Cesar's decisive intervention, he fled from Ostia, where he was prisoner, to Naples. In this city the great Captain Gonzalvo of Cordoba, who had received him with the offer of a safe conduct guaranteeing his liberty, showed him all the consideration due to his high rank. But following upon an order of the King of Spain he was obliged, in spite of his given word, to arrest him and send him to Spain. He remained a prisoner in that country in the Castle of Medina del Campo until October, 1506. He then managed to escape to the Kingdom of Navarre, whose ruler was his brother-in-law. He died a few months later, fighting almost alone against a group of rebels to his King.

It is difficult to arrive at a judgement as to the political capacity of Cesar Borgia. When he found himself left alone by Alexander's death, still very young, he was seriously ill, and there was reason to suppose that the effects of this illness lasted for some months. By the time he was fully recovered, he was almost entirely disarmed and surrounded by a world of enemies. He has left us the explanation of his weakness and therefore of his defeat in the phrase he uttered to Machiavelli in Rome: "I had made provision for everything except that at the Pope's death I should be close to death myself." Yet his attitude in these first moments was better than the one he adopted later. It is comprehensible that he should have helped the election of Cardinal Piccolomini, but not that he should have given his aid, decisive as it turned out, to elect Giuliano della Rovere. The truth is that he found himself faced with difficulties which only a man of constancy, habituated to continuous labor and alive with spiritual ardor, could have overcome. And men possess these qualities, only if they have acquired them by a hard and laborious existence. But Cesar, as he says himself, was the manufacture of Alexander VI. He showed boldness and ability only in isolated acts, and for short periods; for fundamentally he loved pleasure and long repose too much to be able to sustain continual conflicts. When Alexander saw him refusing to receive ambassadors and sleeping all day, he murmured glumly: "What will happen to him after our death?" And in this also Alexander saw things with dazzling lucidity.

As to the other so-called children of the Pope, the second Duke of Gandia, who was murdered in Alexander's lifetime, left a numerous and respected family. The third duke, who bore his father's name, had as his eldest son the child who was later St. Francis Borgia. Jofre, the youngest, after having been at Cesar's side in the first difficult moments after the Pope's death, withdrew to his estates at Naples. He was able to keep all he had acquired because King Ferdinand confirmed him in all his rights. At the death of Sancia his wife, he married a del Mila, a relation of the Spanish branch of the family. And later one of his grand-daughters entered the Spanish branch, marrying a Borgia of the Gandia family, and as she was herself the last of the Neapolitan branch, she brought her husband the Italian titles and estates. Thus the Borgia Pope had, at least in the realm of nepotism, left something solid and resistant which did not die with him nor with Cesar's fortunes.

In the sphere of politics, after an interruption, there was a return to his tradition. Once the period of madness was over in which the Church's own servants worked for its ruin, Julius II was able to follow in Alexander's footsteps. The tyrants were once again attacked, Venice was thrust back on the Adriatic coast as far as Ravenna, and the Bentivoglios, who had been saved in 1502 by the conspiracy of La Magione, were expelled from their territory and from the wealthy city of Bologna.

But the work Alexander had accomplished for the good of the Church and the good of Italy was only half resumed in the violent and incoherent efforts of Julius II. From these efforts, there resulted advantages only for the Church, and these limited. Julius II rebuilt the Church's authority upon the ruin of Italy and to the prejudice of the Papacy as a universal institution. Alexander's political conception and political action had involved a far vaster and nobler plan than the small matter of the annexation of some slight territory to a Rome whose prestige was gone.

On Other Supposed Children of Alexander VI

W<small>HILE</small> some authors hold that Alexander VI had only two daughters, Geronima and Lucretia, others present a third, Isabella.

She is not supposed to be a full sister of the others, and in consequence she is not held to be Vannozza's. In fact, she was not Rodrigo's either; she was only a relation and probably from the poor branch of the Borgias.

Two pieces of evidence are supposed to support Rodrigo's paternity. One is a contract of marriage, the other a phrase from Bruchard's *Journal*. The first document says, that in the presence of the notary Agostino de Martini, Pietro, son of Giovanni Matucci, and Isabella Borgia have agreed to marry; and that she is to bring a dowry of two thousand ducats. The dowry is to be made up of a house and land valued at eight hundred ducats, another house valued at seven hundred, and five hundred ducats in cash. A notation on the document says that the act was signed in the Vice-Chancellor's office, in the presence of the Protonotaries, Borgia and Agnelli and Antonio de Porcaris, and Jacopo Casanova.[1] The Vice-Chancellor himself is not mentioned as present, the dowry could hardly be more insignificant, and throughout the text of the contract of marriage there is nothing about Cardinal Borgia save that someone of the same family name was present and that the document was signed in his office. We know that the Borgia clan, both in Spain and in Italy, was very numerous, and that at that time in both countries a rich relation often lent his house on such occasions to poorer or less important relations. The custom still exists and extends even to servants of a certain standing or held in special affection. The document in question is dated April 1, 1483, but it was actually included much later and is not an authentic original. None the less its context seems to me pretty convincing evidence that what it contains is true. Only it contains nothing on the matter of Alexander VI's paternity. On the contrary, it seems almost clamorously obvious that the girl with such a dowry was no daughter of the wealthy Cardinal Borgia.

To come to Bruchard's phrase, it would have more value if interpolations were not so frequent in his *Journal,* and if, on this particular matter, the *Journal* did not contain certain defects of form not customary in the Vatican master of ceremonies. Here is the phrase. "In the month of October or November, 1501, was received [at the Vatican] Matucci a Roman, a son of Pietro Matucci, a Roman citizen, and nephew of his holiness the Pope by one of his daughters, wife of the said Pietro, chancellor of the city."[2] De Roo considers that this is evidently an interpolation, for the very precise Bruchard never uses the expression "in the month of," but always gives the exact day, that being the form in which his *Journal* is written. Still less would he give a period of two months within which an act is supposed to have happened. Finally, de Roo observes that Bruchard never mentions the year in the body of the text but only at the head.

Whether these arguments seem over subtle or not, it is certain that the contract of marriage, and the total absence of information before or after, force us to reject the idea that this girl was the Pope's daughter, an idea which has nothing to support it save a phrase from Bruchard's journal which has been for centuries manhandled by copyists.[3]

We come now to the children supposed to have been born when Alexander VI was Pope and over sixty years of age. I have already mentioned the accusation that he had had three or four children by Giulia Farnese. The accusation, as we have seen, is fantastic, since Giulia had only one child, a daughter, whom she married to a nephew of Julius II at a time when that Pope's hatred of Alexander was so great that he had his bedroom changed so as not to see Alexander's portrait.

So we are left with Giovanni Borgia (the *Infans romanus*), and also a certain Rodrigo Borgia, even less known. This Rodrigo must have been born when the Pope was already dead, or at any rate at the point of death at seventy-two. It is true that the Venetian ambassador wrote at the time: "The pope is getting younger every day," but I doubt if this is what he meant. The only evidence for the story is a bull of Leo X, dated 1515. In fact, against all Vatican usage, it is not a bull, but a kind of omnibus of bulls, for it resolves a whole crowd of questions. In lifts the excommunication from the youthful Rodrigo Borgia—who was then twelve—legitimizes him, names him abbot of the Benedictine Monastery of Vietri near Salerno—although at that time he was still a layman and not a cleric—and authorizes him to receive from then onwards secular and regular benefices. The bull does not actually say that this Rodrigo was the son of Alexander

VI, it merely says that he was the son of a Sovereign Pontiff; it does not give his exact age, but says that he was twelve or thereabouts on August 15, 1515. The eighteenth of August of that year was the twelfth anniversary of Alexander's death.

But note that this bull, like one we have already noticed, is inscribed in a register with blank pages, and a large space left for the date, so that this might be inserted as desired; and in fact it was completed later by another hand, with the signature of the attesting scribe in the wrong place. The whole thing is plainly a later forgery.[4] Gregorovius has followed up the life of this Rodrigo and discovered that he had another brother, a Bishop. It seems unfair that he too is not included among Alexander VI's children. But he is not. The ambassador of Ferrara writes from Pausilippa, near Naples, and mentions the death of this Rodrigo Borgia adding simply that he belonged to the Borgia family but without making any allusion to the dead Pope, who was at that time fair target for every man's abuse.

Let us now examine what is historically known of the *Infans romanus*. Cesar Borgia had a son by an unmarried woman in Rome. The child was brought to the Pope his grandfather, who with his habitual sensibility or even sentimentality received the child and soon came to love it tenderly. He made it the companion of Lucretia's son, and had both children go about with him in public. His incorrigible nepotism, based upon his view that while a pope lives he has all the rights of a temporal prince, caused him to make the little Giovanni Duke of Nepi. A bull of September 10, 1501, informs us that Cardinals Antonietto Pallavicini, Giovanni di San Georgio, Ippolito d'Este and

419

Francesco de Borgia are named his guardians, because the child was illegitimate, born of the love of the noble lord Cesar Borgia, a married man, for an unmarried woman. And the Pope using the right conferred upon him by his apostolic authority legalized the situation.[5] In another bull, in the month of October, he made different provision for the child's guardianship, but repeated the fact of his relation to Cesar.[6] Prior to these bulls—the first has been attacked as false, but this does not matter here—he had in the College of Cardinals ordered the publication of a bull according to which Giovanni Borgia is legitimated as Cesar's son, with rights of primogeniture.

There have been discovered in the Vatican orders for payment in which the Pope continues to call this Giovanni his nephew.[7] His guardians used Cesar's armorial bearing for the child, who was governor of Nepi, and they had the same bearings engraved upon the coinage of Camerino, of which the child was also ruler.

But we find in Bruchard a phrase which might seem to indicate that Giovanni was the Pope's own son. We find the same thing, in an equally vague form, in a dispatch of Giustiniani: the Venetian ambassador, while calling him Cesar's son, mentions that certain people regarded him as the Pope's child.[8] Sigusmundi dei Conti assumes that he is the Pope's son.

Certain documents discovered by Gregorovius make the question rather less clear than it had been without them. Two contradictory bulls, issued the same day and bearing the same date inform us: one that Giovanni Borgia is Cesar's son and that by this bull he is legitimated; the other that he is the son of the very Sovereign Pontiff who dictated both bulls. The most curious element is that one of the two bulls admits its own futility, since the legitimation (in so far as Cesar is treated as father) had already been solemnly declared. Why then should Alexander VI have issued this futile legitimation on the very day on which he annulled it? Historians, thus faced with the unexplainable, have recourse to the most absurd explanations. Gregorovius thinks that the Pope, not willing to admit the child as his son, yet wished to recognize him as Cesar's son. But in the bull, the Pope is recognizing a son of his own, and not a son of Cesar *as* his own. Portigliotti thinks Lucretia had insisted upon it, for Portigliotti takes the papal incest for granted. And Frederick, Baron Corvo, advances the explanation that this vigorous sincere Pontiff did it for the sake of honor, being incapable of maintaining a lie.[9] But then why, on the very same day, repeat the lie of Cesar's paternity? De Roo sets out all the technical reasons which lead him to conclude that the two bulls are forged; but why in that case did the forger amuse himself by forging two contradictory documents? An enemy of the Pope would have been content to forge the second, in which Alexander VI declared himself the father of Giovanni, without giving himself the bother of forging another, which neutralized its effect and which anyhow accomplished nothing since there was already a genuine bull affirming the same thing.

Nor can we suppose that there were two independent forgers at work, doing the same mean thing on the same day, since the second document refers to the first. Nor again can it be held that the document making Cesar the father is authentic while the one about Alexander VI is false, because it is precisely the first that is superfluous and contrary to juridical forms.

There remains but one explanation, a simple theory but probable enough in itself. In 1535 there was a legal action in which this Giovanni was defending his claims to the Duchy of Nepi. An unscrupulous lawyer, ignorant of the documents in the Vatican, but anxious to use one or other paternity according as the argument might make it the more useful, simply forged both bulls, meaning as I have said to use the one that turned out most helpful. Giovanni lost his case, precisely because the court considered that the two bulls cancelled each other out. What is certain is that Alexander VI had no hand in either of them. His intelligence and his knowledge of the affair would have prevented him from issuing an unnecessary confirmation of the child's legitimacy and immediately annulling this by an admission which served nobody, least of all the child whom he was so anxious to defend.

Notes

CHAPTER I

1. Fabroni: *Vita Laurentii* (Vol. II, p. 390): Letter of Lorenzo the Magnificent to Innocent VIII.
2. Benedetto Croce: *La Spagna nella vita Italiana*. This scholarly work contains a very full résumé of the book *De Educatione* of Antonio de Ferrariis (pages 113 to 121).
3. Fleury: *Histoire ecclésiastique*. LXLIII, no. 17.
4. Randon Brown, in *Ragguagli sulla vita di Marin Sanudo*, has said that a portrait has been made of the Borgias which is in itself a picture of the corruption of the fifteenth and sixteenth centuries.
5. Villari-Pasquale: *Savonarole* (English translation, p. 60).

CHAPTER II

1. Villanueva: *Viage literario a las Iglesias de España*. Vol. II, p. 213.
2. Villanueva. As above, in a passage from a document of a certain Master Diago.
3. Continuation of Platina: *De Vita et Moribus summorum Pontificum Historia*.
4. The name of Lanzol appears under different forms: Lanzol, Llanzol, Lenzuoli, etc.
5. Because of the confusion in the orthography of the period, the name was written variously in Spanish and in Italian: Borja, Borge, Boria, Borjia, Borza, Borigia, finally taking the form of Borgia.
6. Sanchiz y Sivera: *Bulletin de l'académie royale de l'histoire* (Vol. 84, p. 1924). Giuseppe Portigliotti, in his work: *Les Borgia*, says erroneously on page 15: it was his uncle Calixtus III, who, when raising him to the purple at the age of twenty-five, caused him to give up the obscure

patronymic of Lanzol for his own, upon which the tiara had conferred such splendor and celebrity.

7. Portigliotti: *Les Borgia,* French translation, p. 16.

8. On this topic, see Gaspar Escolano: *Historiae Valentinae.*

9. Most authors give 1431 as the date of the birth of Alexander VI, relying on Bruchard, who in his *Journal* says that the Pope, on the first day of 1498, informed the cardinals that he had then completed sixty-six years of his age, having been born in the first year of the pontificate of Eugenius IV. But the same Bruchard, a little further on, says that in 1503 his colleague Bernardino was appointed by the same Pope who was then seventy-one. The Vatican documents consulted by De Roo for his book on Pope Alexander VI incline me to believe that he was born in 1432, not in 1431.

10. Pope Nicholas V declares in this bull that he was led to accord these special favors because of *"Vitae ac morum honestas aliaque laudabilia probitatis et virtutum."* We need attach no great importance to these words, but it is to be noted that the exaggerated ecclesiastical language then customary has a good deal of importance from the point of view of the information it contains. At this period, while Nicholas V was thus speaking of the young Rodrigo, the legend has him figuring among bandits and Spanish lawyers.

11. We shall often use this word "benefice." It is to be understood in the canonical sense. A benefice is the continuing right granted by the Church to receive an annual (or other periodic) payment for a spiritual charge.

12. Many of the bulls of Nicholas V concern the young Rodrigo. To the prebends given him by Cardinal Alfonso Borgia must be added the benefices granted by the Pope. In the commission authorizing him to live elsewhere than in the place of his benefices, the Pope says that he is authorizing the Canon of Valencia, his dear son, "seu in Roma curia residendo aut in litterarum studio."

12a. Becchetti has fallen into this error (*Istoria de quattro ultimi secoli della Chiesa,* Vol. VI, p. 217). Other writers

have made the same mistake, but Gregorovius allows that
he attended the University of Bologna for seven years.

13. This Jason del Maino was an orator of Milan, who congratulated Alexander on his election to the papacy. In
his pompous discourse, he indicated that the Pope had
by then spent forty-four years in Italy.

14. In a bull of Nicholas V it is said that in the year 1453
Rodrigo de *Boria* studied at Bologna (Secret Archives of
the Vatican, register 428. Nicholas V, *de Curia,* book
XXIII, folio 65).

   The part concerning the investigation of the secret
archives of the Vatican has been printed by Peter de Roo
(*op. cit.*). From now on, I shall omit this indication, but
I must express my gratitude to this most careful investigator.

15. Ximeno: *Escritores del Reyno de Valencia,* VI, Chap. 23,
says that he was graduated as first in his year.

15a. These books are entitled: "*Glossae Roderici Portuensis in
regulas Cancellariae et Constitutiones Innocentii VIII de
Beneficiis*" and "*De Cardinalium excellentia et Officio vica-
cancellarii.*"

16. R. Rodocanachi, in *Une cour princière au Vatican,* p. 140.

17. These bulls are found in the secret archives of the Vatican
(Calixtus III, *De curia:* I, Vol. V, Regestae 440).

18. Fabroni (as above).

19. Von Pastor, V, I. *Document 67.*

CHAPTER III

1. "The Sovereign Pontiff has highly felicitated Your Eminence, and everybody in the College of Cardinals admits
that great obligations are owed to you . . . The whole
court of Rome would greatly rejoice at your return . . .
Your presence would cause great joy (to Calixtus III) . . .
I don't know what will be decided in regard to your return (to Rome), but if I can do anything to advance it,
I shall not be found wanting . . ." Letter of Eneas
Silvius Piccolomini, Cardinal of Siena (later Pope Pius II)
to Cardinal Rodrigo Borgia, April 1, 1457.

In *Opera Omnia* of Eneas Silvius Piccolomini, Epistola 257.

2. Jacopo de Volterra is an author who wrote before the death of Alexander VI, and even before he was Pope; he wrote a *Diarium Romanum* from the pontificate of Sixtus IV to that of Julius II; but only the first part concerning the period of Sixtus IV has come down to us. He is an unbiased writer with a good historical sense. Certain of the letters of Cardinal Ammanati-Piccolomini are from his hand, for he was the secretary of the Cardinal. It is a fact that must not be overlooked that those who wrote in these conditions and whose texts have not been the object of later alteration speak well of Alexander VI, or at least not ill.

3. Words reproduced by Leonetti: *Papa Alessandro VI*, Vol. 1, p. 106.

4. "Multis annis eximia virtutis eclectissima et exactissima diligentia." Bull 13, of June, 1482. Secret Archives of the Vatican, Sixtus IV, Vol. LXXV, register 620, folio 145.

5. Rodocanachi, following here other earlier writers, says that the election was due entirely to Giuliano della Rovere (*Une cour princière au Vatican*, p. 82).

6. Romanin: *Storia documentata di Venezia*. In the fourth volume, the author treats of the Venetian policy at this period.

7. Ludwig Von Pastor reproduces a document on this last point (*Geschichte der Päpste*, document 67). I have used the German, English and Italian editions indifferently for my references according to the edition available in the place I happened to be working.

8. Raffaele Maffei da Volterra: *Commentariorum Urbanorum*.

9. Jacopo Gherardi de Volterra: *Diarium Romanum* (page 48), Muratori edition.

CHAPTER IV

1. Portigliotti (*op. cit.*, page 49) says: "Rodrigo promised to correct his ways, and in another letter to the Cardinal of Pavia, he likewise promised to amend and swore to lead a

life conformable to good morals." No trace has been found of this letter.

2. Portigliotti reproduces Von Pastor on this point.

3. We have said above that Sixtus IV was elected by "accession," and that Cardinal Borgia, who had voted against him, changed his vote at the last moment to accede to him, which would seem to prove that he did not use intrigue to get him elected.

4. All these documents are found in: *Cardinalis Papiensis Epistolae de Ammanati Piccolomini.* De Roo, in the work already cited, has published the original draft, with corrections in the hand of the author, of the letter which Ammanati sent to Borgia in November, 1476. This draft is found in the Secret Archives of the Vatican.

5. Secret Archives of the Vatican: *Innocentius VIII,* register 682, folio 251. De Roo (*op. cit.*) reproduces the entire text of this bull in an appendix to volume II.

CHAPTER V

1. To understand the public state of mind at that day, it is sufficient to remember that the Florentines: Machiavelli, Vettori and Guicciardini, each in his own way, wanted the Turks to invade Italy "to give those priests a good lesson."

2. Jacopo de Volterra in *Diarium Romanum.*

3. Isabella and Ferdinand were related in the third degree of consanguinity.

4. Villanueva: *Viage literario a las Iglesias de España* (Appendix to volume IV, p. 306).

5. William Thomas Walsh: *Isabella of Spain,* p. 76.

6. Prescott: *History of Ferdinand and Isabella* (Vol. I, page 159).

7. This discourse is found in the *Epistolae et Commentarii* of Cardinal Ammanati, who kept, besides his own papers, such documents as seemed to him interesting.

8. Secret Archives of the Vatican. *Sixtus IV. Bullarium* (Book II, Vol. VII, register 552, folio 95).

9. "Exigit tuae eximiae virtutis integritas et probata in rebus commissis sinceritas" . . . (See De Roo: p. 442, vol. II).

CHAPTER VI

1. Ardicino della Porta died a little later, in November of this same year 1492.
2. It is odd that France and Naples should have backed the same candidate: but even if we do not accept the story of the deposit of money in favor of Giuliana della Rovere, it is certain that these two powers, though in rivalry, agreed on the particular matter of the papal election.
3. This incident with Cardinal La Balue has led Gregorovius and others to say that Rodrigo Borgia was of the Spanish party and La Balue of the French party. But there was then no Spanish party; there were only partisans of the kings of Naples who were in process of becoming Italianized. Rodrigo was not a friend of the kings of Naples, but in this incident he was supporting the cause of peace.
4. Camillo Beneimbene, in a poem on the election of Alexander VI, says:

> *Ut sensere Deum mox suffragantia vota*
> *In te convertunt animis concordibus unum.*

(Vatican Library. Ottobiana. Cod. 2280. Fol. 165).
This was likewise what was told to their respective governments by Filippo Valori, representative of Florence, and Manfredo Manfredi, representative of the Duke of Ferrara. In the discourses pronounced in honor of the new Pope, this unanimity is clear. It is to be found in the orators of Florence, Lucca, Genoa, Mantua, and Milan. The contemporary historians Geronimo Porzio, Giovanni Stella, and Sigismondi dei Conti say the same thing.

   The most recent authors also accept the theory of unanimity. (See Tulio M. Cestero: *Cesare Borgia,* page 73.)
5. Rodocanachi (*op. cit.*, page 137) sets down both opinions and says that after Gherardo's vote, which decided the election, all the cardinals were anxious to concur in the triumph of the Pope already elected, and that those who

had so far voted against him gave him their vote by accession. This probably is substantially what happened, but it could not have happened in this form, for once the requisite majority was obtained, the voting was regarded as finished. If we must enter the realm of hypothesis, a realm so dear to historians, it may have happened thus: when it was known through private conversation that Borgia had the majority, there was an agreement to give him a unanimous vote. If so, this would exclude all hypothesis of simony, for an unbought voter does not spontaneously, and apart from the necessity of the public good, add his vote to that of the corrupt.

6. He had been present in the Sacred College at the nomination of all the existing cardinals, and had helped many of them to achieve the honor. In a friendly letter, Lorenzo the Magnificent thanks him for having thus lent his aid to the nomination of his son, Giovanni, and assures him of his constant gratitude.

7. On the other hand, Infessura gives the Borgia palace to Cardinal Orsini, which proves that he was ignorant of what the whole of Rome then knew, a thing that has been handed down to us in an authentic document.

This Stefano Infessura wrote his *Diarium Romanae Urbis*, which ends in 1494. He was the type of slanderer, as Reumont calls him. His political passions were violent. He was employed by the Roman Senate and was fiercely anti-papal, as he proved by attacking all the Popes.

8. Burchard, Bruchard, Burckardi, etc. . . . Master of Ceremonies of the Vatican, wrote a *Liber Notarum*, or *Diarium*, or *Rerum Urbanorum Commentarii*. We possess only twenty-five and a half pages of the original of this work, which are at the Vatican. We know nothing more of the rest of the manuscript since 1508. At that period it was in the hands of Paris de Grassis, his successor in the office of Master of Ceremonies; the latter said that he could make nothing of the work, which must have been "copied by the devil," and that "only the Sibyl could interpret it." The pages still in the Vatican make his rather vigorous language fully comprehensible.

429

But in numerous libraries copies of this manuscript are found. Partial publications were made until L. Thuasne, 1883-86, produced a complete edition. Two scholars in this field: Cardinal Ehrle, the Vatican librarian, and E. Stevenson pronounced a severe judgement upon the value of this edition: "No one has called the attention of scholars to the inadequacy of the text printed by Thuasne, which is very far from being a complete edition. On the contrary, it contains a great number of errors."

Subsequently to Thuasne, Enrico Celani published a more complete text, based principally on a new copy found in the Vatican, which treats only of the years from the last illness of Alexander VI to the death of Bruchard himself, and on the manuscript in the library of Munich. This edition, though better than Thuasne, is yet not very accurate. The Munich copy was copied from another copy, and not, as some have thought, from the original; then it was altered in its turn. Panvinio, who was in charge of its redaction, wished to make it a completer historical work than that left by the author more than a half century earlier.

Copyists of that day were scholars. They had strong opinions upon subjects which had cost them so much effort and so much patience. The difficulty of interpreting Bruchard's manuscript made it easier for the critical conscience of the copyist to introduce alterations arising from his own considerable knowledge. Interpolations, generally regarded as such, are very numerous. There are, in fact, massive insertions in Infessura's *Journal*, especially in relation to the conclave which elected Rodrigo Borgia. Thus, there are included documents that Bruchard could not have known; lists of personages, including cardinals noted as still alive, whereas the genuine *Liber Notarum* gives them as dead. We read dystichs on Alexander VI, inserted by the hand of Paris de Grassis, and quite obviously by certain others after the death of Bruchard. They have even gone so far, in connection with the Jubilee of 1500, as to reproduce a humorous tale by Boccaccio. In copies of the end of the 16th century and the century

Notes

following, we find the agreement signed in Rome between the Pope and Charles VIII, which is not to be found in any of the earlier copies.

If interpolations on such a scale exist, as by unanimous opinion they do, is it not extremely likely that others also were slipped in—isolated phrases, abusive epithets, obscene incidents, which seem not to correspond with Bruchard's own taste or the tone of his book?

One must use the *"Liber Notarum"* with prudence.

9. Thuasne. Vol. III, pages 21 et seq.
10. Pietro Martyre: *Opus epistolarum* (letter of July 19, 1492).
11. Hartmann Schedel treats only the beginning of this Pontificate.
12. Johannis Stella: *Vitae ducentorum et trigenta summorum pontificum a beato Petro usque ad Julium secundum modernum Pontificem.* Leonetti (volume II) reproduces the part concerning the life of Alexander VI.

CHAPTER VII

1. Gregorovius: *Storia della Citta di Roma* (Book XIII, Chap. 4, page 30).
2. Von Pastor: *Geschichte der Päpste*—Gregorovius: *Lucretia Borgia*—Creighton: *History of the Papacy during the Reformation.* And, among the ancients, Hartmann Schedel, Geronimo Porzio, Nardo, etc. To say nothing of Infessura himself.
3. Nardi: *Ystorie Florentinae* (Book I, page 9).
4. State Archives: Venice. Despatch of August 14, 1492.
5. "Praestans animi magnitudo quae mortales credere omne antecellere. Magna quaedam de te, rara, ardua, singularia, incredibilia, inaudita, pollicentur."
6. The publication of this discourse took place shortly after it was pronounced. There is a copy in the Vittorio-Emmanuele library in Rome. It is a fact of some evidential value that the works printed at this period, of which we have original copies, always speak well of Alexander VI.
7. F. Gothein. II: *Rinascimento nell' Italia Meridionale* (Italian translation, 1915, p. 235).

8. Francesco Trinchera: *Codice Aragones*. Volume II, second part, pages 41-48. The letter was addressed to Antonio d'Alessandro, orator of Ferrante in Spain, but must have been shown to the sovereigns of Castile.

9. Trinchera, in the work already cited, includes all these documents. We should note, in particular, the letter of July 13, 1493, addressed to Antonio d'Alessandro.

10. Trinchera: *Codice Aragones* (Volume II, second part). In particular, the letter of Ferrante to his son, the prince of Altamura, July 11, 1493.

11. King Ferrante himself says: "E quello sia per darli dal canto suo havendo sua Sta lo bono modo che ha ad beneficarlo et bene collocarlo, como ad sua Sta specta." (Letter to Prince of Altamura already cited.)

12. Infessura gives as certain the marriage with Juan de Centellas. Giovanni Andrea Boccaccio affirms, on the contrary, that a marriage had been celebrated with Gaspar de Procida. Lucretia was then eleven years old. Later authors give both marriages as certain.

13. In reality, the authors posterior to those of the time have copied Infessura on this particular point. But, as Infessura is not considered a credible and creditable authority, they fall back on Boccaccio's phrase, doing violence to its plain meaning. It is worth noting that Infessura is so well informed that, for example, he calls Sforza Alessandro instead of Giovanni.

14. *Statuta et novae reformationes Urbis Romae* (Book IV, folio 1).

15. Ut supra.

16. The spelling of the time, suppressing the diphthongs, writes "cetera" and not "coetera."

CHAPTER VIII

1. Tommaso Tommasi (his true name is Gregorio Leti) wrote a *Vita del Duca Valentino*. He is one of the first authors to speak of the Borgias.

2. In fact, Thuasne is here merely reproducing a document

from the collection of the Duke of Osuna. But this collection is crammed with documents written *after* the event. Yet, it caused Von Pastor to say that the Borgia Popes' cause was irremediably lost after this publication. It is probable that Pastor did not closely examine the documents.

3. Portigliotti et Borgia: *"de nobis tunc episcopo Portuen. S. R. E. Vice-cancellerio genitos et muliere vidua."*

4. Paolo Giovio was personally acquainted with the mother of Giovanni, Cesar, Lucretia, and Jofre de Borgia.

5. A. Belli: *Ospitale della Donne di Santa Maria della Consolazione.* 1835.

6. Mantagne: *Revue des Questions historiques* (Vol. XI, page 189).

7. De Roo: *Op. cit.* (Vol. I, page 152).

8. Forcella: *Iscrizioni* (Vol. I, page 335, no. 1276).

9. Page 24.

CHAPTER IX

1. Tommasini's opinion of the manuscripts of Infessura: "Di tutti questi manoscritti assai diverso e il valore. I piu antichi e pregevoli recano nel testo la lezione schietta favorevole alle causa popolare e Colonnense, cui lo scrittore e devoto, gli altri l'ingarbugliano e soventa l'alterano secondo contraria inclinazione degli ammanuensi, favoreggiando la fazione ecclesiastica de Orsini."

2. Sigismondo del Conti: *Le Storia dei suoi tempie* (Vol. II, page 61).

3. The most significant example is given us by the letters of Machiavelli to Vettori and others: especially that in which he speaks of his life of St. Cassian, and that in which he relates a certain ignoble adventure. Many biographers of Machiavelli have attributed to these merely literary compositions the value of historical truths.

4. Rodocanachi: *Op. cit.*

5. I must admit that in my book on Machiavelli, where I treat the Borgias only indirectly, I regarded as true the general opinion of the amours of Alexander VI and of

the other accusations generally admitted, although they are clearly false to the eyes of one who examines things directly as I have done in the present work.

CHAPTER X

1. Stefano Infessura: *Journal* (published by Tommasini). Page 296. "The Cardinal de Monreale is son of the said Pope Alexander."

2. The king declared that he had acted "animo indefesso ac viriliter."

3. Fidel Fita: *Estudios Historicos* (page 224). "Et vestri respectu atque meritis prenominatos germanos," and, at the beginning of the Ordinance: "Nobiles et dilecti nostri, domini Pedrus Ludovicus de Borja, alumnus et camarlengus noster, Cesar de Borja, Yohannes de Borja, Germani."

4. Fidel Fita: *Op. cit.* (Vol. VI, page 126).

5. Fidel Fita: *Op. cit.* (Vol. VI, page 212).

6. Fidel Fita: *Archives of Osuna*.

7. Gregorovius: *Lucretia Borgia*, appendix.

8. Portigliotti: *Op. cit.* (Page 248 and following).

9. After having indicated the cause alleged by the Pope for annulling the marriage, i.e. impotence, Giovanni Sforza said to the Ambassador: "Anzi haverla conoscinta infinite volte, ma che Papa no ge la ha tolta per altro se non per usar con lei."

10. Leonetti: *Op. cit.*

11. Portigliotti: *Op. cit.* (Page 249, French edition).

12. Zurita: *History of King Ferdinand* (Book V, Chap. 42, page 298).

13. De Roo: *Op. cit.* (Vol. I, page 258). This author asserts that the said bull is of May 18, 1489, and that it is to be found in the Secret Archives of the Vatican (Register 770: Innocent VIII commun., year V, Book LXXIII, folio 255).

14. Collection Dupuy: Cod. 28, fol. 17, Bibliothèque Nationale de Paris.

15. Vienna: State Archives, Cod. II. "Conceptum missivem, etc.," fol. 252.

Notes

16. National Archives, Cod. K. 188, no. 154, Paris. Extract from the registers of the Privy Council of the King.

17. Luigi Fumi: *Alessandro Borgia e il Valentino in Orvieto.* An historical note, according to unpublished documents, concerning the marriage of Francesco Gamurri and Anna Giulietti (p. 74), Library of Orvieto.

18. Leonetti: *Op. cit.* (Vol. I, page 197). Leonetti proceeds to a complete examination of the use of the word "nephew," applied to Giovanni, Cesar, Lucretia and Jofre.

19. Reproduced by Leonetti: *Op. cit.* (Vol. I, page 197): "*Cujus (Cesar) ipse fratris nepos esse dicebatur.*"

20. Zurita: *Op. cit.* (Book I, Chap. 22, page 28).

21. *Les Borgia* (page 564). "*Nipote de uno Fratello di Nostro Signore.*"

22. Frederick Baron Corvo: *History of the Borgias* (page 296).

23. Gregorovius: *Lucretia Borgia.*

24. Gregorovius: Ibidem.

25. The entire work of Von Pastor: *The History of the Popes from the End of the Middle Ages,* is, in the section devoted to Alexander VI, entirely shadowed by this question of the children. If this violation by a Pope of his obligation of chastity had not affected Von Pastor's Catholic mind, I am convinced that his judgement upon the Pope generally would have been different, and that his account would have followed another course.

CHAPTER XI

1. Henry Hauser and Augustin Renaudet: *Les débuts de l'age moderne* (page 71).

2. Pierre Champion: *Le Roi Louis XI* (page 28). The words between quotation marks which are reproduced in this work are in a preamble to a chancellory document of the period.

3. Alberi: *Relazioni Venete* (Series I, Vol. 4, pages 15 and 16).

4. Maximilian was the Emperor of Germany, but, not yet having been crowned, bore simply the title of King of the Romans.

5. Francesco della Casa, the Florentine ambassador, says that Basche was avaricious and easily corrupted.
6. Giuliano della Rovere had tried to obtain a similar offensive against the Pope—the summoning of a general council by the intermediary of the King of Naples. As the king refused to follow his advice through fear of the dangers that such an action would have involved, the cardinal abandoned him and went over to the enemy: he went to France to work for the fall of the Aragonese rulers of Naples.
7. An allusion to Pietro de Medici.
8. Dispatches of Sebastien Badoer. Codex D. X. L. VII and VIII, at the Marciana library.
9. A Florentine diplomat expresses the treacherous conduct common at the time by the verb: *Ludovicheggiare.*

CHAPTER XII

1. Trinchera, in his preface to the unpublished documents published by him under the title *Codice Aragonese* says: "It is clear from our documents that the Italian princes, while criticizing the Pope's conduct in their diplomatic correspondence, otherwise showed him their esteem and respect in words and in act."
2. Sigismondi dei Conti: *Le Storie dei Suoi Tempi.*
3. "Domine Orator, vedremo quel che fará il re christianisimo, se metteremo in le so man diamandando misericordia."
4. The document we have just summarized is found (with a few insignificant differences) in Thuasne and in the *Archives de la Bibliothèque Nationale*, of Paris.
5. Archives of Vienna, De Roo, page 99.
6. Dispatches of Pirovano, August 16, 1493. (State Archives, Venice.)
7. Cherrier, in his *Histoire de Charles VIII* (Vol. I, page 384) says, "Un bref du 1er février autorisa le Roi très-chrétien à venir en Italie, etc." But Cherrier did not sufficiently carefully examine the brief in question for it says: "Since our well-beloved son, Charles, having come into our city with his armies, wishes to continue his march . . ."

436

Notes

CHAPTER XIII

1. Zurita: *History of King Ferdinand* (Book I, Chap. 42, page 54).
2. It has been said that this flight had been planned in advance and that when Cesar Borgia's baggage was opened, it was found full of stones. The flight may have been premeditated, given the character Cesar later showed as captain and prince. But there was no pretense about the baggage: it was sent directly to Rome with all it contained.
3. Si ammalo, fo divulgato da cataro, el cual li era disceso in uno ochio e nel estomago (Sanudo: *Journal,* Vol. II, p. 243).
4. This personage, prose-writer and poet, courtier and statesman, ambassador and chancellor, is one of the witnesses to whom the court of History has accorded highest credit in the leading case of the Borgias. Erasmo Percopo, in his *Vita di Giovanni Pontano*, denies that Pontano uttered the discourse in question. But he is compelled to admit that in the *Asinus* Pontano attacks his former masters.
5. Philippe de Commines: *Mémoires,* Vol. II, page 397: "Tout se mit à faire bonne chière, et joustes, et fêtes." Commines was then the ambassador of the King of France to Venice.
6. "Et principalement à m'y envoyer gens à ce que ju puisse garder les passages des montagnes . . . et sauver la personne du Roy" . . . (Mémoires of Commines: *Annotations et éclaircissements,* pages 418-419).
7. Sanudo: *Journal,* Vol. I, page 252, July 1496.
8. "Giornale ferrarese" of Bernardino Zambotti (Collection *Rerum Italicarum Scriptores.* Fascicules of 1935). This is one more example to prove that Diaries and Memoirs, while they give the tone and savor of the period, must not be regarded as a source of information to be accepted without considerable checking.
9. Marchese de Ferrara, di la Casa di Maganza,
   Tu perdera il stato al dispetto dil re di Franza.
       (Verse reproduced by Sanudo.)
10. Commines: *Mémoires* (Vol. II, page 482).

CHAPTER XIV

1. Sansovino: *L'Historia di Casa Orsina*, page 124.
2. Sanudo, reproduced by Romanin (*Op. cit.*, Vol. V, page 99, note). There is nothing about this question of Gorizia in the printed work of Sanudo, but Romanin copies it from the manuscript.
3. Philippe de Commines: *Mémoires* (Vol. II, Book 8, Chap. 25). "Le Pape Alexandre, qui règne de présent, estoit en grande practique, de tous poincts à se renger de siens comme malcontent de Venissiens: et avoit messagier secret, que ju conduisis en la dicte chambre de Roy notre sire peu avant sa dicte mort."
4. Letter of Girolamo Savonarola to the emperors and kings of France and Spain.
5. Ut supra.
6. Villari: *Op. cit*. Thuasne: *Op. cit*.
7. Letter of the Seigniory to the informer Bouxi, its representative in Rome.
8. Lucas: *Girolamo Savonarola* (page 347).

CHAPTER XV

1. Zurita: *Op. cit.*, Book I, Chap. 28, page 34.
2. It is incorrect to say that the Duke of Gandia also was to have gone to Naples to receive the investiture of the Duchy of Benevento, since this investiture had to be given him by the Pope, not by the King of Naples.
3. This account is taken in its entirety from the two most detailed accounts which were written immediately upon the event. One is by Bruchard (*Journal*, Vol. II), and the other by Gian Carlo Scalona, Mantuan ambassador to Rome.
4. "Non decet Majestates vestras Catholicas pati atque permittere ut quidquam periculi statui Sanctae Romanae Ecclesiae ab ipso duce Valentino, dum in vestra tutela est oriatur . . ." (Secret Archives of the Vatican: *Julii II brevia* (Arm. 39, Vol. 22, folio 52). Reproduced by de Roo.

5. Capello arrived at Rome May 23, 1499. He had as successors Marino Giorgi in 1500, then for a very short time, Marco Dandolo. Finally, much later, came Antonio Giustiniani.

6. Leopold Ranke: *History of the Papacy in the 16th and 17th Centuries* (French edition, page 75).

7. Among other errors, Branca de Telini asserts that the French conquered the Spaniards in the war of Naples, whereas it is the simplest fact that the French were definitively expelled from the kingdom of Naples.

CHAPTER XVI

1. Bruchard: *Liber Notarum* (under the date of June 4, 1497). This is also stated in a dispatch of Donato Aretino, the representative of Este, to Cardinal Ippolito d'Este. In it he mentions that Lucretia went off to the convent without informing her family. In his *History of Italy*, Pietro Balan says erroneously that Lucretia went to the convent after the assassination of the Duke of Gandia.

2. In the Archives of Milan there is an abundant correspondence on this subject between Cardinal Ascanio Sforza, Ludovico Moro and his representative at Rome, Stefano Taverna. From this correspondence the fact of the impotence of Giovanni Sforza emerges clearly. He was invited to meet Lucretia at Nepi (a territory governed by Ascanio) to consummate the marriage, and he refused.

3. As to the asserted relations between the Duke of Gandia or Cesar with their sister Lucretia, there is no proof at all save rumors and vague slanders. It helps us to evaluate it to remember that Giovanni Sforza, who was looking for any pretext to accuse Lucretia, never makes the faintest allusion to it—nor indeed to that invented pregnancy which, had it been true, would have absolved him as husband from all blame, given the evident adultery of his wife.

4. Bruchard: *Liber Notarum* (under the date of February 14, 1498). Bruchard adds that much was said of this death in Rome, which is only natural since the dead man was an official in close personal contact with Alexander VI.

5. It was written two years and nine months after the death of Perotto. And that part of the *Journal* of Sanudo which reproduced the story of Capello was written much later.
6. Pietro Delfino: *Epistolarum Volumen* (Book V, letter 37).
7. In this project of reform there are a certain number of articles treating of the duties of princes and kings in relation to the Church. I omit them, because they have no direct bearing upon my present study.

CHAPTER XVII

1. Biagio Buonaccorsi: *Diario dei successi dall'anno 1498 fine all'anno 1512* (i.e. during the period when Buonaccorsi was employed by the Seigniory), pages 9 and 10. Buonaccorsi says that Frederick had privily informed his daughter that she must not consent until he had been given what he asked.
2. *Bibliothèque nationale*, Paris (*Fonds français*, Cod. 293, fol. 1).

CHAPTER XVIII

1. *Bibliothèque Nationale*, Paris (*Fonds latins*, Cod. 5974). (*Fonds français:* Cod. 2711 and 20, 176 and 20, 177).— The first two *Codes* deal with the dissolution of the marriage of Louis XII and Jeanne of France. The last two contain the documents relative to the Royal house of France, revised by the Frères de Sainte-Marthe.
2. Alvisi: *Cesare Borgia* (pages 83 et seq.).
3. It is a thankless task, in writing the story of the Borgias, to have to correct the lies of the Legend, step by step. But I must point out here that it is quite inaccurate to say that in these discussions of marriages, the Pope undertook to give the cardinal's hat to Cesar's brother-in-law, the son of the King of Navarre. Armand d'Alberti, who was protonotary and son of the king, was a candidate for the cardinalate, and he actually obtained it two years after Cesar's marriage.

440

Notes

4. Maximilian, king of the Romans, said one day (July 14, 1502) to the Venetian ambassador, Francesco Capello: "One can have no confidence in the King of France because every day he swears upon the Crucifix and the Consecrated Host to carry out his promises, and the moment he turns his back, he remembers them no more, and does the exact opposite of what he had promised." Cited by Romanin: *Storia documentata di Venezia* (vol. V, page 130).

5. *Secreta*, October 26, 1498.

6. Machiavelli: *Il Principe* (chap. VII).

7. Zurita: *Op. cit.* (page 165, chap. 38, L. III).

8. Biagio Buonaccorsi: *Op. cit.* (page 22).

9. Secret Archives of the State of Venice, August 24, 1499. Letter to the king of Spain.

10. Naturally, his death was attributed to the Pope. It is, in fact, so attributed by Rafaele de Volterra after Alexander's own death, but Bruchard says that Giacomo Caetani died on July 9, 1500, that Cardinal Farnese presided at his interment in the Church of San Bartolommeo in Rome, where the mother, sisters, and other members of the family saw the body, the coffin being open. Paolo Giovio also has Nicola Caetani assassinated by Alexander on the same occasion. But Nicola had died six years earlier.

CHAPTER XIX

1. Vitelli and Baglione, like the Orsini, were then considerable personages. Signorelli, in a painting in the Cathedral of Orvieto which shows the Anti-Christ preaching his theories, depicts among the audience Dante, Petrarch, and also Vitelli and Baglione.

2. Barberini Library, Cod. XXXII, p. 242, under the title: "*Acta contra Principes et Barones.*"

3. Bruchard: *Liber Notarum* (under the date of July 5-25, 1500).

4. Alvisi: *Cesare Borgia*, page 108.

5. Biagio Buonaccorsi: *Op. cit.*, page 51. Lucretia "married the Duke of Bisceglia, who, one night, leaving the Vatican,

was attacked upon the steps of the Palace and wounded to death. He ultimately died of his wounds."

6. Bruchard: *Liber Notarum*, page 240 (August 11-23, 1500).

7. In his monograph entitled: *"Alexander VI, Caesar Borgia und die ermordung des Herzogs von Bisellis,"* Hagen bases Cesar's guilt principally upon the dispatch of Paolo Capello of August 23, 1500, which is found in Sanudo (*Diarium*, page 685). I do not understand how any faith can be placed in the evidence of Paolo Capello, given that his work is crammed with historical errors, generally recognized as such.

8. A contrary opinion is to be found in Cipolla: *Le Signorie dal 1300 al 1530* (page 778). And also in many authors of secondary importance.

CHAPTER XX

1. In this period and apropos of Vitellozzo, there is an incident which reveals the character of Alexander VI. Vitellozzo, on his way to attack Piombino, passed through Orvieto, committing many depredations. The people of Orvieto complained to the Pope. Alexander was angry and cried: "So that is the task of our soldiers—to devastate the territories of the Church! By my faith, I tell you I shall punish Vitellozzo for the wrongs he has inflicted upon you not less severely than if he had despoiled my own bedroom." And in fact he wished to expel Vitellozzo from the papal army; and only refrained from doing so on the request of the people of Orvieto, who forgave the condottiere. (Fumi: *Op. cit.*, page 49.)

2. Summary by Romanin: *Op. cit.*, Vol. V, page 122, of the Secret Archives, vol. XXXVIII, p. 4. Meeting of May 7, 1500.

3. *Instructions d'Édouart au Duc de Valentinoys, August 8, 1501.* Bibliothèque Nationale, Paris.

4. "Quasi ficus fatua non cupata."

5. *De re aulica*, Book I, chap. 87.

442

6. Dispatch of February 1, 1502, of the ambassador Constabili to the Duke of Ferrara.
7. "Hinc est quod sicut ars impressoria litterarum utilissima habetur ad faciliorem multiplicationem laborum probatorum et. utilium, ite plurimum damnosa foret si illius artifices ea perverse utérentur passim imprimendo quae perniciosa sunt." . . .
8. Villari: *Dispacci di Giustiniana,* page 49.

CHAPTER XXI

1. Today, the Barberini Library has been incorporated into the Vatican Library. The report made by the two bishops quoted and by the theologian de Mondia is found in the Barberini catalogue. Lat. 2876, Cod. XXXVI, 10. The title of the file is: *Acta consistorialia a die 6 junij 1498 usque ad 5am julij 1499, tempore Alexandri VI.* And the document referred to is found 'in folio 7 et seq. under the heading: *Inquisitio contra Episcopum Calagusitanum.*
2. Manuscript of the Foundation of San Jacopo (vol. I).
3. Dispatch of February 1, 1502, of ambassador Constabili to the Duke of Ferrara.
4. "Cum ex antiqua consuetudine et observantia romanae curiae, quaecumbona et pecunia curialium qui beneficia ecclesiastica obtinent ad cameram apostolicam pertineant."
5. Alvisi: *Cesare Borgia* (pages 82-83).
6. Bembo: *Historiae Venetae.* Book V, page 185.
7. Bruchard: *Op. cit.* (page 283). In this part of the *Liber Notarum,* or *Diarium,* as elsewhere in other sections, we find proof that Bruchard did not write his notes day by day, and that the greater part of what we read under his name was not written by him. In fact, in the particular case of the inheritance of Cardinal Zeno, we find the whole matter of the difference dividing Venice and the Pope treated under the first ten days of May, at which time Zeno's death was barely known in Rome.
7a. Sanudo: *Diarium* (chap. IV, page 19).
8. Villari: *Dispacci Giustiniani* (vol. II, page 351).
9. Bruchard: *Liber Notarum* (page 295). Cardinal *"Lopez*

*noluit testari, sed reliquit omnia bona sua dispositioni et
mero arbitrio ss. d. n. Papae."*

10. Vedriani: *Vita dei Cardinali Modenesi* (page 20 et seq.).
11. Bruchard (pages 331 and 332).
12. The dispatches of Giustiniani of which we are speaking
    were written between July 12 and July 22, 1502.
13. In a number of different documents which pass for copies
    of Bruchard's *Journal*, we find these epigrams and many
    others. But apparently Bruchard never put them into his
    notes, for in the oldest manuscript of the work still ex-
    istent, there is no trace of them. Their insertion is one
    proof more of the untrustworthiness of the copyists.
14. L. Collison-Morley: *The Story of the Borgias* (page 237).

CHAPTER XXII

1. Sanudo: *Diarium* IV, page 195.
2. In one of the manuscripts of Bruchard, the one called the
   Monacense manuscript, all that relates to this episode has
   been removed. No one would have removed it for love of
   the Borgias. So that we must conclude—since the manuscript in question is the least inaccurate—that the passage
   was removed because it was held to be an interpolation and
   that proof of this was to hand at the moment.

CHAPTER XXIII

1. Alvisi: *Op. cit.* (pages 227 and following).
2. *Storia di San Giovanni Gerosolomitano*, Vol. II, page 559.
3. Villari: *Dispacci di Giustiniani* (Vol. I, page 134).
4. Villari: *Dispacci di Giustiniani* (Vol. I, pages 61-62).
5. Alvis: *Op. cit.* (pages 243-44), is based upon the *Istorie* of
   G. Gambi.
6. Bruchard: *Liber Notarum* (page 320). "Papa vero cum
   galea sua non potuit attingere portum, ex quo omnes in
   galea perterriti et ex turbatione maris commoti, hinc inde
   in galea sunt prostrati, solo papa dempto qui in sede sua,
   in puppi firmiter et intrepide sedens prospexit omnia."
7. Machiavelli: *Legazione al Duca Valentino.*

Notes

CHAPTER XXIV

1. According to Sanudo, Capello, the Venetian ambassador who was in Rome, says that the Florentines cut off Vitello's head and then tried him. (Col. Alberi: *Relazioni Veneti*, series II, Vol. III et seq.)
2. Machiavelli himself writes some years later that Cesar went to clear himself before the king of the accusations brought against him.
3. Dispatch of Giustiniani of August 7, 1502.
4. This Monseigneur Trozo, whom we shall meet again in tragic circumstances, is cited in different documents under the names of Troches, Troccio, Trocces, Trozo, etc. . . .
5. Inventory of Jeanne de Serre, cited by Alvisi: *Cesare Borgia* (p. 312).
6. See Luzio: *Isabella de Este e i Borgia* (page 110); and Luzio and Renier: *Mantova e Urbino* (page 113); Zambotti Bernardino: *Giornale Ferrarese,* January 6, 1503, page 344.
7. Zambotti: As above, page 345.
8. Machiavelli: *Opere* (Vol. V, page 387).
9. Bruchard: *Liber Notarum* (page 343).
10. *Turris None* (Bruchard: *ut supra*).
11. Villari: *Dispacci di Giustiniani* (Vol. II, page 305).
12. Citta di Castello or Civita Castellana.

CHAPTER XXV

1. Funck-Brentano: *The Renaissance* (pages 329 and 330).
2. The slogan "Fuori i Barbari" was never uttered by Julius II.
3. Archives of Florence: *Lettere ai Dieci* (April-May 1503).
4. Cesi Roberto: *"Dispacci degli Ambasciatori Veneti alla Corie di Roma presso Giulio II."* (Note on page 8 in the preface.)
5. Giustiniani's dispatches number 1,223 and begin under the date of May 4, 1502. Of the time of Alexander VI, these dispatches cover only a year, two months, and a few days.

Pasquale Villari has published them in summary. Though I have read them for the most part *in extenso,* my references will be to Villari, to render verification easier for the reader, save in certain instances. These dispatches are preserved among the Secret Documentation of the Senate, but we are dealing with a copy made in the 16th century. There are some in the documentation of the "Dieci," which are authentic. I shall not cite the book of Villari or the Archives when I give the date of the dispatch, for this latter indication should suffice. When the reader can deduce the date of the dispatch for himself, I shall not put any note.

6. Archives of Florence: *Lettere ai Dieci,* 1503.
7. Villari: *Dispacci di Giustiniani,* July 20, 1502 (Vol. I, pages 61-62).
8. This allusion is to the ultramontane sovereigns.
9. Cesi: *Op. cit.* (pages 7 et seq.).
10. Villari: *Dispacci,* Vol. II, page 70.
10a. Dispatch of Giustiniani of May 10, 1503.
11. Dispatch of Giustiniani of May 3, 1503.
12. Dispatch of Giustiniani of March 29, 1503.
13. State Archives of Venice. Register 54 a, c, 76 t. Communication to the most Christian king by the intermediary of the ambassador of Venice in France.
14. Dispatch of Giustiniani of July 26, 1503.
15. Romanin: *Storia documentata di Venezia,* Vol. V.
16. Roberto Cesi: *Dispacci degli Ambasciatori Veneziani alla Corte di Roma presso Giulio II* (page 13).
17. Luniz: Reicharchiv contains the treaties referred to here.

CHAPTER XXVI

1. Zurita: *Op. cit.,* Book IV, Chap. 68, page 242.
2. Dispatch of Giustiniani of July 4, 1503.
3. Villari: Dispatch of Giustiniani of March 8, 1503.
4. Tommaso di Silvestre: *Chronicles.*
5. Gebhart: *Adrian Von Corneto.* This prelate, who had been very useful to Alexander VI, was exiled by Julius II, and under Leo X, deprived of all his titles and benefices.

6. Dispatch of Giustiniani of August 11.
7. Bruchard: *Liber Notarum* (page 352).
8. "Facies erat sicut pannus vel morus nigerrimus, livaris tota plena, nasus plenus, et amplissimum lingua duplex in ore, que labia tota implebat, os apertum et adeo horribile quod nemo videns unquam adesse talem dixerit."

   The rapid decomposition of the body may be regarded as evidence against the theory that the death was caused by poison—at any rate the legendary cantarella of the Borgias; for it is said that this powder contained arsenic, and arsenic retards decomposition. Those who have copied Bruchard's *Journal* have added to the horrible description above certain phrases to render Alexander's corpse more repugnant still.
9. These verses are in the Monacense manuscript of the *Liber Notarum*, interpolated many years later after the death of Bruchard.
10. *State Archives*, Secr:, reg. 39 c. 106.
11. Sanudo: *Journal* (Vol. V, page 66). The party who favored the immediate conquest of the Romagna was led by Giorgio Emo. The party who favored a more gradual conquest was led by Foscari and Morosini. The first party triumphed, sending into the Romagna Paolo Manfroni, Filippo Albanese and Gian Francesco Caracciolo with men and money.
12. "Once the news of the Pope's death was received . . . all the Italian lords started into action, and the *poor* lords expelled from their States by Cesar began to raise their heads in the high hope of returning to their States with the aid of various powers (Potentati)." (Priuli: *Journal*, page 285).—This author describes the Roman barons as *dignissimi*. (Priuli: *ut supra*.)
13. Giustiniani, in a dispatch, assures the Pope that his republic (Venice) knew how to keep its word not only to the living but to the dead.—Thus guaranteeing by these words that he could die in peace, because the republic would always be interested in Cesar. Giustiniani was the principal instrument in the persecution of Cesar.

447

APPENDIX

1. *Archives historiques du Capitole* (of Rome). **Credenza XIV, Vol. 72, folio 333 (de Roo).**
2. Bruchard: *Op. cit.*
3. It is in this part that Bruchard's *Journal* contains the strongest accusations against the Pope and Cesar Borgia.
4. De Roo: *Op. cit.* (Vol. V, page 256).
5. Secret Archives of the Vatican: *Alexander VI.* Reg. 871, fol. 196 bis.
6. Secret Archives of the Vatican: *Alexander VI.* Book V, reg. 871, fol. 744.
7. Secret Archives of the Vatican: Division com. 1501-1503, arm. 29, no. 54, fol. 189½: *"Dilecto filio infanti Johanne Borgia, nostro secundum carnem nepote."* See Gregorovius: *Lucretia Borgia* for another document from the archives of Modena.
8. Villari: *Dispacci di Giustiniani* (Vol. I, page 109).
9. Frederick Baron Corvo: *A History of the Borgia.* This is a very original book, which contains some errors, but many fewer than other books which are more celebrated.

Index

Index

451

Index

Index

454

Index